PENGUIN BOOKS

# HOME RUN

John Nichol is a former RAF flight lieutenant whose Tornado bomber was shot down on a mission over Iraq during the first Gulf War in 1991. He was captured and made a prisoner of war. He is the bestselling co-author of *Tornado Down* and, with Tony Rennell, *The Last Escape* and *Tail-End Charlies*, and author of five novels. He is also a journalist and widely quoted military commentator. His website is at www.johnnichol.com.

Tony Rennell is the author of *Last Days of Glory: The Death of Queen Victoria* and co-author of *When Daddy Came Home*, a highly praised study of demobilization in 1945, and with John Nichol *The Last Escape* and *Tail-End Charlies*. Now a freelance writer, he was formerly associate editor of the *Sunday Times* and the *Mail on Sunday*.

D0766708

# Home Run

*Escape from Nazi Europe*

JOHN NICHOL AND TONY RENNELL

PENGUIN BOOKS

PENGUIN BOOKS

Published by the Penguin Group
Penguin Books Ltd, 80 Strand, London WC2R ORL, England
Penguin Group (USA) Inc., 375 Hudson Street, New York, New York 10014, USA
Penguin Group (Canada), 90 Eglinton Avenue East, Suite 700, Toronto, Ontario, Canada M4P 2Y3
(a division of Pearson Penguin Canada Inc.)
Penguin Ireland, 25 St Stephen's Green, Dublin 2, Ireland
(a division of Penguin Books Ltd)
Penguin Group (Australia), 250 Camberwell Road, Camberwell, Victoria 3124, Australia
(a division of Pearson Australia Group Pty Ltd)
Penguin Books India Pvt Ltd, 11 Community Centre, Panchsheel Park, New Delhi – 110 017, India
Penguin Group (NZ), 67 Apollo Drive, Rosedale, North Shore 0632, New Zealand
(a division of Pearson New Zealand Ltd)
Penguin Books (South Africa) (Pty) Ltd, 24 Sturdee Avenue, Rosebank, Johannesburg 2196, South Africa

Penguin Books Ltd, Registered Offices: 80 Strand, London WC2R ORL, England

www.penguin.com

First published by Viking 2007
Published in Penguin Books 2008
4

Copyright © John Nichol and Tony Rennell, 2007
All rights reserved

The moral right of the authors has been asserted

Typeset by Rowland Phototypesetting Ltd, Bury St Edmunds, Suffolk
Printed in England by Clays Ltd, St Ives plc

ISBN: 978–0–141–02419–6

www.greenpenguin.co.uk

Penguin Books is committed to a sustainable future
for our business, our readers and our planet.
The book in your hands is made from paper
certified by the Forest Stewardship Council.

For Harry & Sophie

In memory of Dédée de Jongh – '*Postman*'
Born 1916. Died 13 October 2007, aged 90


This book is dedicated to all of the 'helpers' who were willing to risk everything to assist British and American evaders on the run during the Second World War. Their courage and fortitude ensured so many men made that incredible 'home run'.

# Contents

# Illustrations

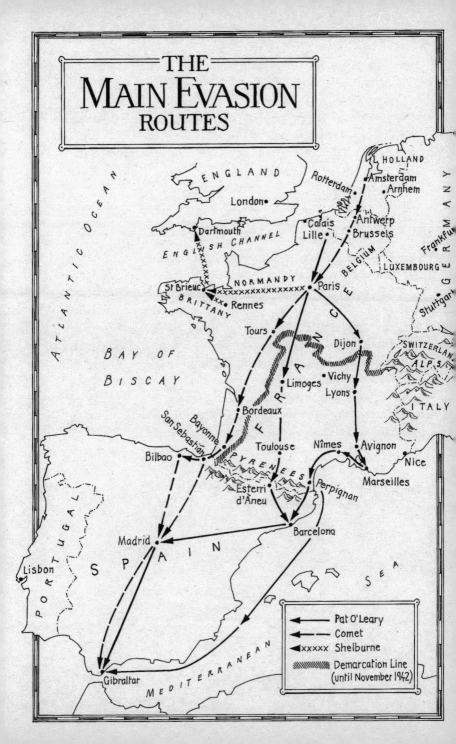

# THE MAIN EVASION ROUTES

ATLANTIC OCEAN

ENGLAND

London •

HOLLAND

Rotterdam • Amsterdam • Arnhem

Dartmouth

ENGLISH CHANNEL

Calais • Antwerp
Lille • Brussels

GERMANY

Frankfurt

St Brieuc
BRITTANY
Rennes

NORMANDY

Paris

BELGIUM

LUXEMBOURG

Stuttgart

BAY OF BISCAY

Tours

Dijon

SWITZERLAND

FRANCE

Limoges • Vichy
Lyons

ALPS

Bordeaux

San Sebastián
Bilbao

Bayonne

Toulouse

ITALY

Nîmes • Avignon
Nice

PYRENEES

Esterri
d'Àneu

Perpignan

Marseilles

PORTUGAL

Madrid

SPAIN

Barcelona

MEDITERRANEAN

SEA

Lisbon

Gibraltar

| | |
|---|---|
| ←——— | Pat O'Leary |
| ◄– – – | Comet |
| ◄×××× | Shelburne |
| ～～～ | Demarcation Line (until November 1942) |

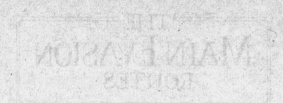

# Acknowledgements

There are many people who willingly gave us their expertise and time whilst we wrote this book. We have tried to acknowledge them all but we apologize to anyone we neglect to mention. Our heartfelt thanks go to:

Diana Morgan from the Royal Air Forces Escaping Society, who provided much information on the evaders, sent letters requesting information to all of her members and allowed us to join them at their annual dinner.

Frank Haslam, who provided many of the initial points of contact to veterans' groups and societies.

Roger Stanton, secretary of the WWII Escape Lines Memorial Society, who invited us to attend their annual service and dinner and offered much expert advice.

Scott Goodall for a delightful personal introduction to one of the escape routes across the Pyrenees.

Lieutenant Colonel Clarke M. Brandt (USA Ret.) and Trish Young, who provided countless written accounts from American veterans and assisted in contacting many more.

Larry Grauerholz from the US Air Forces Escape & Evasion Society for answering many queries and facilitating contacts to his members.

Dr Peter Liddle, Trevor Mumford and Cathy Pugh from the Second World War Experience Centre, Leeds for transcribing and providing many of their archived interviews.

Peter Elliot from the RAF Museum for his assistance in searching the museum's archives.

The staff of the National Archives, Kew, the London Library and the British Library.

Rod Suddaby and Katharine Martin from the Imperial War

Museum in London for their assistance in finding many accounts detailing evaders' experiences.

John Clinch for his excellent website charting many aspects of the early evaders' stories: www.belgiumww2.info.

The remarkable 'marketplace' booksellers on Amazon.com, whose access to publications old, lost and obscure is one of the wonders of the internet.

Martin Gladman, whose excellent second-hand bookshop in West Finchley was the first place of call for this project, as for the other books we have written. Sadly, like so many others in his precious trade, he had to close in December 2005, another blow to Britain's book culture. We will miss his expertise.

Andrew Merton for the many useful books in his family's library at Le Trident.

Barbara Hadley, whose farmhouse in the French countryside was a haven and an inspiration.

Eleo Gordon, our publisher and mentor at Viking Penguin, for her unbridled enthusiasm, unrivalled expertise and keenest of eyes; Trevor Horwood, our meticulous and ever-helpful copy-editor; and all our other friends at Penguin, especially Stephanie Collie, Juliet Annan, Carly Cook and the wonderful team who produce, market, sell and publicize our books.

Many friends and colleagues for advice and support, among them our agent Mark Lucas, Rowland White, Tom Bower, Paul Carter, Simon Freeman, Sarah Helm, Bob Low, Brian MacArthur, Andrew Pierce, Amanda Platell, Rob Ryan, Barry Turner.

The brilliant surgeons, doctors and nurses of the Royal Free Hospital, London, without whom *Home Run* (as well as one of the authors) might have come to a premature end.

Our wives, Suzannah and Sarah, and our children, Sophie, Becky, Tom and Harry; we thank them for their unconditional love, support and advice.

Finally, we send our greatest thanks to the evaders and helpers themselves and their families. They delved into their past to relate their experiences and emotions with great fortitude. We are eternally grateful to them.

# Preface

'Hiding, always hiding! What a monotonous and horrible business!'
  *An evader in Holland*[1]

'Strangers gave me their beds, their food, their friendship; they risked
their lives for my safety. What more could a man ask of a fellow human?'
  *English soldier on the run*[2]

On a dark winter's night in 1944, a young couple stood arm in
arm on the swaying platform at the rear of a Brussels tram, clinging
desperately to the shadows. Their eyes were down, their faces taut
as they tried to conceal their fear of discovery. As the crowded
carriage clattered through the Belgian capital, against their shoulders pressed two German army lieutenants in smart uniforms, every
inch the conquerors and 'master race' they professed to be. Such
close contact with the enemy shook 20-year-old Terry Bolter. 'I
was like a scared rabbit,' he would recall.[3] A single paralysing
thought lodged in his mind – what if these two officers of Hitler's
occupying forces realized that the man standing next to them was
a British airman on the run in Nazi Europe and the tall teenage
girl with long black hair and brown eyes was a member of the
local Resistance helping him? The slightest suspicion and pistols
would slip from the Germans' leather holsters. Papers would be
demanded. And then, would Bolter's false documents identifying
him as Cyrille van der Elyst, a butter merchant from Limbourg,
stand up to scrutiny? Would he collapse under questioning and
confess the truth – that he was a bomb aimer from an RAF Halifax
which had been shot down returning from a raid on Frankfurt two
months earlier?

He could guess what his own fate would be. There would be a

period of danger when, in his civilian clothes, he would be threatened, told he was a spy, beyond the protection of the Geneva
Convention, liable to be shot out of hand. But he knew the odds
were that he would eventually end up in a prisoner-of-war camp
in Germany, a captive but alive. Not so Francine, the pretty
19-year-old art student by his side. She would pay the severest
price for doing what she considered her patriotic duty. All over
the Belgian capital – as in every town and village in Nazi-occupied
Europe – posters proclaimed the penalty for helping Allied airmen
to escape capture. She would be executed, probably after months
of torture. So too would her family and friends. The best any of
them could hope for was deportation to a concentration camp.
The knowledge of how much more their helpers would suffer if
caught was an extra burden for the thousands of evaders who did
their best to remain at liberty and get back to England in those
dark days of the Second World War.

The tram came to a halt. The German officers, busy with their
own conversation, sure in their superiority, barely noticed as the
anxious couple brushed past them and hurried down the steps to
the dimly lit street. A bell clanged and the tram moved off. Bolter
and Francine ducked into a pitch-black side street and she clutched
at his arm. 'What a story you'll be able to tell when you get
back home,' she whispered. He had stood beside the enemy and
survived. It was a small victory, a moment to savour. Just then, it
began to rain heavily and they hurried along deserted streets,
through the cold winter downpour, to the safety – if such a thing
existed in war-ravaged Europe – of her mother's home in rue Van
Eyck.

Sixty years later, rain is falling in torrents in an altogether different place. We are in Stratford-upon-Avon – the quintessence of
peaceful Middle England. A lifetime has passed by since that dark
and wet night in February 1944. But the memories of it are as
sharp as ever for Terry Bolter. On the streets of the town centre
pedestrians dash from shop to shop, dodging the fierce showers
of an English spring to load up with food from well-stocked
supermarkets and clothes and luxuries from stores overflowing

with goods of every kind. The scene is a far cry from the rationed, threadbare Europe he knew six decades ago. The world has moved on to better times. But not inside our hotel. There, beneath the old-world wooden beams, the talk is of times of danger, a world at war which, like a tidal wave, swept up young men in their prime and dumped them down in situations of conflict and fear they could never have imagined. They sank or swam. A few of the 'swimmers' are gathered to relive the past, for this is the annual convention of what remains of the Royal Air Forces Escaping Society.[4] Once, thousands of men were entitled to membership but over the decades their numbers have dwindled. Now just two dozen old men — all in their eighties, some fit and sprightly for their age, others clinging on to walking sticks or in wheelchairs — meet. They wear the silkworm-motif tie of men who have gambled their lives on the gossamer fabric of a parachute, their sudden and unwanted descent to earth just the first of many brushes with danger and death before they got home.

They are an exclusive band. They always were. In the Second World War a quarter of a million Allied soldiers and airmen — British, American, Australian, Canadian, and others — were stranded behind enemy lines and became prisoners of war, filling scores of camps in eastern Germany and Poland, as far from their home as the Germans could put them. Just a few thousand — somewhere between 3,000 and 5,000[5] — evaded capture, stayed free and made that home run back to Britain. This book is their story. They fought the most intimate of wars in the enemy's own backyard. They hid in hovels and châteaux, smart city flats and coal miners' cottages. They walked hundreds of miles, swam raging rivers in the dark, climbed mountains, sneaked past German barracks and frontier posts, talked their way through checkpoints and snap inspections or, more often, posed as deaf mutes and said nothing. Many chanced their luck on the railways where Gestapo agents and collaborationist local police roamed the corridors on the lookout for runaways. Just as many thousands tried and failed. Caught in the Nazi dragnet which covered the continent from the tip of Holland to the Pyrenees, often betrayed by those they thought friends, they were bundled into captivity – or worse. Unknown numbers were caught and summarily executed, their very presence on occupied soil a symbol of resistance to the invader and an affront to the Germans' sense of invincibility.

They needed coolness, courage, determination – and, above all, luck by the barrel. They had to be infinitely patient, yet ready to spring into action at a moment's notice. They had to trust their helpers completely, yet fear every stranger and suspect every would-be friend. Bolter is typical of the breed. Here in Stratford-upon-Avon, as young Francine had predicted all those years before, he has *his* story to tell. A mischievous smile flickers across his face as he talks, the daredevil youth he once was resurfacing through the mask of age. But these are not schoolboy pranks he is recalling. They were desperate situations in which his life was on the line. He is a self-assured man, charming but resolute, brooking no interruption, taking few questions, as the authors sit listening. He would be the first to admit he is not the easiest of men. By nature he is, in the parlance of his generation, a fully paid-up member of 'the awkward squad'. But it is hard to resist the conclusion that this very stubbornness and refusal to conform are why he is still alive. Those characteristics are what snatched him from imminent danger and kept him free all those years ago.

We are back in 1944 and Bolter is in hiding in Brussels in the home of a Resistance worker he knew as Adrian. An active fighter who regularly left the house on missions to assassinate Belgian citizens collaborating with the German occupiers, Adrian was a dangerous companion, though, on the surface, his lifestyle appeared completely normal. His wife and baby daughter shared the family home. Granny was on the first floor. Bolter was up in the attic.

But when I arrived the first thing Adrian did was to show me the coal cellar. Down there he shovelled away some soot on the floor to reveal a small trap door which he lifted up. We descended wooden steps into a small room with a sandy bottom. Six paces covered its length but there was plenty of headroom. It was lit by electric lights, which revealed a dazzling display of colour. Flags of the Allied nations, ready for Liberation Day, covered the walls. Small arms and ammunition stolen from the Germans were everywhere, enough to have Adrian executed several times over if he was caught. 'Terry,' he said, 'this is where you will hide if the Germans come. You will be quite safe here.' I was not so sure. I thought it was an incredibly dangerous place to be.

Bolter's caution was justified.

Up in my attic room several nights later, before going to bed I stood on a chair and pushed open the skylight. It was unusually clear for a February sky. I could see the Plough, with its pointers showing the way to the North Star, which I had often taken shots of on the way back to base from a bombing raid. Polaris was an old friend, a link with my former life in England. Sometimes I could not believe I was in occupied Belgium. These sorts of things could not be happening to me.

The next morning I was awakened early by the insistent ringing of the doorbell. It vibrated throughout the house, persistent and menacing. Below in the street a half-circle of men stood around the front door. There were the bulges of weapons in their pockets. One had a Sten gun under his raincoat. 'Open up! Open up!' they shouted in broken French.

Lulu, Adrian's wife, rushed up the stairs and into my room. 'Terry, Terry, get up at once. The Gestapo are here.' Now I felt real fear, but not the numbing sort that paralyses you. I threw on my clothes in record time, stuffing my nightshirt into my trousers, with a raincoat, scarf and trilby on top. I was ready just as Adrian came tearing up the stairs to tell me I still had time to dash down to the coal cellar and hide. 'What are *you* doing, Adrian?' I asked. 'I'm going over the roof tops!' he said. 'Well, I'm coming with you,' I replied.

Later Bolter would discover that when the Gestapo got inside the house, the first place they made for was the coal cellar and the supposedly concealed trap door. They knew about the secret room where, if he had followed instructions, he would have been hiding. They had been tipped off by persons unknown, another example of the betrayal that blighted so much Resistance activity and led to the capture of so many Allied evaders. Had he gone through with the original plan, he would have been caught, he says, 'like a rat in a trap'. For now, though, he had two guns in his pockets, which he would use if cornered, and the Gestapo still had to lay their hands on him. Escape was his only thought. 'I still had a chance.'

On the top landing, Adrian flung up the window at the back of the house. Bolter looked over his shoulder and could see they were four storeys up. 'Pedestrians in the street below looked disconcertingly small.' The nearest houses were six feet away, across a chasm. Adrian crouched in the window and edged out onto the sill, hesitated there for a second and then leapt.

He landed on the flat roof of the adjacent house, which miraculously was lower than our window ledge. It was a wonderful leap, weighted down as he was by heavy weapons. Then it was my turn. I stood poised on the sill, looked down and then hastily across at the adjacent roof and sprang across. Adrian caught me in his arms as I landed.

The pair of fugitives quickly prised open a skylight and lowered themselves into the building. The noise of their entry woke the household and pandemonium broke out below.

Young women appeared wearing practically nothing at all followed by middle-aged men, also in a state of undress, who should have been at home with their wives. We had landed in a brothel!

Adrian drew his revolvers and motioned to the scantily clad prostitutes and their red-faced clients to raise their hands. 'The Gestapo are after us,' he announced. 'If you do nothing, say nothing, you will be quite safe.' Then, while Bolter kept them all covered with his revolvers, he set off downstairs to check if it was safe to leave. He came back to give the all-clear and the two of them then went down to the front door. Nervously they peered outside.

No Gestapo. They were still round the corner at Adrian's house. We went out fast from that house of ill repute, into the street, first left, first right, first left, first right, jumped on to a passing tramcar and we were away.

I felt a deep sense of relief. We were safe . . . for the moment. It was too soon to be sure. We got off at the first stop and went across the road into a café where Adrian ordered two cognacs. He then repeated the order and I felt distinctly better.

The Resistance man's chief concern was to get 'the Englishman', as he called Bolter, away from the scene and into another hiding place. They went first to Adrian's parents' home but it was too dangerous to stay. One step ahead of the Gestapo, Adrian's mother ushered Bolter through the streets to the house of a couple named Dubois, knocked on the door and waited anxiously as the slow shuffle of bedroom slippers came down the hall. The door opened and Adrian's mother pushed him inside, slamming the front door behind them. The elderly couple appeared unafraid and unconcerned at having an English airman under their roof. Like so many of their countrymen, young and old and across all social classes, they were simply glad to help. Their hatred of the German invaders – and their intense gratitude to the British for continuing the struggle against *les sales Boches* after their own country had been forced into surrender – outweighed the threat of reprisals. They were well prepared for 'visitors' like him. Mme Dubois ushered Bolter to the dining room. 'This will be your hiding place if the Gestapo come here, monsieur,' she told him. 'But where, madame?' he asked. 'Here!' she said, and pushed a concealed button in the wall.

The bookcase which a moment before had stood solidly against the wall, now swung away from it to reveal a small cavity behind, just enough for a man to sit in by drawing up his knees under his chin. I tried it, and inside it was dark and intensely uncomfortable. My whole body went numb in just a few minutes. She left it open, ready for use. If we needed it at all we should need it in a desperate hurry.

For now, however, Mme Dubois – plump, with rosy cheeks, in Bolter's recollection, a plain and simple Belgian housewife with no pretence to heroism – got on with her normal life, busying herself preparing breakfast and hot coffee as if this was any other morning. 'I found her preoccupation with domestic things soothing after what I had just been through.'

He was soothed in a different way when, later that day, Adrian arrived with his cousin, a beautiful girl in her early twenties with blonde hair and vivid blue eyes. Her name was Marie and she was ecstatic to meet *un aviateur anglais*. It had been a cherished ambition of hers throughout the occupation. 'Bonjour, Monsieur Terry,' she said in a low, husky voice. 'I have pledged myself to kiss the first English flyer I see.'

*

In this history, there are two strands of heroism. The first is that of evaders like Terry Bolter, the other is that displayed by the Francines and Adrians, the many thousands of ordinary men and women, the 'helpers', who risked their lives to hide Allied servicemen on the run.[6] At Stratford-upon-Avon they are represented by Nadine Dumon, petite, smart, her youthful looks and grooming belying the fact that she is in her eighty-third year. Her beautiful hands with long, elegant fingers are those of a woman a quarter of her age. Appalled by her country's fall to the German blitzkrieg of 1940, she fought back in the only way she could – she became a courier for a Resistance-run escape line, escorting men from safe house to safe house, delivering them to the railway station, accompanying them on the train journey if necessary. She learned to operate under the noses of an enemy who was alert, ruthless and very well informed. Resistance groups were regularly – and far too easily – infiltrated by enemy agents. From the start of her clandestine activities the teenage Nadine, a doctor's daughter, knew that one day the fist crashing on the door and the pummelling of rifle butts would be for her, and it would all be over. But still she continued, a guiding light for dozens of Allied evaders. And, as we will see, they did come for her; the Gestapo took her away, her one-woman battle was over and a new one just to stay alive about to begin. As she begins this part of her story we are awed by her quiet composure, her dignity, her lack of rancour. This woman survived Ravensbruck, the vile Nazi concentration camp exclusively for women. She still bristles at the memory of how she was betrayed to the Nazis by a fellow countryman, a man she thought was a friend. For once those fingers, normally relaxed, are twisted together in anguish. But as for what happened after that, she just shrugs. 'If you are alive, you are alive,' she says. 'And if you are dead, then . . .'

Nadine lived through unimaginable horror and returned home at the end of the war. But thousands like her in Belgium, Holland and France did not. They died for their belief in freedom and their determination to do *something*, to make a contribution, however small, on behalf of their overrun and terrorized nation, anything that would strike a blow against the Germans. Of his helpers, Bolter told us, 'Each one took a personal decision to risk his or her life. They were very brave people indeed.' And there were large numbers of them. A successful evader might pass through scores of homes and the hands of hundreds of people on his journey from first forced landing to finally reaching home. It was incumbent on each evader to protect those who sheltered, guided and protected them. Standing orders for RAF men who found themselves in enemy territory and dependent on local people for their survival emphasized that they should 'never write anything down. *Remember everything but write nothing.*'

One address on a scrap of paper can result in the tracing of many helpers. Never discuss your previous helpers with those with whom you find yourself next. Security must be of the highest order. There have been cases where evaders and escapers have sent post cards back to helpers thanking them. The motive may have been good but the supreme stupidity of their actions is almost incredible. Do nothing which can endanger your helpers' lives. They do what they do without thought of reward. All they ask is that you do not talk. They trust their lives to your hands. Do not betray that trust.[7]

This underground fight carried on by those helpers against the invaders of their country has remained a barely acknowledged part of Second World War lore, generally passed over in the official histories and the more popular military accounts. Tales of special operations, of secret agents dropped behind the lines, of Resistance fighters and guerrilla raids, take precedence. But, in truth, the Resistance achieved little by force until the final twelve months of the war, its acts of sabotage and attacks on German forces ending in such severe reprisals on civilians that their worth was highly questionable. But helping Allied soldiers and airmen to escape was an ongoing positive and constructive act of defiance against the Germans. In France in particular, the shame of abject defeat in 1940 stung thousands of its citizens into clandestine action. The French surrender and then their collaboration with the invader remains a slur to this day, hurled across the Channel, a glib accusation of cowardice.[8] Few of those who trade in such insults are aware of the undercover struggle by brave, self-sacrificing men and women to get Allied evaders home. This was the real fightback against oppression. The likes of Nadine refused to take defeat lying down. They stood up to challenge the oppressor in the only effective way they could.

And their actions wounded the Germans. Back in London, as we will see as this story unfolds, rescuing evaders was a small-fry operation in the minds of generals and politicians, a side issue to the main task of winning the war. The Whitehall team supporting the escape organizations was of one-man-and-a-dog proportions, occupying a single small room in the War Office and starved of money, resources, people and respect. But, on the ground, the impact of evaders at loose was immense. Hunting them down became an obsession for the Gestapo and the SS. The Luftwaffe commander, Hermann Goering, was incensed when he realized how many highly trained Allied airmen were getting home to be fed back into the very same war machine that day after day and night after night was making a mockery of his air defences and his fighter squadrons. Goering set his own teams of special air force investigators to track down and destroy the escape lines that were causing him so much trouble and embarrassment. It is to the shame of British Intelligence and the Special Operations Executive – too busy pursuing more glamorous (if less effective) covert activities in occupied Europe – that they gave less credence to the role evaders could play than the enemy did.

The very fact that men could get home was also a vital boost to the morale of airmen whose lives were constantly at risk in the relentless bombing campaign against Germany from 1941 until the very end of the war. The crews of Bomber Command knew all too well how poor were their chances of survival. They had only to look at the empty bunks in their billets at the end of each operation. By the time the fighting was over they had suffered an attrition rate of 50 per cent, more than any other single Allied military command, on land, at sea or in the air.[9] But they were briefed to believe they could survive. And most chose to believe it, however terrifying the prospect of baling out from a burning aircraft and the likelihood of falling straight into the enemy's hands. Hope was preferable to despair. More than one airman landed feet-first in France with his mind firmly set on seducing all the pretty (and available) foreign girls he was sure he was about to meet.

In reality, the girls they encountered were not as sexually precocious as boys brought up on tales of the Folies Bergère might have imagined. Most men knew little about the countries they landed in. Today we live in a society where travel abroad is commonplace. The 1940s were different. Few in the armed forces, officers included, had ever been in a foreign country before. The vast majority spoke English and nothing else. Out of the blue, their feet were planted in the soil of lands that were quite alien to them. Their first problem was to make themselves understood. Instructors told them not to worry too much about this. 'The difficulties of language are not as great as you might imagine,' they were told. 'One escaper travelled through Germany posing as a Norwegian businessman, and the only Norwegian he knew was "I am sorry, I have no cigarettes." Another got out of Germany knowing only *auf Wiedersehen*, which he used on every occasion.'[10] But the witty reassurances of the briefing room when safe at home with your squadron seemed hollow when faced with the sense of shock, loss and loneliness of actually being on the ground in a strange, bewildering and frightening environment. Since their initial landing was likely to be in the countryside, it meant having to communicate with peasant workers who found them just as strange and threatening. One airman who landed in Holland could only summon up the words 'Churchill, Wilhelmina [the Dutch queen in exile], *kamerad*' to win over the anxious local farmer he approached, desperate for food, water and shelter after three days of trying to fend for himself.

There was a complete lack of communication. He and his wife were afraid, fully aware of the dangers of harbouring me. Nobody spoke. I made a fuss of their children, kissed the baby, gave the mother my silk flying gloves and her husband a ten-guilder note. In return I was given an old pair of shoes and something to eat and drink. Then they got rid of me by taking me to a neighbouring farm a few fields away. The man then hastily returned to his home with a sigh of relief at having solved his problem.[11]

The problem of whom to trust was an acute one. In France in particular, evaders found themselves swirling around in a maelstrom of conflicting loyalties. The French had surrendered to the Germans and agreed a humiliating armistice in which half the country was under enemy occupation and the other half a puppet state run by one-time patriots who had, in the eyes of many, turned traitor. But to whom did a loyal French man or woman owe his allegiance? To the Free French forces exiled in London under Charles de Gaulle, dedicated to kicking out the Germans? Or the authorities in the provincial town of Vichy headed by Marshal Henri Philippe Pétain, a First World War hero who had made a shameful deal with the conquerors? Some made their choice clear – such as the extreme collaborationists who filled the ranks of the dreaded Milice, the Nazi paramilitary force set up by Vichy to hound Jews, communists, Resistance workers and anyone else opposed to the regime. The ordinary police, however, and government officials too, were often Allied sympathizers, defending the status quo on the surface while helping the Resistance in secret. But which was which? It was a dilemma that faced every evader and his helpers, and one in which the wrong decision could be, and often was, fatal. For much of the war the French people were in such a state of moral and ideological confusion that an evader's chances of staying free depended on the whims of individuals who did not know for sure where their loyalties lay. They and their helpers had to take immense risks. On a train journey, carrying a bag of Resistance documents, Nadine Dumon had to pass a customs official at the Belgian border. She took a chance:

I opened the case and told him in a quiet voice that under my pyjamas and spare clothes were papers. 'What papers?' he asked. 'Papers for the other side,' I whispered. 'Ah!' he said, 'That's good,' and he closed the case and let me go. I was very lucky.

But in other places, at other times, evaders and their helpers could be astonishingly open about themselves. One airman on the run recalled trying to board a crowded bus in Brittany with another evader. Local women were pushing and shoving their way ahead of them. As the driver began to shut the door, the airman shouted out in exasperation that the women should make room for '*des aviateurs anglais*'.

That was good enough for the driver, who crammed us in somehow at the back of the bus and slammed the door behind us. Someone on board heard who we were and told us that when we got to the town we were heading for, we should check in with a man named Pierre who would be sitting in the Grand Café on the corner of the main square. We did and were immediately given shelter in his home. But God knows what would have happened if the person on the bus had been a collaborator.[12]

On such thin threads hung the lives of Allied evaders and their helpers.

★

*Home Run* is not a chronicle of every escape line, of which there were dozens at different times, some small and local, others extensive and criss-crossing Europe. Most were infiltrated and broken but then revived and carried on by different people under different names. To plot those changes was not our purpose. Instead we have tried to recreate the life of men on the run during a savage occupation through the recollections and the words of those who experienced it. This is the story of their odysseys. The bulk of them were airmen, but the story is not entirely theirs because the trails they took home had been blazed by others as early as 1940. At briefings for aircrew by RAF instructors towards the end of the war there was a favourite anecdote, guaranteed to raise a laugh, about a sergeant pilot who baled out over France and came down close to a *convent* – cue for giggles and ribald comments from the men-boys in the audience.

He had not been on the ground for more than a few minutes when several nuns rushed out and hustled him inside. He was given civilian clothes and in due course was allowed into the grounds, where he posed as a gardener. On his first day, he caught sight of an exceptionally pretty nun and all thoughts of escape and evasion departed as he envisaged many happy days in front of him if only he could win himself into the good graces of this most attractive young lady. With this in mind he made tentative advances towards her but was dismayed at the complete lack of response. Refusing to give up, however, he continued his efforts in a clumsy mixture of French and English, until 'she' finally turned to him with an angry grunt and said: 'Don't be a damned fool. I'm an English soldier and I've been here since Dunkirk . . . !'[13]

A true story? Almost certainly not. But the raucous, boyish belly-laughter that the punchline inevitably raised was a tonic – and the chance that it could just possibly happen was a fillip to morale for men going into action.

But this apocryphal tale contained one essential truth. There were indeed British soldiers who had bedded down in France after being stranded there in 1940. Others had pioneered the routes home. And that is why we begin our story on the beaches of northern France in the aftermath of the Dunkirk evacuation. There the remnants of the British Expeditionary Force watched the last of the rescue ships disappear out to sea and turned to face a German army rapidly closing in on them. Some brave souls told themselves, 'No one is going to make a prisoner out of me. *I am going home, whatever it takes!*'

# 1. Left Behind

Battle weary and bloodstained, Private Gordon Instone stood on the beach at Calais and stared towards England. Here he was at the point on the continent of Europe closest to the mainland of Great Britain. A mere twenty-one miles of calm, blue-grey sea separated him and his comrades-in-arms from home. But it might as well have been an ocean. 'The Channel stretched before us like a great lake, terminated by the cliffs of Dover which on that perfect, cloudless day we could see quite clearly in the distance,' he would recall.[1] There was safety, tantalizingly close but hopelessly out of reach.

It was late May 1940 and Instone had been in France for three months, one of the quarter of a million volunteers and Territorials making up the BEF, the British Expeditionary Force sent by a confident government in London to bolster the French army and see off the military threat from Adolf Hitler's Germany. But Hitler had outwitted them all. More to the point, his armies had out-flanked them, the Wehrmacht's troops and tanks curling past the static defences of the Maginot Line, then bursting through Luxembourg and Belgium, not so much a fist, more an outstretched hand of iron, the long fingers stabbing to the south and west, menacing and all-conquering. Resistance crumbled.

With no answer to the fierce blitzkrieg attack, the BEF fell back until it reached the coast of northern France. A desperate evacuation began at Dunkirk. In Calais, just a few miles to the south, Instone had been doing his bit to hold off the German armour, buying the time needed by the Royal Navy and the hastily assembled armada of small ships to get so many of the hundreds of thousands of stranded soldiers off the Dunkirk beaches. 'Every hour counted in which we could deny the main coastal road to the German tanks.' But now Calais's harbour and *gare maritime* were in flames around him and the stalling was over. It was every man for himself. He hurried to the waterfront, hoping beyond hope that there might be a ship waiting, then waded out into the sea up to his armpits to escape the non-stop enemy mortar and shellfire raking the sands. The men from his unit gathered round and decided their only hope was to make their way along the coast to Dunkirk. Perhaps there would still be boats there. Perhaps.

We started to walk along the beach but each time a shell whined overhead we threw ourselves flat until our battle-dresses were covered with sand. Steadily our numbers diminished as the insatiable mortars took their toll. One after another men staggered and fell, their painful moans and cries for help following us pitifully along the beach. Gunner Williams was hit in both legs. He was conscious and smiled as I knelt beside him, but I could do nothing for him.

I threw down my rifle and trudged on as best I could but the pace grew slower and the heat more intense. This was my third day without sleep and I was numbed with fatigue. About a hundred of us were left and were halfway to Dunkirk when a German tank blocked our way. Its turret turned towards us and one of the crew jumped out with a revolver. We raised our hands, prisoners of the Third Reich.

It was not a prospect Instone found easy to accept. Tired and dismayed as he was, marching away inland with a backward glance at the Channel he had hoped would be his passage home, he was determined that, whatever his German captors might be telling him, his war was not over.

On another stretch of that bloody beach, Second Lieutenant William Dothie was also staring longingly across at his homeland just a few miles away and wondering how he could get there. A Royal Artillery subaltern, he had retreated from Lille and then St Omer along roads clogged with demoralized British and French soldiers and civilian refugees fleeing the fighting. Now he and his battery had reached the sea, and there was nowhere else to run. Shells and mortar from German tanks filled the air. Screaming planes rained down bombs. For a while Dothie and his men had held their ground on the edge of Calais, though quickly losing a sergeant and a bombardier to vicious sniper fire. He managed to rally the rest, mounting a counter-attack, bravely – hopelessly – leading a raid against two dug-in enemy tanks. With just one Bren gun and two anti-tank rifles they had driven off the enemy's armour. But not for long. The panzers returned in greater numbers and the unstoppable German advance continued.

Falling back to the wide, flat beach, Dothie found himself among hundreds of British soldiers lying exhausted on the sand, all fight drained out of them, their rifles and steel helmets strewn around them. There was an air of complete despair. But Dothie glimpsed hope. Offshore he could see ships on the water a mile or so out. He thought they must be British – one looked like a Royal Navy destroyer. But his frantic signals from the beach went unanswered and a desperate thought crossed his mind: he would swim to them, raise the alarm, bring them to the rescue. Stripping off his uniform, he ran into the waves and struck out for the only help in sight. He struggled in the tricky, deceptively calm waters. 'A current carried me away from the ship,' he recalled in the official report he gave to a military intelligence officer many months later, 'and I had to return to land. When I got back to the beach it was deserted.'[2] His uniform had also gone and he stood there dripping wet in just his underclothes. He was cold, exposed, alone and frightened – experiencing the same emotions as the many thousands of stranded Allied soldiers and downed airmen who would be lost in German-occupied Europe from this point on until the war ended five years later.

He pulled himself together and assessed his situation. The men he had left there on the beach must have surrendered and been taken into captivity, but Dothie determined to stay free as long as he could. He picked up a blanket left lying on the beach, wrapped it round himself and then headed inland to find shelter. At the first house he came to he knocked on the door and was relieved when the Frenchman who answered it offered help. A hot drink and a new set of clothes had the young lieutenant off on his way to find somewhere to hide. He settled in a deserted farmhouse and lay in

the dark, gripping tightly a revolver he had found, as one German
tank after another cruised by on the road outside. Two nights went
by, then he saw figures approaching. He cocked the gun, ready to
shoot his way out of trouble or to die. But the three men emerging
out of the darkness were fellow British officers, and they had a
plan to evade the enemy completely. They were going to head
deep into the countryside and try to lose themselves among the
local French population.

Dothie teamed up with them and the next night the small group
crept through fields, down side roads and along a canal. They
knocked on doors trying to find help and somewhere to sleep but
the heavy German presence in the area now had the locals afraid.
They were sent on their way. Finally, they bedded down in a small
hut. When Dothie woke the next morning it was to stare straight
into the eyes of a German soldier. He was a prisoner. Was it a
chance discovery or had they been betrayed? He never knew as
he and his comrades were bundled into a lorry and taken to a
makeshift POW camp on a football ground. There, thousands of
British soldiers sat or lay on the ground, dejected, hungry, thirsty,
stripped of their arms and their dignity. Another new arrival
recalled this 'dismal sight' – a morass of exhausted bodies covering
the grass, which was churning into mud under them.[3] A private
who showed a glimmer of defiance was battered with rifle butts
by German soldiers, then booted into submission. Control over
their own lives had gone; they were subject to the whim of others.
It was the first harsh lesson of captivity. Dothie kept his head down
– for now. His short time as an evader was over, but he would
have his chance again.

Meanwhile, Lieutenant Jimmy Langley of the Coldstream
Guards was dug in outside Dunkirk, under orders to defend its
perimeter to the last man. The odds against him were immense,
the battle already unequal. The desperate situation provoked a
sporting response from his commanding officer. A British soldier
armed with just a Bren gun could easily take down the Stuka
dive-bombers that were peppering the retreating army, the brigadier told his men. 'Take them from the shoulder, like a high

pheasant,' he ordered. 'Give them plenty of lead. Five pounds to any man who brings one down.' Langley never got the chance. His immediate enemy was not in the air but on the ground and closing. His platoon was holding a canal bridge, allowing others – 'a bedraggled, leaderless rabble' – to cross on their way to the evacuation beaches eight miles further on. He watched infuriated as French troops, all self-discipline gone, pitched their weapons into the canal. He admired the French 'and in the years to come I was to owe them debts of gratitude I can never hope to pay. But they were not at their best on that hot day in May 1940. When I remonstrated they shrugged their shoulders and said that France had lost the war and the sooner they could surrender without being shot the better. They frequently added what stupid fools we were to go on fighting.'[4]

But fight on they did, though the Germans were now barely a hundred yards away and putting up an almost continuous artillery bombardment. Over a radio they heard an interview with a soldier claiming to be the last man taken off the beaches. 'The impression he conveyed was that he had held back the advancing Germans single-handedly before jumping into a boat.' It caused a moment of bleak humour among the Guards, still under orders not to retreat. Three quarters of them would be dead in the next twenty-four hours.

From a cottage in which he was taking cover, Langley sniped at anything that moved in front of him. But the enemy had his measure, and as he stopped to reload a shell burst on the roof above him. 'There was a frightful crash and a great wave of heat, dust and debris knocked me over. I heard a small voice saying, "I've been hit," and suddenly realized it was mine.' His left arm hung limply, bloodied and useless, the bones mangled, the flesh studded with splinters. Gangrene was a certainty, amputation inevitable. For now, though, medics patched him up as best they could and carried him off in a wheelbarrow to a field ambulance. The ambulance, filled with wounded men, then stumbled its way through the town of Dunkirk and onto the sand dunes. From his stretcher Langley could see the sea a few hundred yards away and a lifeboat with a man in naval uniform manning it. So the radio report of the last man having gone was wrong. Was he about to get a passage home after all? His condition ruled out rescue. 'Can you get off the stretcher?' the sailor asked, but Langley was unable to lift himself up. It was no good, the sailor told him. Walking wounded only were allowed – those were the orders. A stretcher would take the space for four men. 'I was just too damned tired to sit up, stand up or argue,' Langley recalled as his chance of escape slipped away.

The ambulance drove him back into the town and to a large house in its own grounds serving now as a hospital. The next day the Germans were at the gates. Langley, concerned by rumours that the Germans were under orders to take no prisoners, went to confront them. Two orderlies carried him outside, where he lay on his stretcher, fully expecting to die, as a tired, dust-caked enemy platoon approached. Nervously he offered up his cigarette case and a silver hip-flask of whisky while drawing their attention to the Red Cross flag flying over the house. The German in charge saluted and Langley felt relief. 'We were not going to be massacred. But I was now a prisoner of war.'

*

Port by port and beach by beach, the Channel coast was mopped up by the German advance. The Dunkirk operation ended, the sand dunes there littered with the burnt-out debris of an entire army, the bodies of tens of thousands of soldiers washing to and fro in the gentle breakers on the beach. But upwards of 330,000 British and French fighting men had got away in seven miraculous days, struggling back across the Channel, wounded, shocked, demoralized but alive to fight another day. Winston Churchill proclaimed the retreat a victory, though in truth it was more a triumph of spin-doctoring. The impression was given that the BEF was home, bloodied but unbowed. Only the dead, the wounded and the captured remained behind. The fact that 150,000 British troops were still on French soil and fighting to find a way back across the water was glossed over.

The focal point for rescue now became the small fishing port of St Valéry-en-Caux between Dieppe and Le Havre, where 10,000 men of the 51st Highland Division were waiting for a similar armada to the one at Dunkirk to take them back across the water. Lost in fog, it never arrived. The few ships that did make it took off a little over 2,000 British troops, just a fifth of those waiting for rescue. Then there was another mass surrender at Dieppe. German tanks beat the Royal Navy to the port and perched on either side of the harbour to stop British warships from entering to take off waiting troops. Five thousand more soldiers went into captivity to join the 8,000 from St Valéry. Now the German army drove relentlessly south and west, pushing a mass of stranded British servicemen in front of it. They were a raggle-taggle army of backroom boys – cooks, mechanics, clerks, signallers and so on. Getting the fighting men home had been the priority at Dunkirk. The support troops – as many as 120,000 of them – had been left to fend for themselves. Their only hope of rescue now was via Brittany and the west-coast ports between St Nazaire and Brest. All along France's Atlantic coastline in the middle of June 1940, last-ditch efforts were being made at one harbour after another to scramble away the final remnants of the British army. Terrible casualties were inflicted, notably when the 16,000-ton Cunard liner *Lancastria*, converted to an emergency troopship, was sunk by dive-bombers as she set out from St Nazaire. Three thousand men died in what was Britain's greatest maritime disaster, the death toll double the number who died on the *Titanic*. Nevertheless, by Sunday 16 June 1940 the evacuation begun on the beaches at Dunkirk three weeks earlier was over. The operation was a success – 186,000 British, French and Polish soldiers were snatched away just in time.

A senior RAF officer boarded the very last ship to leave from the port of Brest after driving across the whole width of France, from Nancy on the eastern border where he had been a liaison officer with the French air force. It was a nightmare 400-mile journey through a country collapsing around him as streams of French civilians fled from the German invaders. France, the writer

Antoine de Saint-Exupéry declared, was 'like a giant anthill kicked over by a boot',[5] millions of refugees filling the roads in cars, on buses, lorries, wagons, mules and horses. Squadron Leader Patrick Barlow saw 'drunk men on horseback, old women driving cows, pathetic household bundles carried on carts drawn by motor tractors, fowls in crates slung between the wheels, canaries in cages on wheelbarrows, panting Alsatian dogs pulling perambulators with babies or bundles inside, little boys carrying huge loads – and all sweating in the intense heat'.[6] The French government had run south too, split between the few who wanted to continue the fight and the majority, led by Pétain, arguing for surrender and an accommodation with the Germans, an armistice with the invader. Meanwhile, in Paris the Germans had commandeered the Champs Elysées and the swastika flew from the Arc de Triomphe.

It was a close call for Barlow and his passengers as the German front line, never more than ten miles away, now closed in. On the very last leg of their dash to safety they drove without lights through the dark night, gripping revolvers and machine guns, ready to shoot their way through any German patrols they ran into. By some miracle they made it to the harbour at Brest, ditched their car and ran to climb on board the *Lady of Man*, one of three Isle of Man ferries drawn up at the dock. As Barlow reached the top of the gangplank he turned to see a tearful French family watching from the quay – an old gentleman with the rosette of the Légion d'Honneur in his buttonhole, his white-haired wife and their little granddaughter dressed in traditional Breton white headdress and pinafore. Like thousands of their countrymen and women, they had tried to join the exodus but had been turned back. There was no room for civilians, they were told. 'Are you British going?' the old woman called out plaintively. 'We are so frightened about what is going to happen to us now.' Barlow mumbled an inadequate excuse but the memory of them and their obvious despair was still locked in his head as the little ship headed out to sea, taking him to England and to safety. What sort of a life would they have under the heel of German occupation? What horrors was he leaving them to?

But in the same way as France was being abandoned to its fate, so were the many thousands of British soldiers for whom there had also been no escape. One of those left behind was Private Peter Scott Janes. A grocer's assistant from Surrey, he had been told by a sergeant during basic training that he would make a good killer with rifle and bayonet, but had then been co-opted into the more peaceful pursuit of an officer's batman. At St Valéry he had been on the brink of finding out if the sergeant's assessment of his latent talent was true or not. But the enemy kept their distance, picking off the defending British and French soldiers with sniper fire and shells. He watched a pal – 'Richardson, the best-looking lad in our class' – die, 'his whole face blown away, his scalp hanging down like a ghastly lid, his head a pool of brain-speckled blood. I looked at his rifle and saw it was unused. He had never fired a shot, never in practice and never in war.'[7] Janes still had his Bren gun and 700 rounds of ammunition but he too never got to use them. 'We were told to unload our guns and throw away our knives and bayonets. The Division had surrendered. We were dumb with the misery of it all as we took our guns apart. Then we were marched away by the Germans. It strikes at one's very soul to find oneself a prisoner. I lay down with my face on the wet ground. My brain would not work at all.'

He was herded at gunpoint into a vast six-acre field, filling up with the thousands of others surrounded and trapped at St Valéry. They were held in this makeshift POW camp for days before being marshalled to their feet and directed eastward away from the coast and towards Germany and long-term internment. The German guards made no attempt to conceal their contempt for their captives. They were also dangerously trigger-happy, and rifle shots rang out as a few brave souls attempted to slip away from the column. Everyone was tense. Janes went to relieve himself in a hedge and a slug from a Luger smashed the branches just inches above his head. His mind filled with crazy thoughts – 'of Death and God, of steak and kidney pies and of Richardson and his white brains on the ground'. He hurried back into the line. There was no point in trying to escape, he decided. There were no boats at the

Channel coast to run to and the only other way home, he worked out, was via Spain, an impossible 400 miles away to the south.

In another of the temporary internment camps now dotting northern France, a soldier with a background so utterly different from Janes's that he might have been the inhabitant of another planet was coming to the same conclusion about Spain, though with a more optimistic slant on it. Major Chandos Sydney Cedric Brudenell-Bruce, the Earl of Cardigan, was from a family of long military distinction – if 'distinction' is the right word for leading the suicidal charge of the Light Brigade in the Crimean War, as his ancestor, the 7th Earl, had done a century earlier. The 36-year-old aristocrat had been caught up in the retreat of the Belgian army and surrendered after throwing his revolver into a duck pond, an action he now regretted as he stewed behind barbed wire, listening to German guards crowing that England too would fall to the Wehrmacht in a fortnight. He decided not to believe their stories that King George VI, his wife and daughters had fled to Canada but it was nonetheless hard to see much hope. 'I see a grim picture of the war dragging on for years,' he wrote in his diary, 'and myself at last being released, a man over 40, decrepit in body as a result of meagre feeding and with a mind completely out of touch, a poor wreck and a stranger to his family and friends.'[8] What lifted his spirits was when an escaper was returned to the compound after a fortnight on the loose. 'Apparently he had no great difficulty in remaining at liberty until he unfortunately blundered into the hands of the Germans again. It seems he made a practice of lying up by day in ruined and deserted villages and of moving only at night. He was generally able to find food.'

The man's only big mistake, Cardigan concluded, was that he had headed towards the Channel in the hope of finding a boat to row himself back to England. He wondered 'what would have happened if the fellow had made for the south instead. Assuming the concentration of German troops to be less dense in the inland areas, it seems quite possible that he might have got clean away. All this revives my own ambition, always present in a vague form at the back of my mind, to attempt an escape.'

Cardigan's chance came as the prisoners were being transported east. He was in the back of an open lorry, the German guards so sure of themselves, so filled with the self-confidence of victory in battle, that they took to sitting inside the cab instead of closely watching their captives. Cardigan eased his way to the tailgate, hoping for a moment when he could jump without being seen by German soldiers in the lorry behind. It was an anxious and frustrating business because whenever a gap opened up, the lorry he was in was travelling too fast and when it slowed the one behind caught up.

Then luck turned in my favour. We were on the outskirts of Tournai when our lorry slowed down at a cross-roads and the driver came almost to a standstill to ask some Belgians the way. This was it. With more agility than I knew myself to possess, I slipped over the tail-board and the lorry moved on, leaving me standing alone. Several of my friends were gazing at me open-mouthed. I called out to them to tell the Germans I had jumped out five miles back. I raised my hand in a quick farewell salute and dodged off the road, scouting for some sort of cover. I felt as conspicuous as if I were dressed in a bathing suit in Piccadilly Circus! I must 'go to ground' and quickly.

I sprinted round behind a wall and threw myself into a patch of greenery. Stinging nettles! And I had to lie low in them for six hours until sunset. But at least I was free. After a weary spell of waiting in which I had to fight down an attack of panic, I heard someone pushing through the nettles towards me. I braced myself for the barrel of a gun to be thrust in my face but it was a Belgian civilian who appeared. He told me he had seen me jump from the lorry. 'I am worried what will happen to you if the Germans find you,' he said. 'They shoot everyone who is found in khaki uniform.'

Cardigan now faced the fundamental dilemma that every single evader in occupied Europe was to experience – could he trust this man who was offering him help? 'He seemed genuinely friendly – or was he a fifth columnist who would turn me in to the Germans?' Brusquely he told the man to go away, but kept the beer and chocolate he had brought. And when no Germans or policemen came to arrest him, he presumed the man was genuine. As dusk fell the villager returned, bringing a change of clothes. Here was the evader's second dilemma. If he remained in military uniform he was certain to be spotted and caught. But if he dressed as a civilian he risked being taken for a spy and shot. He and the Belgian argued the point until Cardigan gave in. He stripped off his uniform and pulled on a pair of striped black trousers, full of holes and too short at the ankle, and a shabby jacket that had seen better times. 'The general effect was of a disreputable Belgian waiter on a day off.' Together he and his new friend walked to the man's house, where he stayed the night on a bed in an attic, sleeping fitfully. 'Previously I had slept through air raids but now, with the prospect of a German search party finding me at any moment, sleep would not come. The first light of dawn appeared, heralded by the sound of bugles from a nearby German barracks. It was time to leave.'

He went south, as he had always planned to do. He would head for the Mediterranean and then hope to find his way to the Pyrenees and across into neutral Spain. He did not know it but this was a pioneering decision as he set out on the route home that many evaders after him would follow. He was encouraged in this plan by rumours among the prisoners that France had now been divided in two. The precise details of the armistice between the French and the Germans were not known but there was a general belief among the evaders that 'there is an area somewhere to the south which will not be occupied, and within which the French government will maintain some sort of independence. It is not clear whether any route exists by which one could get home; but it would at least be an immensely valuable first step if one could get outside the limits of the German occupation.'

Cardigan began what would be a heroic one-man journey, much of it on foot, through back roads and small villages, across fields, streams and rivers. He passed over the border from Belgium back into France and then followed a canal until a German soldier angrily turned him away – the towpath was a military zone and *verboten*! But the good news in this was that the German did not recognize him as an outsider, a man on the run, though the locals he passed did – and sidled up to offer help. And advice. Yes, they told him, in his ragged clothes, he looked like a bona fide itinerant but his bearing and his gait gave him away. 'You are too much like an Englishman,' one newly acquired friend told him. He was tall and thin where most Frenchmen of his height and age were stout. And he walked oddly, 'taking long strides, with my head up in the air and looking from side to side as much as to say "What sort of place is this?" A Frenchman is quite different. He knows where he is going and plods along looking straight in front of him.' The earl listened and, with his freedom and his life depending on it, threw off his Englishness as best he could, stifling the manner bred into him at his ancestral home, at Eton and at Oxford.

It was hard to kick the habits of a lifetime. Early one lovely morning he stopped to admire the vista around him – 'the sun breaking through some low-lying clouds and beautiful shafts and streams of light radiating upwards' – as he might have done on the family estate in Wiltshire. Suddenly he realized he was being stared at intently by a German soldier on a motorcycle. 'I hastily moved off. Tramps are not normally susceptible to the beauties of nature. I must remember in future to restrain myself from un-tramp-like behaviour.' He did his best to avoid towns where German forces were concentrated, taking long detours across fields and down country lanes rather than go brazenly through the centre of a town. It was not always possible – 'one village was positively packed with Germans, many strolling up and down the street, others stripped to the waist and jogging along in running shorts. A big house was marked by a huge Nazi flag, the swastika against a blood-red background. From a garden came the crack of revolver shots as some officers engaged in shooting practice.' Eyes straight ahead, he pressed on, thankful not to be their target.

But he was not always able to avoid the Germans. On a bridge one day he was stopped by sentries demanding his identity papers. He had none and could only act stupid, stalling, explaining in faltering French that he had lost them. His stammer – a natural affliction made worse by his anxiety – actually came to his aid. The German soldiers tired of his babble, decided he was a harmless half-wit and sent him on his way. 'I raised my battered cap, added to their bewilderment with a string of apologies and thanks and stumped off across the bridge.'

But there were terrible times too when his spirit flagged and he was close to giving up. He starved, going for days without finding food if the locals he met were too scared to help him. He was exhausted, a hundred hard miles under his belt but his goal still too far away to contemplate. One night, hungry, tired and alone, the very thought of another day on the road was too much for him:

I may not be able to stand another 24 hours. No man can walk for long with bad feet, insufficient sleep, no water and no food. Lacking help, there can only be one end to it – surrender. The grim choice will have to be made between becoming once again a prisoner who eats and drinks or remaining a free man who starves!

Then, at his lowest moment, help came. In desperation he walked up to a remote farmhouse and announced himself to be an English officer trying to escape. Eggs, bread and ham were put in front of him. There was fresh milk to gulp down, followed by a chance to wash and bandage his sore feet. His offer to pay – he was carrying some £40 in francs, a considerable sum, which he had hidden from his German captors – was brushed aside. Quite the opposite. A 20-franc note was thrust into *his* hand. Such kindness and generosity revived his spirits and he went on his way feeling a new man.

*

Every man's escape and evasion was different. No two were ever the same. So, where Cardigan chose action and set out on the arduous road to Spain, Peter Janes decided to stay in northern France and hide. His escape from a line of prisoners being marched under escort to Germany was pure chance. For him there was no forethought, no calculated leap from a moving lorry. A girl simply grabbed his hand and tugged him away. Until that point, Janes's opinion of the French had been a poor one. After he and his men had thrown down their arms at St Valéry he had been disgusted by the sudden change of heart by the local French people, refusing even to offer the British water now they were captives. Then, when France's armistice with Germany was announced, he watched in further disgust as French soldiers hugged each other and cheered what was a shameful defeat as if it were a Napoleonic victory. But it was now several days later and the reality of being defeated had apparently sunk in because the road the POWs trudged along was lined with sympathetic French people offering up gifts of food, cigarettes, soap, towels and razors. In a mining village a man had just thrust a glass of beer into Janes's hand when a girl hissed '*Allez, allez, tout de suite,*' seized his hand and hauled him behind a wall. There she gave him a shirt and trousers to put over his uniform and hurried him away to a house 200 yards away. Revived with coffee and rum, Janes was then taken to a farmhouse in the country and hidden.

At first he expected to be back with his regiment behind friendly lines within a few days. He thought the surrender at St Valéry had been an isolated local incident and that the BEF still had a presence on the continent. He did not know about Dunkirk and the whole-sale evacuation from France. His ignorance was not surprising – and typical of the chaotic state of affairs in the countries now falling to the Nazi invaders.

Listening to the news from London on the illicit radio of the family hiding him, Janes realized those lines no longer existed and he was a long way from safety. He decided there was no good reason to leave. He was lodged with a local miner 'and am very comfortable indeed'. He was well fed and sheltered, and his only worry was that the people hiding him might get into trouble. But they seemed unperturbed. He was taken to meet friends and family members. All the village seemed to know about him. A fortnight went by and he felt himself becoming a part of the place. He might have been homesick, but there were three Scots soldiers in a village nearby, evaders like him, and he visited them whenever he wanted the company of his own countrymen. There was also an Englishman, a teacher named Teddy who had lived in the area for years, and Janes spent time with him.

Teddy, though, sounded the only discordant note. He lived in fear of being picked up as an alien and interned.

He has the crazy idea of trying to walk to Portugal or Switzerland in the hope of getting home to England and asked me if I would care to join him. The distance to Portugal is roughly 1,400 kilometres. Heaven only knows how he will keep himself in food and, above all, boots all that way. It will take five weeks at least. And Spain is Fascist [under Franco] and may quite possibly be in the war on the wrong side by then. And he will be in danger of being caught every minute of the day. True he is a civilian and has a passport but I don't think that that will help him a lot. Not me. If I travel at all I want to go north or else west to America. Neither is possible yet or likely to be for a bit.

An epic march to Spain or Switzerland through occupied territory may have seemed impossible to Peter Janes, but many evaders would attempt the journey as the war progressed. Perhaps there were other attractions persuading him to stay put – the number of pretty French girls he was getting to know, for example. He was a ladies' man, always had been. He had a steady girlfriend back home – her name was Doreen but he called her 'Babe' – though this had not stopped him kissing as many girls as he could in his home town in the weeks immediately before going off to war. Now, with the added allure of being a foreigner and a fugitive, he had a harem of teenage admirers around him. There was Mathilde, his host's teenage daughter, and Gilberte, another friend, and Hélène, whom he called the 'little lady' and considered 'breathtakingly lovely' with her light brown hair, slightly sun-browned skin 'and the cleavage of her dress!' For a red-blooded 21-year-old with time on his hands, there was little more that life could offer. And the Germans? They patrolled the main roads but were not hard to avoid. They pounced on Teddy and took him away to be interned but seemed oblivious to the presence of other foreign bodies in the area. So Janes stayed, and as high summer turned to autumn he helped with the harvest, listened to news of the Battle of Britain on the radio and quietly got on with his life.

★

Janes had decided against trying to escape from France – for now at least – but other British soldiers at liberty were doggedly heading for home – and taking the shortest route they could think of rather than the long way round via Spain. Captain Leslie Hulls had also been forced to surrender in the débâcle at St Valéry-en-Caux. He had been quickly shuttled away from the coast by lorry and was in a makeshift camp fifty miles north of Paris waiting for a train for Germany and a long incarceration. He had been a prisoner of the Turks in the First World War and shuddered at the thought of another stretch of time behind barbed wire. At the same time he knew that escaping meant leaving the comfort of comrades and comparative safety for unknown hazards on the outside. He weighed the matter and decided to make a break for it. He traded his distinctive Burberry overcoat for something less obviously English and borrowed a beret from a French soldier. He chose a navy man as a companion – Commander Elkins had a compass and knew how to navigate by the stars. Since they planned to make for the coast of Normandy and find a boat, his seafaring skills would be a double bonus. Hulls's contribution was his own invaluable experience – he had once lived in France, spoke the language and knew the geography.[9]

Getting away from the camp proved the least of their problems. Early one evening, while other POWs distracted the bored guards with conversation, Hulls and Elkins crawled under the wire and into bushes. They lay low until it was dark and then set out across country in a south-westerly direction towards the Seine. The high crops in the fields slowed their progress but also gave them cover as they put as many miles as they could between themselves and the camp that first night. They were helped by a woodcutter they approached – 'I could see he was *the right type of man*,' Hulls wrote in his official report. He told them they easily passed muster among the countless refugees on the road and would do better to travel openly in the day rather than risk being caught out during the night-time curfew. He gave them the address of a small hotel in Rouen where they would be safe.

But when they got to the city, they found it was a hive of suspicion. The streets were thick with German soldiers. Under martial law, civilians were being held as hostages to guarantee good behaviour. The contacts they met were nervous, fearing the men might be undercover policemen or agents provocateurs. They would not be the last evaders to have to prove their authenticity to their would-be helpers, not always an easy task. A knife across the throat awaited any who failed the test. But eventually they were taken at their word, provided with bicycles and slipped across the Seine on an unsupervised ferry to avoid the military checkpoints on the bridges. They cycled out into the Normandy countryside, into a completely different atmosphere.

Away from the city the war seemed to have left no mark at all. Against all expectation there was scarcely a German soldier to be seen and they reached the coast without interruption or worry. Spirits soared at the sight of fishing boats bobbing on the sea and the prospect of England just eighty miles away. But the view was deceptive. In one port after another they discovered the Germans had been, done their work and departed. The harbour at Ouistre- ham just outside Caen was blocked with sunken craft. Elsewhere, lines of small boats pulled up on beaches looked promising but close inspection showed their hulls deliberately holed beyond repair. They were unusable. Just as damaging was the legacy of fear the Germans had left. When the two English officers sought help from fishermen they were turned away. Anyone caught helping them would be shot. It was an effective deterrent.

However, not everyone was cowed by the German threat of summary execution. In the village of Lion-sur-Mer Hulls and Elkins were directed to a Professor Mercier, a scientist in charge of a government marine research laboratory. For his work, he had an eighteen-foot yacht, which was moored offshore, and when the two men approached him he came up with an answer not untypical of the French at this time. He could not help them openly, he declared, but he would do nothing to stop them stealing it. He even left charts and extra equipment out for them. Then the local mayor entered into the plot, agreeing to pull his police patrol off the beach on the night the two Englishmen planned to get away. In his official report of the escape, Hulls made no mention of their feelings as they waited to embark. But it is hard to think they were not apprehensive. The Channel was no easy crossing. Its waters may be familiar to travellers today, when powerful ferries plough their way over as a matter of course. But sixty-five years ago this stretch of sea, prone to dangerous currents and sudden changes of weather, was a formidable natural obstacle. Enemy gunboats and spotter planes patrolling the coast were an added risk. Even if they survived the elements, there was the threat of being blown out of the water – by their own side as much as by the Germans. When and if they reached the English coast, shore gunners on alert for a Nazi invasion might be tempted to fire first at an unidentified craft and ask questions afterwards.

Aware of the dangers they faced, the two men set out. As darkness fell they rowed out from the shore in a dinghy and climbed aboard the yacht. The sea was already choppy; a storm was blowing up. Elkins was mystified by the rigging of the mainsail, jib and mizzen. Though a naval man, he had never seen anything quite like it. It took time to familiarize himself before they could set sail. Then the engine refused to start, and two hours went by getting it going – 'the worst two hours we had spent', according to Hulls. It finally spluttered into life, but ran for just five minutes before overheating and dying. As the sun came up they saw, to their relief, they were just far enough from the shore to be safely out of sight.

Their problems, however, were only beginning. Hulls recorded 'bad weather, desperate with engine and gear' as all that day they battled the winds and current pushing them back towards the French coast. Not until the late afternoon did the wind veer – 'a godsend' – and at last head them north towards home. 'The next morning we sighted land, which turned out to be the Isle of Wight.

But then the wind turned against us and we had to approach slowly to Selsey Bill. We had anticipated being picked up by some steamer in the Channel but met no boat of any description. We finally sailed right into Hayling Island [near Portsmouth] and ran the boat ashore there.' It had been a battle against the sea for Hulls and Elkins but they had completed a successful 'home run' to safety.

So too had Lieutenant William Dothie. After surrendering on the beach at Calais he had found himself in a long, despairing column of prisoners force-marched towards the German border. Each step was taking them closer to permanent captivity. If he wanted to escape, he would have to act before it was too late. He seized his opportunity as they filed through the main street of a village, slipping into a narrow passage between two houses and racing across a field to an abandoned farmhouse. He heard shots behind him. The German guards patrolling up and down the column on bicycles were encouraging the stragglers at the rear by taking pot-shots at them. They had not noticed his dash for freedom. The column moved on without him. That night he slept in a barn and next morning stayed hiding there, keeping watch on the nearby village and its comings and goings, assessing his chances of finding help there.

Suddenly he was confronted by two German soldiers. Intent on his observation of the village, he had not noticed them come into the farmyard. Somehow he managed to keep his head. Boldly he introduced himself as the farmer; they saluted and asked to buy some eggs. He realized his stumbling French was marginally better than theirs. They suspected nothing. The soldiers took their eggs, exchanged for some tobacco, and left. He had passed his first test. To the enemy at least, he could pass for a Frenchman. He made a decision that his safest course of action was to do nothing. He would stay where he was, bed down in this farm as long as he could, wait until he was good and ready to make a proper escape. He spun a line to the people in the village, telling them he had taken over the running of the farm at the request of its absentee owner, though it was clear they did not believe him. 'I think they realized I was English by my accent but they said nothing.' His disguise was so good that Germans from an artillery battery camped in the woods nearby kept coming to him for eggs. 'To keep them away I began to deliver to them!'

His trips outside the farm had another purpose – he was on the lookout for a bicycle. Eventually he 'spotted one in a farmyard and quietly took it without being seen. I then packed a bag with food and set off. I knew that going back to Calais was not a good idea. I headed for Brittany.' In corduroy trousers and a beret he was indistinguishable from a French peasant, but he felt his real nationality and his true identity must be screaming out to anyone who saw him. Passing through his first town he fully expected a cry to halt, a rifle cocked in his direction and a swift end to his freedom. But he sailed through, past Germans and locals alike, unexceptional and unnoticed. His confidence high, he even tackled bridges manned by steel-helmeted guards. The one time he was stopped, he explained to a German officer that he was a Breton heading home. There was no reason for the officer to query this. The roads were thronged with travellers in these early days after the fall of France. It would be a while before the occupying forces settled in and took a firmer grip. Until then a man on the road – as long as he obeyed the curfew at night – was nothing out of the ordinary.

For a week he cycled across France, ticking off the towns he passed on a Michelin guide he had managed to obtain. Then he spent a week on the north Brittany coast, riding between seaside villages, picking his spot and his moment. He lighted on the hamlet of Bréhec, where a jetty poked out into the sea. A sailing boat was alongside. He didn't wait to reconnoitre or plan. 'I just got on, adjusted the rudder and sails and got away without being seen.' Plain sailing? Hardly, because the wind and currents took him not north to the English coast but east to the Channel Islands – to find the Germans had just landed and taken possession. Warned just in time by two fishermen, he pushed on from Jersey to Alderney and then steered out into the Channel. He seemed to be making good progress but in fact was going in a circle. Half-swamped by rough seas, he found himself back in Alderney.

Dispirited, he made the short passage back to the French mainland

and, exhausted, ran the boat onto a beach at Cap de la Hague near Cherbourg. It was now a case of starting all over again. Or should he give up? 'My face was black from the sun and salt, and my clothes consisted of a shirt, corduroy trousers cut off at the knees and army boots. I had given up hope and expected to be arrested as a suspicious character.'

He was walking through a village when a door opened. A woman invited him in to rest, eat, change his clothes. He stayed with her and her husband, amid their growing anxiety about what would happen to them if he was found. After a week he left them in peace and hid out in fishing huts and empty houses before getting a job on a farm, posing as a Frenchman. Ten German marines were billeted on the same farm, and he would engage them in conversation. They never suspected him – his French was better than theirs – though the farmer did become increasingly anxious, urging the Englishman on his way. He should go south to the Mediterranean coast and make his escape from France there, he was told. But Dothie decided to give the Channel one last try. He managed to find a tiny sailing boat, intact though decrepit, and, despite his fears that it would sink, he set out on the 2 a.m. tide. The wind let him down, pushing him back to port.

Back on land, the pressure on him to go was growing. Everyone in the village knew about him. It was only a matter of time before the police came for him. He needed a boat with a motor if he was ever to make it out to sea and luckily he found one and the petrol to power it. Once again he launched himself into the unknown. The crossing was smooth and his passage easy – until, with the Isle of Wight in sight, he ran out of petrol. 'I made a sail from a piece of sacking but the wind dropped and the current took me westwards along the coast away from the Isle of Wight.' Then the wind sprang up again but veered constantly and he was washed backwards and forwards. England was in sight just a mile or so away but he was being pushed and pulled away from it. A Royal Navy patrol ship came to his rescue. Sailors hoisted him on board and he was on his way to dry *English* land at last.

★

Once home, Dothie – like Hulls, Elkins and the other BEF veterans who managed to escape and slip back across the Channel – was directed to an office in London for a special debriefing. A small section of Military Intelligence known as MI9 was there to glean what information it could about what they had seen. That summer of 1940, Britain stood in fear of an invasion. Any military details these men could recall, particularly of German units massing in the Pas de Calais region, might be important. It was also a chance to add pieces to the complex jigsaw of what had happened and was still happening across the Channel to their comrades. Details of their capture, who they had seen behind the barbed wire, how they were treated, where they were taken – all had significance. From their experiences, a dossier was also being drawn up of dos and don'ts for British servicemen on the run in occupied Europe. The War Office had had a department dealing with POW camps during the First World War and this was revived shortly after the outbreak of the second under a middle-aged ex-infantry major, Norman Crockatt, a tall, imposing man, 'clear-headed, quick-witted, a good organizer, a good judge of men and no respecter of red tape', according to those who knew him.[10] He set up shop in Room 424 of the Metropole hotel in Northumberland Avenue, next to Whitehall. Long before there were any POWs to actually concern him, he defined his job as monitoring activities in the internment camps that, in the long war ahead, would inevitably be set up in Germany, but, just as importantly, to help in whatever way he could men escaping from them or avoiding capture in the first place.

From the start Crockatt's was a Cinderella department, squeezed of money and tending to attract detractors rather than active supporters in the War Office. The haughty Admiralty could not see the point of it and to the army and air force what it did was a side issue to their operations. MI9 would also brush up uncomfortably against the Foreign Office's Diplomatic Service. All these Ugly Sisters tried to bully and meddle with its activities at some point or another, and it took all Crockatt's skills to keep his little independent unit from being constantly overwhelmed. Even greater interference came from MI6, the secret service, whose driving force was the formidable and much-feared Colonel Sir Claude Dansey. History did not help Crockatt here, and there was a particular ghost he never laid to rest – that of Nurse Edith Cavell. The spies at MI6 never let him forget how, in the First World War, their operations in Belgium had been compromised when she, though one of their undercover agents, embroiled herself in helping British soldiers to escape. These activities drew attention to her, she was caught by the Germans and shot by a firing squad. The all-powerful and self-regarding MI6 was determined that this overlapping of roles, leading to the loss of an agent in the field, should not happen again. Spying had priority; escapers and evaders must wait in line. The fact that men making it home from occupied areas gleaned important intelligence along the way was a blurring of this facile distinction that was never totally resolved. One MI9 veteran would recall departmental battles with 'Uncle Claude' as fierce as any against the Germans. MI9 was also drawn into the senseless power struggles and personality clashes involving MI6 and other undercover outfits, the Special Operations Executive (SOE) and the Political Warfare Executive (PWE). But MI9 had to tread carefully. As its historians put it: 'What Dansey wanted done was done and what he wanted undone was undone. He could have broken Crockatt as easily as he blew his own nose, and Crockatt knew it.'[11] That the lives of thousands of brave men and women came to depend on a unit with such a precarious existence in Whitehall is one of the less laudable aspects of this story.

For now, though, in the summer of 1940, the intrigue and the infighting lay in the future. Men were returning from behind the lines with valuable stories to tell. With space limited at Room 424 in the Metropole, a floor was taken at another requisitioned London hotel, the Great Central, now transformed into the 'London Transit Camp', opposite Marylebone station. 'Home runners' like Dothie climbed its wide staircase to the second floor and in elegant bedrooms, now bare except for a table and chairs, were interrogated on every last detail of their journey home. Some, like Hulls, wrote down their own accounts, but others repeated their stories for an officer to record. No time was wasted. From the very top – Winston Churchill himself – came a humanitarian order to cut through red tape. Interviews should be swiftly conducted and the men with the guts to make it back were sent off to be reunited with their families within forty-eight hours.

The information they supplied was collated, and MI9 drew up one of its first notes of advice for men on the run.[12] Some was trite – 'great care should be taken in approaching civilians for help' – but unrealistic in that it gave no indication how to distinguish the safe from the unsafe. Not that there was any such guaranteed sign but the advice as it stood was obvious. More practical – if just as obvious – was the suggestion for men in uniform to travel at night but for those who managed to acquire civilian clothes to move openly in the day. 'Main roads can be used and large towns can be passed through in reasonable safety. Side roads and small villages should be avoided, as a stranger excites suspicion.' This, it might be said, was not what the Earl of Cardigan had experienced, but then by this time he had not reached home to tell his story. But other lessons he was picking up from experience had already been learnt by others and passed on:

Do not march in a military fashion, but adopt a tired slouch.

Try and 'collect' a bicycle. They proved invaluable to several escapers.

Do not wear a wrist watch. Carry it in your pocket.

Sling your haversack: French peasants commonly carry one in this way, but never as a pack on their backs.

Do not use a cane or walking-stick: it is a British custom.

Get rid of army boots and adopt a pair of rope-soled shoes as worn by peasants, if procurable.

French peasants are generally clean-shaven, though a slight growth of beard is not uncommon.

A beret is a very effective disguise.

Village priests are likely to be helpful. Care should be exercised in approaching them and one should avoid being seen talking to them. Slip into the confessional box in the church and approach the priest in sacristy after service. First mass at 5 a.m. Listen for church bell.

It was pointed out that the average German soldier's grasp of French was limited and they were generally unable to tell an Englishman speaking it, however poorly, from the bad French of a Flemish-speaker from Belgium. Posing as a Belgian refugee was recommended. On the other hand, German *officers* tended to speak and understand French very well. But the vast movement of refugees in France gave an opportunity to mingle with the civilian crowds and 'fade into the landscape'. As for the best route home, the advice was still to head for the northern French and Belgian coasts and find a boat. It was outdated the moment it was issued, as evaders on the ground were now finding out for themselves.

★

The German grip was tightening more than ever on the coastal towns. Serviceable boats capable of making it across the Channel were increasingly difficult to find. Fleeing north was no longer the way. South was the direction. Any man who wanted to get home now would have to go that way round. Which was why Wing Commander Basil Embry was now in Paris, sitting at a round marble-topped table under a striped awning and ordering a coffee. He glanced down at himself, dressed like a tramp, tattered coat, broken shoes, hands dirty, face unshaven. Then he looked around him. Paris! It was hard to believe he was here at a pavement café, taking his ease, or at least pretending to do so. The streets were thronged with people on their way to work, the road filled with streams of cyclists. Then, from the nearby Champs Elysées, came the sound of a band as column after column of jackbooted German infantry, bayonets fixed, marched triumphantly down the middle of this most symbolic of all French boulevards, a concrete embodiment of national pride now being trampled on by a barbarian force. Swastika flags swayed in the midsummer breeze. The occupier was making his mark. The crowds watched in silence, 'sullen, stupefied by their conquerors' tramping feet, stunned by defeat', as Embry noted.[13]

His own presence as a witness to the full humiliation of France's defeat continued to astonish him. Just three weeks had passed since he had been drinking beer with his fellow pilots in the mess at Wattisham in the quiet Suffolk countryside. So much had happened since then, it seemed a lifetime ago, in another world. Everything in his well-ordered existence had been turned upside down. Now here he was, bedraggled, exhausted, in rags, not only on the run in an enemy country but wanted for murder.

Embry was unusual in being an air casualty of the fighting in northern France. Churchill kept his air force largely away from the Dunkirk evacuation, knowing he would need his fighter squadrons intact for the battle for Britain that would inevitably follow the battle for France. But bombers had a job to do and Embry's squadron of Blenheims had been ordered into the air against the advancing German tanks. He didn't need to fly that day. He had just been promoted to a new command, a whole RAF station to run instead of just a single squadron, and no one would have blamed him if he had decided to sit this one out. But, on the spur of the moment, he opted for one last sortie with his boys. They roared over the Channel, past Calais, already in flames 6,000 feet below, and homed in on an armoured German column. The puffs of anti-aircraft shells took him by surprise. The aircraft shuddered from a hit – 'like a punch to the solar plexus' – stalled and its nose tipped down. The gunner was dead in his turret from the flak, the navigator had already baled out, and Embry followed.

Head-first he went, counted three and pulled his ripcord. He looked down and saw beneath his feet the canvas roofs of lorries in the convoy he had just bombed. He was about to drop straight on top of one of them. A tug at the parachute lines steered him away, across the column and down into a field. He flung off the 'chute and ran for the nearest hedge just as a German motorcycle and sidecar turned from the road onto a farm track and headed in his direction. The realization of the danger he was in hit him like a shock wave. 'They were *Germans*, armed, my enemies. I had tried to destroy them from the air. But now I was on the ground without a weapon of any kind. It was their turn to do the killing.' He ducked down into a field of corn and watched as the soldiers stopped at a nearby farm. He saw an old man lift his arm and point in his direction. The soldiers came towards him, their automatic rifles levelled. He stood up. 'The game was up.'

The capture was almost friendly. Hands high, he was searched, then offered water and a cigarette. They helped him into the sidecar and gave him goggles to protect his eyes from the dust. On the way he saw what was left of his plane, oily smoke rising from the wreckage. His leg began to hurt and for the first time he realized he had been hit. For the Germans, Embry was a curiosity and they treated him with quite unexpected courtesy. He was ushered to an open-top staff car where someone wanted to speak to him. Inside sat General Heinz Guderian, commander-in-chief of the German tanks corps, the architect of the blitzkrieg attack that was even now sweeping all before it. He invited Embry to get in and then gently interrogated him as they drove to his field headquarters. Soldiers came to attention and saluted as they motored down the road like royalty. Lulled, an exhausted Embry fell asleep and Guderian laid his own greatcoat over the English airman to keep him warm.

Even after the general had handed him over and driven off, the courtesies continued. At a requisitioned château he watched German soldiers handing out chocolate to local children. Laughter filled the air. This was not the enemy he had expected. What was going on? Then came the sting in the scorpion's tail, the alert to the realities of his situation. 'Try to escape and you will be shot in five seconds,' he was warned.

But try he did. He had told himself from the outset that he would not go submissively into detention, and when the niceties of chats with the general were over and he was transferred to a holding camp and then joined the miserable trek of POWs towards Germany, he was even more determined. If he needed any more persuading it came when a rumour swept along the line that Germany was not their destination. They were being marched to an execution ground to be liquidated. He worked himself into the middle of the column, waited until there were no guards in sight and then dived into a ditch. He lay in water, his heart thumping, counting to 120. Then he crawled up and looked to see the tail of the column winding away without him. He was euphoric as he ran for a copse in the distance.

But once there his mood changed. Suddenly he was a hunted creature and the realization almost felled him. 'You're lost. You're liable to be shot on sight.' The doubts ran riot in his mind. 'You're alone in a world you don't know. Your clothes are soaked through. You don't stand a chance. Now be sensible. Play safe. Go and give yourself up.' It would be so easy. Just a few hundred yards away, some steel-helmeted soldiers from the column had returned. They were looking for him. All he had to do was stand up. But then the duty drummed into him over years of military training kicked in. It was his job to escape, to stay free, not to submit. He grabbed a stick and dug away at the soft ground beneath him, fashioning a hole to hide in. Then he pulled branches and briars over himself and lay still in what was now a slimy pit filling up with rank-smelling water. He heard German voices nearby and tensed himself for a gun barrel sticking into his head. But nothing happened. It was getting dark. The voices drifted into the distance. He heard a car engine fire and move away. He looked up and saw nothing, no one. Embry stumbled away into the night, the words of a half-remembered psalm now ringing in his head – 'Yea, though I walk through the valley of death, I will fear no evil . . .'

Locals rescued the fugitive, took him in, warmed him up, dried him out, fed him, let him sleep. Then he went on his way. He, like others at the time, thought he could get back to British lines. The news passed to him by a schoolmaster he met that the British army had gone was a body blow. But then he realized that the same military might that had overrun France would now be aimed at England. It was even more imperative to get back now, to join in the defence of his country. He would walk to the coast, find a boat, row home if he had to. But first he would have to hide his RAF uniform. In the middle of a field of beet he spied a scarecrow dressed in an overcoat, dark grey, high-buttoned, with holes in the side and a torn sleeve. He put it on over his uniform, but the blue rings of his rank still showed at his wrists, so he took off the jacket, ripped it into four pieces and buried it in the ground. He knew the significance of the moment. Caught in civilian clothes, he could be shot as a spy.

But the disguise worked. As he made his way along tracks and roads, he passed the test of encounters with German soldiers. He concocted a cover story – he was Belgian and he was a refugee simply doing his best to get away from the fighting. Those German soldiers who stopped him shrugged and let him go on his way. Could his luck last? It seemed so, until a lorry passed him on an open country road and screeched to a halt. Five SS troopers jumped down. One of them clubbed him to the ground. '*Je suis belge,*' he protested. 'That is a lie. You are an English soldier,' the sergeant in charge said and lashed out with his boot. Where were his papers? He had none, he said. They threw him in the back of the lorry and drove to their platoon base in a farmhouse for more questioning, more beatings. 'If we find out you're English . . .' the sergeant said, drawing his hand menacingly across his throat. They locked him in a room and as he stewed on his situation, despair overtook him. He was finished. Soon it would all be over – 'a dirty, disgraceful end, bullied and beaten and shot to death by little German corner-boys!'

The thought raised his hackles. Angry now instead of scared, he kicked the door and shouted for some water. A soldier, slight of frame, opened the door, held out a cup . . . and Embry hit him. He told his biographer many years afterwards:

My knuckles met his jaw, his head went back and his legs gave way. I kicked him in the stomach before he reached the floor and when he was down kicked him again. I snatched up his rifle from the ground and made for the door. I ran out into the corridor and saw a second German on guard. Before he could turn I lifted the rifle and brought the butt down on his head. He collapsed in a heap. I leapt over him and out into the yard where a third German, buckets of water in his hands, was standing in his shirt sleeves, whistling. I swung the rifle again and the whistle faded from his lips as it hit his temple. He and the buckets went sprawling. I looked around. No one else was in sight. No one came running but I thought I heard the sound of a car, so I flung the rifle away and dived into a heap of drying manure to hide.

Embry lay concealed for several hours but nobody came to the farm. Eventually he crawled out of the yard, through a fence, then took to his heels. Miles away he found a deserted house – it was one of the few blessings for evaders at this particular time that so many people had dropped everything and run from the Germans, leaving home after home like a beached *Mary Celeste*. In the kitchen he nosed out a lump of mouldering pork in an earthenware crock. It was sustenance of a sort, along with eggs from the hen coop, a lettuce from the garden and the dregs of home-made cider, sharp and sour, from an old barrel. 'What more could any man desire?' he asked himself. But his satisfaction was short lived; soon afterwards he was stopped by a German patrol as he was walking through a village and asked for his papers. He realized his usual cover story would not do. If the bodies at the farm had been discovered, the Germans would be looking for a 'Belgian'. So this time, grabbing at straws, he said he was an Irishman, a Republican, as fierce an enemy of the British as it was possible to be. It was a wild, improbable tale but he spun it with verve. He had been active in the IRA, a master of sabotage and terror attacks, he'd been imprisoned in England, he had escaped and fled to Belgium. They didn't buy it . . . well, not completely. They needed to make checks, they said, to refer the matter to higher authority. They locked him up. In the cell, his mind stewed again, imagining the worst. Of course, the simplest of inquiries would expose him, and wouldn't he then be linked to the killings at the farm?

As he foresaw his fate, a sentry came to the door and ushered him out and through the village, towards open countryside. Embry's mind raced ahead – he must be on his way to be shot, in whatever wood or field the local German administration used as their execution ground. He plotted his escape. When he got the chance he would hit the guard and run. As they reached the last house, he gathered his strength. The German stopped. But his rifle stayed slung on his shoulder and he pointed his finger down the road. 'Go,' he said. 'Just go.' Embry went. The bullet he half expected in the back never came. So had they believed his pre-posterous story after all? Or could they just not be bothered dealing with him? It didn't matter. He was free again.

★

Embry's intention was still to get to the coast and find a friendly French fisherman to take him over the Channel. It wasn't far now. A farmer he chanced on gave him the name of a man who might help at Cayeux-sur-Mer. Embry was jubilant. He walked the last few miles on a cloud. Home seemed closer now than it had ever been. Those hopes were quickly dashed. There was no fisherman to help him. As everywhere else along the coast, the harbour was closed, fishing banned and the hull of even the smallest dinghy smashed in. There was no way home this way, not any more. And so he had come to Paris, travelling the best part of a hundred miles from the coast, on foot, then on a stolen bicycle. He knew the city had fallen to the Germans, but where else was he to go? In Paris, he told himself, he would present himself at the embassy of the United States – not in the war at this stage (and not for another eighteen months). He'd been a Belgian and an Irishman, now he would be an American to get himself home.

To be in the French capital as it fell to the Nazis was extraordi-nary. But then, in the history of the Second World War evaders, it never ceases to amaze how many of them roamed its streets, hiding in its back alleys but also tramping its tourist sights as if they were on a Thomas Cook holiday rather than in an enemy capital. They rubbed shoulders with that other group of visitors eager to explore its charms, its art, its history – German soldiers. As they rode the Métro, some men on the run even took a dangerous delight in jostling those they met in the grey uniform of the Wehrmacht, simply because they could. In a situation where you were powerless it was a small, childish way of reasserting some control.

Paris would become a hub of the escape lines which – as we

will see – were to develop quickly and become a core part of this story. But in the summer of 1940 no such organizations existed. Men like Embry had no safe houses to go to, no guides he could trust. Anyone might turn him in. He was not alone in this situation. Other evaders from the battle on the northern coastline were also arriving there. Signaller John Christie came by train to the Gare du Nord, where the first thing he saw was a pre-war travel poster with a picture of York Minster and the words 'Visitez York!' His companion, a Yorkshireman, whispered out of the side of his mouth: 'Wish to hell I could!' They left the station and, in Christie's words, 'let fate take its course'.[14] In a small bar in a run-down area they confessed who they were to the *patronne*, were greeted with open arms, fed egg and chips and hidden for the night. Then they made for the American embassy. To their surprise there was no cordon of German soldiers outside, no one to stop them. The reception inside was friendly. A woman delegated to look after British affairs noted their details and gave them some money – 600 francs each.[15] But her urgent advice was to 'beat it out of town' fast. The embassy had learned that the Germans were about to launch a crackdown on foreigners.

There was only one way to go that made any sense. A Paris newspaper helpfully printed across its centre pages a map of the new France, showing its readers the demarcation line between the occupied and unoccupied zones. The coastal areas in the north and west were also ring-fenced, out of bounds to anyone without specific permission to be there. But the Mediterranean coast was wide open and beckoning. They went to the Gare d'Austerlitz, bought tickets and made their way south by train, the first of many.

Embry was by now also going in the same direction, though under his own steam. At the American embassy he had tried to bluff his way as a US citizen, hoping to hoax the officials into repatriating him. He announced himself as a Henry J. Walker from New York City, peppering his fictitious account of what had happened to him to the woman at the bureau with lots of 'aw shucks', 'goddams' and 'yes, ma'ams'. She listened, unimpressed, then leaned over the counter and whispered: 'If I were you I would go away and clean myself up and then come back and speak the truth!' He did as she said and came back openly as Wing Commander Basil Embry of the Royal Air Force. With the money she gave him he bought a bicycle and took the road out of the city towards the place which was now becoming the magnet for every single person seeking the back door out of France . . . the teeming, untameable, vagabond port of Marseilles.

## 2. The Back Door

The demarcation line between German-occupied France and the truncated but nominally independent new state in the south was a beacon of hope for the early evaders. It proved to be a deceptive one. The Earl of Cardigan approached it not knowing what to expect. Would there be sentries to pass, a river or a canal to cross? He had no idea. He had been on the road for close on four weeks. The first stage of his journey to freedom was almost over, if only he could cross that line. It was easier than he ever imagined. The frontier turned out to be a road infrequently patrolled, and a local showed him where and when to slip over without being spotted. 'It was childishly simple, almost an anti-climax. I stepped out from behind a cottage, took a quick glance in either direction and then walked quickly across the main road. I followed a path between two cottages and kept going for another mile across some fields. Only then did I feel safe. I sat down in a field. But what was great was that it was an *unoccupied* field.'[1]

That night he rested in a barn and the enormity of his achievement at last hit him. He wrote in his diary:

I AM ACROSS THE BOUNDARY! I must have walked more than 300 miles in all; I have certainly been moving through the German lines for 25 continuous days. I am still very far from home, but I *have* succeeded in the first of the tasks which I set myself – to elude pursuit and to get clean away. Now I am ready to face a new set of perplexities.

He was not complacent.

There are still plenty of difficulties ahead! I am now in a country – Unoccupied France – which has apparently severed its relations with Great Britain. Officially, the people here are not friends but potential enemies: I must walk warily among them. I am still in rags; I am about 300 miles from the Mediterranean coast; and my total wealth remaining is equivalent to £1. The outlook still bristles with complications.

The fact was that the unoccupied part of France, though administered from Vichy, had very little real independence. German soldiers patrolled both sides of the border – as Gordon Instone quickly discovered. After surrendering on the beach between Calais and Dunkirk, he had escaped from the march of POWs into Germany, tried and failed to steal a boat home from the Channel coast, then travelled to Paris before heading south. He was posing as a French soldier and had discharge papers which he forged himself. They passed their first scrutiny by a German NCO and a French policeman, and he was then able to get a ration card and a travel permit. But the papers turned out not to be valid once he was beyond the demarcation line. Two German soldiers stopped him and ordered him back into the occupied zone. He was taken to a station to be put on a train back to Paris. Left in the waiting room, he decided to make his escape. He sauntered out of the door and down the platform as casually as he could, trying not to draw attention to himself.

But German soldiers on another platform spotted me, one blew a whistle and they began racing across the railway line in my direction. Luckily for me, a goods train pulled in and stopped them. The few minutes' respite was what I needed. I ran for my life, and as I did so I could hear the echoing of their boots as they clattered down a subway between the platforms.

Ahead of me I saw a crowd of country women. I rushed headlong towards them and pushed my way in among them, panting out urgently: '*Evadé anglais! Aidez-moi, s'il vous plaît!*' They heard the shouts and running feet of the German guards, and, taking in the situation, they all closed in around me. I bent down low, concealed by their long skirts, ample figures and their large market baskets held high above me. We all moved off slowly down the platform in a little convoy with me in the middle, through a small gate and out onto the road beyond.[2]

But it was a mistake for Britons on the run to assume every French man or woman they met would be their automatic ally as they had been for Instone on this occasion. And they could never be sure whose side the officials and police of the Vichy-run French government were on. Private Derrick Peterson was several miles into 'free' France when a French patrol found him and two companions. They were marched back to the border 'and the officer actually cycled on ahead to the German guards and personally handed us over'.[3] What shocked Peterson was that he had been on the run since Dieppe and had been sheltered by numerous French people for weeks while hiding in the north. He could only conclude that the officer was 'a fifth-columnist, either directly in league with the enemy or one of the few Frenchmen fooled by German propaganda and embittered against England'.

The mood of the local population was often difficult to divine. One officer ran across a Frenchman who told him: 'I hate the British. You killed my great-grandfather at Trafalgar.'[4] Such resentment was certain to spread after 3 July 1940, the day when, on the other side of the Mediterranean, the British navy sank French warships at anchor off Mers el-Kebir, near Oran, Algeria, to stop them falling into German hands. Three battleships were destroyed and 1,300 French sailors killed.

John Christie heard the news while under cover with a French family and realized it was 'a complication we needed as much as a hole in the head'.[5] His hosts were understanding. 'They accepted it as necessary in war. But I knew all Frenchmen wouldn't look on it in the same light.' The Germans made the most of the propaganda opportunity. Lurid posters denouncing the British 'betrayal' appeared on public notice boards. An indignant Instone risked his fragile freedom by tearing them down. A film about the attack was also shown in French cinemas, and an English army captain who went to see it was surprised by how little impact it made on the French audience.[6] They seemed much more taken by the main feature – *Gunga Din*, a homage to British military prowess in India. They roared their approval of that.

★

It was in Marseilles that the French cinemagoers made their anti-German feelings clear – hardly surprising in this city that had traditionally been a law unto itself, though law*less* would probably be a more fitting description. The city had always been considered a den of thieves. Now it was teeming with desperate people and those who would exploit them, a honey pot for the sticky fingered as hundreds of thousands of the newly dispossessed congregated there to be conned, robbed, murdered. The port, the streets, the hotels and boarding houses swarmed with every kind of displaced person, hoping to get a passage on one of the scores of steamships moored in the docks, if only they could slip past the French troops and policemen patrolling the quays for stowaways and illegal emigrants. There were refugees from the occupation of the north looking for a new life overseas. There were British residents of the Riviera – the rich, but also their penniless nannies and governesses – now classified as enemy aliens and trying to avoid internment. There were deserters and discharged soldiers of a dozen nationalities. There were Jews and German communists who had fled to France to escape the Nazis and now found their lives at risk again under the swastika. There were French men and women, ashamed by their country's surrender and its government's descent into collaboration and eager to continue the fight by joining the newly formed Free French forces under Charles de Gaulle in London.

Above all, there was that small army of British soldiers (and a handful of airmen) who had avoided the German round-up on the Channel coast and had come south to find a way back home. They crowded the waterfront streets and open-air bars and cafés, eking out what little money they could muster, the air ringing with loud English voices gossiping, arguing, plotting how they could get a passage across the Mediterranean to Spain or Gibraltar or even North Africa. Many were in a very bad state – weak, starved and exhausted after battling their way for hundreds of miles to try and make their way home. Some still carried festering wounds from the fighting in the north.

They were easy prey. One soldier paid good money to a ship's cook to smuggle him on board and hide him in a lifeboat until the ship was out at sea. He lay concealed for two days, hungry and almost paralysed with cramp, and then emerged to discover the ship was still in dock and not due to sail for another five weeks![7] Another soldier paid 10,000 francs to a very shifty character for a passage to Casablanca – twice as much as the man charged to carry out a murder! – but the ship he was slipped aboard took him to Tunis instead. It took him a year to get home.[8] Gangsters, spivs and double-dealers ran a thriving black market in identity papers, passports, exit visas, entry permits, tickets for ships. Bureaucracy bottled up every transaction. You couldn't get a boat ticket without an exit stamp or an exit stamp unless you had a ticket out. And an exit visa couldn't be issued without an entry permit into another country. Some of the paper that was traded was genuine; most was not. A bureau on rue Féréol sold Chinese visas for 100 francs, a price that most of the émigrés could afford, and thousands queued to get a stamp – unaware that, when translated, the words in Mandarin on it read: 'It is strictly forbidden for the bearer of this document, under any circumstance and at any time, to set foot on Chinese soil.'[9] Others paid a small fortune for fake tickets. Even reputable shipping agencies apparently sold bogus passages to the United States and Canada on ships that didn't exist or were already full.[10]

Meanwhile, German spies and Gestapo policemen were everywhere, interfering and infiltrating. So too were undercover agents from many other countries – not least those working for London.

Though the Vichy government broke off diplomatic relations with Britain as a result of the Oran attack, the attitude of its officials in Marseilles remained ambiguous. In theory, the British servicemen were now in a neutral country and should be interned for the duration of the war. Indeed, new laws demanded every effort to stop them getting home. A key clause in the armistice agreement the Vichy government made with Berlin stated that 'the French government will prevent members of the armed forces leaving the country to England or to any other foreign country whatsoever'.[11] Accordingly, on 14 July 1940 the Vichy government issued an order for all British servicemen at large to be interned in Fort St Jean, a medieval prison-like barracks in Marseilles harbour. Some of those on the streets were rounded up in a general sweep. Others arriving from the north went to the fort voluntarily after being told it was the safest place to be.

Some found life in the fort not to their liking at all. The men shared their barracks with the French Foreign Legion, infamous for its toughness, and one English inmate described it as cold and sinister, epitomized by the motto carved in the stone above the entrance – 'Legionnaires, you ask for death and I will give it to you'.[12] But others thought the fort surprisingly hospitable. John Christie was glad for three meals a day and a generous ration of red wine. The internees were also allowed out into Marseilles in the evenings as long as they gave their word to return. He considered his treatment there 'no different from our own army. It was a very mild form of internment.' But none of them had much intention of staying, and the freedom they had gave them plenty of opportunity to plot how to make their getaway from French soil.

The sea was still the favoured route – particularly after two sergeants escaped, got to the Pyrenees but could find no way over – and hours were whiled away devising madcap schemes for a mass exodus. Gordon Instone, now an internee there, came upon three army officers who had pooled their resources and, astonishingly, bought a schooner for 100,000 francs. This was to be a spectacular escape. They planned to cram all of 100 men – almost the entire British contingent of the fort – on board, sail out into the Mediterranean and hope to be picked up by a passing Royal Navy ship. Sentries were bribed and the huge party scrambled down the walls of the fort in groups of ten one night and gathered at a boathouse in the harbour. That was as far as they got. The weather turned nasty and a storm made it impossible even to get on board. Just before dawn, all 100 of them crept back into the fort, bitterly disappointed. There was also a plan to hijack a small liner berthed in the harbour, pile everyone on board and make a dash for the open sea. But a venture like this would almost certainly mean having to arm themselves and fight their way out if necessary, a dangerous precedent which not only threatened the lives of those caught up in such a battle but would undermine the status of all other Britons on the run.

The strangest escape plan of all involved Coldstream Guards officer Jimmy Langley – whom we last encountered lying outside a field hospital in Dunkirk, his arm shattered and gangrenous, waiting to surrender to a German platoon. He went into captivity, where a British army surgeon amputated the arm, and was then held in various hospitals while he recovered. Several times he narrowly missed being classified as fit enough to be transferred to a prisoner-of-war camp in Germany, and when he thought his luck was about to run out and he was earmarked for the next transit, he absconded. Ignoring posters newly pasted onto public walls warning that any British soldier who did not give himself up immediately would be shot out of hand, he took the now time-honoured route south to Marseilles. There he gave himself up to the French authorities and was interned in Fort St Jean. But on a visit into the city he was picked out by a local Marseilles gangster and made an extraordinary offer. Over a sumptuous dinner at a restaurant, the Frenchman explained that his boss, the most powerful mob leader in a city notorious for its criminal fraternity, had secured an ocean-going tug to ferry stranded British soldiers down the Mediterranean coast and land them on the British-owned rock of Gibraltar. He would supply the crew, provisions and even an armed escort to deal with any interference from, say, the Italian navy. The French authorities had already been paid off to look the other way. In return he wanted no money . . . just a favour in the future, a guarantee that after the war the British government would do nothing to hamper his criminal 'activities'. Langley agreed – though fully aware such a pledge was beyond his powers to honour. A date was fixed, the men in Fort St Jean were alerted and briefed for their passage home . . . and then, at the very last minute, the gangster pulled out. He explained that the Vichy government had made an offer *he* could not refuse – he and his *capo* could have carte blanche to do as they pleased now on condition that they didn't help the British to escape. Full of apologies, he withdrew his offer.

But still an escape by sea remained a glimmer in the eyes of everyone trapped in Marseilles – and some individuals certainly slipped away by ship. Christie went with a draft of French Foreign Legionnaires from Fort St Jean. He and his best mate managed to lay their hands on two of the distinctive uniforms of the Legion and, dressed accordingly, simply marched up the gangplank of a troopship heading across to North Africa. Legionnaire friends they had made at the fort protected them, though there were uncomfortable moments as they sailed into Oran the next day, right past the wreckage of the French navy:

The ship picked its way slowly to avoid warships which had heeled over or were sunk with only their superstructure above water. The most spectacular sight was a submarine with its stern down in the water and its bow high in the air draped across a breakwater. I was very conscious it was our navy that had knocked six bells out of them.

On land, Christie and his companion took their places in the Legion column marching to barracks, then peeled away and discarded their uniforms. They took a train to Casablanca and after many months managed to hide in the hold of a coaster going to Lisbon. Two days out to sea, the ship was stopped by a British destroyer and searched for contraband. The stowaways stepped forward to identify themselves and that evening were in Gibraltar.

But such escapes were exceptional and the reality was that getting away from Marseilles by sea was becoming almost impossible. But there was another way, thanks to a quiet and courageous Scotsman who had begun to play a crucial part in the lives of the evaders. He brought some order to the chaotic happenings on the streets of Marseilles and in Fort St Jean and, at great personal risk, laid the foundations for the first properly organized escape line out of France. His name was Donald Caskie.

★

The Revd Caskie came from the Hebridean island of Islay and for five years had been the minister of the Church of Scotland kirk in Paris. He had had little choice but to leave. On the Sunday before the German army arrived in the French capital he openly denounced Hitler from the pulpit. 'They shall reap the whirlwind,' he thundered, knowing full well there were spies and collaborators sitting in the congregation who would report his words to the invaders. The service over, he locked the church doors, gave the key to the owner of a café next door for safe keeping and joined the exodus. He intended going back home to Scotland and so headed for Bordeaux on the Atlantic coast to find a ship, one of those many thousands of refugees jamming the roads, at the mercy of German dive-bombers, driven on by fear and panic. But there were no ships at Bordeaux – the last one had just sailed – and so he cycled south to the port of Bayonne. He was in time – a ship was waiting, a place was being kept for him. But his urge to run had gone, replaced by a sense that his duty lay in staying, not leaving.

For days I had walked, trotted, run, halted, meditated, prayed, starved and staggered across France – and all to reach a ship. Instead I watched the last one steam out of Bayonne. I saw it go. Scotland had been so near and now I was cut off from it, forever maybe. My heart sank, but surely in deciding to stay in France I was doing the right thing?[13]

At the time, he had no idea where that duty would take him but, after accepting a chance lift in a car, the very next day he stood among the frantic crowds on the Marseilles waterfront. He was shocked by the sight of British soldiers huddled on the pavement. He had found his flock. He wandered among them, offering consolation where he could. 'Comfort ye my people . . . My new vocation came with the clarity of crystal.' An instinct took him to the American consulate:

The door was open. I walked up the stairs and a hand was laid on my shoulder. 'Padre, we've been looking for you.' I turned, and a man regarded me intently. 'My name is Dean,' he said, 'and I'm the former British consul in Nice. We need you to help starving soldiers and airmen from Dunkirk. Can you do anything for them? I feel sure you can.' I grasped his hand.

Caskie now did something that, in the circumstances, was either foolish or inspired. He gingerly approached the French police for help in setting up a refuge for British servicemen – officially their enemies. 'Audacity offered the only hope of a permanent solution,' he would recall. The police were sympathetic – that ambiguity again – but already under the influence and the surveillance of the Gestapo. They could not sanction what he wanted, blaming 'our new masters . . .' and shrugging their shoulders. But a compromise was possible. He was given permission to provide help and accommodation to British *civilians*. There was the British Seamen's Mission building in the Vieux Port standing empty. He could use that, 'But give help to one British soldier and you will be interned,' he was told. 'Trust no one. You will be watched. And beware of paid agents and sudden raids.' A delighted Caskie made his way to the deserted Mission, used £200 he had in his wallet to hire beds and blankets and pinned a notice on the front door – 'Now open to British civilians and seamen ONLY.' It was a blatant deceit, but one which did not trouble the clergyman's conscience. 'I had a job to do for servicemen and plans were already formulating in my mind.'

Quickly the word travelled along the narrow streets and back alleys of Marseilles and his first customers, tired and desperate for food and shelter, were on his doorstep almost at once. The word spread much further too. Soldiers on the run were still arriving from the north and many seemed already to have heard of him. They made straight for the Mission.

My first task with each new arrival was to hide him until I could furnish him with non-combatant papers and prepare him for dispatch to Spain. The Mission was under constant surveillance and my only armour was the grace of God and my native gumption. Everywhere I went I was being watched and followed. Raids on the house began a few days after I requisitioned it, at six o'clock in the morning. Fortunately the raiders caught no one in uniform or without papers. But they conveyed an unmistakable impression that they would return.

And return they did, often. But Caskie had been busy, constructing secret hiding places: 'We discovered the shallow space between floorboards could contain a man and gently prised boards up all over the building, fitted them so that they would slide out and into position without trouble, and thus created "holes" in which our men could shelter. We also utilised spaces behind cupboards and under the roof.'

He provided civilian clothes for those who, remarkably given how far they had travelled in an enemy-occupied land, were still in the uniforms they had been wearing at Dunkirk, Calais or St Valéry. Some clothes were kept in stockpiles hidden in the cellar beneath the coal but others had to be bought secretly in the city's Arab bazaar. Under cover of night Caskie would smuggle small groups there to be fitted with second-hand suits, shirts, socks and shoes.

On the way there we would keep to the darker streets, and walk close to the walls. But the return to the Mission was more leisurely, with the men now in their job-lot civvies. Each carried a bundle of the rags of khaki or air force blue in which he had arrived. The Arabs feared to have them in their premises even to burn, and so long as a thread of service cloth was in the Mission it imperilled each one of us and the whole organization. So we made our way to the walls of the old harbour and dumped the outmoded wardrobes into the blue Mediterranean.

Caskie's next task was to obtain civilian papers for the men in his charge so they could stay openly at the Mission before leaving on the next leg of their journey – travelling along the coast the 200 miles to Perpignan and then over the mountains and into neutral Spain – with a reasonable chance of not being caught. In this he was helped by the American consul, a man forced by the

politics of the time to play a game of bluff. His officials were
obliged to advise any English soldiers who arrived at the Marseilles
consulate asking for help to give themselves up to the French
authorities for internment. John Christie was one of many who
were thus pointed in the direction of Fort St Jean. But secretly the
consul was an ally of Caskie's and an unstinting source of documents and passports. The result was that, when the Vichy police
came calling, there would be thirty or so men with papers to
show – while a dozen or more lay stashed and hushed under the
floorboards.

The cat-and-mouse game he played with the police – 'living
like a hare in the heather' as Caskie himself put it – was a constant
worry. The sudden pounding on the door, the intimidation, the
checking of papers, the searches, the fear that a small but fatal error
might give the game away – through it all the pastor struggled to
keep his head and his freedom. He walked a tightrope and it was
a miracle he stayed aloft as long as he did. After the war there were
suggestions that the French authorities must have allowed his
Mission to stay open as a way of keeping tabs on what the British
were up to.[14] On the other hand, his security was superb. John
Christie and his group visited the Mission once a week to pick up
the 'dole' allotted to them by the US consul and had no idea
that, behind the innocent cover of ping-pong tables and churchy
women volunteers sewing and knitting, men just like them were
in hiding there.

Caskie did take extra risks, however, in the way he funded what
soon became a costly operation. It was permitted to receive gifts
of food from the crews of American ships who used the Mission
legitimately as a place to stay. Guessing what was going on and the
other mouths Caskie had to feed, they would come with sacks of
potatoes, rice, boxes of sardines, bags of sugar and so on. Donations
of money also arrived, ostensibly from wealthy expatriates in Nice,
Cannes and Monte Carlo. But Caskie knew full well that the
visitor who took coffee with him and then left an envelope with
850,000 francs in it was from British Intelligence. Though there
was clearly a Nurse Cavell-type blurring of the lines here, the

secret service encouraged his activities and gave him a list of subjects on which any information he could glean from the evaders who passed through the Mission would be very useful. Caskie agreed to cooperate.[15] He had no qualms when it came to helping the men on the run to whom he had now dedicated his entire life.

A more formal link with the intelligence services was also being forged by an army officer who had now joined Caskie in his endeavours. Captain Ian Garrow was a Seaforth Highlander who had led his men safely south from Dunkirk after missing the evacuation. He was already moving on to Perpignan and home when his conscience persuaded him to turn back. The sight of the disconsolate gangs of British servicemen hanging around the streets of Marseilles had upset him and, like Caskie, he decided it was his duty to stay and help them. He took on the difficult job of finding trustworthy guides who would escort the 'packages' – as the men in transit were called – to the Pyrenees and over the mountains. His choices did not always please Caskie. He thought too many of them were mercenary, working solely for the money, and therefore not trustworthy in the clergyman's eyes. What he did not know was that complex international politics were playing a part here. The obvious communities to trawl for loyal guides were Basque nationalists and republicans and anarchists who had fought against Franco in the Spanish Civil War – their hatred of fascism and therefore their loyalty to the Allies would be assured. But in London the ever-nervous officials at the Foreign Office had ruled out using any groups opposed to the regime in Madrid for fear of compromising Spain's neutrality. So, in constructing escape lines across the Pyrenees, deals were deliberately done with cash-conscious smugglers and people-traffickers. To keep the diplomats happy, the lives of men on the run were put in the hands of rogues. As Caskie noted of one guide he met, 'his demeanour made his attitude plain – that if something went wrong with our finances and his pay was delayed he would not hesitate to recoup himself by claiming rewards from the Germans'.

But Caskie had to bite back his concerns. Under Garrow's influence, the escape line was faster and more efficient (helped

along too by Jimmy Langley, who had slipped out of Fort St Jean
to join the organization). More and more parties were now setting
off from the Mission to the mountains. Caskie made his preparations for each departure in secret, deciding in his mind who
among his flock would be going but not telling anyone. This
way he avoided leaks and also disappointment in the event of a
cancellation. He would wait for his instructions from Garrow,
then, quietly, in the dead of night, assemble the chosen few.

The starting time was always 2 a.m., and at midnight I wakened the
travellers and whispered orders to them. They acted quickly and on
their stockinged feet followed me to my room with their gear. Then I
thoroughly searched them. It was essential that if captured no one should
be carrying evidence that might incriminate not only the Mission but
the whole escape route.

I also made each of them pledge that if he were captured he would
not involve the Mission in any way, no matter what happened. It was a
harsh instruction, I knew, but I lived with the knowledge that hundreds
of men making for Marseilles would be mortally endangered if the enemy
discovered us. The Mission was a springboard to freedom for those men,
their sole hope, and must be preserved as long as possible.

These preliminaries over, I explained the escape route in detail. Before
the tap on the door that announced the coming of the guide, we offered
a short prayer. A quick reconnaissance followed and then, if the coast
was clear, I bade them Godspeed. The system functioned perfectly and
20 to 25 men each week were sent to freedom.

Their chances of making it home were significantly improved
because, on the other side of the Pyrenees, operations were now
gearing up to receive them. A fireside chat in one of the smartest
enclaves of London had seen to that.

★

Afternoon tea and toast in a bachelor flat above an oyster bar in
St James's Street, London. From his comfortable chintz-covered
armchair, Claude Dansey, assistant chief of the British Intelligence

Service, looked his guest straight in the eye as he outlined the problem. The German blitzkrieg in northern Europe had overrun his networks, smashed years of work. A back door was now needed into France through neutral Portugal and Spain. His visitor, a young diplomat named Donald Darling, was ordered to go there immediately and organize it. His role was to be a dual one. Not only was he to set up intelligence links for MI6 but also, guided by MI9 (who had been instructed by Dansey, its overall master), he was to establish escape routes for the British soldiers trapped in Marseilles.

Dansey concealed the real reason for his sudden concern for these men, a switch from his previous insistence on keeping spying and evading activities apart. He felt threatened by the setting up of a new secret service, separate from his, to work underground in occupied Europe and, through sabotage and acts of resistance, to 'set Europe alight', in Churchill's hyperbolic words. SOE, the Special Operations Executive, was a challenge not just to the Germans but to Dansey's control of clandestine operations. He couldn't stop it but he could extend his own empire to offset it. Out of Whitehall inter-departmental rivalry came a major boost to the chances of British servicemen lost in France actually getting home.

For the next week Darling was pumped full of codes and security procedures and then put aboard a blacked-out DC3 aircraft in blinding rain at Northolt airfield and flown to Lisbon. His credentials to the British ambassador there presented him as the new 'vice-consul', but that didn't fool anyone. 'I won't ask you your business here,' the ambassador said knowingly as they drove in the embassy Rolls-Royce for lunch. 'Thank you, sir,' Darling – codenamed 'Sunday' – replied. Three days later he arrived in Barcelona, to a totally different reception – outright hostility. In their eagerness not to offend Spanish neutrality, British diplomats in Spain lived in a state of paranoia. 'You can't stay here,' the Barcelona consul-general told him. 'We are constantly watched.' It was the same when he arrived at the embassy in Madrid. The ambassador, Sir Samuel Hoare, told him to leave at once. 'I was at a loss to know how to deal with this scared man,' Darling reported later.[16] He would get no help here from diplomats who saw their job as doing nothing to upset the Spanish.[17] His planning would have to be done from Lisbon.

From there, he made contact with pro-British sympathizers in Barcelona and then with Ian Garrow in Marseilles, busy establishing his growing band of mountain guides. From his end, Darling, who knew the Pyrenees well from his youth, was doing the same, offering guides £40 for each British officer they brought over the mountains, £20 for an 'OR' (other rank) – fees he and Dansey had fixed with the Treasury in London. He had also recruited a rare ally among the diplomats. Michael Creswell, an attaché at the embassy in Madrid, ignored his ambassador's misgivings and, with the codename of 'Monday' to Darling's 'Sunday', set himself the task of helping British servicemen who had got over the mountains only to fall foul of the Spanish authorities. Spain was by no means the safe haven many evaders hoped it would be. The Franco government's sympathies lay with Germany and it pursued a policy of aggressive neutrality towards Allied fighters. Any found within its borders, hoping to reach Gibraltar and home, could expect to be treated harshly. There was even a concentration camp waiting for them – as Major the Earl of Cardigan, one of the first to get into Spain, was discovering.

The earl's journey from northern France, much of it on foot and all of it entirely on his own, had brought him to Marseilles on a sweltering sunny day. He lay low for a few days in a small hotel but sensed the Vichy police net around him. 'Is there any way I can slip through the meshes?' he wrote in his diary. He rejected the blandishments of some English officers he met to join them in Fort St Jean. The prospect of bars, even if French, not German, appalled him. Preferring 'my present precarious but real freedom' to French hospitality of indeterminate length, he bought a bicycle – brand new, 1,000 francs – and pedalled towards Spain. A gendarme stopped him en route. Cardigan confessed to being English but was sent on his way. 'He did not know what to do with me,' he wrote.

The Pyrenees began to loom out of the mist in the distance,

and as he pedalled closer he pondered precisely how he was going to get over them. 'They look formidable.' In a small village he was directed up a winding valley. Another policeman stopped him. 'I'm just a tourist on a cycling holiday,' Cardigan protested, and was allowed to proceed. Then the road ran out and, shouldering the bicycle, he began to climb up through trees and then over rock and scree towards the ridge he believed was the border. Sheep bells jangled in the distance. A sheepdog barked. His eyes strained for the silhouette of a sentry. He rested, set off again at dawn and in the light of day he could now see that he was over the top. His route lay ahead, exhilaratingly downhill. He was in Spain! The days had turned into weeks and the weeks into months since he had put his hands over his head in surrender in Belgium. He had walked hundreds of miles, begged, stolen, played the idiot, anything to stay free. And now he was. He reached a road and got back on the bicycle. Gerona lay ahead, then Barcelona three days' ride away. He sped along joyfully, past mule carts and peasants on donkeys. Then in the main street of a small town a man in a green uniform stepped out and stopped him. The police officer's demand for papers deflated Cardigan's joy. He had none. He was arrested and taken all the way back to the border. There he confessed everything to the Spanish immigration officer. Yes, he had sneaked over the mountains. Yes, he was an English soldier. His honesty cleared the air but not his name. He was thrown into a cell to await formal deportation back to France.

And then, quite by chance, he was reprieved. He heard an English voice in the police station. Someone – there is no record but it could easily have been Creswell or one of his agents – was inquiring about British subjects being held there.

I was only able to have a few moments' conversation with this visitor but I quickly gave him my name and particulars of my arrest. He pressed 25 pesetas into my hand and a few bars of chocolate and urged me to be patient. I was to remember that from now on diplomatic machinery would be operating on my behalf.

Instead of being escorted back to France, Cardigan was marched to a stone-walled fortress full of detainees of a dozen different nationalities, a medley of Europe's flotsam and jetsam all washed up together, including a number of other British soldiers like him.[18] There he stayed in the most primitive of conditions – open latrines, stone floors to sleep on with not even straw or blankets. The guards fingered the triggers of their rifles purposefully. There was no doubt they would shoot anyone who tried to escape. The incarceration continued, amid rumours of release. There was jubilant talk that the consul in Barcelona was coming to get the British contingent. Instead, after ten days, they were told they were going to the place everyone escaping via Spain would come to dread – the concentration camp at Miranda del Ebro.

It was 300 miles away on the other side of the peninsula, closer to the Bay of Biscay than the Mediterranean, and the prisoners were roped together to shuffle through the streets to the railway station. They travelled in cattle trucks, with a single tin of sardines for every three men to sustain them for the twenty-four-hour journey. The *deposito* at Miranda was a world of its own. At first glance it looked like a disused holiday camp,[19] but the barbed wire, floodlights and tough conditions quickly dispelled that illusion. Heads were shaved bare – to Cardigan's horror he looked like a convict – and guards carried sticks to beat anyone who complained. The latrines emptied into a stream that was also the wash place. They were set to work like slaves in ancient Egypt, moving gravel and sand in the blazing sun for hours on end. Each night they were forced to salute the lowering flag of Franco's fascist state. Discipline was strict. Offenders would be marched round the parade ground with a sack of stones tied to their backs. Five prisoners who were caught trying to escape were shot dead, one a French youth of just sixteen. Cardigan could only watch in horror from a distance as guards surrounded a figure and bounced him from rifle butt to bayonet and back again. Then the figure was pushed out of the circle, rifles were raised and 'the sound of a ragged volley came to my ears. What possible excuse can there be for torturing a man who has already been recaptured and then shooting him? Such a thing could only be done by barbarians.'

Cardigan was soon out of the barbarians' hands, though not soon enough for his liking. An official – Creswell?[20] – came from the embassy in Madrid to take a group of fifteen British soldiers away. A disappointed Cardigan was not on the list, but ten days later, on 20 September, it was his turn. A telegram came authorizing his immediate release along with all the other Britons, and the next morning he was tucking into a breakfast of kidneys, bacon, toast and marmalade in the flat of the military attaché at the embassy in Madrid. The following day he crossed the border from Spain into Gibraltar. A sergeant saluted him. 'Would you like a cup of tea, sir?' After 100 of the toughest, most exacting days of his life, the earl was back on British soil.

The arrangements made for evaders arriving in Spain improved considerably from this point on. Cardigan's had been a solo effort, without organized help from anyone, and was all the more remarkable for that. But now the escape line set up by Darling began to operate with increasing efficiency. Every effort was made to meet those arriving over the mountains and prevent them falling into Spanish hands. Not that they were home yet. There was one last, difficult leg where discovery was still a possibility. Concealed under tarpaulins on lorries, sometimes hidden in the boots of cars or posing as students on a charabanc outing, the men would then be driven the length of Spain – a tortuous journey on ancient roads and through towns still scarred by the Civil War fighting. Checkpoints barred the way, police patrols demanded papers and permits, but most made it to La Linea and the crossing out of Spain and into Gibraltar. Only then could they truly say they were safe. Gibraltar also became Darling's base. Lisbon had just been too far away, too out of touch with what was happening on the ground. 'Sunday' moved to the Rock to pull the levers on his increasingly complex underground railway.

★

Back on the other side of the Pyrenees, matters had taken a turn for the better too. Realizing that it was too risky to rely on the Seamen's Mission alone as a refuge for soldiers on the run, Garrow had begun sniffing out other helpers and safe houses among the pro-British community in the city. It was a chancy business. One wrong move could bring down the entire operation. Every contact had to be tested, credentials cross-checked – and all at a time of shifting, uncertain loyalties when many people in France believed the British beaten and the war over and were leaning towards collaboration.

Women were his best recruits. An American girl nicknamed 'Tex' hid evaders under her hotel bed; rich Australian-born Nancy Fiocca,[21] codenamed 'White Mouse', took them into her home for champagne and caviar. Then there was Elizabeth Haden-Guest, Estonian by birth, British by marriage, who had been interned in northern France as an alien, threatened with deportation to Germany and then escaped with her three-year-old son to the unoccupied zone. Her vivid account of pushing the boy on his hands and knees under barbed wire and the eyes of German sentries gave her a certain notoriety in Marseilles. Garrow met her and she became his girl about town, message carrier and finder of food and shelter for new arrivals. She established contacts in a string of brothels, which made excellent safe houses. Garrow's team also included the crucial figure of Louis Nouveau, a middle-aged local business-man who took it on himself to raise money. He secured loans, which were underwritten by the War Office and the Treasury in London. The escape line begun by Caskie had moved on to an altogether more sophisticated level.

It was now to go up several more notches, ironically thanks to a botched operation by SOE. Two of its agents were landed on a beach, Canet-Plage, just outside Perpignan, from HMS *Fidelity*, a heavily armed trawler used for clandestine missions. The launch that dropped them turned turtle in a squall on its way back out to sea. One crewman managed to swim ashore, where he was arrested by a local gendarme. He made up a story. His name, he said, was Patrick O'Leary and he was a Canadian airman shot down in

France and trying to get home. He was detained and sent to the barracks at St Hippolyte-du-Fort, an internment camp near the southern city of Nîmes which now housed all the British prisoners who until recently had been held in Marseilles. Fort St Jean had proved too easy to flee from and Marseilles too much of a magnet for its inmates. The French authorities were taking a tougher approach to the British servicemen in their midst and enforcing a much more rigorous form of detention.

The resourceful O'Leary had an immediate impact on the inmates of St Hippolyte as he set about organizing escapes. Caskie, who had appointed himself visiting chaplain to the camp, met him, was impressed and told Garrow about him. A secret rendezvous was arranged. They hit it off straight away, the English captain recognizing a like mind, a kindred spirit, an adventurer and a doer like himself. O'Leary admitted the truth – his real name was Albert-Marie Guérisse, he had been a doctor in the Belgian army, had escaped to England when his country fell to the Germans and been recruited by SOE. He had joined the crew of *Fidelity* with the rank of lieutenant commander, taking the *nom de guerre* of Patrick Albert O'Leary to protect the identity of his family back in Belgium if he were ever captured by the Germans. Garrow had this story checked in London and then decided this was a man he wanted to join his operation.

O'Leary escaped from St Hippolyte-du-Fort, sawing through a bar and climbing out of a cell window on one side of the barracks while the other 250 British inmates mounted a mock mass escape attempt on the other as a diversion. Chased by guards, he was hidden by nuns before eventually arriving at Garrow's hideaway, a flat above a doctor's surgery in Marseilles. At this stage O'Leary probably believed he was on his way back to London to resume his SOE job. Instead Garrow persuaded him there was more pressing work to be done here. There may have been an argument but it was settled when together they listened to a coded message from London on the European network of the BBC: '*Adolphe doit rester – je répète – Adolphe doit rester.*' It was the order for O'Leary to stay. It had been sanctioned by Dansey, his finger in every pie, though the MI6 chief remained wary. He never trusted the Belgian completely (then again, 'Colonel Z' never trusted anyone). He gave his approval perhaps for no other reason than it gave him the minor inter-departmental victory of grabbing an agent from the rival SOE. But it was a breakthrough in the escape line's fortunes.

In the cool and charismatic O'Leary/Guérisse the organization had found the dynamo who would electrify its activities. Darling recognized the qualities of the new recruit immediately. 'With O'Leary established in Marseilles,' he noted, 'I feel we are at last getting somewhere.' The Revd Caskie was also an instant fan, noting that, though the newcomer was frail in appearance, this was not a man to mess with. He had powerful shoulders and muscular hands: 'I suspect he could strangle a strong man as easily as I might stick a stamp.' He quickly established a reputation for exceptional fearlessness and daring. There was an air of mystery about him too that had an impact on everyone he encountered. One member of his organization recalled: 'He didn't so much walk into a room or a café as manifest himself, simply arrive. He had suddenly come among you, and it was disconcerting for those with anything to hide or fear. Yet his presence brought a sense of all being under control and stamped authority on whatever was being planned or discussed.'[22] Able to pass more easily as a Frenchman than Garrow ever could, he began to travel widely outside the Marseilles area, finding helpers, setting up routes and safe houses, establishing links to Paris and beyond. Soon the workers for what was eventually dubbed the Pat Line were providing an unbroken chain of contacts from northern France all the way into Spain.

One of these contacts was a ginger-haired, freckled-faced British soldier named Sergeant Harold Cole. After the Dunkirk débâcle, he had established himself under cover in Lille and was now bringing parties of men, nine and ten at a time, down to the Mediterranean coast on a regular basis. He showed conspicuous skill and courage, finding routes across the demarcation line, talking his way through control points and spot checks despite his halting French. Once in Marseilles he would take his charges to an agreed rendezvous – a bar, a newspaper kiosk, just a bench in a public park – and then leave. A helper would then appear to take them to a safe house. This way each link in the chain was kept separate from the next. Then Cole would meet Garrow and O'Leary and they would discuss plans and agree on the timing of the next delivery. Money would also change hands – for Cole's expenses. The line was never cheap to run. There were train tickets and lodgings to be paid for, couriers and contacts to be compensated, officials and policemen to be bribed. The meetings were not always comfortable. There was something caddish and not quite right about the debonair Cole, with his moustache, plus-fours and 'I say, old chap' language. His weakness for the ladies was a liability too. Caskie disliked him intensely, thought him 'fishy', too pleased with himself. O'Leary was also set on edge one day – 'smelt a nasty smell', as he put it later – when Cole asked for an unusually large sum of money, 50,000 francs.

Garrow dismissed their suspicions. Cole was his ideal courier, he maintained. 'He has this uncanny ability to get men through. Lots of chaps swear they owe their lives to him. He amazes them with his cheeky schemes for outwitting the guards along the way.'[23] And, yes, he liked to travel in the company of pretty girls, but they were so useful at diverting attention from the evaders. And as for Caskie's instinct that there was something 'missing' in Cole, something he was concealing, well, anyone doing this sort of work needed a fair bit of deceit in their make-up. There was sense in Garrow's argument. Undercover work threw up a strange breed of people. Time would tell whether he was right in his generous assessment of Cole.

Not that Garrow would get the chance to find out for himself because not long afterwards he was arrested. It surprised no one. He was tall, head and shoulders above most men, and had always been a most unlikely candidate for an undercover role. He was such a conspicuous figure in Marseilles and the work he was doing so obvious that it was a miracle he had stayed free for as long as he did. The first time Langley met Garrow in June 1940 he concluded he 'did not seem likely to survive very long'. But it was not until October 1941 that the French finally moved on him. Until then they 'simply could not believe that the British Intelligence service could ever employ anyone whose physical appearance alone made him an impossible choice for an agent', according to Langley. They spent their time looking for the real mastermind behind the escape organization before finally concluding that it was Garrow after all. That was when they acted.

Pressure on the network was already growing at the time. Elizabeth Haden-Guest had spent an uncomfortable but temporary time in detention. O'Leary was also stopped by the police and frog-marched into custody for four days of interrogation. Both were released. Their papers were in order and nothing could be proved against them. But Garrow was gone for good. He was picked up on the street while going to meet two local policemen he hoped to turn and recruit. He had taken one chance too many, the curse of all evaders and those who helped them. Garrow said nothing under interrogation, was sentenced to ten years in jail and taken away to a top-security prison in the Dordogne. O'Leary took command of the line, stepping up its work. He would in time have 250 men and women working for it. Forgers turned out fake identity cards, food coupons, all the paper needed for a man on the run to fool an inquisitive policeman. A tailor was skilled in making any sort of uniform as a disguise. Communication, always crucial, always dangerous, was maintained through a chain of dead-letter boxes from one end of France to the other.

O'Leary had eyes and ears everywhere. But there was one thing he did not know – that what he was doing was being duplicated elsewhere. Marseilles–Perpignan–Barcelona was not the only back-door route out of France. On France's Atlantic coast, stranded British servicemen were also collecting and being successfully shepherded across the mountains – and all thanks to a slip of a girl and her friends.

★

Not one of the servicemen who managed to get back to Britain in the period after Dunkirk would have stood any sort of chance without the aid of brave souls who decided to defy the Germans and the forces collaborating with them. As we saw in Chapter 1, men on the run sometimes had doors slammed in their faces by people too frightened to offer help but equally they benefited from many spontaneous gestures of support, whether a simple bowl of soup, a change of clothing or a bed for the night. Some helpers went further, taking men in at great risk to themselves and hiding them for months on end. But to a small minority of the very brave, the saving of Allied lives and the returning of those men to their homeland to fight again was a duty, a cause to which they were utterly committed. For them, assisting evaders became a way of life.

To fight back in this way was never an easy decision to make. When German soldiers entered Belgium, Anne Brusselmans' first instinct was to flee. She and her husband scooped up their family and drove hurriedly to the coast. They crossed the border into France, reached Boulogne but could not get a boat to England. The tidal wave of the invasion swept over them. Dejected, they made their way back to Brussels and their home, an upper-floor apartment at 127 Chaussée d'Ixelles.

Shortly after their return, the pastor of their local church came to call. Could Anne, who was half English, help? Would she translate the nightly news broadcasts from the BBC and pass them round? Listening to foreign radio was banned, distributing its content an even greater crime. She risked jail or worse, but she said yes. That night she tuned in and made the first of what would add up to around 1,500 reports over the next four years. Months later there was another knock at the apartment door. The pastor was back with a member of his congregation, a military man. Her help was wanted again. Allied airmen were providing the only resistance to Hitler in the whole of Europe, making bombing sorties to Germany, hitting the enemy where it hurt. But they were taking heavy casualties. Bombers were being shot down and their crews baling out over Holland and Belgium. They needed shelter and a chance to get home. Again, Anne Brusselmans said yes, though to be caught doing this could mean a death sentence.

Her husband Julien was party to the decision but children

Yvonne and Jacques were not. They did not catch on for a while, though Yvonne clearly remembered the day that a man called Jack with a particular liking for tea came to stay and she was told he was a Flemish cousin who did not speak French so they would have to converse in English. The British airman stayed a fortnight while in the street outside a German military band marched up and down and the sound of drums and fifes and martial music filled the flat. A neighbour, known to be a collaborator, praised Hitler to Anne. With a secret to keep, she bit her lip. Jack eventually went on his way. Anne was told nothing of his journey ahead but, reasoning that he would have to swim across at least one river, she sent him off with a bag containing a change of clothes. That night the children slept in their own bed again instead of on the couch – until the next time.

Jack was the first of dozens of 'Flemish cousins' who came and went in 10-year-old Yvonne's life. 'After 32, my credence wore thin,' she wrote later. 'Where did all these cousins come from? They had never been to our house before.' She was told the truth one day after sheltering in the cellar under the house during an air raid:

Not having much to do down there I opened this container of wheat my mother had for baking bread and ran my fingers through the contents. Deep down I uncovered a metal box and inside were loads of false documents and photographs of my so-called Flemish cousins. It was then that Mother let me into the secret. She told me simply: 'If we can do our part, one day we shall be free again.'[24]

Finding food for illicit guests was a constant problem. Belgium was being stripped of supplies, its home-produced potatoes and coal commandeered and sent by the trainload eastward to feed and fuel the conqueror's families and homes. In Brussels eggs were a rarity, sardines a treat, meat virtually unknown. People in the capital took trains into the country to scavenge for vegetables. One mother winced at having to make chips from swede, a root normally reserved for pigs, and pancakes from 'chestnut flour'.[25] Any extras had to come from the black market, so if the Brusselmans were to feed their visitors they had to dig deeply into their own pockets. They had been saving to buy a house of their own. The money was now put to a different use.

Seventeen-year-old Nadine Dumon was prepared to make sacrifices too.[26] A quiet girl, on the surface one most unlikely to be a firebrand, she was driven by indignation at the Germans invading her country and taking away her freedom. She turned thought into action when her mother, a nurse, came home one day with a drawing mocking Hitler.

I decided to make copies of it and put them in other people's letter boxes to spread the message. I went far and wide on my bicycle to do this. Then my mother introduced me to someone who asked if I would do the same thing with a clandestine newspaper called *Libre Belgique*. My father, a doctor, was in the Resistance organizing acts of sabotage against the Germans and he also used me as a courier to pass information about possible targets. So that's how it started. I knew how dangerous it was, that I could be arrested and tortured. But I was very cold blooded and I could think and react quickly. I told myself I would never say anything no matter what they did to me. I didn't really think they would shoot a woman. But I was wrong.[27]

All the family were involved in dangerous, anti-Nazi activities of one kind or another but never discussed details with each other. It was better not to know. Before the war her parents had been very strict with their teenage daughter – she wasn't allowed a boyfriend – but now when she went out they didn't ask where she was going or who she was seeing. 'We were very conscious of security. You had to be careful whom you spoke to and what you said. I knew for sure that my friends were not collaborators but even so I told them nothing, not a word.' Then she advanced from a bearer of messages to a transporter of people:

One day a man we didn't know, a headmaster in a local primary school, came to see us. He introduced himself as Frédéric de Jongh and told us that his daughter, Andrée, was organizing the escape of British servicemen from Brussels and needed help. We didn't know how to react. Could we trust him, or was this a trap? But we instinctively felt he was all right and so I agreed. I had one condition. I told M. de Jongh, 'I will do anything you want but not kill. So no guns, not even for protection.' That was my rule.[28] My first job was to pick up a soldier who was hiding in our area and guide him to another safe place. It was difficult because I didn't speak English and he didn't speak French and we communicated by sign language. I took him on a tram through Brussels and dropped him off. It was as simple as that. I wasn't scared. It just seemed like an adventure.

Nadine did not know it at the time but she had just joined what was to be one of the most successful escape lines of the Second World War – dubbed the Comet Line (though not until after the war) because of the speed with which it got men home to England. Its inspiration and founding genius was that same Andrée – known to everyone as Dédée – whose father had now recruited Nadine.

Dédée was in her mid-twenties but looked younger, just another girl in ankle socks, pretty enough but with nothing to distinguish her or make her stand out in a crowd. Her ordinariness was her disguise. It hid a steeliness and courage to carry out extraordinary deeds. She began her travels in the summer of 1941 by helping a dozen young Belgian soldiers and a plump middle-aged English-woman named Miss Richards to get over the River Somme on the first leg of their journey to England. The men wanted to join the fight against Germany, Miss Richards to avoid internment as an enemy alien. Ducking under German searchlights Dédée swam backwards and forwards, pushing an inflated tyre that served as a raft for those who could not swim. There was a moment of extreme danger when Miss Richards had to remove her skirt, and her stark white bloomers were like a beacon in the night. But Dédée's words of encouragement calmed any panic during the two hours it took to get everyone across. The operation completed, she sent the party on under the guidance of a friend, a young man named Arnold de Pée.

But on the next trip – with a smaller group that included Colin Culpar, an evader from St Valéry – she went the whole distance herself, down to the town of Bayonne on the south-west coast of France.[29] There she hired a veteran smuggler to guide the party through the tricky mountainous landscape, past German sentries and border patrols and into Spain. To his surprise, she insisted on going too. She had a mission. The previous trip had ended in disaster. The Belgian would-be soldiers (and possibly Miss Richards too) were not in Britain swelling the forces of freedom but languishing in the Miranda del Ebro concentration camp. A mechanism would have to be put in place on the Spanish side of the border for those crossing to be collected and protected.

The next day she presented herself at the British consulate in Bilbao, explained that her family had been helping British evaders since Dunkirk, that she had put in place a chain of safe houses all the way from Belgium and was prepared to pass more British servicemen along it. She would accompany each party herself and in return she wanted reassurance that they would be looked after once they arrived in Spain. She made it clear that the line would be hers and hers alone. She wasn't asking for direction, she wouldn't disclose any information and there was no way she would accept orders from anyone else. She simply wanted to be recognized and her out-of-pocket expenses paid. And, for a start, could she be reimbursed for the cost of ferrying Culpar – 6,000 Belgian francs plus the 1,400 pesetas charged by the mountain guide? She had had to borrow money from a relative to pay his way.

Her pitch – from such a sweet and ineffectual-looking girl – was greeted with incredulity and then scepticism. Surely she was far too fragile to have made the mountain crossing – though a quick check established that she had. But was she a German plant, an infiltrator? After a long discussion she persuaded the British official she was genuine, and that she could deliver on her promises. He paid her for Culpar and then kept her waiting for a fortnight while he consulted MI9 in London about what to do next with this most unlikely of undercover workers.

The immediate response was not good. Dansey said she had to

be a phoney and castigated the official in Bilbao for paying her any money at all. He distrusted all women, thought they had no place in his organization.[30] But MI9's Norman Crockatt decided she merited proper inquiry rather than being dismissed out of hand by male prejudice and set his snoopers on her trail. Everything checked out. 'Sunday' reported that the de Jongh name had appeared in reports from successful evaders and bravely offered the opinion that Dansey was in danger of 'looking a gift horse in the mouth'. Then Creswell came from Madrid to inspect her and was impressed. Dansey gave reluctant permission, and Dédée – with the new codename 'Postman' – was directed back to Brussels to bring the next batch of evaders down in a month's time. But there was one stricture. Belgians (and presumably middle-aged ladies) were not wanted. She was to concentrate her efforts on retrieving missing British airmen.

MI9 had suddenly discovered a real purpose for itself. The Cinderella organization had its invitation to the ball and, though it would never achieve the superstar status or the glamour of, for example, SOE, nor attract huge resources of money or staff, it was nevertheless now firmly established with a job to do. Until then the rescue of men from occupied Europe had been largely humanitarian – and that purpose was running out as the number trapped in Marseilles dwindled. The emphasis switched. Now MI9 was seen as having an important and utterly pragmatic contribution to make to the war. In its nightly onslaught against Hitler's cities and factories, the RAF was sustaining massive casualties. A beleaguered Britain – for so long mounting the only active opposition to the Third Reich – was in danger of running out of trained pilots, navigators and all the other crew to fly the bombers that were damaging the enemy in his own backyard. It took two years to train a pilot, make him battle ready. If those who had been shot down on their missions could be helped to get home, they would have a valuable contribution to make to the war effort.

Wing Commander Basil Embry's return played an important role here. He had escaped twice from German custody, killing three of his captors in the process. He had succeeded in cycling south from Paris to Marseilles, but had missed a boat home from there by minutes. He finally got over the Spanish border in the boot of a diplomatic car, still sporting the jacket he had stolen from a scarecrow in a Belgian field. He wore it with great pride when back with his squadron in Suffolk as he related his adventures. His success in getting home highlighted the real potential that lay in gearing up escape lines and preparing bomber crews for the possibility of evading the enemy. His enthusiastic telling and retelling of the story was the key. The official history of MI9 records that 'his was a personality so vigorous and so forceful that people listened to him and remembered what he said. His example and his energy did much to fix evasion firmly in the heads both of MI9's staff and of the Air Ministry's as a mode of war to which they would need to pay full heed.'[31] Dansey moaned – to be expected – about 'the apparent inability of the RAF to remain airborne over enemy-occupied territory' and how his job of spying on the Germans was being fouled up by MI9's having to act 'as nursemaids to people who seem totally incapable of getting back on their own'.[32] But he gave his blessing to increased efforts by putting Jimmy Langley on the job. The one-armed Langley, wounded at Dunkirk, had, after his stint as one of Ian Garrow's sidekicks in Marseilles, got home the cushy way – officially repatriated on medical grounds because of his injury. But his first-hand experience of being an evader was invaluable.

Dédée had by now left Bilbao and trekked back across the Pyrenees into France to make arrangements for the first group of airmen. She ran into difficulties and danger straight away. In Bayonne she discovered her friend de Pée had been arrested. Back in Brussels her family had had a visit from the Gestapo asking about her. It was clearly not safe to go home so she contacted her father and he agreed to take over the running of the line in the Belgian capital while she would operate from Valenciennes, just over the border in France. To her father she would send a message innocent-sounding enough for a schoolteacher – *Envoie-moi des enfants* (Send me some children).[33] Evaders would then be brought there for her to transport on to the south-west.

This was why Frédéric de Jongh had contacted Nadine Dumon and enlisted her help. Her work had begun escorting evaders around Brussels but soon she was going further afield, making regular trips to Paris by train with her 'packages'. They must have made a curious sight, the tiny, five-foot teenager in the company of several strapping men, all towering over her. On the train they travelled third class in compartments with hard wooden bench seats, but she felt safer there. And they travelled at night – 'less chance of being questioned'. The girl matured quickly – her life depended on it. Before the war she had rarely travelled at all, just to the seaside with her parents. Now she found herself in Paris, nursemaiding adult men through unpredictable dangers. At the Gare du Nord a glamorous girl approached and asked one of her group, none of whom spoke French, for change for the telephone. The sharp-eyed Nadine had noticed the girl talking to two German soldiers a few seconds earlier. She darted forward and pushed a franc into the girl's hand. Crisis, just one of many, over.

For those like Nadine who helped evaders, it was like that all the time, constantly on the alert, suspicious of everyone and everything. The men she was escorting did not always understand.

Once I was waiting with an American airman in a doorway in Paris and I suddenly got the feeling we were being watched. I told him but he just laughed. 'We're not in a detective story, mademoiselle!' he scoffed. Our contact was late coming for us anyway, and I was getting worried, so I insisted we moved. That was the rule – you never waited more than half an hour. It was too dangerous. We began to walk away, down a street which was absolutely empty. The American laughed at me again for being so jumpy. But suddenly I spotted a man lurking at a junction. Something wasn't right. He began walking towards us. I grabbed the American and ran. We got to the Luxembourg Gardens and I saw a door in a wall where the gardeners kept their tools. We jumped inside and I peered out to see the man come puffing up, looking around, searching for us. He had slicked-back hair and was in a dark suit. I think he was a collaborator, a spy for the Germans.

Sixty years on, as she told the authors this story, Nadine could still see his face in her mind – 'Slicked-back hair reminds me of some very bad men.' She shuddered at the memory – though, as we shall see in Chapter 10, there were far, far more terrible incidents to come in her young life as a helper of evading airmen.

The drama wasn't over. We couldn't go back to the original rendezvous so we took the Métro to an emergency address I had been given. I rang the doorbell but the woman who answered told me to go away. 'The Germans have just been,' she said. She gave me another address, where we hid in an attic. It was very small with just a single bed. But there was milk, chocolate, biscuits, bread and water, which was great because we had had nothing to eat all day. The next day someone arrived and took the American away and I was free to go. But it was after curfew when I got back to Brussels and I was stopped by a gendarme. He was going to arrest me but I pleaded with him to let me go. I smiled sweetly and told him I had been out with my boyfriend but my parents didn't know and I'd stayed too late and now I was in trouble and . . . He said he understood and he would let me off, just this once, and I hurried off home.

In all, Nadine took twenty evaders on that trip to Paris. She met Dédée there and they became firm friends. 'I looked up to her, admired her. She said I should come with her across the Pyrenees and I was going to but I never got the chance.' And, although security was always a priority and it was best not to know the next person in the chain, Nadine also knew the Brusselmans family and went to their apartment to pick up some of her 'packages'.

The Maréchals were also part of the network. Elsie, London-born and married to Georges, a Belgian, had lived in Belgium for twenty years before the Germans arrived and put herself forward to help soldiers and airmen from her native land the moment she heard of their plight. The next thing a priest arrived at her house in civilian clothes.

He had been given our address and came to see if the accommodation was suitable. But shortly after he discovered he was being watched by the Gestapo and was forced to flee. He said that if he was not able to return with Englishmen, a young girl would come in his place. A few days later she did. It was Dédée, 'our Colonel', as we came to call her, because she was always so full of energy and enthusiasm.[34]

Elsie Maréchal's first guest – 'our first attempt at patriotic work' – was a flop. He turned out not to be a Canadian airman who had been tortured by the Gestapo, as he claimed, but a Belgian who had escaped from a mental home. But genuine evaders soon arrived. Elsie recruited her 18-year-old daughter, also called Elsie, fresh from school and about to embark on her training as a nurse – ironically at the Institut Edith Cavell – to seek out supplies for the RAF boys now passing regularly through their home. They all needed little things such as combs, toothbrushes and soap. Shoes were a constant request. Elsie was a lot like Dédée – bilingual, clever, committed and looking so much younger than she really was that it was relatively easy to pass unnoticed by the Germans. She quickly graduated to even more vital work – establishing the very first link in the Comet chain. She travelled out into the countryside and approached the priest or schoolmaster in little villages. It was dangerous work sounding out strangers. 'I would arrive and the man didn't know who I was or if I was from the Germans,' she recalled. 'I would talk about this and that, a bit of everything, for a while until I could sense which side he was on.' Those who passed the test were then asked directly to help. They were told that, if an aircraft came down in their area and the crew needed hiding, then this was whom they should contact.

Local communities were thus alerted to look out for downed Allied airmen arriving out of the blue and instructed how to guide them into safe hands. From northern Europe to Gibraltar, a line now stretched out that could return them home and back into the war from which they had been so suddenly and so violently ejected. However, whether the lost boys of the RAF were as ready as their rescuers for this dangerous odyssey was an entirely different matter.

For all MI9's efforts to prepare them, most airmen who found themselves hurriedly exiting from a plane over occupied Europe were making a leap in the dark in every sense.

## 3. Feet First

On an impulse, navigator Bert Spiller checked his parachute that afternoon at RAF Elsham Wolds in Lincolnshire. He was about to set out on his fiftieth operation, the end of his second tour of duty, some achievement for a pink-faced youngster of twenty-one but with no more than a fuzz of hair yet showing on his upper lip. There was another sort of fuzz in his head that day – the previous night he had been in the saloon bar of the Gladiator, downing pints of bitter with the others. Hangovers were becoming increasingly common among some bomber crews in the autumn of 1942 as casualty figures mounted from the nightly assault on enemy cities. You had to do something to try to blot out the fact that you could be next. Spiller had come through forty-nine missions unscathed, apart from two front teeth that fell out of gums rotted by frostbite at 22,000 feet. He prayed the target for this last sortie would not be Berlin, the Big City as they all called it, or one of those equally heavily defended conurbations in the Ruhr, Germany's industrial belt. A softer centre in the south would do – Stuttgart, perhaps, or Munich. He got his wish. It was to be Milan – 'a lovely doddle over France, the Alps in moonlight, an easy Eyetie target, followed by a warm bed'.[1] They didn't get any better than that, he told himself.

He looked at his parachute and saw that it was two days overdue for a safety check and repacking. 'It wasn't really a hazard but it gave me a chance to chat up Brenda, the WAAF packer.' He gave her the eye across the enormous packing table. 'How about coming to Brigg or Scunthorpe with me if I get back from the gates of Hell?' he asked. She smiled sweetly as she delivered the expected rejection: 'The only pulling you'll do is on that rip ring on the chute.' Spiller did as he was told and the yards of pure white silk blossomed out onto the table. She began repacking it – 'a wonder-

ful art' – and told him to come back for it later. He sighed and
slouched towards the door, stopping briefly as she called gently
after him, 'Be careful.'

She had seen a good many go, including her husband, and knew what
the risks were. She and her like, all the ground staff who worked
sometimes at all hours so that we could take the hero's part and strut
about when all went well, were the salt of the earth.

Out at dispersal, in the cold night air he lined up with the rest
of the crew round the Halifax bomber's tail-wheel and splashed
the contents of his bladder over it, a ritual along with the good-luck
charms – a WAAF scarf and a French soldier's cap badge acquired
in 1940 – that he always stuffed in the pocket of his flying jacket.
Then the skipper led them on board D-Donald and they were
underway. Up into the darkness they climbed, heading south to
Essex, then over the Thames estuary glimmering below and the
Kent Downs, leaving Dungeness behind for the emptiness of the
Channel and the enemy coast ahead. Butterflies fluttered in Spiller's
stomach – as always. His throat went dry – as always. He took a
swig from his flask. Suddenly a bomber ahead of them in the
formation was coned by searchlights and flak guns opened up as
they crossed into Normandy. Explosions buffeted the thin metal
fuselage. The skipper pushed her nose up, gaining height, gambling
that there was no other plane in the darkness above them to crash
into. It paid off as D-Donald broke through sporadic cloud at
9,500 feet into a clear night under a thin crescent moon. 'France
stretched out interminably beneath us, and we revelled in our luck,
lulled by the ease and quietness of the journey as we drifted on.'
When the attack came it was sudden and fatal:

The aircraft shuddered and began to yaw to port, in a slow diving turn.
A fiery missile zinged across my navigation table. The skipper announced
that the port engines and wing were on fire. 'Stand by to abandon aircraft
if need be.' The front cabin was brilliantly illuminated by flames and I
could see the skipper bent over the controls, desperately trying to keep

us in the air. The dive became steeper, and Fitz, the engineer, pulled up the side flap of my helmet and, against the roaring whine outside, shouted 'We've got to bale out!' Woolly, the radio operator, and Peewee, the bomb aimer, were crouching round the escape hatch, parachutes already attached and helmets off. The angle of the aircraft was becoming steeper by the second. I tore my helmet and scarf off and lurched towards them. Peewee cupped his hand over my ear, screaming: 'The bloody hatch is jammed.'

It took three hefty kicks before the panel gave way, flying away into the slipstream as the plane sped faster and faster into a near-vertical dive.

I watched Woolly and Peewee disappear into the night, then clipped on my own chute and clawed my way to the hatch – to discover in a blinding flash of horror that I had put it on upside down. Seconds passed like years as I readjusted it. As I did so I glanced into the cockpit. In the eerie bright red light, the skipper's face was stony, like a gargoyle. Then Fitz tapped my head and put his thumb up. I sat over the hatch, dropped my legs outside into the tremendous tug of the slipstream and went. Immediately I was in complete silence. I cartwheeled through the air, feeling the dampness of cloud all about me. One . . . two . . . three . . . I pulled the rip ring.

Still in the cloud, I swung first one way then the other, semi-conscious because my head had taken the full force of the opening parachute. Peering down, I could see no breaks in the cloud. I was floating for ages in a strange silent world as the cold and wet ate through my overalls. Then, as if by magic, the cloud disappeared and the dark earth lay below, an odd light showing here and there. No way of telling what sort of area I would land in. I would have to trust to luck. I wasn't scared but my head was teeming with thoughts of what I now had to do. I knew roughly where we were and had a little bit of French because this was about to be my second time in France. I had been with the advanced air striking force in 1940, the war we lost. I'd got home then. Could I do it again? I knew I had to get away, find some help. The thoughts crowded my mind, but the ground was coming up pretty fast now and as the last few feet dissolved, I felt a fresh flash of pain as I finally made contact.

A terrifying drop through the air after a life-and-death struggle to get clear from a blazing plane was how almost all airmen on the run in occupied Europe began their remarkable adventure. Nothing could have prepared them for it. Parachute training was primitive and peremptory. Harry Levy, an RAF wireless operator, recalled climbing a ladder to a tiny platform high inside the roof of a hangar. 'Looking down at the tiny figures on the stone floor below, I felt a tight ball of fear in my stomach, but with a long line of men behind me, there was no question of turning back. I stepped off.'[2] Some might have had a similar descent from the basket of a tethered balloon or rolled from the back of a slow-moving lorry after a few tips on how to spread the impact of landing. Most had been drilled in escape procedure, but exiting from a stationary plane on the ground bore little resemblance to the reality of fire, fear and fury of a fuselage in a vertical dive at terminal velocity with split seconds and inches the difference between living and dying.

Almost every man who went through the escape hatch was doing so for the very first time. Some were terrified. The radio operator in Ed Burley's B-17 froze at the escape hatch and the gunners queuing behind him to jump had to prise his hands from the sides, 'slug' him and throw him out.[3] They pulled his ripcord just before he went through the hole and he survived. But thousands of others died, panicked into paralysis or trapped, buckles caught on spars, limbs jammed, radio headsets snagged, bodies pinned to the floor or ceiling by the centrifugal force of the spin, helplessly screaming into the ground, the luckier ones blown instantly to oblivion in a mid-air fuel explosion.

George Duffee remembered gravity pinning him to the floor of his stricken Halifax on the outward leg of a trip to the Ruhr valley. He was a newly qualified pilot just back from post-training leave, straight off the train from home and immediately rostered, as were all rookie pilots, to fly his first operation as an observer in a veteran crew. In the briefing room he had felt every inch the embarrassed new boy he was, as the old hands – in reality just months ahead of him in age and experience – nonchalantly went through the familiar routine, dragging on cigarettes and chatting like playboys about the 'popsies' they had been with the night before. They teased him, anything to ease the tension. He was not to know they were as nervous as he was. More so probably. They knew what lay ahead. He could only guess. Joking stopped when they were in the air. Now only the skipper's commands rang out to break the silence of the night. Duffee felt 'very much alone' in the all-embracing darkness over the North Sea, as if suspended in mid-air. He could not believe that 'it was only this morning that I had kissed my mother goodbye'.[4] Ahead, the quiet night sky was now exploding with the glare of searchlights and orange bursts of flak. Suddenly he felt 'hunted'. An aircraft exploded to his left. 'My God,' he thought, 'what an end, just snuffed out.' He dismissed the thought, stifled the fear, as they flew on to their target. Then it was 'Bombs gone!' and they were on their way home.

Suddenly – like an electric light being switched on in a room – three searchlights clamped their beams on us. The pilot immediately executed a violent weaving manoeuvre, trying to shake off those menacing fingers. He lost them. 'Nice work, skipper,' the rear gunner called out, and at that very moment a burst of cannon fire raked the starboard engine, which burst into flame. We spiralled earthwards. 'Abandon aircraft!' called the skipper as the dive got steeper. I was thrown violently into the nose and when I tried to get up I couldn't. Gravity was pinning me to the floor as we plunged at a sickening speed earthwards. Down, down. I couldn't move. The roar increased to a high-pitched shriek as the whole aircraft shuddered terribly. My mind was filled with thoughts of my mother, my childhood, my old headmaster. I seemed to re-live my whole life. And then what? Soon I would know.

But then I roused myself. A voice in my head said: 'Why are you waiting to die when you have only just begun to live? Why just sit here in resignation? Try, man, try!' I puffed and strained and struggled to force my knees over the escape hatch and felt the cool blast of air blowing in from the outside. This revived me a little and I gathered all my strength and leaned and rushed forwards and downwards. Suddenly all was silent and I was tumbling earthwards.

There was a technique to getting out of a bomber in a terminal dive. It was taught in training, though the calm procedure carried out step by step in practice on an airfield or coldly committed to the pages of a manual bore little relation to the reality, which was beyond any imagination. Survival was hit and miss in every sense, instant and instinctive. Most men knew their chances of getting clean away were slight. Escape hatches were awkwardly placed and narrow, the panels in the fuselage difficult to shift against the pressure of the outside air. Time was the critical factor. The speed with which a normal trip could turn into a nightmare of helplessness and terror was phenomenal. In his Lancaster, K-King, radio operator Sergeant Fred Gardiner should have been safer than most. He was manning 'Monica', codename for an experimental tail radar supposed to give warning of an attack, a few precious lifesaving seconds to react. The beep from the machine never came.

The attack was from astern and slightly below and was heart-stopping. In a few horrific seconds the aircraft was filled with flashes, bangs and the smell of cordite as gunfire ripped through from end to end. Tracer bullets flashed under the navigator's seat. There was an ominous silence from the rear gunner's turret. Holes and torn metal appeared. My immediate thought was that this was it. I was going to die.[5]

The bomb aimer jettisoned the 4,000lb 'cookie' they were carrying, intended for Mannheim, not even waiting to open the bomb doors but letting it crash through them.

Every second counted. There was no time to disconnect the oxygen line and intercom cord to my helmet so I discarded the lot. The fuselage was now on fire, with flames coming from the floor on both sides. Our incendiaries must have ignited and fire was licking round the ammunition boxes containing 10,000 machine-gun rounds. The enemy fighter was still firing on us from directly astern.

I grabbed my parachute and snapped it on to the two hooks on the harness as I made for the rear door. I grasped the handle, twisted, the door opened and then reclosed on my thumb. I pushed again and this time it flew wide open. The training suddenly came back to me. Kneel on the door sill and roll out head first to avoid being struck by the tailplane. Wait until clear, not necessarily to the legendary count of ten, then pull the ripcord. I put my head out into the slipstream, moving at 200 mph. I couldn't breathe in it. I tried to face the other way but that was just as bad. But this was no time to hesitate. I rolled out.

The inferno of K-King roared away into the darkness. In a second or two it had gone. Completely disorientated, I pulled the metal handle of the ripcord, there was a violent jolt, then utter silence as I hung under the canopy in a clear sky. There was very little moon but the sky above had the usual starlit glow. In one direction the horizon was particularly bright as the attack on Mannheim was pressed home by the rest of our bombers. I was now aware of having bare feet. The jolt had removed my wool-lined flying boots and my socks too. Looking down there was nothing but inky blackness. Unprepared, I struck the ground, hands and feet together, with a thud which knocked me breathless. Luckily the ground was soggy. Even luckier I had been perilously close to some buzzing electricity lines. But here I was sitting on soft grass. It had been a close thing but I was alive.

Terry Bolter's exit from a blazing bomber was even more of a miracle. A Messerschmitt 109 caught them close to the Belgian border on the way back from Frankfurt. The wing tank was about to explode, the pilot told them all to get out, the aircraft bucked and bomb aimer Bolter was thrown into the Halifax's perspex nose cone. Lying there on his stomach as the plane went into a dive, he stared ahead transfixed.

We dropped through the sky like a massive piece of lead, screaming down with the sound of wind and engines for harsh and throbbing accompaniment. The rest of the crew were silent. There was nothing to say that mattered any more. We could not get out. I put my left hand across my eyes and waited for the ground to come up. But my other hand was dashing against the perspex nose, out of frustration I think, or anxiety, or just for something to do on that endless journey down. And then the perspex cracked open in front of me. A hole appeared and I fell out. I pulled the ripcord and a mass of billowy silk opened above me. Bits of the aircraft fell past as I twisted round, and then the Halifax roared by a few thousand feet away, on its last flight to earth. A burst of orange flame leapt up as it hit the ground three miles away and the stratus cloud I was floating down through was tinged with red. Above the wind in my ears I could hear myself saying, 'You were lucky to get out of that.'[6]

For many airmen, that journey floating down to the ground was filled with strange sensations. From the hell of a burning fuselage and the last intense claustrophobia, the closing in of imminent death, they were suddenly ejected into peace and tranquillity. Reaching the ground took longer than it should have done. The standing instruction was to free fall for as long as possible. If you pulled the ripcord too soon there was the danger of the parachute being ignited by flames from the aircraft. Many experienced airmen had watched in horror as comrades tumbled from stricken planes to certain death, their parachutes on fire. Also, if you held your nerve and put off the moment when the 'chute billowed out, then you were less likely to be spotted by watchers on the ground. But a delay like that took a cooler head than most had in the circumstances. They yanked the ripcord at once, desperate for the relief of the canopy opening.

Most recalled the descent as a dreamlike drift into the nightmare awaiting them on the ground, though Wayne Eveland of the 614th Bombardment Squadron did not get even that moment of calm before the storm. He was co-piloting a B-17 with a rookie crew on their first mission, going along as their commanding officer to steady their nerves and assess their abilities. En route to Bordeaux, they were Tail-End Charlie, flying low and last in the formation. German fighters cut them out of the pack like the slowest buffalo in the herd. Eveland stayed at the controls – that was the pilot's lot in an emergency – holding the bucking Fortress as straight as he could to give the rest of the ten-man crew time to bale out. Every time he tried to leave his seat for the escape hatch, the nose reared up and he had to grab the column again to steady her. By the time he got to the bottom door, the plane was upside down and instead of dropping through he had to summon his last reserves of strength to pull himself up and out.

I pulled the ripcord, the 'chute worked beautifully and I found myself gently floating toward the earth. What a beautiful feeling! But then a German fighter spotted me, circled round and came at me head on. What looked like flashing Christmas-tree lights arced towards me. There was no noise but I knew *he was shooting at me!* I pulled frantically at the shrouds to try and slip out of his way. I made a terribly fervent but profane prayer: 'Dear God, don't let that son-of-a-bitch kill me.' The Lord must have been listening because after several passes the fighter left and I continued my swinging fall toward earth.

Now I had time to look at the ground. I was over a wooded area with large evergreens, closely spaced. As I landed, the tree branches lifted one corner of my 'chute, emptying the air and dropping me many feet to the ground. I hit it with a shattering thud. I remembered the Intelligence briefings to hide the 'chute and get away from the place of impact as quickly as possible. My mind locked in on that single thought and I started to run, only to be thudded back to the ground again. I got up, tried once more, and again I was jerked back to the ground. I finally sat down, cleared my head a little bit from my hard landing, and realized that I hadn't disengaged myself from my parachute harness. I did, and then started to hide the parachute when I heard shouting and dogs barking . . .[7]

Not all those who escaped from a plane did so by parachute from thousands of feet. 'Collie' Collins was making a low-level attack on a power station in the Pas de Calais when his twin-engined, three-man Boston bomber was hit. He shouldn't even have been there. He had been rostered for a day off, or so he thought, and therefore had had a good time out in Norwich the night before. Then, unexpectedly, he was hauled from his bed to fly. A few hours later, at 200 feet over the town of Béthune, he flew into light flak.

It was a bloody shock. A large chunk of the rudder disappeared and the starboard engine was on fire. Then the other engine began to cough. The next few minutes seemed like years as we jettisoned our bomb load on to a railway line and prepared to crash land. We hit some electricity cables, which caused blue flashes, but they didn't matter because we were on fire anyway. Ahead I could see trees, poplars 30 to 40 feet high. I tried to steer over them but we went through the tops. Then I saw a ploughed field and dropped the Boston into the soft earth as gently as I could. We were travelling for quite a distance before stopping just six feet from a copse. We were bloody lucky. A wheel was on fire and rolled towards the trees as I scrambled out of the cockpit with Harold Milford, my navigator. Then we rushed round to the tail in time to see the wireless operator, George Nicholls, coming through the escape hatch. All three of us beat a hasty retreat over a road and into a field of corn stubble.[8]

The first act was over, the fire and the fury, the heat of the action finished. The drama, though, was only just beginning. A cold and bleak reality was about to set in, one for which most were completely unprepared.

★

When airmen adrift behind enemy lines got back – if they got back – they were asked by MI9 whether the preparatory advice it had given them had been useful. The file of debriefing reports shows that most evaders gave only qualified endorsement – 'Yes, but the information did not apply to me', or, 'Yes, but I had no opportunity to put it into practice.' The anecdotal record tells the same story. It seems the majority of airmen, whether in training or on active service, gave little thought to how they would survive if they were ever shot down. Most paid scant attention to the few lectures they were given on the subject or took seriously the evasion exercises they were very occasionally sent on. 'Nothing was drummed into us,' said 'Collie' Collins. Their commanders – at squadron level and right on up to the top – were similarly unenthused and unenthusiastic. They had enough on their plates getting men and planes to battle-readiness. They had to teach them formation flying, low-level flying, aerial gunnery and bomb aiming. They had to feed them, brief them, service their aircraft. Against all this, preparing them on how to run away had a very low priority.[9] This was neither shocking nor wrong but all of a piece with the mindset needed to fight the war, by both the leaders and the led.

Only in films do gladiators salute the emperor as 'those who are about to die'. Dying, being shot down, being wounded, being on the run, being a prisoner of war – these were generally taboo subjects in the briefing room and in the mess. Many of those who fought that war in the air testify that these matters so central to everything that was happening to them were not up for discussion, even among the closest of friends. 'We made jokes, we said to each other, "If you don't come back, can I have your shoes or your hat?" – things like that,' recalled George Fernyhough. 'I told this bloke he could have my iron and when I was shot down he took it. My wife was cross. She wrote to the CO and got it back. But we never talked about the possibilities of being shot down or being an evader. It was something you told yourself just wouldn't happen to you.'[10] Fear, the most natural and understandable of instincts, had to be buried in the sand of unknowing, of not wanting to know. And rightly so, otherwise the job would have been impossible. Bomb aimer Terry Bolter and his mates saw themselves as a crack crew, and therefore 'we didn't think about getting shot down. We just thought about getting there, hitting the target and coming back again and then going into York to dance and have a good time.' As we will see shortly, however, this made the horror of facing reality on the ground all the greater. For now, though, its effect was to make men indifferent to those who wanted to prepare them for the worst.[11]

Some insist they had no evasion training or lectures at all.[12] Of those who did, most half-listened, and remembered the most extraordinary things. Frank Haslam was told by an airman who had successfully evaded and came to his squadron to relate his experiences that the first thing to do on hitting the ground was 'to relieve yourself'. Evacuating bladder and bowels 'was a chance to gather yourself together, to calm down, to make a plan. He was right – as I discovered for myself.'[13] A different, if equally bizarre, message was received by George Fernyhough through the haze of an intelligence officer's briefing. 'In France you can sleep with a man, you can sleep with his wife, you can sleep with his daughter – but don't pinch his bicycle because if you do, you're off to the knacker's yard.' He also recalled a lecture concentrating on what to do if you baled out near Paris – 'and the advice was that a brothel was as good a place as any to go to. And then, just my luck, I came down in Holland!' Even a veteran like Bert Spiller was left in ignorance. After forty-nine ops, he still had as little idea as a rookie on his first flight what to do if he was ever on the run. 'There hadn't been any lectures. They didn't tell us about making contact with the Resistance or how to get out of an area, how to hide, what to avoid. Nobody told us about escape lines. I was never told of anything like that.'

During training, Tom Wingham actually went on an evasion exercise, though it was a farce. 'They stuck us on a truck after dark, took us out in the country and dropped us off with instructions to make our way back to base. We were told that instructors would be at various points hoping to catch us. I worked out that once the instructors had caught enough to feel they had done their job they would pack up, so I laid up and waited until the last minute and arrived back without being seen. I saw it as just an exercise rather than something real that I might one day have to put into action. This was never going to happen to me.' He did, however, remember being told to be wary of priests and religious institutions in France because they were often right wing and not trustworthy – the complete opposite of the advice Bolter got. He was told to approach teachers, priests and farmers but avoid anyone looking prosperous because they might be linked to the Gestapo. Bolter, anyway, had other things on his mind. Sixty years later he admitted the chief attraction of the intelligence officer's lectures was the number of fanciable Waafs he got to meet there.

To be fair, some did listen intently and took on board all they were told. John 'Ginger' Brown and his navigator were inspired by a 'cracking' intelligence officer. 'He told us the first thing you do as soon as you hit the ground is to hide your parachute but then get away from the scene as soon as you possibly can. And you have to put your life in the hands of any local people who are willing to help you. Afterwards the navigator and I would chat over what we had learned.'[14] Then again, Sergeant Dix of 158 Squadron said the training he had received had been of no value at all, particularly the course he had been sent on in unarmed combat.[15] He clearly found it extraordinary that anyone could have thought downed airmen would be able to fight their way out of trouble with their fists or a few judo throws – and who can blame him?

The half-hearted response, by the crews of the RAF and their commanders alike, to its efforts to inform and prepare them cannot have been good for morale at MI9. It was under-staffed, under-resourced and unappreciated . . . and yet still its Cinderellas continued trying to sweep up the detritus, the cast-offs, of the increasingly forceful and costly bomber war. By now it had left the confines of the Metropole hotel and was set up in Wilton Park, a pleasant country house in the Chilterns west of London known officially as Camp 20. There RAF intelligence officers came to hear lectures on evasion techniques which they would take back to their squadrons and repeat to their men, with differing responses, as we have seen above. Successful evaders also toured the airfields telling their stories, offering advice and helpful hints from their experience, though only those who could be trusted to be discreet were allowed to do this. Passing on too much information had a down side. Strictly against the orders given at his debriefing, one returning airman gave the name and address of a French farmer and his wife who had sheltered him to his best friend. The friend wrote the details on a piece of paper, which he slipped into his wallet and forgot about. Many months later, this second man was shot down, captured by the Germans, searched and the note found. The French couple were arrested and shot.[16]

An MI9 bulletin also gave a forceful reminder that 'successful evaders are forbidden to relate their adventures to war correspondents or any other unauthorized persons. Germans read our papers. Accounts of successful evasions which become known to them make the paths of future evaders more difficult.'[17] If this seemed obvious, it wasn't, even to some of the brightest and best informed in the land. After evading through France, Spain and Portugal, two army majors found themselves sharing a plane from Lisbon to London with Sir Walter Monckton, director general of the Ministry of Information. When he heard their story he was very excited and wanted them to go on the radio as soon as they got back and broadcast it as a morale-booster to the nation. MI9 had to step in to stop such foolhardiness, threatening, as it did, to compromise escape lines that had only barely begun to operate.[18]

Such an encounter would only have encouraged the dim view the intelligence services held of politicians. Even of Churchill himself, if the use MI9 made of the Old Man's youthful experiences was anything to go by. Its official bulletins giving advice for evaders were combined in thick folders marked 'Most Secret' in red and 'To be kept under lock and key when not in use'. The cover was devoted to 'A warning from the past':

He was in plain clothes, his instinct was to escape. Here was the risk: as he appeared at the top of the walls, shots might ring out. He heaved himself up. His waistcoat hooked on to something. He freed it. He saw a sudden glow in the cupped hands of a sentry lighting a cigarette. He dropped into the garden and crept into some bushes. To his horror he realized he had left his food, tablets, map and compass on the wrong side of the wall, as a result of which he later suffered considerably. This prisoner, who escaped in the Boer War, is now the BRITISH PRIME MINISTER. BUT THE MORAL IS STILL THE SAME. *ALWAYS CARRY YOUR ESCAPE AIDS WITH YOU.*[19]

It was a wise warning. Escape aids were issued to every crew setting out to cross enemy territory and were masterpieces of inventiveness and ingenuity, largely the work of MI9's own mad boffin, an early version of 'Q' in the James Bond films, named Clayton Hutton.[20] He had been a pilot in the First World War, then a national newspaper journalist and after that worked in the film industry. He was fascinated by magicians, illusionists and escapologists and had discovered the secret of how the great Harry Houdini managed to extricate himself from a sealed wooden box.[21] Now he turned his bizarre interest to helping British soldiers and airmen get out of occupied Europe.

Public schoolboys, wittingly, and a German general, unwittingly, helped him. He distributed a pile of fifty books on escape in the First World War to the sixth formers at Rugby school and in four days they came back with the consensus conclusion that maps were the key to getting home. This confirmed the view of the Wehrmacht commander-in-chief, Walther von Brauchitsch, expressed in a lecture on spying and sabotage in Berlin just before the second war and based on what he had been told of the escape activities of French POWs in the first. 'The most vital preparations,' the general had said, 'consisted in obtaining mapping materials, compasses, forged permits, wire cutters and a supply of food.'[22] So 'Clutty' secured the cooperation of map-makers Bartholomews, a friend in the textile business and another in printing. The result was maps on thin white silk, each eighteen inches square, which could be easily hidden in a man's flying kit.[23] Their only drawback was the propensity of airmen to give them to their girlfriends as scarves.

His next coup was miniature compasses, manufactured by Messrs Blunt, a venerable firm of instrument makers in the Old Kent Road. They came in all shapes and sizes, some disguised as buttons and collar studs, others secreted away inside pipe stems and fountain pens. MI9's history records that 2,358,853 were made. Even simpler was to magnetize the clip of a propelling pencil and punch a small hole half-way along on which to balance it. Razor blades sold in the Naafi were magnetized – north was indicated by the

G of Gillette, the manufacturer's name. Special bootlaces made of serrated wire converted into miniature saws. Then there was the escape boot. Ordinary fleece-lined flying boots were loved by airmen because they kept their feet warm in the crippling cold at 20,000 feet. But down on the ground their bulkiness was a handicap to running and their military appearance an instant giveaway. Hutton built a boot with a strip of webbing round the ankle and a small knife hidden in the cloth at the top. The leggings of the boot could easily be cut away, leaving a pair of plain black walking shoes. Piling ingenuity on ingenuity, the leggings sliced down the middle and could be restitched to make a fleecy waistcoat, while the heel was hollow with a sliding panel and could be used as a hiding place. According to the history of MI9, the boot was not a great success, even though Air Chief Marshal Sir Arthur Harris, head of Bomber Command, personally endorsed it and pilots pestered Hutton to be supplied with it. Apparently, with all its hidden modifications, it tended to leak – water inwards on the ground and heat outwards in the air. Nonetheless, airman after airman left a record of his appreciation of the special boot. It served its purpose in the first few frantic hours after touching down and racing to leave the scene, even if the men were glad to switch to shoes provided by their rescuers soon after.

But the greatest product from Hutton's conveyor belt of brilliant ideas was his escape kit, a flat tin that slipped into the front pocket of battledress trousers or the breast pocket of the jacket. Inside, carefully packed to make use of every last millimetre of space, was a cornucopia. There were twenty-four malted-milk tablets, boiled sweets, a bar of chocolate, ten Benzedrine tablets, matches, water-purifying pills, razor, needle, thread, fishing hook and line, a rubber water container and fifty cigarettes to smoke or barter with. Here was everything a man would need to survive hidden for forty-eight hours, time enough for the hue and cry seeking him to die down. One of those consulted on its contents was Wing Commander Basil Embry, whose return from France we have already plotted. Doing the rounds to relate his experiences, he called on Hutton and wished fervently he had had some of his escape aids when he was on the run. 'I would have committed a felony for a map and murder for a biscuit after three days without food,'[24] he commented. He considered Hutton a genius – 'a man of action and ideas who never allows a difficulty to stand in his way. All aircrew are indebted to him for what he did in the cause of escape.' Embry bemoaned the bureaucracy that meant he had been lost in France without even a compass. Early in the war some staff busybody had decreed that compasses should not be hidden in buttons 'because if the Germans discovered such deception all uniform buttons would be cut off from prisoners' uniforms and officers would look slovenly'. This was the sort of nonsense Hutton battled with constantly.

He was at his happiest working away in his own private hideaway, a hut on the edge of a disused graveyard at Wilton Park, letting his imagination and his inventiveness run free as he experimented with escape aids, lethal blowpipes, anti-tank grenades and any number of madcap schemes to further the war effort. It was outside of his laboratory that he ran into problems. There were difficulties with the Ministry of Food and the Quartermaster's department over the contents of his escape kits, and with the Equipment branch of the RAF over his special boots. MI9's lowly position in the pecking order gave him little help. 'Time and again I had to abandon some vital project or other to answer letters from civil servants whose imbecile queries suggested they had not yet realized the state of emergency the country was in,' Hutton wrote. Britain was fighting for its survival and 'these blinkered pen-pushers quibbled over pennies and halfpennies'. He often dug into his own pocket to pay for things he needed urgently and forgot to get the money back. He reckoned his country owed him close on £1,000 – a considerable amount of money, the price of a house – by the war's end.

Hutton was to find allies in his crazy ventures after the United States joined the war against Hitler in December 1941. Crockatt opened up all MI9's secrets to the intelligence community in Washington, which set up a department known as MIS-X to do the same work for the American armed forces. Its home was Fort

Hunt in Virginia, twenty miles south of the capital. When General Carl Spaatz brought the US Eighth Air Force to England and established it at bases in East Anglia to run daylight bombing raids into Europe, he asked to see Crockatt and was most impressed by his schemes to help evaders. He drafted one of his senior men to MI9 to participate in its 'shenanigans'.[25] But, like MI9, MIS-X was also to have its problems with higher authority. In Washington, the chief of the war staff, General George Marshall, and the Secretary of War, Henry Stimson, thought it of no consequence and dismissed its work as more to do with science fiction than military strategy. They did not kill it off but their lack of enthusiasm slowed its development and severely limited its budget.

Nonetheless, intelligence officers came to Fort Hunt from the fast-growing air-training bases in America's western states to hear escape and evasion lectures and then take them back to their men. The messages seem to have been listened to with more attention by the American aircrews than by their British counterparts. USAF Sergeant George Buckner recalled that when he had to jump, 'reaction was automatic. All the correct moves were etched in my mind. Those drills and procedures for exit stood me in good stead.'[26] When Ed Burley, a bombardier with the 331st Bomb Squadron, arrived in England, the first thing he did was buy a pair of walking shoes made of sturdy Scottish leather. He recalled an instructor back in Texas saying standard GI shoes would be dangerously conspicuous if he was ever behind German lines. His friends scoffed at him but he changed into them every time he took to the air. 'I knew that casualties were averaging five to six per cent for every mission flown, and since we had to fly twenty-five missions before rotating back to the States, it didn't take a mathematical wizard to work out that statistically it would be impossible to finish a tour of duty without being shot down. Death or injury never entered my head but I was mentally prepared to bale out and physically prepared with my shoes.'[27]

But some advice offered to US airmen proved hopelessly wrong, reflecting difficulties in grasping the realities of Europe. On the run, Major Wayne Eveland tried to follow the training he had been given to travel only at night, stick to the woods and avoid making contact with anyone. But the thick forests of south-west France were not like those of the Colorado he grew up in. His crashing around in the dark simply set all the dogs in the area barking and he soon realized he had no chance of surviving if he did not seek help. He broke cover, travelled in the day 'and cussed that intelligence officer, wishing that smart bastard could have been with me to see what it was really like'.[28]

Of course the information MI9 and MIS-X dished out was only as good as the information coming in, and there was more of that as more men returned from occupied Europe. But it was, by definition, almost always out of date and could be disastrously wrong. Small details were hard to get right, and yet precision could be the difference between life and death. George Fernyhough recalled that the recommended photograph of himself he had sewn into his battledress for use on forged documents would have been fine for an identity card in France, but unfortunately he came down in Holland and it was the wrong size for Dutch documents. The difficulties MI9 faced were illustrated by the constantly chang-ing sheaf of documents required for everyday life in the fascist-run countries. In Vichy France, any man travelling outside his own town or village was supposed to have on his person (a) an identity card stating name, parentage, date and place of birth and marital state, plus photograph and thumbprint; (b) a work permit, showing trade and place of employment; (c) a ration card; (d) a tobacco card (whether a smoker or not); (e) if near the coast or frontier, a special permit to be there; (f) demobilization papers; (g) a medical certificate giving exemption from forced labour in Germany; (h) if driving a car or lorry, a licence and an insurance certificate; and (i) if travelling by train, a seat reservation and a ticket.[29] These nine pieces of paper could be demanded by any policeman or soldier at any time. More often than not, the inspections were cursory but equally they could be thorough, and one document out of date, incorrectly stamped or clearly faked could spell trouble.

General advice urged quickness of action and organization as the key to getting away.

Speed off the mark often decides whether or not an airman can reach cover before the enemy arrives on the scene. The crew of a multi-engined bomber should divide into parties of not more than two. The navigator should inform the crew of their approximate position. Each party must then endeavour to find a hiding place. The search for them will rarely cover more than a five-mile radius from the crashed aircraft, and anywhere outside this area should be comparatively safe. The evader should carry out minor alterations to his uniform to make it resemble as far as possible civilian clothing.[30]

But this seemed to presume that crew all came down in the same place, whereas the reality was that they were usually scattered over many miles. Some advice was extraordinarily precise. There were instructions on how to start the engine of a German aircraft or a Norwegian boat, how to identify the destination of a goods train in Germany and France, which routes into Switzerland to avoid, the brothel in Stettin where help could be sought. Some was really helpful – 'When jumping from a train do so from the right side of the carriage in the direction which the train is travelling, thus obliging any guard leaning from a window to fire off his left shoulder.' But the manual could also be hopelessly vague – 'Try to avoid being seen without arousing suspicion by being too furtive.'

Some advice had the wisdom of ancient military aphorisms – 'Moonlight and woods give the same advantages to the enemy as to the evader' and 'A startled enemy sentry is just as frightened as the evader' could have come from Sun Tzu's *Art of War*. Other advice was plain confusing, as on whether a man could use violence: 'Once evasion has begun and a man has adopted the guise of a civilian, all arms and weapons must be discarded and force must no longer be employed. This does not rule out the rare occurrence where an evader may have to *dispose* of an enemy. But even then this method will only be used if and when the lives of helpers are not thereby jeopardized and there are no eye-witnesses.'[31] It could be unreasonable in its expectations: 'It is the duty of every evader to bring back information on all he has observed. This information must be memorized and nothing should be written down since discovery by the enemy of notes or sketches might lead to the evader's condemnation as a spy.'

In this latter injunction lay a fundamental problem. Nothing was to be written down. An airman was supposed to go into battle carrying nothing personal to identify him, no letters, not even a girlfriend's photograph. And certainly not the reams of advice and instructions to help him survive. As a bulletin signed by Crockatt himself said categorically: 'The above should be read out to selected crews by information officers when orders are being issued for flying over France. Under no circumstances should anything in writing on this subject be carried on the man or in the aircraft.' Wise as this was, it left many men utterly bewildered when their feet touched down on enemy ground and they felt the cold clutch at the heart of being alone and vulnerable as never before.

★

'I shall never forget the silence of those first few moments after landing,' wrote Hugh Dormer. 'I was alone in a small field. The moonlight was flooding down and I could see for miles. The grass was drenched in dew. It seemed impossible that one was in the middle of France. The night was of peace. It had nothing to do with war. Down in a village the dogs were barking furiously and I heard whistles as though gendarmes were out.'[32] As in *Henry V*, the inspirational Shakespeare play he always carried with him, he thought of all those people sleeping in their beds in England. He knew the danger he was in.

If one is caught by the Germans, one is tortured incessantly and scientifically until by pain and hunger the will is broken and priceless information is finally extracted. It is all done so secretly that the world will never know whether you faced your torturers with closed lips to the end or broke down and screamed for mercy at the first blow. And the result either way will be the same – death, shoddy and ignominious, like a rat hunted to exhaustion by its persecutors.

Dormer was different from most men dropping into occupied France. He was an SOE agent on a sabotage mission, he had chosen to go, he had been trained for undercover work, he had been before. His poignant thoughts, his apprehension and fear, were those of a professional, steeled for this sort of activity. By comparison, the average airman was an amateur thrown into the deepest of deep water to sink or swim. For most, the shock was profound. Landing in France, navigator Ralph McKee of the 305th Bomb Group was overwhelmed by the thought that 'just a few minutes ago I had been part of a smoothly functioning bomber crew, able to make decisions and command power. Now, I had been projected into a cold, hostile environment and I was at the mercy of nature and the enemy. It seemed impossible that the peaceful, orderly countryside around me belonged to an enemy conqueror and that I was a hunted animal.'[33] He was lucky. Two French boys crawled through a hedge to greet him, put him on a bicycle and escorted him through a village. 'Several German soldiers were lounging in the street. They glanced but took no special notice, even though I was wearing American flying coveralls and a flight jacket with a brightly coloured squadron insignia on the left breast.' Within half an hour of touching down he was hunkered down in a hayloft, sipping wine while his new friends dragged deeply on Lucky Strike cigarettes.

Terry Bolter, without such a genial welcoming committee to greet him, wiped the mud from his eyes, quickly buried his parachute in a bank of soft earth and then set out across open countryside. He limped; as had happened to so many others, a boot had come off in the drop. It was a serious handicap but after seeing the headlights of lorries and the torches of a German search party in the distance he forced himself on. He then lay up in a barn until dawn. 'Overhead I could hear RAF bombers on their way back to England.' He couldn't be sure but he thought he was in Belgium. The last of the navigator's calls before they were hit had said they were passing over Bonn. They must have made it beyond the German border before the crash, he told himself. He ran through his escape kit, checked the compass, spread out the silk map on the grass. He waited until it got dark again, preparing himself for the moment he knew must come when he would have to emerge from hiding and try to find help.

This was always a moment of truth. One evader said: 'It's a gamble, perhaps with your life, certainly with your freedom. You know it's a risk but whether you do it in the first hour or the first week, you have got to make contact with somebody. I remember saying to myself: "This, old son, is where you leave it to the angels." '[34] Another felt 'like a door-to-door salesman making split-second judgements on the people who answered our knock. If all the signs looked good I went straight into my sales pitch as a British serviceman on the run and grateful for any food they could spare.'[35] Bolter was brazen. He spotted a cyclist, stepped out into the road and in schoolboy French said he was an English flyer.

The swarthy face broke into a smile and the dark eyes lit up. 'But of course, monsieur. My name is Gaston. I am a member of the Belgian Resistance. I was nearby when your aircraft crashed. The Germans stopped me and forced me to help pull out the dead bodies of your crew.' I had struck lucky the first time, great. He looked a nice type, very genuine. It never occurred to me that he might be lying. I had been isolated for the past twelve hours in hostile territory with Germans searching for me. You have to trust someone. You have no alternative. Where else are you going to turn? I lay hidden again as he went off on his bicycle and came back with some food and a spare shoe. I put my white roll-top sweater on top of my RAF blouse and with a black beret on my head felt I could easily pass for a farm labourer on his way home.

Gaston, of course, had taken a chance too and had every reason to be suspicious of the Englishman, if that was what he really was. Bolter was taken to a field behind a farm where a haystack had been hollowed out in the middle. In a hiding place the size of a room he ate, drank some wine and dozed before being subjected to a sharp interrogation to establish that he was genuine and not a German impostor trying to infiltrate the escape lines. A few hours

later he had bathed and was tucked up between clean sheets in a
soft bed in a farmer's house. 'I was very thankful just to be alive,
to have a hiding place, food, warmth, shelter. I knew I had to be
patient, to wait and to do as I was told.' He fell asleep thinking of
the young widow he had been courting back in York for the past
couple of months and felt sorry that 'some other bloke is going to
get the benefit of all my work!'

George Duffee's mind was elsewhere too. As he had floated
down to earth from his exploding bomber – a casualty on his very
first op – he had felt this couldn't really be happening to him.
Surely it was a bad dream and he would wake up soon in his bed
at home. He crumpled into the ground and lay there beneath the
canopy of his parachute, still in a reverie, telling himself that 'this
was the soil of England and I was safe. I must just lie awhile and
think. Noise of aircraft flying high above. Aircraft? Yes, that was
it. I had been shot down and had baled out. But it wasn't really
me. No, the real me was secure in my bed, and this was just a
flight of my all too vivid imagination.' He had to fight himself to
accept the truth. The soil on his hands was real. This was no
dream. This was happening to him.

I must think. I must get away. The strong impulse to run came over me
but I had this feeling that if I stood up, someone would shoot me.
Slowly, inch by inch, I began crawling to a hedge at the side of the field.
When I got there I stood up. I felt for my emergency food box and felt
the smooth surface of the casing in my pocket. I knew I must walk to
put as much distance as I could between myself and the crash scene.
According to my rough calculation, I was very close to the Dutch–
German border, on the Dutch side.

He stopped by a cornfield and rested during daylight, soaking
up the sun, saving his energy. 'I thought of home and what my
family were doing. Did they already know what had happened to
me? I dozed and thought about the happy days I had spent in
America during my training and wondered if it would all be wasted
and I would soon be thrown into a prison camp.'[36] As night fell

he set off walking again, past isolated farmhouses, through dark woods, over streams and fields. He resisted the strong temptation to look through the window of a house. He slept, hidden in a hedge, through another day and was woken by a strange noise – the clattering of two men in clogs. He *was* in Holland, then!

I extracted a few Horlicks tablets from my escape kit and sucked them. They were very sustaining. Then a bar of full milk chocolate. Delicious. I chewed thoughtfully on a piece of gum. Far away I could hear a train racing along a rail, a lorry changing gear, the mooing of a cow. That night I travelled further, skirting villages and keeping to the shadows. Hiding like a common fugitive and always listening, walking and listening, all night long. Exhaustion sent me in search of another hiding place, this time a dried-up ditch. I slept away the hour before daybreak, and was woken, heart pounding, by a rifle shot in the woods behind me. I lay very still hardly daring to breathe. Then I peeped cautiously above the level of the road and there, not twenty yards away, was a German soldier armed with a rifle guarding a lorry. One of the invincible Master Race. His comrades were searching the wood and the surrounding countryside. I could hear the crunch of their boots as they strolled about. They shouted to each other as I lay there hardly daring to draw breath. I was so still that a field mouse ran on to my chest, stayed looking at me and then ran down my leg.

Eventually the enemy patrol left and Duffee could relax. But this first sighting of the enemy, though the soldiers he saw were old and hardly impressive, had unnerved him. This was not unusual or surprising. Lieutenant Howard Harris, an American bomb aimer, came down on the outskirts of Paris, falling into woodland near Orly airport. He covered himself in leaves in a ravine and straight away could hear a platoon of German soldiers combing the undergrowth for him. 'At times they were less than ten feet away. If they hadn't been so noisy, whistling and shouting, they could have heard my heart beating.'[37] This moment, the first close encounter with an enemy who up until then had been an abstraction rather than a physical reality, was when panic could overwhelm with disastrous results. The temptation to run was huge. Terry Bolter's first sight of a German was looking round at a pair of jackboots beside him on a Brussels tram. He edged away, overcome by 'a surge of fear' at the closeness. 'I had signed up to fight them from the air, not on the ground,' he recalled. Fortunately the soldiers didn't notice his panic reaction. Another evader pushed open the door of a church, thinking he was safe, and swallowed hard as German soldiers in the congregation turned and stared at him. It took a supreme effort to control the urge to run. Yet another had his first brush with '*les Boches*' on a crowded train. He was pushed up against a squad of soldiers, complete with rifles, and one asked him the time. He had the cool common sense to bite back the terror he felt inside and flash the face of his wristwatch in the German's eyes.[38]

Duffee lay in his ditch and was happy just to have survived his first close brush with the Germans but he knew that if he was to continue to stay out of their way he would have to seek help. He was desperately hungry too and so when night came he approached a house and peeped through the window at a woman sewing, her man sitting eating.

I knocked on the door, imagining their startled look from one to the other. Were they expecting visitors? The door was opened by the man and I walked straight in. 'I am a British pilot,' I said. He was nervous, suspicious. I showed him my flying badge and he picked out the letters, R-A-F. They continued to stare at me nervously. I used the phrase card from my escape kit to ask for civilian clothes and shoes, offering my battledress and flying boots in return. Rummaging in an outer room, the wife produced brown trousers, a tattered coat and well-worn wooden shoes. She placed these before me. Nothing was said. I changed out of my uniform and put on the clothes, uttered my warmest thanks, shook the man by the hand and as quickly as I had entered, I left.

The next day he came across a group of children on their way to school and swung in behind them.

They were so busy chasing each other, they had no eyes for the shock-haired, unshaven, rather tired-looking individual following them. We passed a German soldier, who took no notice of me. Then we came to a village, the children disappeared into school and I went into a café. I made signs asking for something to drink and the woman there gave me a glass of water. I asked if she spoke English and she said no, but she would fetch the teacher from the school. She vanished and I was left wondering if she would come back with the police but she returned with a quiet young man who listened without comment as I told him my story. 'How can I be sure you are an English pilot?' he asked when I had finished, so I showed him the remains of my escape kit. By now other villagers had gathered in the café and there was furtive discussion among them. But eventually the schoolteacher smiled. 'Yes, I believe you,' he said, 'and we shall help you.'

The airman was taken to a farm. 'I was overjoyed at gaining help so soon. By some miraculous chance I had made contact with one of the many wonderful underground organizations in occupied Holland.' It was not until after the war that Duffee discovered how close he came to death that day. His interrogation in the café had been touch and go, and a pistol had been levelled at him throughout. For a while the consensus was that he should be taken round the back and shot. 'Apparently they took a vote on it and I survived by just one vote!' Here was an indication of the dangers facing men on the run. If the German search parties didn't get them, there was every chance that their so-called 'friends' might kill them off. Herbert Pond, a New Zealand pilot, felt the muzzle of a revolver against his head after his story did not check out and was saved only when another airman vouched for him.[39]

Not surprisingly there were many who thought it might be safer to go off meekly into captivity, despite all the pep talks they had had back in the squadron about their duty to try and get home. A Dutch Resistance worker got to one Allied airman before the Germans did and quickly outlined how he planned to hide him and send him on his way home. The man refused the offer of help. The air battle in which he had been shot down and the parachute jump had been enough for him. Nor did he want people risking their lives on his behalf. 'Where can I turn myself in as a prisoner of war?' he asked. He was pointed in the direction of the police station.[40] Most downed airmen, of course, did not get any choice in the matter. The Germans were never slow at pinpointing crashed aircraft and getting to the vicinity quickly. Search parties picked up dazed, disorientated and injured airmen before they had time to get far. 'Collie' Collins peeped out from the ditch in which he was hiding and was horrified to see his navigator and wireless operator walking along a farm track, out in the open and utterly exposed. He glanced at his watch and realized it was precisely two hours and twenty minutes since he and his crew had taken off from their base in Norfolk. That was how quickly fortunes changed in the air war.

I watched them suddenly make a run for the nearest cover, a couple of haystacks. Then I spotted the German motorcycle and sidecar that was after them. A soldier walked slowly to where they were hiding, there were three shots and they came out. It was just tough shit. And there was nothing I could have done about it. I wasn't going to tackle armed Germans. I stayed in the ditch and that was the last I saw of Harold Milford. He was one of those fifty RAF officers shot by the Gestapo after the 'Great Escape' from Stalag Luft III.

Fred Gardiner might easily have surrendered to the first Germans who challenged him. The fight had gone out of him on the way down from his doomed Lancaster. He lost his boots and socks, sprained his ankle, bruised his arm and mislaid his watch. Utterly demoralized to find himself in hostile territory he was all for giving himself up. So what if he became a prisoner of war? It would improve his chance of surviving it.

The flying had been hard, and, to be honest, I was relieved at the thought of not having to go on any more ops. I had been on five and I couldn't stand the flak night after night. You couldn't opt out unless you went LMF [requested to be stood down from duties],[41] and that was even worse. No, my war was over and I was glad. As for my chances of getting home, that was just too monumental to comprehend. I was alone in an enemy-occupied land, and things looked very bleak. But we had been told to try and I thought I'd have a go. Strangely enough I wasn't afraid. The experience of being trapped in the plane and then somehow getting out when I was sure I was going to die had used up all my fear. After that, nothing could scare me.

Gardiner stumbled towards a cottage where, in the early morning, wisps of smoke were rising from a chimney. Should he knock? The decision was made for him when he heard a truck approaching. It could only be Germans – who else would have petrol? This was his moment of truth. All he had to do was stand there and be taken into captivity. Instead some instinct took over and he shoved open the door, stepped inside and watched from the window as an army vehicle drove by. Soldiers, rifles between their knees, were sitting in the back. 'It was my first sight of "the enemy". Until then they were remote figures. Now they were very, very real.' And just as real was the little old widow into whose impoverished, stone-floored home he had strayed. She burst into tears. Her middle-aged son rushed to comfort her – and to greet the airman enthusiastically. 'He produced socks and boots and an old black raincoat to cover my uniform. Then he indicated I should follow him. We crossed the road and went to another cottage. Soon I was eating a slice from the biggest plum pie I had ever seen. They told me I was in Belgium.'

Half the village must have come to see the fugitive and shake his hand. A doctor checked him over and gave him money. Then two young men on bicycles came to escort him to another hamlet where he was given a room for the night. Here again he could have given up. An old man came and told him his chances of getting away were slim and he would be better walking into the *gendarmerie* and surrendering. 'I thought about it but by now I was in civilian clothes and had made a start as an evader. I decided to get on with it.' Only later, as he made a back-door getaway from the house with a Resistance fighter codenamed Raymond, did he learn the old man was a collaborator. Just in time he was hurried away, to find sanctuary in the house of a priest. There, over black bread and a cup of bitter acorn coffee – meagre fare but wholly typical in those hard times – he learned from the *abbé* that he was close to the French border. Gardiner tuned into the illegal radio hidden in the priest's desk and heard that his was one of nine planes shot down that night on the Mannheim raid. As he listened, he looked out of the window of the priest's study and, to his horror, saw two uniformed policemen at the front door. It was too late to hide. So the game was up after all, just when he had decided to go for it. But this was one of those confusing moments for evaders because the gendarmes were patriots and friends. They saluted him, delighted to meet this brave English flyer.

That night, Gardiner was moved again, a cassock over his shoulders as he and the *abbé* hurried through rain down a country lane to a wood.

The priest stopped and gave a low whistle. It was answered by someone in the darkness. A man came forward – it was Raymond, a pistol in his hand. He had one for me too. I was aghast at the idea of firing it – which was pretty strange given that I had been flying in a war and dealing out death and destruction from a distance. But I really didn't want to use a pistol. That would be much too close up, too personal. Then again, the situation I was in was really perilous. I was out in a wood after curfew with a Resistance fighter, armed and disguised as a clergyman. If I was caught, I was in real trouble. It got worse as I followed Raymond and we crept past an army hut. Suddenly the door was flung open, light streamed out, and German soldiers emerged talking and laughing. We crouched in a ditch as they mounted cycles and rode off a few yards away from us. Raymond had his gun on them until they disappeared into the distance.

Gardiner was passed down a chain of safe houses. Not that these could ever be totally free of danger. And, given the large number of German soldiers billeted on the local population, in a surprising number of cases evaders were forced to live cheek by jowl with the enemy hunting them. It was far from unknown for boys in blue to be tucked away in the attic above bedrooms where soldiers in grey and olive-green slept. One airman, Kenneth Skidmore, spent many weeks in a flat in Paris knowing full well that in the apartment above lived a high-ranking Wehrmacht officer and his family. He could hear the daughter playing classical music on the piano and, rather mischievously and incautiously, he would sometimes counter her with a little music playing of his own. He even shared the lift with the girl, who acknowledged him with a smile. But Gardiner had no such genteel *divertissement* or freedom of movement. In his safe houses he was often confined to a small room for days on end and felt like a prisoner, with nothing to do, nothing to read, and no radio. But he knew not to make a fuss. And he was constantly aware of the danger his hosts were putting themselves in on his behalf. If caught, he would probably end up in a POW camp, 'but they would be tortured and possibly killed. They were very proud and patriotic. One young woman kissed me on both cheeks with some emotion. They saw in me the evidence that they still had allies carrying on the fight against the hated occupying Germans.'

But the risks they took were very real. When a British air gunner was found in the home of the Hoogvliet family in a coastal village outside Rotterdam, the head of the household and his son were tied to stakes in the garden and shot in front of the whole village. In Zaandam, a suburb of Amsterdam, nine Americans were seen to bale out from a plane. An SS commander had four local men executed and another eighteen arrested as hostages to suffer the same fate if the airmen were not produced. If that failed to flush them out, he threatened to drive round the area in a car and machine-gun 150 people randomly. After a painful discussion, the Resistance crumbled, and enough of the crew were handed over to keep the Germans happy.[42] Not surprisingly, Marguerite Brouard, just fifteen when her mother became active in the Resistance in Paris and began hiding Allied airmen, recalled times when she was 'very, very frightened':

We knew the dangers, that we could be tortured, executed or sent to concentration camps. My mother was extra worried because she knew the Germans would torture her children to get her to talk. But we did it because we wanted the Germans out of our country. We weren't soldiers. We were just ordinary civilians surrounded by the enemy and fighting a war as best we could. I was proud and happy to do my bit.[43]

In a French village, 'Collie' Collins was given refuge by a jolly, buxom farmer's daughter named Yolande with similarly patriotic views. She found him stripped to his underpants and washing mud off himself in a water tank in her backyard after a night in a ditch. She hid him, and even fooled a patrol of German soldiers who came to the house that there was no one there. But then her little brother whispered to friends at school about 'the English airman', the word travelled and, though he had already gone, she was arrested by the Germans. Their interrogation was hard on her. The friendly, laughing 17-year-old turned out to have a weak heart and she died a few days later. Collins was by then in a different town and staring at a public notice offering 25,000 francs (£140) and the return of two French POWs from Germany for his capture. The offer to trade flesh for flesh was an attractive one. After the fall of France and Belgium, hundreds of thousands of soldiers and young men had been shipped at gunpoint to Germany as slave labour. An English stranger for the return of two loved ones was a tempting deal. That so many mothers, wives and sisters resisted it is remarkable. That others could not was a sign of the times and the terrible tearing of loyalties.

Meanwhile, Gardiner was finally settled in the attic room of a family who spoke English and for the first time since he baled out had someone to talk to. Until then his 'conversations' had all been in sign language. Now there was even a pretty teenage daughter to flirt with. The house was large, standing in its own grounds in a small town, and his hosts wealthy, stocking their larder with black-market eggs and meat. He was offered Turkish cigarettes, an unheard-of luxury. As he settled into this comfortable lifestyle, a Resistance leader visited and out of the blue punched him hard in the stomach. The Englishman slumped, but was safe. The sudden blow was a test of his real identity, a way of finding out if he would lapse instinctively into German swear words. Gardiner now passed several weeks like so many evaders, just watching and waiting. The high drama of being on the run only ever came in fits and bursts. The real skill required was not to be brave but to be patient.

For some this verged on the unbearable. George Duffee, still trapped in Holland, recalled half-losing his mind:

Weeks passed, weeks of waiting and of tension. It was an ordeal. Little exercise, no English literature, and a house full of children who must not know I was there in case they let something slip to their friends. During the day it wasn't too bad because they were at school and I could move about the house but the evenings were torturous. The children would be downstairs and I would be in the spare room upstairs, keeping as quiet as possible. All the time I was there the children only saw me once, when it was explained to them that I was a distant uncle who was a little 'wrong' in the head. Each night I would hear them say their prayers before going to bed in the next room to me. Then I would breathe as quietly as I could and lie quite still until I thought they were asleep. Only then could I relax a little. In those many hours of exasperation, fantastic thoughts drifted through my mind. I picked up the threads of religion, what I believed in and why. I even tried in my elementary way to diagnose the cause of war, the rights and wrongs of bombing. I also had day dreams of being whisked off the next night and flown back home. Then I got a change of scene. I was moved to another house and stayed there . . . for ten more dreary days and nights. The monotony was broken occasionally by passing regiments of German soldiers singing their marching song, '*Wir Fahren Gegen Engeland*' ['We're sailing against England']. I thought: if only I could come with you!

At least Fred Gardiner had some human conversation and company to keep his spirits up. The only person he had to be careful of was the cleaning lady who came to the house in the morning.

My room in the attic was pleasant and comfortable and I had to remain there each morning when she was around. She never learned of my presence and when she was told after the war she was astonished. After she had gone, I had the run of the house as long as I kept away from the windows. I could also venture into the garden but kept a wary eye on passers-by. There were two English books in the house – *Little Lord Fauntleroy* and Dickens's *The Old Curiosity Shop*. I also played the piano, quietly. I had plenty of time to speculate on my chances of returning home safely. It was a daunting prospect – walking the whole length of France and then over the Pyrenees into Spain. Alternatively there was the well-guarded border into Switzerland, which meant internment until the end of the war, as yet nowhere in sight. My mind went back to the training talks we had had on evasion. It had been so hard to visualize what the speakers were talking about and yet here I was in that exact situation. It felt utterly incredible and unreal.

But real it was, and soon he would have to relinquish the safety of this 'safe house'. Some evaders stayed put, bedding down with families for years and seeing out the war posing as Belgian or French peasants. (They had some explaining to do to the military authorities at home when the war was over.) But most knew they could not get too comfortable, though Gardiner was tempted. 'You begin to forget you're an evader. You are just existing in a different place and a different time. I didn't live with the constant tension of being captured. I just got on with this new life.' But then one night he was wakened by RAF bombers roaring overhead. 'I sat by the open window to listen, my thoughts with my comrades in the darkness above. I felt very alone. By then I had been on the go for over a fortnight and I knew I had to get home if I could.' Soon after, the Resistance leader arrived with an identity card, 'a good forgery, on which I was named as Jean Joseph Jacques, a farm worker. The "official" stamp was rather blurred but at least it was a document to produce should I be challenged.'

It was time to move on, to complete the journey. It would be a long slog with uncertainty at every corner and then that daunting trip over the mountains. But he had to try.

# 4. Over the Top

The young woman stood up as the express train slowed and pulled into the station at Bayonne, on the south-western coast of France. Dédée de Jongh straightened her hat in the mirror and glanced round casually, checking that her three 'packages' had got the message. Sergeant Jack Newton, gunner from a Wellington bomber, stood up too, pushing a copy of *Le Figaro* into his overcoat pocket. He had been buried in its pages for hours now, not understanding a word, just keeping his head down, anything to discourage other passengers from striking up a conversation.[1] From time to time on the journey from Paris he had peeled and eaten an orange – a messy process which Dédée had told him was also a deterrent to the nosy. But he had decided against pretending to be deaf and dumb, a ploy adopted by many evaders as they travelled the public transport networks in occupied Europe. Sometimes the number of people so afflicted all in the same place must have seemed like the result of a suspiciously strange plague. It was a wonder they got away with it.[2] Suddenly a German soldier banged against him, pushing his way to the door. Newton let him go.

These were dangerous moments, when a wrong gesture, a misplaced word, an English 'sorry' or an 'excuse me' could slip out and blow his cover. Many evaders had such blood-chilling encounters with the enemy on French trains, literally cheek-to-cheek. Fred Gardiner recalled being crushed against an army officer's Iron Cross as the German squeezed passed him in a corridor with a curt '*Excusez-moi*'. It amused the Englishman no end to think that, if the enemy soldier had had X-ray vision, he would have seen through to the PT vest he was wearing under his shirt with an RAF crest and his name, rank and number on it.

Newton kept the Belgian girl in sight as she stepped down onto the platform and headed away from the ticket barrier where gendarmes and secret police were demanding papers and towards the station café. There, another girl was waiting to meet them, a pretty blonde teenager. Dédée and the girl embraced, then indicated to Newton and the two other airmen to follow. Through the lavatories was a back way out of the station. A locked door opened directly onto the street. The girls had a key. It was that simple. Soon they were on a tram to the nearby town of Anglet and the home of the woman who, after Dédée, was the second most important figure in the Comet escape line, Tante Go.

Aunt Go's real name was Elvire de Greef. She was Belgian, like Dédée, and had fled from the Germans when they invaded her country. She had intended to cross the sea to England but got as far as the Basque coast and then stopped running. With her husband and two teenage children she settled on an abandoned farm fifteen miles from the Spanish border. For hundreds of evaders, the de Greefs' shabby, nondescript house between Bayonne and St Jean-de-Luz, grey paint peeling from its walls, would be the last stop, the final safe house before they tackled the dangerous journey over the mountains. The whole de Greef family was involved in the operation. Tante Go's husband Fernand worked as an interpreter in the office of the local German commander, where he had little trouble stealing blank ID cards, travel permits and stamps. And it was Janine, their daughter, who had met Dédée and her party at Bayonne station. As they trudged from the tram terminus at Anglet out along the road to the farmhouse, Newton stared fixedly at the peaks of the Pyrenees away to the south. They looked impossibly high. Dédée had warned them it would be no picnic up there in the mountains, clambering up narrow, steep paths, through dense fog, heavy rain and snow, walking in absolute silence for fear of alerting German border patrols. Freedom was on the other side. So near yet so far away – the tantalizing motto of every evader. His mind went back over the incredible journey that had brought him here. He was very, very lucky to have made it even this far.[3]

His bomber, G-George, was on its way back from a raid on Aachen when either flak or an enemy fighter – he never knew which – blew the starboard engine. As they lost height, the skipper could have made the North Sea but not the English coast. Rather than a cold and wet ditching in those treacherous waters, he decided on a dry landing on a dark and deserted airfield he spotted below, just outside Antwerp. They flopped down on the enemy runway, skidding past rows of parked Dorniers and Messerschmitts, expecting a hail of bullets at any second. Nothing. They came to a halt, dropped the ladder onto the runway and scrambled down, expecting to be surrounded by armed Germans. Nothing. Not until the crew exploded flares in the Wellington to destroy it and G-George started to burn was there any activity. They heard shouts in the distance, lorry engines revving, and ran pell-mell for the perimeter fence. Then, splitting into two groups, they just kept on running, in the case of Newton straight into the arms of the Resistance.

The other group would all be captured and spend the rest of the war in prisoner-of-war camps, but a passing cyclist spotted Newton and his two companions in a field. ''Allo, are you English airmen?' he called out. 'I am with the Resistance.' Soon they were whisked away, kitted out in civilian clothes and lodged in a farmhouse. The speed of it all left Newton bewildered. He found it hard to grasp this total change in his life in just a few hours – from free man to fugitive, dependent on strangers, suddenly in an alien world, danger everywhere. He sat bereft and scared, thinking of Mary, his wife of five months. Would he ever see her again? He didn't see how. Thoughts of being captured troubled him. Torture! On the squadron there had been talk of Nazi atrocities. Would he be able to stand up to ill treatment? He doubted it.

In fact the greater danger to him was from his rescuers in the Resistance. They were bemused. How had a British bomber come to land undetected on a Luftwaffe airfield and its crew escape? It sounded too preposterous. They had to be impostors. It was not long since the Germans had pulled a crashed Wellington bomber out of the River Meuse, stripped the uniforms from the drowned crew, dressed six of their own English-speakers in them and sent them to infiltrate the escape line. The Resistance had soon cottoned on to them and dealt with them. But was this the Germans trying the same trick again? A furious debate ensued. Some thought it better to kill them, even if they were genuine, rather than risk the security of the whole organization. If that argument had prevailed, Jack Newton's life would have ended there and then, his body buried in a back garden in Liège, where he had been taken for questioning. It was a close call. He was subjected to a vigorous cross-examination, quizzed on his home in London, down to the number of the bus that ran at the end of the road – it was the 74 between Baker Street and the Zoo – and details of particular forms he had to fill in at his squadron.[4] During all this it dawned on him that his life was at stake and one wrong answer might condemn him. His replies passed muster when they were checked with MI9 in London – unlike those from the earlier impostor crew. He and his men were in the clear.

Meanwhile, incensed by the cheek of the bomber landing at a Luftwaffe airfield, the Gestapo had stepped up the hunt for the crew of G-George. Patrols were everywhere, and his rescuers were extremely edgy. Newton had now been separated from his two fellow evaders and found himself locked alone in attics and cellars as he was moved from house to house so often he lost count. The prolonged confinement frustrated him so much he committed the evader's cardinal sin – he lost his patience. Left alone in a suburban house, forbidden even to go near the window, he rebelled. First he sat defiantly (and stupidly) in the window, then he moved into the garden to smell the flowers, next he decided a short stroll could do no harm. Out through the garden gate he sauntered, down a lane . . . and straight into the path of a German soldier. A challenge rang out, a rifle was raised, his papers demanded. As if in a dream (or so he recalled), he walked towards the German with only one option – he hit the soldier hard in the face with his fist and the man crumpled and fell unconscious. Newton ran back to the house and told his hosts what he had done. He was smuggled away instantly to another refuge. Fortunately nothing came of his encounter with the German. He had got away with his act of folly, though the risk to the organization hiding him could have been serious indeed. Now he was lodged with a monk the size of Friar Tuck who packed two Colt revolvers in a belt beneath his cassock. He explained that one gun was for any Germans who got in his way and the other for himself if he failed to hold them off. There was no doubt he would use it on Newton too if he compromised the escape line again.

Not that he was alone in stepping out of line. Many evaders had a sense of unreality about the situation they were in. To one, Harry Levy, it seemed as if they were in a film or an adventure book.[5] Putting on a trilby hat with the brim pulled down over his eyes to be guided through Brussels made him feel 'like Spencer Tracy and James Mason rolled into one. Two peaked-hatted German officers were standing at my side on the tram, yet their very presence intensified my perverse pleasure. I was thinking, "If only they knew who I was . . . !"'[6] Elizabeth Haden-Guest, who hid many evaders in homes in Marseilles and Cannes, recalled how some just didn't grasp what was happening to them.

Remember they were just ordinary, very young chaps who often had been having breakfast in England only three or four hours earlier. Many of them still had that morning's newspaper on them. One minute they were up in the air, loaded with bombs. And the next, there they were dressed up in other people's clothes, slopping around in somebody else's bedroom slippers, eating strange food, confined to a small room, and told by strangers to keep quiet. Everything was shrouded in secrecy, no names were given, and all plans were kept from them.[7]

The 'Brylcreem Boys' – RAF men – in particular could be difficult.

They were the glamorous members of the armed forces and some were inclined to see themselves as important people, that *they* were the ones whose lives counted most. After all it was they who had just been shot down, and were escaping. Some gave the impression they thought the civilians who now had them in charge should perhaps be grateful to them.

Some took silly risks. On a tram in Bordeaux USAAF airman Wayne Eveland, by now dirty and bedraggled, deliberately jostled a snappily dressed German officer. 'I gave him several intentional bumps, coordinated with the movement of the trolley. It was a shameful lack of judgement on my part but the situation amused me.'[8] It was as absurd as another emboldened evader, disguised as a French peasant, driving a dodgem car in a small-town fairground and deliberately trying to crash into cars with German soldiers at the wheel. Simpler pleasures could be just as risky. In the coal-mining village in northern France where he was being hidden, 'Collie' Collins persuaded the woman in whose home he was staying to take him shopping in the nearby town of Béthune. He had a drink in a café and bought grapes in the market but his presence set tongues wagging. For that he was severely lectured by the local Resistance chief and confined to an attic room.

Others who wouldn't toe the line faced sterner punishment. At one stage in Paris the Germans imposed a severe clampdown at railway stations, and travelling south became extremely difficult for a while. Close on a hundred Allied evaders were trapped in safe houses in the French capital. Boredom got the better of some of them and they slipped out of their hiding places to have fun in cafés and clubs. The situation threatened to get out of hand, and horrified Resistance chiefs sent a frantic call to MI6 in London for instructions on what to do with the miscreants. The hard-nosed Colonel Dansey sent back a two-word message: 'Kill them'.[9] Their lives were spared only because the German restrictions eased and the lines began to move again. But stories like this would have a profound effect on evaders. Terry Bolter heard rumours that some of his fellow countrymen holed up in Belgium made 'a bloody nuisance' of themselves and were driven to a quarry by their Resistance minders and executed.[10] Did it really happen? There is no corroboration but, given Dansey's documented attitude, it could well be true. And if not, the story had the desired effect. 'I stayed very much out of trouble,' said Bolter, echoing the vast majority of evaders. 'I did as I was told.'

Jack Newton was now on the move. He had false papers at last, adorned with his photograph, taken, incredibly, in a photo booth in a Brussels department store. 'I sat there in Bon Marché,' he recalled, 'put the money in the machine and ten minutes later out popped the sheet of snaps into the delivery slot.' It seemed such an absurd thing to be doing as a fugitive in an enemy land. Once again he had to pinch himself to grasp that this was really happening. But then, translated into M. Jacques Dumonceau, a commercial traveller from Dax in south-west France, he was on his way south by train. Before that he had his first meeting with Dédée. He and the two other airmen he had been teamed up with – an Australian and a Pole – stared at their youthful guide in disbelief. Newton took an instant fancy to her in her light blue floral dress and dark jumper. But the Australian was dismayed. 'Do our lives depend on this schoolgirl?' he asked sourly. But she quickly asserted her authority. She promised to get them to Spain. 'It will be tough and dangerous, but you are brave boys,' she cajoled them. Newton recalled feeling humbled by her. 'We were flying bombers over Germany and crashing in her country and here was this girl saying "I'll get you home", and risking her life to do so. What she was doing was more dangerous than anything I was up to.'

What Newton did not realize was that the three of them were about to be the first travellers on the fully fledged Comet Line. Dédée had made her agreement with the British consul in Bilbao to bring RAF evaders across to Spain. Newton and the others were 'Package One', 'Package Two' and 'Package Three' – the first of the 110 deliveries she would make. And now here they were in the foothills of the Pyrenees, at Tante Go's house, resting before the final leg. He could relax, the tension of travelling in an enemy-occupied land over for a while. 'What a relief it was to be off the streets after feeling vulnerable for so long, to be able to speak some English, no more charades . . . for the time being.' He was worried more than ever by what would happen if he was caught here in the heavily policed and guarded border country. This was a forbidden zone, constantly patrolled. Every stranger was a suspected escaper. The chances of being stopped were high.

And he knew so much more now – thirty or forty helpers along the way, all with names and addresses the Gestapo could thumb-screw out of him. 'If I was tortured, the Jerries would have a field day with me.' The physical journey ahead troubled him too. Did he have the stamina for the mountains? Was he fit enough? Or brave enough? He feared this ordeal more than brushing shoulders with German soldiers on a train. Sensing his anxiety, Dédée and Tante Go sat beside him to encourage him. He would be fine, they said. 'And if you run out of steam, well, our Basque guide Florentino Goicoechea will carry you on his shoulders. You'll see.'

For three days they waited anxiously at Tante Go's as winter storms from the Atlantic lashed the mountains. But then the weather broke. Sun lit up the peaks. The wind eased. It was time to cross the start line. They began on bicycles, strung out over a mile or so, Janine out ahead scouting the way with her brother Frédéric, on the lookout for German patrols. Into St Jean-de-Luz they went, then down roads littered with the debris of the storms and onto muddy country tracks to the village of Urrugne and a cottage up in the hills at the head of a valley. There they dumped the bikes, warmed up on hot soup and waited for Florentino. When this giant of a man arrived, there were squeals of delight from Janine and Dédée. Amid hugs and huge embraces for the girls, the mountain guide reached out to shake Newton's hand. 'It was like putting your fingers in a car-crusher,' the airman recalled. The craggy-faced and weatherbeaten Florentino was tougher than any man he had ever come across, his huge body fortified by years of goat's cheese, rough red wine and cognac. He knew every inch of the mountains, was as much at home there as the sheep. Yet, surprisingly, he yielded control of operations completely to little Dédée, the girl from Brussels. She was the boss. He led the way but she made the decisions.

'*Salut!*' A final glass of wine was raised in a mutual toast as they set out into the darkness. Newton and the other 'packages' had exchanged their boots for espadrilles, the local rope-soled shoes which gave the best grip on the mountain tracks. Each carried a light backpack with wine and snacks inside. Florentino and – to the airmen's shame – Dédée shouldered bigger ones with extra supplies. Soon they were up above the mist and into a clear, starlit night, marching through pine woods at first, then on narrowing, steepening tracks and finally onto loose scree. Newton stumbled and fell frequently but picked himself up and pressed on, gasping for breath in the thinning air, feeling queasy, getting tired.

I need a break, but Florentino won't hear of it. We must press on. Only after another 30 minutes does he think it is safe to stop, and we all collapse on our backs. I have walked the Fells and the Lakes in England and the Scottish Highlands but they are nothing like this. A swig of wine warms my inside, and the 10-minutes rest allows blood to reach my feet, where it seems to have stopped flowing for quite a while. Dédée sits down beside me, and says that Florentino worries about German patrols, a serious risk. But sometimes what can be mistaken for Germans is really mountain sheep, which wear small bells that tinkle their whereabouts. 'We've even thought about fitting bells to ourselves to fool the Germans,' says Dédée, unable to withhold a little giggle.

They were at the top of the climb, 3,000 feet up, and now the track lay downhill to the Bidassoa river. It wouldn't be too long now, Newton told himself, as he steered his way down the perilous slope, digging in a wooden stick behind him as a brake. He was eager for what lay ahead – a wade across the icy river, then over a meadow, a railway line and a road and into Spain. He could hear the river roaring in the distance. Not far. But the sound worried Dédée. It must be in spate to be so noisy. Would they be able to cross it? When they reached the torrent it was clear the answer was no. A few hundred yards away, Newton could see frontier guards and the customs post they could easily slip past in the dark. If only they could cross the river – and that was out of the question. No one could survive in the fast-flowing current.[11] The airman was close to tears, cursing his luck. So near and yet so far – the evader's motto again, except this time it seemed more like an epitaph. They had slogged over the mountains for seventeen hours only to be stopped by a small stretch of water. Hopes dashed, spirits low, all they could do was retrace each weary step, all the way back to where they had started.

A few days later they set out from the cottage at Urrugne again, taking a different route this time. The river was still too full to wade over and too fast to swim. They would have to go further upstream and take their chances on an old rope footbridge, floodlit and patrolled by Spanish border guards. It would be very risky but there was no choice. But first they had to climb the mountains again. Newton began confidently, feeling he had conquered his fears the first time and now knew what to expect. But no two days, no two trips, were ever the same in the Pyrenees. Where before they had marched in clear skies, now cloud descended and they were in constant danger of losing sight of the person in front, of missing the track, of falling off the edge. Dédée was an inspiration, dropping back to encourage stragglers, skipping over the boulder-strewn ground with ease. 'My brave boys!' she called them, and they basked in the young girl's praise like lovesick adolescents and redoubled their efforts. Over the top they clambered and then down towards the river again, zig-zagging, trying to keep their balance, fighting back the tiredness and the knowledge that the worst was yet to come. Then ahead, straddling a high-sided gorge and swaying in the wind, they saw the bridge and, on the other side, a customs post manned by two guards. The group took cover. For now they could do nothing but watch and wait. Newton studied the rickety suspended bridge which stood between him and freedom. It was 100 feet in length, with ropes top and bottom and wooden slats, some of which were missing. Below, the river gushed out of control.

It was midnight when Dédée and Florentino decided the guards were asleep in their post. The moment Newton dreaded had come. Florentino scuttled down the bank and stepped out onto the damp slats. Gripping the ropes with his hands, he was nimbly across in seconds. Then he sank to his knees and crawled past the window in the customs post, up and over an embankment and then onto the railway line. Reaching the cover of some trees, he stopped, turned and beckoned Newton to follow.

I take a big gulp, adjust my beret and slowly feel my way down the slope to the bridge. My God, it looks flimsy. But I quickly remind myself that it has taken the weight of Florentino and he is a big man, so it will certainly cope with me. I look down. The water is one hundred feet below, thundering down the gorge. There will be no chance if I fall. It'll be curtains. What if a plank breaks? So many doubts come into my mind, but I know I have to hold my breath and start the walk across. After all, on the far bank I am out of German-occupied France and into neutral Spain. That thought is the incentive I need, and I begin to walk. I focus on the far bank, and keep going very carefully until finally my feet touch down on the other side. There is no sign of life from the customs building but I approach it cautiously, duck, slide by under the window, then over the road, up the embankment, and join our guide a little way along the rail track. 'Bravo,' he says, slapping me heartily on my back.[12]

The others followed, with Dédée in the rear, moving, as the now much-smitten Newton recalled, 'with the lightness of a windblown feather, and the eloquence of a prima ballerina'. She was not even breathless when she joined them. 'Bravo, my brave boys,' she announced, and gave Newton's hand a gentle squeeze. Of course, they were not home and dry yet. There were Spanish guards to dodge if they wanted to avoid being shipped off to the concentration camp at Miranda. But the worst was over. Now it was time for the mighty Florentino to say his farewells and head back across the river and the mountains to await the next party. When he had gone, the airmen's effusive thanks trailing behind him, Dédée directed them to an empty water tower where they were to hide until morning. Then she handed each of them a one-peseta note, their tram fare from a village down in the valley to the British consulate in San Sebastián, with instructions to get off and approach the building only if there were no Spanish guards on duty outside. She then left to make her own way into San Sebastián ahead of them to warn the consul they were coming.

The next morning was one of the most joyous of Jack Newton's life as he rose early and walked through sunny Spanish meadows

to freedom. On the tram into San Sebastián he took out the prayer
book he had carried in his inside top pocket throughout his ordeal.
It had been a present from his wife Mary. 'Not long now, my
darling,' he whispered. 'I'll be home soon.'

★

It was November 1941 when Jack Newton crossed into Spain after
more than three months on the run. It would be a while longer
before he got back to Britain – via the embassy in Madrid, a
diplomatic car ride to Gibraltar and then a flight back up the
Atlantic in a Sutherland flying boat. He 'paid' for his passage by
manning the tail gun. Shortly before his odyssey ended in the MI9
debriefing suite in London in January 1942, another epic journey
was beginning a thousand miles away in eastern Germany. In a
room in Colditz castle, the high security German prisoner-of-
war camp for 'difficult' Allied officers, those with a record for
attempting escapes, Lieutenant Airey Neave slipped on an imitation Wehrmacht overcoat and pulled on shoes with cardboard
leggings blackened to look like jackboots. His belt and holster
were cardboard too, while the swastika and eagle's wings on his
cap badge were carved from old linoleum. A lock was picked, a
door opened and he stepped outside onto a terrace. Snow was
falling. With his companion, a Dutchman named Toni Lutyen,
similarly attired as a German officer, he walked along the terrace
to a spiral staircase, down the steps and past the guardroom to the
courtyard below. Sentries saluted as the two 'officers' marched
through an archway as if on a routine visit to the town. Then they
ducked through a wicket gate down into the castle moat, climbed
up the other side, over a fence and a wall before hurling themselves
into a wood. There they buried their disguises and in the workman's clothes they had on underneath began their trek to freedom.

   Neave had been a prisoner of war since the fall of Calais.
Wounded in the fighting, he was lying on a stretcher at the *gare
maritime* when he was captured. He spent time recovering in
hospital in France, alongside another wounded officer, Jimmy
Langley, but where Langley managed to escape to Marseilles and

from there was repatriated to England, Neave had been shipped to Germany. He had broken out of the brutal Stalag XXA at Thorn in Poland, been recaptured near Warsaw and spent time in Gestapo hands accused of spying before being sent to Colditz. There, his was not the first escape by one of the growing British contingent, but it was the first 'home run' – the first to make it all the way back.[13] He and Lutyen posed as Dutch workers and carried forged papers allowing them to travel by train. They were immensely lucky, making the sort of mistakes that every man on the run was prone to. Neave dozed on a train and began talking in his sleep – in English. Then, drinking coffee in a café in Leipzig while waiting for a connection, he took out a bar of chocolate, a gift in a Red Cross parcel at Colditz, and began to munch on it. There was very nearly a riot. Chocolate was almost unknown in Germany by then. People stared at him, then muttered to each other in envy and suspicion. The pair scuttled away. But otherwise their journey was uneventful as they travelled to Ulm in southern Germany. Their Dutch identities exploited one of the few weaknesses in the Nazi regime that escapers and evaders alike were able to use to their advantage – the fact that the Third Reich and the countries it occupied were filled with a vast floating population of foreign workers. The sight of chocolate might be alarming in Germany, but not the sound of a foreign tongue or accent. Lutyen even got into a friendly conversation with a senior SS officer on the train. A military policeman came into the carriage to check tickets and passes and stared at the two escapers in their odd assortment of clothes. 'I wondered for a moment whether they recognized the colour of the RAF trousers I was wearing,' Neave recalled.[14] But the SS officer intervened on their behalf. '*Fremdarbeiter*' ('foreign workers'), he said peremptorily and brushed the policeman aside. When he left the train at his station he called out to the pair: 'Goodbye, Dutchmen.' The last leg of their journey – to the Swiss border – was the most difficult. The railway and roads were guarded and anyone out in the open was suspect. A troop of Hitler Youth quizzed them but Lutyen talked them out of trouble. They went on foot at night, hid in a ditch by the frontier and watched a sentry march up and down for hours before feeling certain of his movements. Then, camouflaged in white coats stolen from a beekeeper, they crawled across a field of snow on their hands and knees and into neutral Switzerland. From Colditz, 700 miles away, it had taken three days. It would be months, however, before Neave was back in London.

Getting into Switzerland appears not to have been that hard. Private Wilson, escaping from the Channel coast in 1940, had come that way. He had been heading for Marseilles and Spain like almost everyone else on the run but was directed to Geneva by a Dutch refugee who thought going via Spain was too dangerous. He rode his bicycle to the Swiss border, saw a house whose land appeared to be half in one country and half in the other and traded the bike with the householder for permission to creep across his field at the back and into Switzerland.[15] Three years on, it wasn't much harder for American airman Jim Murray. On a moonless night he crawled on his stomach under several rows of barbed-wire fencing while German border guards were looking the other way and thought it just like the exercises he had done in basic military training, 'but fortunately without the live-ammo overhead gun-fire'[16]. No, the problem was getting *out* of Switzerland. Land-locked, totally surrounded by Axis and Axis-held nations and desperate not to offend its powerful neighbours for fear of their tanks driving in, it took its neutrality very seriously. Allied evaders who arrived here would have to see out the rest of the war, admittedly in reasonable comfort, or else make their way home by going back into the danger zone of Vichy France and from there into Spain.

Neave was held under 'hotel arrest' by the Swiss authorities, a pleasant enough existence allowing him some 'mild dissipation', in his own words. But he was wanted back in London. His experiences were too useful to be left languishing. He was smuggled out of Switzerland into France, then on to Marseilles, Toulouse and Perpignan by train. Helpers from the Pat Line were with him the whole way, picking him up and passing him on in true 'parcel' fashion. Each, he knew, was risking his or her life, and he was in

awe of their bravery. The fact that he was an escaper gave him no
extra protection. Like any other Englishman on the run he faced
the risk of being caught and interned. But by now the escape line
was operating with an efficiency that Neave found staggering. 'I
had heard rumours in Switzerland but never really believed that
such an organized escape line existed,' he said later. Despite the
odd encounter with a gendarme he was delivered to the eastern
Pyrenees. There, at a house on the coast at Port Vendres, five miles
from the border, business was done. He was astonished to see his
helpers produce bundles of French and Spanish notes from the
linings of their coats, stack them 'like croupiers' on a green baize
table, and then push them over to a wiry local guide with a
nut-brown face sitting on the other side. Neave watched as the
smuggler counted his spoils. 'It was obvious the war had brought
him great prosperity.' And then they set out, a party of eight, up
a steep path into the hills, through slopes of heather and over
shale and stones.

We pulled ourselves from tuft to tuft and then clambered among rocks
where icy streams flowed. My breath came in painful gasps and I felt my
heart would burst. Then suddenly a storm descended on the mountain
like a great bird with outstretched wings. The wind blew so that we
could hardly stand upright and for many hours the rain lashed us with
pitiless force. The mountain path filled with water holes.

An elderly Englishman in the party, a civilian who had been
trapped in Paris by the German conquest, collapsed and had to be
carried. There was a discussion about whether to leave him at a
farmhouse they passed, 'but he cried so piteously we had not the
heart to leave him'. This was no gentle holiday hike, as the thousands of all nationalities who undertook the crossing knew all too
well. Hugh Dormer was a fully trained SOE agent and honed to
top fitness and yet when he made the journey on his way back
from an undercover mission in France the physical exhaustion
coupled with the mental strain utterly drained him. In the dark,
goat tracks suddenly petered out into nothingness, the mist

descended, the slippery ground fell away into vertical falls on either side. And all the time the fear of discovery: a barking guard dog, a flashlight in the face, a raised revolver. Not every guide knew his way. Dormer's got lost and, having climbed 4,000 feet, they had to go back down and start again. It was far from unknown for a guide, his pay in his pocket, simply to disappear.

Neave and his party suffered that night, high in the windswept peaks. There were times when getting over the finish line seemed impossible. They would all die or be captured. But by noon the next day, the storm now having blown itself out, they were over the top and walking down through meadows covered in mist. *Spanish* meadows. Neave caught sight of some frontier guards in light green uniforms and distinctive black cocked hats, and there was a moment of panic. But the evaders were not spotted and slipped away in the other direction. And then it was all over. Panting and cursing with exhaustion, they arrived at a country railway station to await the train into Barcelona. There Neave was lodged by the British consul before being packed into the embassy Bentley for the drive to Madrid. He still didn't feel totally safe. 'The danger was not over. I was still a refugee from Hitler, an escaped prisoner of war with no status in a neutral country. My authority for being in Spain did not exist, and in those days the diplomatic plates on a car were of limited protection.' The next day he was put on a coach, nominally part of a student outing, to Gibraltar, and although the Spanish border police argued over the identity and the papers of everyone on board, it was just part of the elaborate charade being played out in the Iberian sunshine. Finally, documents were stamped, the barrier lifted and the hero of Colditz was back on British soil.

He had a story to tell, and on the Rock there were plenty of sailors and soldiers anxious to ply him with drinks to reveal all. An intelligence officer in horn-rimmed glasses pulled him up short. 'Be careful not to say too much,' he was warned. Many men would get the benefit of Neave's experience but not this way. Back in London he was called to the Great Central hotel in Marylebone and wrote an account of his escape, a three-page report preserved now in the National Archives.[17] On the top in pencil someone scrawled 'MC', for the Military Cross he would be awarded for his courage. Neave listed helpful observations for men on the run in Poland and Germany (or anywhere in occupied Europe for that matter) – that cinemas were good places to rest and that eating chocolate or smoking heavily in public drew 'undesirable attention'; that trains could be dangerous, though civilians on them tended not to be asked for their passes; that Germany was full of all those foreign workers whose presence was a cloak for evaders. He had also learned not to write down addresses of helpers – after his first escape he just managed in time to destroy such a note before the Gestapo searched him – nor to sketch military sites. One of his plans had been to hijack a plane and fly to Sweden and to this end he had drawn a rough map of an aerodrome he came across. A Gestapo officer found it on him and threatened to have him shot as a spy.

In the hotel bar he ran into Jimmy Langley and over pink gins they chatted about their times in France. It was no accidental meeting. Langley then whisked him away to Rule's restaurant in Maiden Lane just off the Strand, Colonel Crockatt's favourite watering hole. Over lunch, Neave joined MI9. 'You've seen the people who work for us behind the lines,' Crockatt urged. 'They need money and communications. You are one of the few who have had experience not only of escape but of the Resistance as well. Come and help them.'[18] From Room 900 in the War Office in London, he and Langley would between them run a small outfit known officially as IS9(d), keeping the escape lines fuelled with funds, radio operators and agents. Crockatt rose to leave and shook Neave's hand. 'It won't be a bed of roses. You and Langley will be on your own and many lives will depend on you, so, for God's sake, keep your mouth shut – and get results.'

Langley and Neave now became the sole source of assistance for Allied evaders in occupied Europe and their helpers. Down in the Chilterns where the bulk of MI9 had decamped, the work centred on accruing intelligence about POW camps in Germany, keeping clandestine contact with them and supplying them with escape aids. Here too evasion courses were held, briefing lectures prepared for airmen, advice assessed and updated. But the active job of running the undercover evasion network rested on these two men in a small room on the third floor of the War Office in London. Did Dédée de Jongh and Pat O'Leary and all those other brave French and Belgian souls putting their lives at risk on a daily basis know just how flimsy the back-up in London was? Did they realize that the organization in which they placed their trust was a massive inverted pyramid, resting on that two-man team in Room 900? Probably not.

As he peered round the filing cabinets obscuring light from the only window, Neave concluded: 'In the world of military intelligence, we were extremely small beer.' A sour lecture from Dansey on the 'dangers' the escape lines posed and a stern warning not to meddle in or muddle up 'proper' British Intelligence operations rammed home the message of how unimportant his work was perceived to be in the greater, MI6-driven scheme of things. He was dismayed but undeterred. 'I thought of all those people who had risked their lives to get me back to England.' Let the warring mandarins of the War Office – 'as crazy as Colditz' – get on with their in-fighting, he decided. Out there in occupied Europe were men on the run who needed his help – men with real mountains to climb, not the molehills of Whitehall.

\*

How some of the fugitives failed to be caught as they blundered their way through France was miraculous. Bert Spiller, shot down in eastern France, was advised by a friendly priest who harboured him overnight to take the early morning workers' train to Paris. He mingled with the mass of men at the station and then clambered into a carriage labelled 'No soldiers'. Or so he thought. In fact the sign read 'Wehrmacht only'.

I got a few yards along the corridor when a German soldier collared me and, amid cries of '*Franzosisch Dumkopf*' [stupid Frenchman] and '*Raus!*' [Get out!], I was passed like some rag doll from one soldier to another along the corridor, and finally pushed out of the door by the last one to a chorus of taunting laughter.[19]

He got into another carriage full of workers and surged off the train and through the ticket barrier with them when they arrived in Paris. On the busy streets of the capital he felt bewildered. German soldiers were everywhere. He needed help and, having been well treated by one priest, assumed he could expect the same here. He ducked into a church, knelt at the side of a confessional box and whispered into the grille that he was an English airman. 'Stay here,' the priest said and disappeared, but something in his voice put Spiller on edge. He dodged away to a side door, peeped outside and saw a car draw up at the front and two men in raincoats get out. He hurried away. Luck was on his side then, and again later when he stopped in a park near the Eiffel Tower to eat some bread and cheese.

Munching away, half musing, I heard footsteps and turned to see a body of German soldiers making their way towards me. They looked terribly like a patrol, and the remains of my last mouthful of food took a long time to swallow as they got nearer. Flight was impossible. I would have to brazen it out so I leant back against the seat with arms outstretched. The soldiers were close when they were abruptly brought to a halt. With some relief I noticed that they were not carrying rifles but musical instruments. A smart left turn and they all broke off towards the bandstand and began setting up for a concert. The ludicrousness of the situation appealed to my sense of humour.

He kept walking but as nightfall approached he knew another momentous decision had to be made. Where could he go? Whom could he trust? Evaders' stories sometimes give the impression that they only had to knock on a door to get help. It wasn't like that at all. Hugh Dormer, an Englishman on the run in France, recalled being turned away time and again. Rarely were the people he approached collaborationists; some were frightened even to be seen talking to him, but more often they were simply bemused by his presence – what was an Englishman doing at their door? – and reacted as if they were spectators in some odd game in which they had no wish to be players. George Duffee, by now hiding in Paris, found the atmosphere among the French curious. He could tell they longed to be free, and to take their revenge on the German conquerors one day. But in the meantime 'it was as if a cloak had been thrown over the streets, casting shadows over people's minds, blank expressions on their faces and dullness in their eyes. There was no laughter, only a dull apathy.'

A desperate Spiller now had to chance his arm again among these downcast people, hoping to hit on those in whom there was still a spark of defiance. And, knowing no one to contact, he felt he had little choice but to try another church. This time he struck lucky. The *abbé* had friends in the Resistance. He was safe. Unfortunately, the group he had fallen in with were not the most organized, and Spiller's experiences for the next months were an example of how slow and unsure an evader's progress could be. For some reason the route south seemed barred to him. Either there was trouble down the line or else the group he had fallen in with had no contacts in that direction. Instead there was a complex plan to get him back to England via Holland. After staying in several safe houses in Paris, he was taken by train to Belgium and hidden in the countryside before crossing the Dutch border – and then immediately sent back in a panic because German soldiers were on a high alert and patrolling everywhere. Within days he was back in France lodging with a family in a small country town, confined to one room, time hanging heavily, forced to be patient. Plans were being drawn up to get him home, he was assured. Contact had been made with London where his credentials were being checked. A coded message on the radio – '*Très bien pour chocolat*' – was awaited to signal the OK for his departure for home. That reassured him, made him and his helpers feel part of a proper organization backed by the BBC and all the resources the Allies could muster. It was a good job they remained ignorant about the realities of Room 900 and its two occupants. A month passed before he was woken one night to be told it was time to go. The message had been broadcast. Wheels were in motion. He was suddenly scared. 'Curious how a month of coddling had reduced my resilience.' The pretty teenager sent as his guide was enough to calm his fears. 'Never unhappy in the company of an attractive young lady, I set off with mounting anticipation of a successful run home.'

And now he was fed into the Comet Line, passed from pretty girl to pretty girl. He got a kiss from Emmeline when she handed him over to Constance and played the sweetheart with Nounou, arm in arm, as they swept through the barrier at Brussels station. 'I entered into the spirit of things wholeheartedly,' he recalled with satisfaction. For days he was kept under cover in the Belgian capital, playing tiddlywinks one minute, subjected to a gruelling interrogation the next as Resistance workers double-checked who he was. There had been arrests in the line and the Gestapo were very active. Everyone was very jumpy. But then Spiller was able to go to a department store to get a photograph for his false papers from a public booth. There was a queue, with a German soldier and his girlfriend ahead of him and others behind. He held his nerve, but it seemed odd to him that the Gestapo had not identified this weak point in the system and weren't watching. Sometimes the Nazi state was a mystery in its inconsistencies.

Spiller travelled south as a Dutch student, equipped down to the last detail by his meticulous helpers. There were Dutch cigarettes and coins in his jacket pocket. He had a first-class ticket for the train – another ploy learned from experience by some Comet people. 'It was an example of their colossal cheek, but they also realized that the Germans were impressed by authority and superiority and treated first-class passengers more leniently.' Its truth was demonstrated as he strolled onto the Paris train. The policeman hardly gave him a glance. And in Paris there was Dédée to meet him – 'a strong person, someone you could put immediate trust in, but with that special driving force that champions have. I was very glad she was at my side.' Within hours he was on the overnight express to Bayonne.

Then it was out to Tante Go's house. Here he put his name in the book she kept recording all the servicemen who had passed through on their way to Spain. He counted the names above his. He was 'parcel' number 82. Some names he knew – there was good old Jack Newton for a start, a friend from 12 Squadron, and two navigators, Pipkin and Mellor. 'Knowing they were probably back in England now gave me a tremendous boost of confidence.' The organization had become much slicker in the twelve months since Newton had pioneered the way. Now everyone was issued with local permits – purloined by Tante Go's husband from the German headquarters in Anglet – giving them permission to be in the area. That meant that, instead of cycling all the way into the foothills, they could use the local train as far as St Jean-de-Luz. Now a party of eight, bicycles were waiting for them as they left the station and the eager Spiller leapt onto his and pedalled enthusiastically away. He heard panting behind him and saw Dédée waving desperately, trying to catch him up. He was on the wrong side of the road. Their luck held. Nobody else had noticed but he was acutely aware that yet again a silly mistake had jeopardized his freedom. And who would have paid most for his foolhardiness? 'It brought home to me the slender thread on which our helpers' lives rested. Suitably chastened, I dropped back into the pack.'

Soon they left the bikes and began to trek uphill on foot. In the cottage at Urrugne they feasted on hot milk and bread around a roaring fire as Dédée laid down the rules for the twelve-hour journey ahead. There was to be no smoking, no talking, no coughing, no lagging behind, and any orders must be obeyed without question, even if it meant lying face down in the snow or mud or worse. The arrival of Florentino, pushing through the door in his dark blue fisherman's smock and taking his place round the fire, brought a hush. Each of the evaders sat in front of him as he examined their feet, applied bandages where he thought necessary and then tied on their espadrilles. He checked everyone's clothing, telling Spiller to put his jacket and trousers on inside out so that the black lining would make him all but invisible in the night. There was a last round of meaty soup and then they were off. Spiller recalled his 'sense of mounting excitement that my journey was nearly at an end, that this was the last leg in this strange adventure film I was in. I was about to do something I could never have contemplated myself doing before. There would be dangers – dog patrols, a river to cross – but I was going to go for it and I was going to get out.'

German security was tighter on the mountains since Jack Newton had made his crossing and, instead of the relentless pace he had experienced, now there were frequent halts, a whispered cry of 'Down!' and everyone fell to the ground, faces pressed into cold rock, as the sound of enemy voices in the distance carried through the clear air. Spiller's heart beat rapidly in the expectation of being discovered. 'Minutes went by with the coldness from the ground penetrating the thickest of clothes. But then the danger passed and Florentino was back on his feet beckoning us on. I climbed robot-like, watching my breath condensing in staccato gasps.' The airman spotted a mountain crest ahead and his spirit soared at the thought they were nearing the top. Then his spirit sagged as he saw more crests, one after another, behind the first one.

Wisps of cloud began to cover the stars as we struggled on and met up with a thin powdering of snow. Then we stopped and bread and cheese appeared from the rucksacks borne by Florentino and Dédée, and he passed round his large flask of brandy, making sure we did not take too much. Dédée made us massage each other's calf muscles as we sat. We rose almost like new men for the next stage, making light work of the remaining climb to the top of the world. A fantastic sight awaited us. Spain lay before our eyes, myriads of twinkling lights in the town of Irun, the beam of a lighthouse at Fuenterrabia on the coast and farther in the distance the glow from San Sebastián. I felt like a child looking at a Christmas tree. I was so used to the black-out in England that it also reminded me of what lay ahead when the war was won and we could have as many lights as we wished burning again.

They zig-zagged downhill, the strain now on different leg muscles, bringing curses from those unfit and in pain. Slipping and sliding, they dropped below the tree line and onto softer ground until they reached the river. It was running fast but not so furiously as to be impassable. They took off their trousers and tied them round their necks with the loose ends flapping behind. These would be a handhold for the person behind as they waded across in single file. Spiller's white silk long johns were too conspicuous and Dédée ordered him to remove those too. He did as was told, despite the indignity, 'feeling the cold air around my naked legs and elsewhere'. Then Florentino tied a rope round a tree on the bank and plunged waist deep into the water with it. In the middle he stopped and held the rope taut as he called on the column to begin the crossing. From time to time, a searchlight from a nearby sentry post swept backwards and forwards above their heads.

One by one we entered the icy water holding on to the rope for dear life. I felt the current pushing against my legs, making moving forward a slow process. Out in the middle, Florentino was well up to his waist. By the time the column reached him the water was up to my chest and I was fighting to keep my balance. Then we all held on to the trouser legs in front and went forward as a unit. By now Florentino had let go of the rope and we were at the mercy of the river, swaying to and fro in the rushing torrent. Lights were flashing ahead from cars on the road going to and from Irun, making the whole business seem terribly unreal. We were just over halfway when we came to a halt, and the word was passed to get down against the water. The searchlight dipped towards us before sweeping on towards the bank we had left. We continued our battle with the current, plodding on until all of a sudden the pressure disappeared and we were wading in calm shallows. Then we were able to throw ourselves flat on a soggy meadow before moving quickly to the cover of some low growing trees. We sank exhausted, not caring about the lack of clothing around our legs.

Legs were massaged back into life, trousers and dignity restored, and then the group quietly climbed up and over a railway line to the edge of the road to Irun. Florentino lay in the grass watching the sentries at the frontier post a few hundred yards away. The others piled up behind him. Two cars passed. The guide gave a

frantic go-go signal – like a dispatcher in a plane dropping para-
chutists – and Spiller made the fastest dash of his life. 'I was in a
controlled panic, reaching the other side in seconds, then scrambling up a hill to a hide behind a large rock.' More figures appeared,
one by one, until the whole group was over. 'Welcome to Spain,'
a voice whispered. 'We made it,' gasped Spiller.

There was still a long trek ahead, more Pyrenean peaks to go
over and round, but these were Spanish mountains not French
ones. It made all the difference to tired legs. As the dawn was
breaking they were plunging downhill into pastureland and across
a meadow to a farmhouse where a long table was set out and huge
omelettes were frying in a pan. They ate as their soggy clothes
dried by the fire. Later Dédée took Spiller down a farm track to a
metalled road. A car with diplomatic plates was waiting. 'I was
under the jurisdiction of the British consul. My ordeal was over. I
felt safe. A warm glow came over me.' There were fond kisses –
on the cheeks for Florentino, a very un-English man-to-man
gesture, and then demurely on the hand for Dédée. Spiller held
back out of shyness and respect. But then emotion got the better
of him and he hugged her and planted kisses on her face.

I was so grateful to her. I still am. She had risked her life for me, and
later she nearly died in a German concentration camp. I feel small and
insignificant that she had done that. Back then in 1943, saying goodbye
to her, I knew I would never forget her but it was impossible to
contemplate how important she was and that I would still be thinking
of her 60 years later! There were tears in my eyes as it dawned on me
what I had been through and that I owed her my life. Thanks to her,
'parcel' 82 had been delivered safe and sound.

★

From the Atlantic to the Mediterranean coast, the Pyrenees were
criss-crossed by secret routes, forged since time immemorial by
smugglers and shepherds, bandits and pilgrims. As we have seen,
the journeys from the eastern and western ends – from Bayonne
and from Perpignan – were arduous enough, taking anywhere

between twelve and thirty-six hours and requiring great stamina and courage. To cross anywhere in the middle, however, was to attempt a major life-threatening expedition. But as the German and French authorities grew ever more alert to the exodus over the mountains, more evaders were forced to take these long-haul routes. For them the collecting point was the city of Toulouse, from where they took trains to St Girons, Foix and other small towns in the rugged frontier country. Sergeant Kenneth Skidmore stepped onto the platform and breathed in the cool and sweet mountain air. The sight of snow-capped peaks in the distance was exhilarating. 'Freedom at last,' he thought to himself. Just then a gendarme walked up and demanded his identity card. He handed over a stolen document in the name of a farm worker from Normandy on which his own photograph had been glued.

Taking it from me, he began shaking his head in disbelief. 'Non, non, M'sieur! This will not do!' I protested: '*Mais oui, c'est moi!*', indicating that the photograph was most definitely mine, whilst fully realizing that it was the other details he was questioning. Here I was, so near to freedom, with the mountains tantalizingly close and just waiting to be crossed. Surely the efficiency of this gendarme was not going to stand in my way and upset everything? My emotions were working overtime. What should I do? Perhaps I could overpower him, take his revolver, shoot him if need be. But then my French minder, Johnny, arrived, stood between me and the gendarme and explained that I was an English aviator, escaping home, and that it was imperative the Allies get me back safely. He said I was important to the cause of the freedom of France. France must live on and I was helping to bring this about. The gendarme looked at me. With a smile he gave me back the offending card. Shaking me by the hand he wished me '*Bonne chance*' and a safe journey.[20]

Was this rare good fortune on Skidmore's part? Perhaps, but he was by no means the only airman to be stopped by a local policeman in those border areas, think the game was up and then, to his surprise, be wished God speed on his way. George Duffee, halted at gun-point while cycling in the foothills, was taken to the gendarme's house to toast '*La France, l'Angleterre et la victoire*' before being pointed towards the mountain crossing.

They needed all the good wishes they could get for what lay ahead. Skidmore now embarked on a journey that was nothing less than a nightmare. Six Allied airmen set out, led by professional smugglers. The party should have been much bigger but another group due to join them had, they learned, been arrested at Toulouse. Morale already somewhat dented by this, they were soon battling across ice and snow in the dark and realizing how unprepared they were for the conditions. Not only was their clothing inadequate, they had just two cooked rabbits, two bottles of cognac and four bottles of wine in their haversacks – and these not for long. Most of the provisions were lost in a fall before they had time to eat or drink them. 'We were short of breath and everything else as well. Climbing skill was absent, as was safety equipment. We didn't even have ropes.' They walked for twelve hours without a break, stumbling upwards, muscles screaming. An American airman became delirious, began wandering out of line and eventually dropped to the ground, mumbling that he could not go on. 'He opened his eyes and tried to move but it was no use. He lay immobile in the snow.' The head guide was all for leaving him. Time was vital. He had forced them along at this gruelling pace to be sure of avoiding the regular police patrols on the mountain. The others refused to leave their companion. 'If he did not go, then we stayed. At that the guide picked up the motionless American, slung him over his shoulder and started walking. I was completely staggered. The guide was only small and here he was carrying a man more than his own body weight through the snow.'

After a while the American recovered enough to walk again, supported by the others. By now it was daylight and there was a new danger – snow blindness from the glare. They rested, only to be ravaged by thirst. They had brought no fresh water and cramming snow into their mouths was a health risk. Cognac dried out their mouths even more and stung their cracked lips. And once the sun set they were off again into the night, another seven hours in snow up to their waists. One by one they crept past a hut where a border patrol was sleeping. In doing so, Skidmore lost one of his boots. 'I could hear voices inside and so I did not stop to put it back on but continued in my stockinged feet. Later they became very swollen and I had to cut my boot to get it back on, stuffing straw in the holes and tying it all together with string.' All the time the head guide was harassing and cajoling them – '*Vite, vite! Marchez, marchez!*' – but for the airmen all sense of time and distance had gone. And then the next barrier presented itself – a bridge over a river with a guard on duty. They lay watching the sentry like hawks, counting his steps, his time out of sight. Then they ran like demons, even Skidmore with his frostbitten feet, over and up a near-vertical slope of snow on the other side.

A shot rang out. We had been spotted. My legs began to move faster than I thought possible as we went over the crest and slipped and slithered away until the firing stopped. My legs felt like lumps of lead and my head was singing. That burst of energy had burnt me out and I fell face down in the snow. I have very little recollection after that but I must have hauled myself up and blindly followed the others. Eventually I arrived at a mountain hut where they were waiting for me, and it was only then that I realized I had very nearly fallen over the edge of a precipice.

Now they were up in a real winter wilderness, with just a few animal tracks crossing the glistening beds of snow. By following the tracks they came to surer ground, and to a spring with drinkable water. Refreshed, they established a pleasing rhythm, making good progress . . . until the American collapsed again and lay motionless in the snow.

We thought he had 'had it', but then one of his fellows grasped him by the shoulders, shook him violently and bellowed, 'Man, have you ever prayed in your life? For God's sake pray!' The stillness of the atmosphere was broken. The words penetrated the depths of my soul. I prayed and I am sure the others did too. Then the guy on the ground opened his eyes, scrambled to his feet and began to walk, and he never stopped again until we reached freedom.

And by then that freedom was nearer than any of us expected. We carried on for another 15 hours to reach the top of a magnificent mountain peak. The other side was freedom. We could see it. Ahead was no wall or fence, just a snow-covered mountainside. Not able to contain ourselves, we rolled, slid and skidded down the slope in our hurry to get there. We cheered, sang and hugged and shook each other by the hand. 'We've made it! We've made it!' A few hours later we passed over the border into Andorra.

They rested in a hotel in the small independent state between France and Spain. A doctor dressed blackened, bruised and frost-bitten toes acquired on the five-day hike. Not that the journey was over. After a few days to recover they began again, out of Andorra and into Spain via a bridge. The roadway was guarded and they had to cross from iron strut to iron strut underneath, hanging on to the parapet above and praying the guard would not look down and spot them. Once over they could relax a little as they trudged for another day to a village hotel, and it was there that a lorry arrived from the British consulate in Barcelona to pick them up. 'Oh happy day!' Skidmore wrote in his diary.

★

Not every evader who crossed the Pyrenees did so with the help of escape lines. Pilot 'Collie' Collins got tired of hanging about in northern France, kept under wraps on farms and admonished when he went looking for a little life. He found it difficult to keep the low profile needed for someone in his position. Once he was sitting in a village café when a flight of Allied bombers went over and a local identified them as US Liberators. Before he could stop himself, Collins heard himself piping up in English: 'They're not Liberators, they're bloody Fortresses.' He knew how stupid his outburst was. 'It showed how precarious life was for an evader. One little slip could mean the end.'[21] He decided it was time to move on, and on his own initiative he took the train to Paris and then south to the unoccupied zone. He blundered over the demarcation line – 'I walked straight into a German guard post, but luckily the sentry had taken his dog for a walk.' He had no passes and no identity papers but just blagged his way wherever he went. 'It was all very unplanned as I wandered around France on my own.' He stayed at a hotel, posing as a Swedish soldier in the French Foreign Legion. Nobody challenged him. He chatted happily to anyone he met, told some quite openly he was an English airman on the run, went on a drinking bender with a French soldier in Limoges, narrowly missed a police swoop on the station in Toulouse and ended up in a small mountain village only twenty miles from the Spanish frontier. He slept in a woodcutter's hut, fortified himself with brandy and then began to walk uphill in what he thought was a southerly direction.

Imagine my disgust when after two days I found myself back in the village where I had started. I had gone round in a circle. It was really disheartening. It was dark, there was three feet of snow on the ground and I was frozen stiff. I felt like giving up. I walked into a bar with every intention of doing so. If I had seen a German patrol I would have put my hands up. I would have given up to Adolf Hitler if I had met him. I had gone from being absolutely determined to get home to being so bloody cold and depressed it hurt. And I knew that if I was captured at least I was going to get something to eat and drink and be put somewhere warm and dry. I thought, to hell with getting home to England.

He *did* give up. He presented himself at the *mairie* and was put in a police cell for the night. But then the police chief arrived and took him home, fed him up on steak and chips and set him off in the right direction to avoid German patrols and get to Andorra.

How lucky was that! The person I gave myself up to didn't want me! Apparently, the mayor had telephoned him and told him to arrange to show me the way. A sergeant was sent to take me into the mountains. He pointed out the two highest peaks and told me to make my way between them and keep going. It was December, I was up to my testicles in snow and the wind was gale-force but this time I was determined to get through.

He did, but with no one to advise him or meet him on the other side, he foolishly told the first Spanish frontier guard he met who he was. He was taken off to a filthy prison and then to the concentration camp at Miranda del Ebro. He spent three months in the most pitiful of conditions before he was released to the British authorities and taken to Gibraltar. Back in England, MI9 were so impressed by his solo effort that they asked him to go back, to parachute into France as an agent. 'I told them where to get off!' He was then sent round squadrons all over Britain giving lectures on his experiences, which he took as a punishment for refusing to be recruited. As for those lectures,

I suppose my experiences could have been helpful to somebody else but I don't know if anybody listened. They probably took as much notice as I did of the original one I had. Then I went back onto ops again – did another three tours and over 100 ops.[22] I remember giving my own squadron a talk on what had happened to me and on what to do if you are shot down. But they all thought I was just shooting a line. I didn't care that they didn't believe. Try it yourself then, I thought.

Collins's diffidence about his trans-Pyrenean experience – as well as the indifference of his squadron pals later – should not blind us to what a remarkable achievement his mountain crossing was. Very few men made it on their own, for the very reason that nearly stopped him – the need to have others around to push you beyond your natural limits. Physical conditions on the mountains sometimes defied imagination. US Major Wayne Eveland considered his journey 'the most perilous three days of my life' as he struggled through drifts and blizzards, plunged through ice into rivers, went numb with frostbite. He reckoned himself lucky not to have had both his feet amputated.

There were no paths or roadways, or if there were, we did not dare use them. We would climb each steep and slippery slope, then make our way down the other side – only to find another mountain ahead of us. During rest periods we had to keep one another awake because anyone who fell asleep might never wake up. One of our party pleaded to be left to die. As senior officer, I chewed him out, told him he was not allowed to quit! The rest of us carried and dragged him down to the bottom of one mountain and then up the next. The guides told us: 'Just one more to go,' but we knew they were lying. It didn't matter. It helped to keep us going. They took more drastic measures too. I pulled a muscle in my left upper leg. Each step was agony and I could not keep up. I fell behind. A guide came back, put the muzzle of his rifle at the base of my skull and nudged me forward. I marched – pain or no pain! Near the end I lost consciousness and had to be carried. Thank Heaven the precedent had already been set! No one could be left to die. My companions got me across![23]

The prayers of his wife Dawn back in Montana may have helped too, or so Eveland came to believe. She knew only that he was missing in action but kept the faith that he was alive. She saw him in her dreams – or were they nightmares? – and always he was freezing cold. She imagined he was in Switzerland. Eveland and his party made it, as did fellow American Howard Harris after a similarly arduous winter crossing in which 'we were as near freezing as anyone could be and still be alive'.[24] But that trip, shared with a number of other nationalities, ended in death. As he walked into Andorra, the party strung out over many miles, Harris heard shots and ahead saw two bodies being thrown off a cliff. They were French civilians suspected by the guides of being collaborators infiltrating the escape route on behalf of the Germans.

The Germans were now throwing more and more resources into trying to halt the traffic of Allied airmen back to Britain. At first the trickle of evaders and escapers had been a mild embarrassment, nothing more, and a job for the French authorities rather than the full iron fist of the Third Reich. But as the RAF intensified its bombing offensive against German cities through 1942 and into

1943, joined by a freshly inspired and equipped American Eighth Air Force, the numbers now getting home began seriously to worry German air force chiefs. The Luftwaffe's major logistical problem was always a shortage of men rather than machines, and, with that state of mind, it seemed profligate for so many downed Allied airmen to be getting back to their squadrons. German military intelligence as well as the Gestapo was now directed at severing the escape lines. The routes south to the Pyrenees were seriously risky. On trains, papers were inspected every 100 miles. Eighth Air Force bombardier Ed Burley was travelling from Paris to Bordeaux, seated apart from his guide, a nattily dressed young Frenchman in a full-length raccoon fur coat. Burley glanced around him and, with a shudder of horror, instantly identified another American in the carriage – his distinctive US-issue watch was clearly visible on his wrist and so were his GI socks on his feet. Burley caught the other airman's eye and indicated the problem. 'He caught on immediately and covered up as best he could. For the rest of the trip we neither glanced nor winked at each other. We were both scared, and preoccupied with our own thoughts and worries about what lay ahead.'

What lay ahead was an inspection of papers.

A German officer entered our compartment and asked for my papers. Playing the part of a deaf-mute, I handed my forged one over and he scrutinized them carefully, looking at me several times, comparing me with my photograph. I tried to appear calm even though my heart was pounding, and I looked at him so as not to show fear or give him any reason to think me suspicious. He returned them and, after looking at everyone else's, opened the carriage door to leave. Suddenly he stopped and came back for a second inspection. My papers were returned to me again, he looked at all the others, then went to the door again and called in another officer for a third inspection. I was now completely terrified as I knew something must have triggered this. I felt on a knife's edge of being captured. I prayed. Then the Germans stopped at my guide and the other American and led them away. My guide was very stoic, and showed no emotion, nor did he even glance at me. The American turned white with fear, and as he passed his eyes seemed to plead with me to help him. Obviously that was impossible. No sooner had the compartment door closed than my lower intestines went into a twisting convulsion. When that eased, I realized I was now on my own and I broke out into a cold sweat.

He could not even bear to think about the two who had been taken into custody. The elegant young Frenchman would now undergo torture. Eventually, inevitably, he would be executed. It might be the same for the scared American but more likely, after days, weeks, months of threats and terror he would wind up in a POW camp in eastern Germany. 'I couldn't get this out of my mind. If I were to be captured, would I be able to resist giving the Gestapo the information I had?'[25]

It was a question that fellow-American airman Everett Childs would face for real. After being shot down in eastern France he had been looked after by the Resistance, who had tried numerous ways to get him back to England. There was talk of a plane coming to get him – a constant rumour among evaders but very, very rarely achieved. Switzerland was also on the agenda. He had close call after close call, running from a farmhouse just seconds ahead of a Gestapo raid and on another occasion being inches from discovery in an attic. In the end he went south with two others towards Spain. They got as far as the foothill town of Pau but found it heavily policed by Germans, dangerously so, and with no known contact there they got on the train back to Toulouse. Gestapo agents in their trademark raincoats and wide-brimmed hats ran a documents check. Childs's heart sank – 'Here we go again!' – but his forged papers passed the test. So did those of one of his two companions, 'and your spirits rise because it looks like you're going to get away with it'. The third, carried by George Hill, a Canadian squadron leader, was a fake too far. An old ID card, a stuck-on photograph and an official stamp produced with ink and a raw potato-cut would pass in bad light. But the German held it up and squinted at it closely and all its imperfections were apparent. All three were arrested. Childs was scared.

This middle-aged Gestapo agent was holding a loaded and cocked short-barrel pistol two inches from my ribs and his hand was shaking with excitement at having caught us. I was silently praying that it did not have a hair trigger. But my real fear was about the future. I had heard from the French all about Gestapo methods, the beatings. Thoughts about being shot, about being tortured, all that went through my mind.[26]

They were held in jail, where they witnessed a young Jewish student being savagely beaten up. Then a terrified Childs was half choked by an SS guard – 'his hands were round my throat cutting off my breath' – when he said that Germany was beaten and the Allies would win the war. On a train to Paris they were kicked repeatedly when they peeked out of the window and saw the devastation caused by Allied bombing. In the French capital Childs and his companion were loaded onto an army truck and taken through the streets to one of the most feared places in the whole of France – Fresnes jail, now a German military prison. Its cells held other evaders like them, but also hundreds of Resistance fighters and escape-line helpers. Here they were made to pay for their defiance of the Nazi super-state, most of them with their lives. The exact figures will never be known but there is no doubt that many thousands of patriots died at German hands for daring to help Allied servicemen make a 'home run'. They were usually victims of the most sinister aspect of the otherwise heroic evasion story – treachery and betrayal.

# 5. Betrayed

Nineteen-year-old Nadine Dumon had just got out of bed and was still in her pale yellow pyjamas at her family's Brussels home when the Gestapo broke down the door.

They came at 7 a.m., their cars screeching to a halt outside. My father ran to tell me to get out through the kitchen and up onto our roof terrace but soldiers with guns were already blocking the stairs. They said 'Hands up' – in English, for some reason. I can still see them standing there with their guns. They had helmets on and jackboots.[1]

Sixty-three years on, she relived the moment. 'I remember it all so clearly.' She wasn't scared at first. Her mind was calculating whether she could still get away, whether they would shoot if she made a dash for freedom. Perhaps they wouldn't because they wanted her alive. She had information they needed – she was no good to them dead. She started to laugh – why she couldn't quite recall, probably through nerves – and they told her to stop or they would fire.

And then it occurred to me that they could just shoot me in the leg instead of killing me outright, so I stopped. It was then I realized the game was over, which was exactly the phrase they then used to me. I think ever since I began helping the escape line I had known that one day I would have to pay for what I did. Now it had come.

The teenager was pushed at gunpoint into her bedroom and ordered to get dressed. She asked the soldiers to give her privacy while she changed but they refused to leave, though they did turn their backs as she slipped out of her nightwear. She was told to pack clothes for two or three days, 'but I could tell it was going to be much longer than that'. Then they hurried her down the stairs and out into the street. She was bundled into the back of a car, held firmly in between two hefty Germans. She turned her head to see her father being shoved into another car. She saw a neighbour standing in his doorway watching and smiled and bravely managed to give him a thumbs-up sign. 'You'll be laughing on the other side of your face soon,' one of the Germans said ominously.

I was interrogated all that day, without food or water. They didn't beat me at first, just menaced and threatened me. They said they would kill me unless I told them everything I knew. But they didn't say what they suspected me of. I told them, 'I don't know what you're on about or what you want me to tell you.' Then they got very angry and began to ask about the escape lines. They asked if I knew M. de Jongh [Dédée's father]. They seemed to have a lot of information already but I said I knew nothing. The questioning went on for three or four days, and then I was left in solitary confinement for ten days to reflect on things. Then they started with their questions again, but still I said nothing.

Then came a real blow to her morale as she came face to face with her betrayer.

They brought in a Belgian man, whom I recognized straight away. He had once been introduced to me by M. de Jongh as a Resistance leader. Now this same man was bowing low to the Gestapo officer and accepting his offer of a cigar. 'Do you know this girl?' the German asked. 'Oh yes,' said the man. 'She's Nadine Dumon and she helps airmen get from Brussels to Paris. She's a friend of de Jongh.' I was shocked and very angry that he could betray us all like that. How could a man stoop so low? He then looked me in the eye and said I should tell the Germans everything. 'It's your duty to tell them the truth,' he said. But still I said nothing, though I reckoned it was probably all over for me.

Back in her cell, she had the courage and the presence of mind to concoct a story that would sound plausible to her interrogators without actually giving anyone away. When she was taken back for questioning she confessed.

I told them it was all true, that, yes, I did help men from Brussels to Paris. I made up some contacts – Renée and a man in Paris called Victor. They demanded surnames and addresses and I said I only ever contacted them on the telephone. It was then that they began to beat me. There were many, many interrogations but still I said nothing.

Years later, as she relived her experiences for the authors, she would refuse to go into details about the punishment meted out in that Gestapo hellhole. The memories were still there, probably as vivid as ever, but to open them up was too painful. These were experiences nobody could relive in tranquillity. All she could bring herself to say was that she had withstood the beatings as best she could and was close to giving in when her persecutors stopped.

I was just beginning to think I couldn't hold out any longer when I heard one of them say: 'If the *mädchen* [girl] won't speak, then one of the others will.' It turned out that the traitor who betrayed me had brought about the arrest of 150 people. So they gave up on me. There was never a trial. I was sent to various terrible prisons and eventually to Germany, to Ravensbruck concentration camp.

There, as we will see later, new, unimaginable horrors awaited.

It was August 1942 when Nadine was taken in a major German drive against the Comet Line. This was a massive betrayal, of which there were several in the history of the escape lines, all with terrible and fatal consequences. But every evader, whether part of a formal escape line or not, was prey to collaborators and informers, to 'copper's narks' and nosy neighbours, to an incautious word or an action that gave him away. In the febrile atmosphere of occupied Europe, gossip was a dangerous currency which many unsavoury characters made their trade in.

Catching evaders was, in fact, a big challenge for the Germans, given the vast numbers of workers and refugees of all nationalities on the move all over the continent. Certainly there were weak points in the escape chains – at curfew, at railway stations, on trains themselves and on the demarcation line between occupied and unoccupied France (which disappeared in November 1942 anyway when the Germans took control of the entire country). Here, evaders might be caught by spot checks. But elsewhere, whether in the vastness of the Pyrenees or among the masses of the big cities, normal policing was not the biggest problem for those on the run. In the mountains there were too few troops to man every road and track, and to a degree the same went for the cities. The Germans would throw barriers round blocks of streets and haul everyone off for questioning. The experience would be unpleasant. Hélène de Champlain recalled 'the dull knot of fear as Germans in uniforms with some French collaborators encircled a dozen of us and with shouted commands and the waving of sub-machine guns herded us towards a truck with a tarpaulin top'.[2] But though she carried faked papers in a false name and had been active in the Resistance for three years, she managed to secure her freedom, and so could the wise evader who kept his head.

There were ways to deal with the German presence. Terry Bolter was escorted across Brussels by a helper who told him casually, 'Don't worry if we are held up by German patrols. There are lots of them about. Just put your hands up and do what they tell you.'[3] George Buckner, a US airman, was told by a Resistance veteran to remember that most of the German soldiers he saw in Paris were harmless clerks and staff personnel or on leave and intent only on wine and women. 'Resist the temptation to stare. Ignore them. That is the normal attitude of the French. Germans expect it.' If challenged, 'present your identity card but look bored and avoid direct eye contact'.[4] In general, evaders were rarely as conspicuous as they feared. One recalled queuing in front of a stout German soldier searching bags at a railway station barrier. 'He gestured to the man in front of me to pass through, then turned to me. His expression seemed to harden. I could see the suspicion in his small, pig-like eyes. He could tell I was no Flemish peasant. I felt like a small animal about to be swallowed by a snake. *Then*

*he turned away, his attention shifting to the next passenger, and waved
me on.*'[5]

The real danger for evaders was not stop-and-search operations
like this. It was informers. They were the crucial weapons in the
underground war. Whether in the country or the town, what put
evaders most at risk was people blabbing. Anything out of the
ordinary could be deadly. Someone buying an extra loaf on the
black market might cause a raised eyebrow, a word in the wrong
ear, a denunciation. Bolter was moved on from a safe house when
a counter clerk at the local lending library grew suspicious of
his hostess for borrowing books in English. Amassing as much
information as they could, the Germans went all out to penetrate
the Resistance organizations and escape lines, whether by turning
its members or by planting their own agents. The traitor who
named Nadine Dumon was not an isolated case by any means.
Behind the capture of virtually every Allied soldier and airman on
the run was a betrayal.

★

Sergeant Harry Levy was a Jewish lad from the Mile End Road in
London with more reason than most not to want to be on the run
in Nazi Europe. 'I had a large nose, and for Hitler's goose-stepping
monsters that would have been enough evidence to treat me with
greater cruelty than others.' But this extra danger, the prospect of
a concentration camp, did not stop him from volunteering for
aircrew even before he reached his eighteenth birthday. Nor did
it prompt him to pay special attention to evasion training. Like
every other man who flew in that war, it just wasn't going to
happen to him, though he was well aware that Bomber Command's losses were mounting. He had close scrapes – his Wellington hit by flak, a belly-landing, an overshoot. His fifteenth op was
the final one. As S-Sugar droned towards the North Sea after
bombing the Ruhr, nearly home, he turned his head to see the tail
fins of a Messerschmitt 110 flashing by so close he could make out
the swastika markings. 'As if in a dream I heard the German's guns,
like the slow tapping of a typewriter. I felt a sharp blow on my

chest and a pain in my left thigh. I had been hit.' He lapsed into unconsciousness, then woke to silence. The plane's engines had stopped, though curiously it was still flying straight and level.

I was slumped against the armour-plated shielding. At my feet oil was gushing from pipes. I edged along to the bomb aimer's position and stared at his pale face cradled sideways on the desk, eyes closed. It was the first time I had seen someone dead. I could also see the pilot hanging from his straps, dead too. A basic survival instinct took over. The light from a burning engine cast flickering shadows in the darkened interior as I crawled on all fours along the narrow wooden catwalk to the escape hatch near the rear turret. I kicked out the panel, sat on the edge with my feet dangling in the void and fell out.[6]

It was a remarkable escape. He had cheated death, and he knew it. But his luck stayed with him. Down on the ground, help was offered at the first door he hammered on. An old man with a Lord Kitchener moustache, a teenage girl, her mother – as representative a cross-section of helpers as any airman could hope for. 'You are with friends,' they told him. He was taken to a doctor and his wound tended. Then he was moved to a safe house in Brussels, in the care of a wealthy and well-bred woman. She was nervous. Sitting in her ornate drawing room, she warned him: 'You cannot trust anyone. In his office, my husband employs people he has known for years and has always been kind to them, but he can never be sure that one of them will not betray him.' This was confirmed after a few days when there was an alert. The word was out about Levy. A raid was possible at any moment. He was hurried away to another safe house, in such a panic that firm arrangements had not been finalized and he was not expected. This was a dangerous moment. His guide there and the man who answered the door did not know each other. Unsmiling, they eyed each other with grave suspicion. Then one produced half a playing card, the jack of spades, and laid it on a table. The other man went to a bookcase, took out a book and from its pages produced the other half of the card, an exact match. At last they were convinced of each other's authenticity, that they were part of the same organization. The 'package' was accepted.

Levy settled in with his new 'family', M. and Mme Kauffmann, and was also introduced by them to a young woman known as Vera, rather plain and timid-looking, who surprised him by identifying herself as being with British Intelligence. She said it was her job to check out that he was who he said he was, and she quizzed him, after which, she said, his answers would be sent to London for verification. The next morning he woke in his bedroom in the Kauffmanns' flat feeling pensive. It was seven days since he had been shot down, though so much had happened it felt a great deal more. He went to the bathroom and was drying his face when there was a loud rapping on the door.

I called out, 'Shan't be a minute', but the knocking was repeated, louder this time. I opened it and outside stood two uniformed Germans. One was pointing a pistol at me. I raised my hands above my head, shocked and hardly able to grasp what was happening. I thought I'd been betrayed. But by whom? Outside the bathroom Mme Kauffmann was standing, a simpering smile on her white face. I thought it must have been her. My hands in the air, I pushed past, giving her a scowl. Or perhaps it was Vera who had betrayed me? She was standing in the living room, staring blankly in front of her. The funny thing was that I wasn't really angry. I felt as if I was in a film in which Mme Kauffmann and Vera also had parts. I had this sense not of fear but of curiosity about what was going to happen next.

The two Germans took me out of the house and down the stone steps to a waiting car. They pushed me into the back, and I sat there still wondering if I was in a novel and this was happening to somebody else. But it wasn't. Reality caught up with me. I was overwhelmed with a sense of acceptance. There was nothing I could do. My time as an evader was over. I was not afraid. I knew what fear was. That was what I had experienced on bombing raids over Germany. But in the car, I was merely anxious, faced with the prospect of a prisoner-of-war camp, and other darker, more fearful possibilities, which I chose not to think about.

Levy had been captured by the Geheime Feldpolizei (GFP), the German military police, and he was taken to their headquarters for interrogation. He admitted his name, rank and number and that he was Jewish. He was asked what he had been doing at the Kauffmanns' flat and replied that he had gone there by chance, just knocked on the door, asked for a room for the night. Then they wanted to know who had brought him to Brussels. He lied – 'an old man with a reddish beard'. A German soldier smiled as he typed out the nonsense Levy conjured up and got the Englishman to sign it. 'So am I off to a prisoner-of-war camp now?' Levy then asked. The German shrugged his shoulders. 'There are many questions that have to be answered first. You are in civilian clothes. For all we know you may be a spy.' And Levy was taken to Brussels' St Gilles prison, now run by the German army, which was jealous of its authority and kept the Gestapo at a distance. Nonetheless, it was a beast of a place – 'soundless, bottomless, lifeless'. He began to despair. Why was he here? Why wasn't he on his way to a POW camp? Surely tomorrow . . . 'I lay on my bunk listening for any sound that might signal my release to a prisoner-of-war camp. Only the torment of my empty stomach distracted me from that thought.'

He was left like this for five days, a deliberate period of what the Germans called 'school', intended to soften up the prisoners, teach them a lesson. Then he was taken back to the Feldpolizei for questioning. They wanted to know every detail of who had helped him and where he had stayed. Now the threats were stepped up. He was a spy. The Geneva Convention did not apply to him. They would be within their rights to shoot him. His interrogator trotted out the names of the people he had stayed with in Brussels. 'We have arrested them all. We know much more about this than you imagine. It is very silly of you to think you can deceive us.' And then he was sent back to solitary confinement. This was relieved only when he managed to haul himself up to a barred opening high in the wall of his cell. He could see into the neighbouring wing, hear voices, establish contact. One day he heard his name being called: ''Arry! 'Arry! *Par ici! Par ici.*' From one of the windows opposite a hand was gesticulating. '*C'est moi, 'Arry. C'est Monsieur Kauffmann!*'

And now he learned the truth. Neither the Kauffmanns nor Vera had betrayed him. All three had been arrested along with him – all three were in St Gilles – what no one knew then was that all three would end up in concentration camps. 'I realized how wrong I had been, how unjust my earlier suspicions.' The others in Kauffmann's cell were excited to be talking to an Englishman. When was the Second Front going to start? When was Hitler going to be beaten? Time was a matter of life or death for them. Levy assured them the Second Front would open by the end of the year – it was 1942 and he was wrong by two and a half years! But he gave them hope.

I told them of the thousand-bomber raids the RAF had mounted on Cologne, Essen and Bremen, describing in some detail those I myself had taken part in. I talked of the huge bombs we now carried. We were going to destroy Germany. They gave vent to their feelings with loud and unrestrained cheers.

Levy's incarceration went on week after week.

The wild state of my unwashed, uncombed hair, my gaunt face with its few scattered hairs marking a nascent beard and my skinny frame all seemed to confirm a status of concentration-camp victim rather than that of a prisoner of war. I bore the squalor with stoicism, but the hunger I couldn't ignore. I lived on water and a dark ersatz bread. Occasionally I would be given a piece of sausage or a small, evil-looking roundel of yellow cheese with a fish-like smell. I grew paler and weaker and began suffering from diarrhoea. Increasingly I felt outside the laws of civilization. Nothing that the Germans might do would have surprised me. They had so far committed no wanton act of cruelty. Their attitude was marked by indifference, locking me up in a cell as if I were a letter to be opened later.

Surprisingly, Levy's conditions improved slightly when he made a formal complaint to the prison commandant, demanding to be treated as a military prisoner. He was taken for the first time to be questioned by a Luftwaffe officer. After a month in the prison, it was an important step forward. 'Shouldn't be long before we get you to POW camp,' the enemy officer told him. That night he shouted his good news to Monsieur Kauffmann, who said he too expected to be sent to Germany within a few days, though what awaited him there was something much darker.[7] 'My attempt at comfort, telling him that the war would be over by the end of the year, sounded meaningless,' Levy recalled.

Soon after, Levy was taken from his cell to join a queue of prisoners waiting to see the prison doctor.

The young man next to me was about my own age. He was short and slight of build, his complexion pallid, black hair brushed straight back. His appearance, clean-shaven and smartly dressed, contrasted strongly with my own dishevelled looks. He turned round to look at me, and said in a strong Cockney accent, ' 'Ere, you're bloody English, ain't yer?' I looked at him in surprise. Then I realized this must be Wicks.[8]

I had been warned about this man. Kauffmann and his cell mates had told me how, when the British Expeditionary Force had retreated towards Dunkirk, this English soldier had found refuge in Brussels and had lived there, moving from one apartment to another until six months ago. Then the Germans caught him, and as a result of what he told them, forty-two Belgians had been taken by the Gestapo and the Feldpolizei. Each time someone was arrested, he was taken from St Gilles to identify them.

Now Levy was face to face with this informer.

I said, 'Your name's Wicks, isn't it?' and his face changed from Cockney chirpiness to ferret-like suspicion. 'What if it is?' I told him a little of what I had heard, about how he had been caught and . . . He broke in: 'They didn't catch me, mate. Nobody bloody catches me. I was on the run for nearly two fuckin' years. 'Ad a marvellous time. Girls, booze, bags to eat, the lot.' It was my turn to interrupt. 'But they caught you, didn't they? You wouldn't be in here if they hadn't caught you.'

He retorted: 'Listen, chum, you don't know nuffink about it. It was the bloody Belgians' fault. They was always on at me to escape. Said it was my bloody duty an' all that. Said they couldn't 'ide me any more. Well, in the end I got cheesed off and I 'ad a go at getting away and I got nicked. We got right to the French bloody frontier when they got me. I bin 'ere six bloody months. It don't look as if I'm ever gonna get out. I'd 'ave been all right if they'd 'ave let me alone. They'd never 'ave caught me.'

He admitted telling the Germans all he knew after his arrest: 'What the 'ell was I supposed to do? Let the bastards shoot me? Not bloody likely, mate. You've only got one life, ain't yer?'

Was he the person who had betrayed Levy? Certainly he could have had a hand in it. He had named those who hid him. The Germans would not have pounced at once but watched and waited, trying to catch the entire circle. One name would have led to another, and it could well have been Wicks's confessions that, directly or indirectly, had steered the Germans to the flat where Levy was hiding. But even if this was so, Levy was not willing to condemn the man for it. He had listened with mixed emotions as the Belgians denounced the English soldier.

While I sympathized with those who had risked their lives to help him, only to be repaid by his act of betrayal, an unpleasant shadow touched my mind. How might I have reacted, placed in a similar position? How would I react in the face of any threat of death or torture?[9]

It was a sentiment many evaders would understand. And, anyway, the strong probability was that there was more than one informer. After the war, Levy was told it was a Belgian Resistance leader in the pay of the Germans – probably the same one who denounced Nadine Dumon – who had been directly responsible for his capture. This man had handed out the two halves of the jack of spades that Levy's helpers had matched as proof of their loyalty, unaware that their own chief was the traitor. And Wicks? He survived – as we will see later – true to his maxim that 'You've only got one life, ain't yer?' And his betrayals were small ones compared with one notorious Englishman, whose actions were in a wholly different league. When it came to selling your friends and countrymen down the river, there were few to rival a certain dashing sergeant with an eye for the women.

★

'Harold Cole, alias Rooke, Mason, Cool, Corser *and many more*.' So say the official documents lodged in the United Kingdom's National Archives at Kew on the traitor who very nearly destroyed the Pat O'Leary escape line based in Marseilles. They gave a neat summary of his activities:

Cole went to France as a soldier in 1939, was taken prisoner by the Germans in 1940, escaped and lived first in Lille, then in Marseilles, where he helped escaping British servicemen to reach safety. Re-arrested by the Gestapo in 1941, he was then turned by the SD [Sicherheitsdienst – the Nazi security service] and betrayed a whole French Resistance unit, which resulted in the deaths of over fifty people. At the end of the war, Cole was hunted by MI5, finally being arrested posing as a US Intelligence officer in liberated France, complete with Mercedes vehicle and French mistress. Escaping once more from US custody, Cole was finally discovered in 1946 living under cover in Paris. He was killed in an exchange of gunfire with French police.[10]

Some, but not all, of this detail is accurate, and there are those who believe this 'official' version was only part of the real story. They contend that Cole was in fact a double agent, and in the murky Dansey-driven world he operated in, it has to be admitted that such things were possible. Spies and informers walked on quicksand. It is hard to know where the terra firma of truth was.[11] But the nub of the official account is true – he *did* become a German agent and he *did* do terrible damage to the Pat Line. What is in doubt is whether he was a traitor from the start or whether he was a turncoat. There were many who believed he did a brilliant job to begin with, escorting evaders from the north to the south of France and saving many lives. One young airman who was 'delivered' safely by Cole and stuck up for him would later become an air marshal, a knight and a leading light in the RAF Escaping Society.[12] Another was an RAF squadron leader who had nothing but praise for Cole's coolness and cleverness in hiding him for twelve days in Lille and then smuggling him across the demarcation line. But his manner and his behaviour aroused suspicion in some sections of the escape line right from the start. As early as the autumn of 1941, Revd Donald Caskie of the Seamen's Mission in Marseilles was expressing his doubts to Ian Garrow, the English captain then running the Marseilles line.

Garrow dismissed the clergyman's alarms, expressing complete faith in Cole,[13] but Caskie was not won over. He not only thought Cole a shifty and unpleasant person, he also suspected him of causing the death of a young Yorkshire soldier he had taken a particular pastoral interest in. The story was a tragic one of how war can scar people in the deepest ways. The boy, David, was sombre and sad, prone to sickness and tears. At night in the Mission he would cry for his mother in his sleep and then wake screaming. 'I'll never get home,' he kept saying. He had been in a POW camp in Germany, where he had become friendly with one of the guards – an older man, but they turned out to have much in common because both came from the same rather strict Protestant sect, which set them apart from the others. The guard was in charge of work parties outside the camp and assigned David to one, which gave him his opportunity to escape. One night, on the way back to camp, he slipped away from the column and fled across a field. A guard stood in his way and a panic-stricken David seized an iron bar and battered him until he fell dead. It was only then that David saw the man's face – it was his friend. 'I did not mean to kill him, padre,' the distraught boy said as he finally poured out his guilty secret. Caskie offered him forgiveness as best he could, tried to rebuild the boy's faith and then sent him on the next party leaving for home.

The guide returned to the Mission ten days later to tell me David had been shot and was dead. They had been ambushed. One other soldier had been severely wounded. The rest were in prison. 'Monsieur le Pasteur,' said the guide, 'all would have been well if we had followed the original plan. But I received your letter at Perpignan, and we walked right into a trap.'

But I had sent no letter. I never did anything in writing. If I had a message it was always by word of mouth. But the man insisted he was telling the truth. A letter ostensibly sent by me had told them to change their route. It was now evident that there was a traitor among us, conversant with our activities, and our escape route. We had been tricked by someone inside the organization. My mind focused on Cole.

I reported my suspicions to my superior [Garrow], but he said it could not have been Cole. He had an alibi. On the night in question he was *en route* for Paris and Lille. 'And anyway, padre, he is bringing down a party of RAF men, every one of them worth his weight in gold. It was not him, I know.' I accepted this judgement then but I never have ceased to regret that I was persuaded against my will. Had we relied on my instinct, we would have been spared the most shameful betrayal of our experience.[14]

Caskie's suspicions increased after a tip-off from a sympathizer in the French police that Cole had a girlfriend in Paris who was in league with the Gestapo. 'Be very careful,' the detective added. 'To trust such a man is to invite disaster. In your case, the danger is very, very great.' This was confirmed shortly afterwards when Caskie was followed to a meeting with contacts in the countryside outside Marseilles. 'Turning quickly round, I caught sight of Cole, watching me from behind a clump of bushes. And this at a time when he was supposed to be in the north of France.' It turned out that Cole was often not where he was supposed to be, as Pat O'Leary was next to discover.

It was soon after this incident that – as we saw in Chapter 2 – Garrow was arrested by the French and imprisoned, and O'Leary took charge of the line. He was determined to tackle Cole, a man he too had never trusted. The money he was taking for 'expenses' was worrying, amounting to hundreds of thousands of francs. What was he spending it on? The answer, as O'Leary found out, was not just food and accommodation for evaders, their travel tickets or even the purchase of a lorry that Cole wanted to buy as a safer means of transporting evaders. Money was also going on girls, drinks and parties – and at that very moment he was having a high time in Marseilles when he was supposed to be in northern France gathering the next party of evaders together. O'Leary checked further, travelling north to Lille to talk to loyal helpers there. The group's paymaster, a local businessman, told him they had never received any money from the organization and were deeply suspicious of Cole. Even his identity was a mystery since he was putting himself about as 'Captain Colson', a British Intelligence officer. 'He's not got a very good reputation,' the businessman told O'Leary bluntly. 'People round here are of modest means and they have been surprised by him living it up in the best bars and restaurants. They think it unreasonable that he lives in luxury while they have to rely on charity to hide and feed British troops.'[15] The same message came from everyone O'Leary questioned in Lille, and he set off back to Marseilles ready to sort out this situation. If he had to, he would take 'extreme measures'.

On a cold November day the leaders of the Pat Line met in O'Leary's Marseilles base, the large room above the surgery of Dr George Rodocanachi, a key helper in the organization. There O'Leary confronted Cole, accusing him of cheating the escape line and stealing its money. Later it would be established that Cole had long been a thief. Scotland Yard had him in its files as a convicted con man who liked posing as an army officer. Then, in the army he had absconded with the funds of the sergeants' mess and at the time of Dunkirk had been on the run in France as much from the British military police as from the Germans.[16] A practised liar too, he now began to protest indignantly that he *had* paid the expenses in the north, that he was being falsely accused. But beneath his red hair, his normally florid face had gone white, and it went even paler when O'Leary produced his evidence – the Lille paymaster himself stepped out from a side room. A startled Cole tried to run but O'Leary stopped him with a punch in the face. Cole's demeanour now switched from bluster to blubbing as he lay on the floor and began to plead: 'I admit I've done terrible things. I'm sorry, so sorry, but I have done some good things. I did bring all those men down from the north. You know that.'[17]

The half-dozen Pat Line workers in the room now began to debate what to do with him. Cole's loss of control, instant confession and pleading were as worrying as what he had actually done. This was not a man who would put up any resistance to a Gestapo interrogation. 'We must kill him,' said one, to humanitarian protests from others. They took the still snivelling Cole to the bathroom and locked him in while they argued whether he should live or die. It seemed harsh to shoot a man for embezzlement, yet it was clearly madness to let someone so unreliable and with such extensive knowledge of the organization go free. One compromise was to send him back to England for investigation, and the discussion was veering in this direction when there was a noise from the bathroom. They rushed in to see Cole desperately hauling himself out of the window and across a gap over a five-storey well to another part of the building. They raced downstairs to try to stop him but on the ground floor he dodged out of the front door. Chasing him through the streets would have drawn attention to the house, and there were three evading airmen in the attic that day. They had no choice but to let him go. Cole got away, and as Louis Nouveau, one of those present, put it, 'we were never to see him again'.[18]

His escape was a crisis for O'Leary and his lieutenants. They had to assume he would offer his services to the Germans. *If* he hadn't done so already – there was still Garrow's arrest unaccounted for. At the Seamen's Mission, Caskie got an urgent message from O'Leary to burn any incriminating papers and to cease any activities there that might attract suspicion. All the helpers in the north and on the route south – some fifty families at least – also had to be alerted, not an easy or quick thing to do with uncertain wartime communications. Couriers were dispatched from Marseilles but some who admired Cole refused to accept he could be an embezzler, let alone a traitor. He himself got to some of them first and told them there had been a small difficulty down in Marseilles but it was nothing to worry about. They chose to believe him. Insidiously, the trust on which the integrity of the line depended was breaking down. This was compounded by stupidity in London. O'Leary had radioed a message disclosing Cole's behaviour and declaring his intention to find and 'liquidate' him. From Dansey at MI6 came an inexplicable order – Cole was *not* to be shot but to be 'given a run for his money'. It was a strange order from a man who so readily issued licences to kill in other circumstances and has added to the unresolved mystery of Cole and who he was really working for.

Donald Darling – 'Sunday' – was deputed to give O'Leary the direct order to lay off Cole, though he felt uncomfortable doing so. He had long 'smelt a rat' about Cole and had transmitted his suspicions to Dansey, along with a request for the man's record to be checked. He was told to mind his own business. 'Your summing up of the Cole situation is not appreciated,' Dansey said in a letter. 'Do not write further in this vein.'[19] This was a blow to Darling, who had taken on the responsibility for debriefing all evaders who came through Gibraltar and cross-checking their stories of who had sheltered and guided them.[20] This gave him unrivalled knowledge of the escape lines (so much so that his files were kept in weighted sacks ready to be sunk in the sea in the event of a German invasion of the Rock). With all his knowledge and experience, he was convinced Cole was not to be trusted. Obeying Dansey's instruction to 'reprieve' Cole was a big problem for him. 'I thought it was all very well to sit in London and issue instructions covering a situation only understood by the man on the spot, who was in danger!'[21]

Events quickly showed how wrong Dansey was. In northern France, the Germans began a series of arrests of Pat Line helpers. It seems that Cole fled back to Lille and there, a few weeks after escaping the kangaroo court in Marseilles, he either gave himself up to the Abwehr, the German military intelligence, or was captured by them. Either way, he was in custody and talking his –

and other people's – head off.[22] Did he do so under duress, after torture? Again, no one knows for sure, though it seems unlikely. Ian Dear, a historian of the period, believes it took 'the gentlest of hints'[23] from his German captors of what might happen to him if he did not cooperate for Cole to begin his thirty-page deposition giving every detail of the Pat Line's northern network. Even his interrogator found the ease of Cole's denunciations distasteful. 'One should maintain a bit of self-respect,' he said later.[24]

Among the first of his 'victims' was a priest, Abbé Carpentier, an escape-line hero for the number of Allied soldiers and airmen he had helped in northern France in the past eighteen months, finding places to hide them and forging documents. He had regularly handed men over to Cole to take south and, a saintly man, was now reluctant to believe the warnings from Marseilles that the person he thought his friend was a traitor. So he still welcomed Cole when he arrived at his house with three new 'parcels' and was preparing papers for them when two of them pulled out revolvers and ordered him to put up his hands. They were Gestapo agents.[25] Carpentier was arrested, telling Cole as he was led away: 'I have met many Englishmen in my life but you are the first I have known who would sell his country. Thank God I am not likely to meet another in the short time I have to live.'[26] He was executed, beheaded in Dortmund prison, as was Corporal Bruce Dowding, an Australian soldier who had stayed behind in France as an escape-line helper. He and dozens of others were picked up in this first swoop resulting from Cole's treachery. There would be many more. Some sources put the number of Resistance and escape-line workers betrayed by Cole at 150, of whom a third lost their lives.[27] Some evaders, caught in civilian clothes, were also shot as spies.[28]

O'Leary's line was utterly compromised. A man with intimate knowledge of people and places from one end of France to the other, who probably knew as much as O'Leary did – maybe even more, given how long he had been operating – was now working for the other side. Business shut down in Marseilles. O'Leary, Dr Rodocanachi, Louis Nouveau, all the regular 'conspirators', now kept their heads down, shunned each other's company. Doorbells and telephones went unanswered. There was no communication between safe houses. Inside them, discipline was stricter than ever as evaders in situ kept to their hiding places. Those normally allowed the freedom to play the piano were silenced in case the neighbours heard. Nothing was to be done to attract suspicion. But the entire Marseilles operation was now in danger of falling apart. The Seamen's Mission was closed, its sixty remaining occupants quietly farmed out to safe houses. Caskie himself was arrested – the French detective's warning had been correct – and, under a new law banning foreigners from coastal areas, exiled to Grenoble in the hope that he could cause no trouble there.

As time passed fresh couriers and helpers were recruited to fill the gaps caused by Cole's betrayal. O'Leary found new and trusted agents in the north, a farm on the demarcation line as a safe house and an ideal liaison man between north and south in the person of the *chef de train* on the Paris–Marseilles express. In the south, he built a new network of safe houses with helpers ranging from the Misses Grace and Susie Trenchard, elderly spinsters from the Channel Islands who ran a teashop in Monaco, to Vladimir Bouryschkine, a Russian-born onetime American basketball star, now coach of the Monaco team. O'Leary creaked his line back into operation. The mountains beckoned again. There were also evacuations of as many as fifty evaders at a time by Q-boats – clandestine armed British trawlers – from a beach near Perpignan.[29] Men were on the move again.

Then, in November 1942, political circumstances changed in southern France when the Germans marched over the demarcation line and declared the whole of France now under Nazi rule. For the Allies it was a recognition of their first successes in the rapidly expanding war. After more than two years of military advance and conquest, German armies were on the retreat after British victories over Rommel in the Egyptian desert and American landings in Morocco in North Africa. The Mediterranean was now a real war zone, hence the Wehrmacht's need to seize the coast. But in Marseilles and the other principal cities of Vichy France it was hard to herald this as the first sign of victory as the swastika flew over La Canebière and trucks full of grey-uniformed soldiers filled its streets. There was an immediate difficulty for O'Leary. Three hundred Gestapo and Abwehr agents also arrived, armed with the Vichy police's voluminous files on escape-line and Resistance networks. Plainclothes policemen were everywhere, gathering information. Checks on railway travellers tightened. Where once French people had listened illegally but freely to BBC radio, now they did so in the kitchen or bathroom with taps running to drown the sound. The Germans even paraded their collaborator Cole in the city. O'Leary was outraged by his presence, desperate to get to him to finish the job he and the others had bungled almost a year ago.

There was a more pressing problem, however. Since his arrest and ten-year jail sentence, Ian Garrow had been held in a French prison. Now he smuggled out word that he believed he was about to be transferred to a concentration camp in Germany. Dachau was mentioned. How could O'Leary allow this to happen? Garrow had helped him escape from a French prison. Honour demanded he return the favour for his friend. In London MI9 was uneasy when O'Leary asked for permission to organize a jail break. It would be a dangerous operation and all to save one man. The entire line itself might be put at risk. Dansey and MI9's Jimmy Langley said no to the plan, but Crockatt and Neave agreed with O'Leary that they had a debt of honour to Garrow. They won the argument, a rare triumph over Dansey. An escape was authorized.

But St Hippolyte-du-Fort had been comparatively easy to break out of, as O'Leary and many others had demonstrated. Meauzac prison in the Dordogne was a maximum security jail, its inmates mainly those sentenced to life imprisonment or death. This would be no simple case of dropping over the wall. From what he knew of it, Neave thought it tougher to get out of than Colditz. The only way was through the front gate and that meant subterfuge. Through contacts, O'Leary traced a prison guard with anti-Vichy and anti-German views and offered him a huge bribe of 216,000 francs, equal to six years' pay, to help. Then a fake prison guard's uniform was made by the Pat Line's tailor and smuggled in to Garrow. Early next morning,[30] O'Leary hid with two gunmen just outside the floodlit prison entrance, their pistols pointed at the machine-gun towers at each corner, as the night shift of guards came off duty. There in the middle, saluting the sentries as he left, was the tall, gaunt figure of Garrow. O'Leary watched with great anxiety, fearing that the English captain's distinctive gait would give him away. He was ready with his revolver in his hand for a shoot-out if there had been a challenge. But none came. O'Leary stood up and came alongside Garrow and together they walked down the road from the prison entrance, before diving off into a wood where a car was waiting.

He was hidden for three weeks in the teeth of an intense police hunt which included road blocks throughout the Dordogne and threats to execute hostages. But tucked safely away in Toulouse he was able to build up his strength from the rigours of the French prison before embarking on that very route to home he himself had started two and a half years earlier – to Perpignan and then over the Pyrenees. O'Leary took him to the border and in a shepherd's hut on the Spanish side said his farewells. 'Can this go on much longer?' he asked rhetorically as he waved Garrow off to freedom. It was a good question. From London, Langley sent a message to O'Leary all but ordering him to come back himself before it was too late. He even offered to send a Lysander aircraft to bring him out. 'His reply was a request for another parachute drop of supplies,' Langley recalled. 'I knew then that Pat would never come out and that it was only a matter of time before he paid the price of the magnificent work he had done.'[31]

The escape line was struggling as the German hunt for anyone working for it intensified. Louis Nouveau was forced to flee Marseilles, just one step ahead of the Gestapo. Dr Rodocanachi's surgery and the flat above were believed to be under surveillance as, in the words of Helen Long, the doctor's niece, 'a grey-green plague engulfed Marseilles. Everyone feared his neighbour. People looked warily round in the streets before they carried on a conversation. The dreaded tabs of the Gestapo with SS on the collar caused people to keep their mouths shut and hurry on their way.'[32] O'Leary shifted the centre of his operations to Toulouse.

The sheer reach of the network from Belgium to Spain and the enthusiasm of its helpers meant evaders could travel along it at amazing speed. One pilot who crashed north of Paris was back at his squadron in England in twelve days. But size was a problem too because it increased the opportunities for infiltrators. Some were caught and disposed of. O'Leary had one thrown down a mountain ravine. But plugging all the gaps was difficult. Then there was a major disaster when 21-year-old Tom Groome, the line's recently arrived Australian wireless operator, was pinpointed by a German radio detector van. The country house from which he was broadcasting near the town of Montauban was raided. With his earphones on, Groome did not hear the Gestapo officer come through the door and had no time to snatch up the revolver he kept beside the transmitter before he was overpowered. Groome was ordered to finish the message to London and give no indication that he had been caught. Then he and the young couple from whose house he had been broadcasting were taken away to Gestapo headquarters in Toulouse. There he made an extraordinary dash for freedom, jumping out of a window and into the street thirty feet below. As he hobbled away on a sprained ankle and tried to hide, he was given away to the pursuing Germans by a bystander and hauled back. During questioning, a Gestapo agent pointed a gun at the couple's small baby and threatened to shoot if they refused to talk. Bravely the mother told her persecutors to go ahead, and then kill her afterwards.

The only small piece of good fortune in this sorry story – apart from the baby *not* being shot[33] – was that Groome had managed to fool his captors and, by leaving out the security code letter, indicate to London that the radio was in enemy hands. This dashed the Germans' hopes of themselves manning the line to MI9 and plundering all its secrets. In fact, he turned the situation on its head, leading the Gestapo to believe they had their open line into MI9. A game of bluff and double bluff went on over the air waves, probably saving Groome's life in the short term because his touch was needed on the key. It was a month before the Germans realized they had been outsmarted – though, in truth, MI9 had gained little from the deception, apart from the self-indulgent pleasure that spies got from playing what Neave called 'the wireless game'. Dansey showed his priorities by using the link to tip off the Germans that the chief of police in Genoa hid Allied evaders. It wasn't true but it enabled the MI6 boss to pay off an old, festering grudge he had against the Italian police.

MI9 may have fooled the Germans but it was a small victory given that the enemy had little need of mechanical aids in its battle to break the Pat Line. As if Cole had not caused enough damage, the line was now penetrated by an impostor, a tall, blond Frenchman working for the Germans by the name of Roger le Neveu. He had joined the line as a guide bringing evaders down from Paris and had never been vetted. Few were. It was all very well MI9 being an undernourished Cinderella organization in London but the practical effect of that on the ground – the killing ground, as it became – was that there were few resources the escape-line organizers could call on to check the credentials of people they used. The failure of Dansey's intelligence services in London to provide any professional back-up for this process was a security disaster waiting to happen. When Cole was recruited, they had not even checked on his army record, for which 'lamentable effort' MI9's Langley apologized to O'Leary.[34] Not that criticism for this should be directed at Langley and Neave, who were not provided with the resources to do such a job. And anyway, they were in thrall to a man – Dansey – whose *ex cathedra* judgement, made from an armchair in St James's, was to suspect O'Leary and Dédée de Jongh while letting Harry Cole run free.

In his memoirs, Neave freely admitted: 'If more time had been spent on the security of agents in the field than on internecine squabbles, fewer tragedies would have occurred.' MI9's performance might have been better too if the blinkered and blimpish denizens of Military Intelligence had not been so contemptuous of the 'foreign Johnnies' who were not just the backbone of the escape lines but their head and limbs too. Senior MI6 staff were deeply distrustful of any foreigners, a dangerously negative attitude in the circumstances. No wonder that one weary helper,[35] coping each day with police surveillance and arrests, complained that the British had no idea how difficult it was to persuade guides, couriers and safe-house hosts to keep the faith and keep going. Bob de Graaff, historian of the evasion network in Holland, concluded that MI9's lack of resources was a serious handicap. 'It was forced to use existing lines and trusted individuals far too long.'[36] Signs of infiltration and treachery were overlooked because otherwise it would have meant closing down existing lines entirely and that was not an option.

This sense of desperation left the door wide open to the wily. Le Neveu, a French Foreign Legionnaire, or so he said, was, like so many other recruits, a volunteer whose loyalty was assessed on little more than instinct and then on performance. If he or she delivered, that was often enough to be welcomed on board. Some in the network who met him initially had their doubts. Once this would have been enough to debar him, but the group was desperate for recruits. His girlfriend vouched for him, and she was a trusted Resistance fighter because her brother had been executed by the Germans. Le Neveu should then have been detected on one of his first missions for the Pat Line when, with new restrictions on train tickets suddenly imposed at the Gare d'Austerlitz in Paris, he still managed to obtain the correct passes and get a party of five airmen on board. His action was seen at the time as one of bold ingenuity – just as many of Cole's clever antics at the demarcation line had been. It was only much later that the correct interpretation was put on events – that he could only have got the passes from the Germans so the airmen could continue their journey and all helpers along the way be identified. Le Neveu's success this time also meant he became a trusted member of the line when in fact he was simply compiling a long list of people to denounce and, as Helen Long put it, 'eating his way the length of the line like a canker'.

The disease eventually reached Pat O'Leary. The débâcle began with the arrest of Louis Nouveau, one of Pat Line's longest-serving helpers, who had fled from Marseilles because the Gestapo were

**1**. George Fernyhough *(centre)* and his crew prepare for a training flight in a Whitley bomber in June 1943. He was shot down and on the run less than a year later.

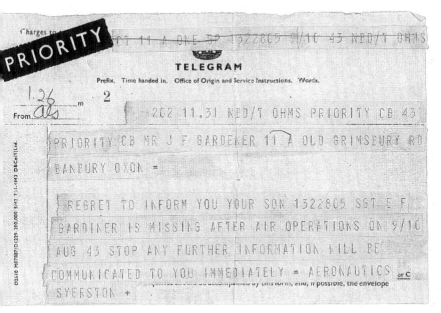

**2**. The dreaded telegram which arrived on so many doorsteps announcing a loved one was missing in action. When his parents received this one, Fred Gardiner was in hiding in Belgium and would return home by SOE aircraft a month later.

**4.** A wartime photo of Andrée de Jongh, known to all as Dedée. She was the driving force behind the Comet Escape Line.

**5.** Florentino Goicoechea, the Comet Line's Pyrenees mountain guide, was fondly remembered by many evaders.

**3**. An RAF intelligence officer uses his artistic skills in an effort to show potential evaders the correct way to act whilst behind the lines.

OU ARE MORE LIKELY NOT TO
ROUSE SUSPICIONS IF YOU SLOUCH
ALONG LIKE THIS —

# AVIS

Toute personne du sexe masculin qui aiderait, directement ou indirectement, les équipages d'avions ennemis descendus en parachute, ou ayant fait un atterrissage forcé, favoriserait leur fuite, les cacherait ou leur viendrait en aide de quelque façon que ce soit sera fusillée sur le champ.

Les femmes qui se rendraient coupables du même délit seront envoyées dans des camps de concentration situés en Allemagne.

Les personnes qui s'empareront d'equipages constraints à atterrir à leur capture, recevront une prime pouvant aller jusqu'à 10,000 francs. Dans certains cas particuliers, cette récompense sera encore augmentée.

*Paris 22 Septembre 1941.*

Le Militarbefehlshaber en France
Signé : von STULPNAGEL
Général d'Infanterie

**6**. The German notice to French civilians threatening severe retribution for helping evaders. And the reward for turning them in. Translation:

Any male person directly or indirectly helping the crews of enemy aircraft landed by parachute, or having effected a forced landing, or assisting in their evasion, or hiding or helping them in any way whatsoever, will be shot immediately.

Women guilty of the same offence will be deported to concentration camps in Germany.

Any persons apprehending crew members having effected a forced landing or contributing to their capture will receive a reward of up to 10,000 francs. In some cases, this reward will be higher.

Paris 22 September 1941. The Military Governor in France, Signed: von STULPNAGEL, Infantry General.

**7.** The remains of Gordon Carter's Halifax bomber are guarded by German soldiers near Landeleau, France, February 1943.

**8.** Gordon and Janine Carter after their reunion and wedding in 1945.

**9**. Gordon and Janine Carter visit Tréboul, the site of his escape by boat, with the authors in 2005.

**10**. The famous Comet Escape Line helper Andrée Dumon, known as Nadine, at the Escape Lines Memorial Society reunion in 2005.

**11.** Airey Neave, 1944.

**12.** Jimmy Langley, 1944.

**13.** Airey Neave hosts a reception at the House of Commons in 1969. *Front row from left to right*, Mrs Langley, Ian Garrow, Jimmy Langley, Airey Neave, Donald Darling, Mrs Neave.

14. Evader David Ward (*left*) with the family who sheltered him in Holland in 1945.

15. RAF officers, liberated in Paris in September 1944, celebrate their freedom.

22/8/44

Dear Madam,

This is written with the purpose of making known the fact that myself & comrade have been extremely well cared for by you & your folk. At all times you have been keen for our welfare & contentment. Also due to your assistance we have made contact which promises to be the means of a safe return to England in the near future. At all times you have acted as a first class patriot. With thanks

Sincerely yours

J.H. Trobe.
Squadron Leader
R.A.2

**16**. Squadron Leader Jack Trobe (George Fernyhough's skipper and evading partner) wrote this letter for Belgian helper Mrs Elza De Mets confirming her assistance and bravery.

on to him and was now working in northern France. Ironically, he had recruited le Neveu, put his complete trust in him only to be caught in the act on a train south with a party of evaders. As a voice with a German accent ordered him to raise his hands, he felt 'as if I was in a lift with a broken cable, falling into an irreparable disaster'.[37] Shortly afterwards, le Neveu invited O'Leary to a meeting, their first. He had information on who was betraying the line, he said, and O'Leary came straight away to the rendezvous at the Super-Bar, a café in Toulouse. Le Neveu was inside drinking what passed for coffee when O'Leary arrived in his usual ghostlike way and took a seat opposite him, facing the door as always. There was no small talk. After le Neveu explained the intricacies of some new identity card the Germans had introduced, O'Leary asked if he knew who the traitor was. 'Yes,' said le Neveu, 'I know him very well,' at which point O'Leary felt a gun sticking in his side. He looked up and six men, virtually everyone else in the café, were pointing revolvers at him. It was the beginning of March 1943. Twenty-one months after he began his work on the escape line, the man with the uncanny survival instincts had walked into a deadly trap. He was taken to St Pierre prison and then to Marseilles, where other members of the organization, Dr Rodocanachi among them, were also being held. London remained in ignorance of what had happened until three weeks later, when another of the arrested group was being taken under escort to Paris with O'Leary and managed to leap from the moving train as it entered a tunnel. He made his way to Switzerland, where he had the British embassy inform MI9 of O'Leary's fate. He also named le Neveu as the traitor and asked for 'all organizations to shoot him on sight'.[38]

This was to be the last MI9 heard of Pat O'Leary for more than a year. It was clear too that the Pat Line had virtually ceased to exist. The job now, as Neave and Ian Garrow decided over long chats into the night in London, was to try to start an entirely new organization with agents nobody knew. This was something they never managed. Smaller groups and lesser networks took up some of the work, but, as Neave wrote, 'the O'Leary organization as we had known it was gone. The War Office insisted that no more agents, no more wireless sets, no more francs and no more reinforcements were to be sent.'[39] Not that it had ever been generous, let alone profligate, with any of these things. If it had been – particularly with wireless operators, over whom Dansey was especially mean, like a miser with a chest of gold – then the Pat Line might have avoided its dismal end. Instead, betrayal – first by Cole and then by le Neveu – plus the increasingly heavy hand of the Gestapo, the Abwehr and the other German intelligence services in France, broke it, slowing to a trickle the once fast-flowing stream of airmen over the mountains from Perpignan. Meanwhile, on the Atlantic side of the Pyrenees, Dédée de Jongh's Comet organization, barely recovered from the capture of Nadine Dumon and her friends, was also being gnawed away by traitors.

★

For Stan Hope, the Christmas of 1942 was not the one he had planned. He had been saving up all the little goodies that came his way on the squadron – the chocolate and raisins handed out at debriefing – to take home to his family in Halifax. They had to go without. His festive season was spent in an attic flat in Brussels hiding from the Germans – and pigging out with strangers on the most wonderful Christmas dinner of his life. Being there was not what he had expected. As a navigator in a photographic reconnaissance squadron, he was spared the riskier pursuits of Bomber and Fighter Command. He didn't give much thought to flak and enemy fighters. Flying high and fast was essential and so was coming back with the pictures. It was a surprise, then, when engine failure brought down his twin-seater Mosquito.

I baled out first. The pilot, my friend Mac, ordered me to go, shook my hand and gave me a thumbs-up before I dropped from the escape hatch. The next time I saw him was after the war. It was almost dark on a winter's night as I floated down into a field of cows. I felt very alone, standing there in the middle of a field in enemy-occupied territory. I had no idea where I was, not even what country I was in. I approached some farm people. They were milking the cows and as soon as they saw me they handed me some hot milk. They told me I was in Belgium and sent me on my way with some sandwiches, which, after walking all night, I ate the next morning while sitting on a railway embankment. A train came along with German soldiers in it and as it slowly passed they all stared at me in my RAF uniform. It felt unreal. The day before I had been drinking in the mess with Mac and now here I was chewing on a sandwich watched by Germans.

But I got away with it and I went to the level-crossing keeper's cottage and was welcomed there with open arms. They found me an old brown jacket, a beret and a scarf and put me on the train to Brussels. There I spent a whole day wandering around. I went to the main stores, bought a paper, then went to a cinema. I wasn't sure what I was doing, just keeping a low profile, I suppose, trying not to be picked up. I'd been in the city as a child and I suppose I naïvely thought I might bump into someone I knew. In the end I went into a café and told the waitress I was RAF. She fetched her boss, who gave me the address of another café and told me to take a tram there. By now it was starting to get dark and I was worried about the curfew. But eventually I got there, ordered a drink and once again explained that I was RAF. I was OK then. They gave me a bed for the night. I had the attic room with a feather mattress and slept like a log.[40]

Hope's haphazard and seemingly aimless wanderings were typical of most evaders' initial experiences, but now he stayed put with a family, became best friends with the son, Maurice – 'we were like long-lost brothers' – went out shopping, to parties, the cinema, a football match. On Christmas Day, he stuffed himself.

I've never been so full in all my life. There were six courses, which ended with ice cream in the shape of a Yule log. It was a wonderful meal. I thought about my family. I was worried that my mother would be suffering in my absence while I was having a very good time. It didn't seem fair but there you are – that's the vagaries of war. I had a ball in Brussels. I used to go out on the tram with Maurice and we would stand next to German soldiers and just laugh. It was risky but I felt luck was on my side. I remember being in the crowd at a football match and getting excited and shouting 'Corner', and Maurice telling me to shush. But everybody else was shouting as well, so it didn't matter.

The good times could not last. Just being there was a risk, for him and for the people sheltering him, and, as January came, they managed to get in touch with the Resistance. A girl came to vet him, plying him with questions about English soccer teams, then he was taken to Paris. He met other aircrew. 'I'll be home by the end of the month,' he told himself as they took the train to Bordeaux. On board he was introduced to Dédée de Jongh.

She looked amazingly young but she was the same age as myself – we were both twenty-six. She was a very lively person, gave you a lot of confidence, told you what to do, knew exactly what she wanted. Perhaps it was unusual for somebody in the military to have a young lady ordering you around, but it didn't pose any problem for me. I felt we were in a line that knew what it was doing and as long as we played ball they would get us home. There were six of us on the train, though we didn't speak to each other. We all had false identification papers, which were checked a couple of times. I remember my heart beating faster when we were face to face with German guards. It was very different from when I was with Maurice in Brussels, laughing at the Germans on the trams. Now they were the enemy in a very real way. But I wasn't too scared and we got through with no problem.

'Tante Go' de Greef greeted them at Bayonne, there was an overnight stop at her house, then the train to St Jean-de-Luz. Hope remembered the tension rising as they headed into the mountains to meet up with Florentino, the guide. The weather was terrible, as bad as the experienced Dédée had ever seen. Heavy rain poured down for hours on end, mud slewed from the slopes like lava and there was a serious worry whether they would have any chance of getting over the swollen Bidassoa river. At the very least they would have to go the long way via the suspension bridge, involving extra hours of climbing in atrocious conditions. Instead of setting out, they hunkered down overnight in the cottage at

Urrugne, and Hope felt worried for the first time. From Brussels everything had been so smooth. A head of steam had been built up, the momentum to take them over the mountains. And now they were weathered in. 'I was desperate to get on with it, desperate to get home. I was worried about the delay. I just wanted to get it all over with.' He was right to be concerned, though he did not know it. Those few hours' delay would prove to be crucial.

The next morning the rain had eased and spirits were high again as they waited for Florentino to join them and begin the trek. 'We'll be over the mountains tonight,' he told himself over a mid-morning breakfast of bread and cheese, 'safe and sound.' Just then there was a roar of engines outside. Suddenly Dédée looked scared. She was about to embark on her thirty-third crossing of the mountains. She hadn't been expecting anyone.

The next thing we heard these heavy steps coming up the stairs. I turned to the others and said as a joke, 'Here come the Gestapo.' But it wasn't the Gestapo, not yet anyway. The door burst open and the barrel of a Schmeisser machine gun poked through. I'd seen one in a film but never in real life. My heart started pounding and I was really afraid. This was it. It was over for me, all over . . .

A dozen French gendarmes swarmed in.[41] Hope had a bread knife in his hand and put it down very slowly and carefully on the table.

I put my hands up. I remember it to this day, all as if it was in slow motion. They took us downstairs, lined us up against the wall and told us we were to be shot as saboteurs. I was resigned to dying. I had known when I joined the RAF that death was a real possibility. But I never thought it would happen this way – and all because some farmhand had wanted to get in on the Comet Line, thought they were making money out of it, and when they turned him down, he went off and told the authorities and we were all caught.

They weren't shot. One of the evading airmen produced his dog tags and said they were all RAF flyers. For the moment they were spared. But there was plenty of rough stuff to come, as Hope guessed and feared.

I had souvenirs on me that I shouldn't have had, photographs and a few addresses of people who had sheltered me. I was anxious to get rid of them but then we were searched and it was all taken from me. A gendarme asked us something and when none of us replied he said: 'Oh you *will* talk.' You begin to realize that this is no longer a game now, you are in real danger.

The one ray of hope was Dédée. Hope remembered how she showed no fear or deference to their captors. 'The way she conducted herself was a great boost to our morale.' She herself was grateful for one thing. Her father was supposed to have been with her on this trip across the mountains. His safety had been increasingly under threat in Paris as the Gestapo closed in and she had decided it was time for him to escape to England along the lifeline he himself had done so much to create. He had come with her and the others on the train and had turned back, reluctantly, when they got to Bayonne and Tante Go ruled that the weather was too bad for a man of his age to make the crossing. 'I shall come with you next time,' he had called out to his daughter as she had left him behind. 'Goodbye, darling.'[42] It was the last time they would ever see each other. But her father's escape from this present predicament was some consolation for Dédée as, in her blue trousers and espadrilles, her hair running with rain, hands clasped to the back of her head, she marched with the others in single file back to St Jean-de-Luz.

On the way Hope tried to pretend he was the Frenchman his false ID card said he was. His language skills were not up to the deception. 'One of the escort spotted it straight away and smacked me across the face. It was terrifying, and you couldn't do a thing about it.' What preyed on his mind – as it did on most others in his position – was that he would not have the strength to resist interrogation when they were handed over to the Germans. 'I was concerned about what they were going to do to us and also about the people who helped us. I worried that I might end up telling them everything they wanted to know. I was in despair about that.'

His worst fears were realized in the Villa Chagrin prison in Bayonne. He was shown a photograph of Florentino (who had not been at the cottage when it was raided), which he refused to identify. He was taken into a corridor and badly beaten up by three guards, then asked once more. He said he wasn't sure, and they hit him again. It was the coldness of it all that stuck in his mind.

This sergeant just sort of shrugged his shoulders as if to say, I've got to do this, it's my orders. It was incredibly frightening – not knowing what they would do, what they were capable of. The threat of violence was always there, and the threat was as bad as the reality. They left you on your own a lot to stew and to worry – and it worked. The interrogations went on for a long time. Once they fetched me at 4 a.m. to identify somebody. I can't remember who it was but I do recall how scared I was. It was a time of fear, despair, anger and loneliness. I was never tortured as such but I was starved, left alone, beaten up once or twice. It wore me down.

Eventually he and the others were taken to Bordeaux. At the station, standing in handcuffs, he saw Dédée – the only time since the arrest. 'I had a black eye and she looked at me and winked as if to say, oh yes, I know what's happened.' The prison at Bordeaux was a rat-infested, stinking hole where they slept on the cell floor. Now in the hands of the Gestapo, they were next taken to Fresnes prison in Paris.

I did 115 days in solitary there. How I kept myself sane I don't really know. I found a bit of metal under the bed and scratched writings on the wall, all sorts of things, poems and plans and meals and everything I could think of. I went back over my RAF service and tried to remember the names of all the people I knew in the squadron and wrote them down on the wall and rubbed them out and then wrote them out again. I kept myself going that way and by trying to kill fleas, which were everywhere. The food was terrible – coffee in the morning, bread and soup at midday, then just coffee again in the evening. I was starving.

I managed to communicate with a prisoner in the cell below me. There was an air-pipe high in the wall and I would stand on a chair and shout down to him. His name was Joe. I also found out how to open the windows and there was a Frenchman who used to shout out whatever news he had picked up. Then other people yelled their bits of news. I caused a sensation when I told everyone we had white bread in England. It went all around the prison. There was only brown bread all over the continent. I said Churchill had promised us white bread all through the war, and everyone thought that was wonderful, a sign of who was going to win.

Interrogations took place at the Gestapo headquarters in avenue Foch. Blindfolded and handcuffed, he was taken there in a van and threatened with torture. 'I was scared to death at being in Gestapo hands. They wanted to know all about the families I had stayed with in Brussels. I told them a yarn, that I had met up with people I knew from before the war, friends of my family, but I couldn't remember their names.' That was when things got really rough for Hope. Two particularly brutal-looking Frenchmen stood menacingly over him as an outsized German officer roared at him that unless he talked he would be taken to the cellar and tortured. He could see in the faces of the Frenchmen what they had in mind. 'I am no hero,' he said sixty years later, 'and I gave in. I gave them the vaguest list of names and addresses of people in Brussels. It was now May 1943, five months since I had been there anyway, and I thought and hoped that everyone would have got away. But they hadn't, and the Gestapo picked them up.'

The family he had spent his wonderful Christmas with were arrested. Maurice, his friend on jaunts round Brussels, was killed. As he told this story in 2005, Hope was overcome with remorse. His voiced tailed off and he began to sob. It didn't matter to him that every other man who had been in his position understood, that in every one of us there was a breaking point and that others, Wicks for example, had given in long before he did. 'I just couldn't face it any more,' he said desperately, the pain as raw as ever. 'I remember begging and pleading with them not to harm my friends but they said nothing. I never found out what precisely happened to Maurice except that he was killed. Knowing him, I'd say he went down fighting. He was aggressive, hated the Germans, probably gave them a lot of trouble.'

Hope was released from Gestapo custody a fortnight later into the hands of the Luftwaffe and spent the rest of the war in a POW camp. 'It was such a relief to be out of the clutches of those people,' he recalled.

Others, however, were firmly in that deadly grip as the Comet Line struggled to survive after Dédée's capture January in 1943. There had been trouble for a year, ever since her schoolteacher father, Frédéric de Jongh, had been forced to flee Brussels when the Gestapo came looking for him. He took over the organization in Paris with Dédée, but there was a setback when his successors in Brussels were arrested and the line foundered until a new Brussels organizer emerged in the upper-class Baron Jean Greindl. Aged thirty-five and a former coffee planter from the Congo, he now ran the Swedish Canteen in Brussels, a Red Cross organization caring for poor and sick children with cod-liver oil and a square meal. He used its once-grand offices, long panelled rooms with tall windows and threadbare curtains, as Comet headquarters as, under the codename Nemo – the submarine captain in Jules Verne's *Twenty Thousand Leagues under the Sea* and apt for an undercover agent – he steadied the line. His maturity was a good foil to its young and sometimes over-hasty volunteers while his management experience streamlined the network of rural collection points for downed airmen which the likes of Elsie Maréchal's teenage daughter had been setting up with school-teachers and priests in country villages.[43]

From MI9 news was flashed of Harold Cole's betrayals of the Pat Line, putting everyone on edge. Security was tightened and Allied airmen ever more closely questioned to weed out infiltrators. The Resistance had some successes here. Marguerite Brouard recalled two suspicious Americans who hid in her home.

We were told to watch them closely as their behaviour had been strange in the previous home they stayed in. Their English was perfect, their stories seemed normal, but they asked too many questions and went through our papers when we were out. We pretended everything was normal and treated them like the others, but after a few days our Resistance comrades took them away. They thought they were being moved to another safe house but in fact they were taken to the Seine and shot as suspected German spies. Their bodies were dumped in the river.[44]

But, more often, spotting an impostor was easier said than done, particularly given the limited support available from MI9 to vet evaders. The questions it supplied to check on an airman – his station, his home, where he had been shot down – were far too general. RAF jargon was one test – if a man didn't know that 'pancake' meant a landing, 'gong' was a medal and 'wingless wonder' an officer who couldn't fly, then he was not the real thing. But none of this was anywhere near foolproof, and Neave admitted that these tests were insufficient to unmask a trained enemy agent.[45] And, anyway, there was rarely a direct radio link to London for quick checks to be made because MI9, under Dansey's direction, was so niggardly with both equipment and operators. In Holland a British crew waited *nine months* under cover (and presumably under suspicion) before London verified their identities.[46] No wonder that the temptation was to rely on intuition – whether a chap looked and sounded right or not.

But intuition was a fickle friend. It had not alerted Nadine Dumon to the Resistance chief who turned traitor and sent the Gestapo to her home. Nor, because they sensed it too late, did it save the Maréchal family a few weeks later when impostors arrived at their home in avenue Voltaire in Brussels. Elsie Maréchal was sitting down to lunch one day when a guide she knew well deposited two men in civilian clothes at her door.

They were introduced as American airmen and spoke good English, but I didn't find them as sympathetic as some of the other fellows we'd had and I could not help feeling a little suspicious about them. The taller one of the two said he came from Jersey City, but he pronounced 'Jersey' with a slight foreign accent. I made up my mind to communicate my reservations to the chief ['Nemo']. The doorbell rang and I was about to send them upstairs to hide when the taller one came towards me with a revolver in his hand, looked me in the eyes for the first time, and said: 'Madame, the game is up.' The two so-called American airmen were Germans in disguise. They'd succeeded in entering the line at its source and had followed it up to Brussels. Sad to say, someone who worked in our line had turned traitor, and so made such a thing possible.[47]

At the door was a German military policeman. He and the two impostors forced her into a chair, then sat around her cradling their revolvers and hissing into her face what deep trouble she was in and how she had better tell the truth. They said her whole family faced arrest, torture and the guillotine. She was taken out to a car and driven away but the policeman stayed behind waiting for the rest of the family. Eight men were there when her teenage daughter, also called Elsie, came home. They told her they had shot her mother and that her body was lying in the kitchen. 'Your turn next,' they snarled. Sixteen-year-old Bobby walked through the door soon after and brother and sister were both taken away.

What Elsie did not know until many years later was that the Germans had started on her daughter even before she got to prison. Having said her mother was dead, they sat around her snapping out questions and slapping her when she refused to answer. Where had she been? Who had she been with? She bought some respite by pretending to take them to a rendezvous with a contact. When they realized she had fooled them they twisted her arms behind her back and shook and hit her. Only then was she taken to St Gilles prison, along with her father, who had also been arrested when he came home. The prison gates slammed behind them and they were trailed through long, echoing, half-lit corridors before being thrown into separate cells. Bobby too was in the prison, acting shocked and dumb, stammering his replies when questioned. His manner disguised cleverness. When they had caught him he had a note in his pocket which named another member of the line. In the back of the car, he had managed to screw it into a ball in his pocket and drop it out of the window. So at least one contact was safe. Others, though, were falling to the subterfuge. A courier from Nemo went to the Maréchals' house, right into the arms of German guards. He tried to run and was shot dead in the street.

In prison the pressure was stepped up on all the Maréchals, particularly after her interrogators discovered that the younger Elsie was a volunteer worker at the Swedish Canteen. This put Count Greindl in the frame. In a blacked-out room, the radio turned up to cover her screams, the teenager was beaten mercilessly with batons and belts for hours to try to get her to implicate him. When she collapsed they revived her with buckets of water and kicks and then started on her again. They switched tack and tried hypnotism, staring intently into her eyes, until she exploded into giggles. They hit her again but still she said nothing. The count, meanwhile, saw his network disintegrating before his eyes. He shut down operations at the Swedish Canteen and moved to a new headquarters. He sent two of his top couriers down the line to safety in England. He could have gone himself but he decided to stay and try to keep the Brussels end of the organization going. After all, at that stage the southern end was intact and men were still getting through. But not for much longer. Just six weeks after the Maréchals were taken French gendarmes drove into the farmyard at Urrugne and Dédée too was a prisoner. Stan Hope was probably right to believe that it was a disgruntled local who had tipped off the authorities about a party of evaders gathering at the Urrugne cottage. The chief suspect was a Basque farmhand Dédée had once used as a guide but dismissed for stealing. But by then the line was so deeply penetrated that it could only have been a matter of time before she was caught. She had known it too but whenever it was suggested she should escape herself she refused. When Greindl spoke to her of quitting, she told him: 'When an airman returns alive and safe he is living proof to his friends that over here there are people to help them if they are shot down. It gives them heart on their raids. We have to go on.'[48]

Arrest after arrest followed hers. Even Tante Go was taken into custody, though her intimate knowledge of the black market in south-west France and the involvement of senior German officers in it was a card she played to secure her release. That was one of the few breaks in the terrible storm clouds hanging over Comet. Another was the Germans' failure to realize the significance of capturing Dédée. She was interrogated twice by the Gestapo and nineteen times by the Luftwaffe's secret police and told them the truth – that she was the head of the organization. She hoped thereby to take the heat off her father, always the chief suspect in the eyes of the Germans. They didn't believe her. Theirs was the same reaction as Dansey's in London or the British consul's in Bilbao to this remarkable young woman. They didn't take her seriously. It saved her life.

But the hunt stepped up for the real boss. In Brussels, Greindl was arrested and brutally beaten with a steel spring but refused to sign a confession that he was Nemo. He was sentenced to death anyway.[49] By now the line had virtually halted. Before the catastrophic raids in Brussels, as many as five parties of evaders a month were hauling their way over the mountains to Spain. After Dédée's arrest, the organization was lucky if one made it. Her father, fortunate still to be free, sought other routes for the growing backlog of evaders, only to find these too had been penetrated. And his luck ran out when a guide who went by the name of Jacques Desoubrie (alias Jean Masson) brought a group of evaders to meet him in Paris and handed them all over, Frédéric de Jongh included, to the Gestapo at the station.[50] Another 100 escape-line helpers were swept up.

★

Both major escape lines, Pat and Comet, were now, if not totally cut, then hanging by a thread. Both continued in lesser forms, with fewer people and diminished results. In London Neave received a telegram from Spain – 'To "Saturday", from "Monday": Deeply regret Florentino reports Dédée arrested. Imprisoned Villa Chagrin at Bayonne. Attempts being organized for her escape.'[51] Desperate plans were indeed being drawn up to free her from jail. She was to be smuggled out in a large soup vat or climb a rope ladder with grappling hooks thrown over the wall. Two of her supporters wanted to put on stolen German uniforms and go in and get her out through a ventilation shaft. All this ingenuity was to no avail. There was to be no repeat of Ian Garrow's rescue. Dédée was taken away by the Gestapo to Paris before any attempt could be made. Neave recorded his disappointment at her loss. 'The moment dreaded for so long had come. We had known she was in danger but it was hard to believe that one who had performed so many miracles should have been taken. She had been a vital flame.'

And this at a time when the combined onslaught on Germany by RAF Bomber Command and the US Eighth Air Force, day and night, was rising to a crescendo. More bombers pounded Hitler's cities more often. Inevitably more fell to enemy action. The Luftwaffe commander, Hermann Goering, had seen the danger evading airmen posed – both by returning home to take up the fight again and as a morale booster to their comrades in the air – and set his police hounds on the case. It has to be said that, as thousands of airmen headed for POW camps rather than home and Resistance workers were thrown into cells and transported to concentration camps in Germany, his blitz on the escape lines was a success. The mountains were all but closed off as a routine way home, and at MI9 Langley and Neave were under severe pressure to come up with a new exit from occupied Europe. Meanwhile, amid the gloom, out there on the evader trail some were discovering that, happily, there could be more to their fugitive lives than betrayal and fear. Different sorts of emotions – altogether healthier ones – were possible too.

# 6. Love on the Run

It was a time to be young and daring, and in the ballrooms and dancehalls of England the tango was still the ultimate in exotic and risqué experiences. The American soldiers and airmen might have arrived and stormed the floors with their loud lindy-hops, all crazy leaps and jumps, legs and arms akimbo, swirling the girls in the air and flashing their underwear, but the drama, intimacy and sexual innuendo of the tango was hard to beat. It was also a hard dance to perform well, but Miss Auriol Bannister, a 20-year-old stunner from Pocklington in Yorkshire, was a Ginger Rogers in the making. Men from the local air bases would queue to be the one to take her in their arms and stare longingly into her eyes in a glide across the floor. But the longing in *her* eyes was for just one of them, a handsome 25-year-old rear gunner called Joe Sankey. His dancing skills, polished at the Tower Ballroom in Blackpool, were a match for hers, and they made a smashing couple, everyone – except Auriol's mother, that is, certain it would end in tears – agreed on that. For several months, whenever he was not on duty, they went everywhere together, did everything together, threw caution to the wartime wind. On their Saturday night out at the cinema on 13 February 1943 she tearfully whispered her secret news – she was pregnant. Her principal worry was what her mother, strict anyway but also a midwife, would say. So they decided instead to confide in her Auntie Ivy, much more of a sympathetic person, always one to go to if you had problems. With Joe's assurance that he would stand by her, Auriol agreed they would meet at Ivy's the next evening – Valentine's Day.

He did not show up. On the afternoon of 14 February he was rostered for a raid on Cologne. He didn't come back.

We were approaching the target when a Junkers-88 night fighter attacked from the rear. We both opened fire and I know I hit him but I also heard the thuds of his hits on our Halifax. Then he came in again and his tracers were coming straight at me. I had to shift my legs smartish to get out of their way. We were well alight when he came back for a third time. The skipper gave the order to bale out but I had difficulty extricating myself from my turret. I had forgotten to take off my oxygen mask and it was not until I unplugged it that I could put on my parachute harness and drop out of the hatch. I sprained my ankle landing in a field but managed to drag my parachute off some barbed wire and hide it. Then I heard a crack and felt liquid running down my neck. My ear drum had burst on the way down.[1]

Sankey had come down in Germany, which for most Allied airmen meant certain capture. Here there was no Resistance or escape line to help them (not at this stage of the war, anyway). But he was lucky to run into a young Dutchman, one of the millions forced from their homes to labour inside the Third Reich. From him he learned that the Dutch border was close and gave him 200 guilders and his flying jacket to guide him there. Once inside Holland he was hidden in local homes and started on his way home. It was a shaky beginning. He was put on a bicycle, an old-fashioned fixed-wheel type he had never ridden before. Two German soldiers laughed as he fell off. 'I kept my nerve, remounted and caught up with the man I was following.' He was hidden in a variety of homes, from a country mansion belonging to Dutch royalty to a windmill, before being settled with a family for three weeks. Here his journey almost came to a sudden end. He was quizzed, as usual, to check his authenticity and was fine until his Resistance interrogator asked what 'a jag party' was. 'I didn't understand what he was saying, and the tension between us rose. Eventually he showed me the question paper, and it was obvious there had been a mistake in translation. He meant "a *stag* party".' The mistranslation could easily have cost him his life.

Determined to return to the girl he loved, the airman now embarked on the classic route home, safe but slow. He was hidden for a fortnight in Antwerp, then in Brussels for nearly two months. Back in Yorkshire, his girl was in despair. All Auriol knew was that he had not turned up at her aunt's house as agreed. She presumed his promise to stick by her had been a lie. The man she loved and whose child she was carrying had abandoned her. Soon she had no choice but to tell her mother, who hit the roof. Leaving her distraught daughter behind, the formidable Mrs Bannister stormed to the RAF station at Melbourne to look for Joe and give him a piece of her mind. At the gate she was directed to the wing commander's office. There she was told that Sergeant Sankey was missing in action. Normally such news would be accompanied by an assurance that this did not necessarily mean he was dead. Letters to relatives always held out hope – a man was missing, yes, his plane had been shot down, but he could well be a prisoner of war or an evader. Only time would tell. But time was not what Mrs Bannister and her unmarried pregnant daughter had. Perhaps she was only being kind, doing what a mother thought best, not wanting her daughter to hold on to hope when there probably was none, but the message she took back home was that Joe was presumed dead and was best forgotten. Looking back on these events a lifetime later, the child born out of this union, Joanna, tried to imagine her mother's distress. 'She never talked to me about it but other members of the family have told me she was very upset. It must have been hard contemplating being a single mum. But in those days, you didn't wear your heart on your sleeve. You just got on with it, and that was what she did.'[2]

But Sankey was far from dead, even if the mother of his unborn child believed so. That summer, four months after being shot down, he was taking his chances on a train to Paris with a Canadian air gunner and two Polish army officers who had escaped from a POW camp. Three Resistance members were tracking them.

We had false ID cards but there was some doubt over whether these were the correct shade of colour. It was decided that when our papers were checked I would go first. If I was stopped then the others would get off the train. At the French border there was no problem with the document, but then we went through customs and a gendarme asked me a question I did not understand. The moment I dreaded had arrived. I just stared at him, stumped. Then one of the Resistance men who had already gone through saw my plight, came back and created a diversion by grumbling loudly to the gendarme. As he brushed past me he whispered – in English! – 'Take your shoes off.' That was what the gendarme had been asking me to do, to check I wasn't smuggling anything inside them. Later I was able to laugh about this but I had had a lucky escape.

In Paris, with the Resistance scares about infiltrators and informers now at fever pitch, there were more checks on his identity. A British undercover agent, identified only as Major X, sat down to play cards with Sankey and afterwards declared him genuine. The spy said he made frequent trips backwards and forwards from England and Sankey asked if he would give a message to his parents that he was alive. It is difficult to think that he didn't request word also to be passed to Auriol, now seven months pregnant. But the major did not keep his promise, and the airman's family and girlfriend were not told he was alive. Sankey's sojourn now took him to Lyons and Carcassonne and then into the Pyrenees for the perilous three-day trek into Andorra with a large party of Frenchmen trying to join de Gaulle's Free French forces in England. It was not an easy hike. 'The first night on the mountain we came under machine-gun and rifle fire. I was seized with terror as the bullets pinged from the rocks and ran bent double to get away until eventually the firing stopped. After we reached Andorra we were shocked to learn that one of the Frenchmen had been executed. He had been a German in disguise.'

As, back in England, Auriol's confinement neared, Joe was at last safe. His thoughts may have been of home, but for the moment he was stuck in Spain, swimming, soaking up the sun and going to a bullfight while he waited for his visa to Gibraltar. It was obtained by bribery, an embassy official handing over a box of cigars and lying to the Spanish police that Sankey was seventeen years old and under military age. On 17 July he left the Rock on a ship, which, two days out, was attacked by German dive-bombers.

Given all he had been through, it seemed the last straw. 'I was blown across the cabin by a blast from a near-miss.' But he survived, docked at Liverpool on 24 July 'and as I stepped ashore, I kissed the ground, as I had promised myself I would'.

His intention was to kiss Auriol too. And more than that – to marry her. The next month he returned in triumph to RAF Melbourne, greeted like a hero as returning airmen always were, an inspiration to everyone. He had it in his head to make the five-mile trip on to her home in Pocklington straight away but cold feet got the better of him. He imagined the reception he would get from Auriol's mother if he just presented himself on the doorstep. He sought his wing commander's advice. In that same office where, six months earlier, his girlfriend's mother had laid down the law, he was shattered to be told there was no point in going to see her. Mrs Bannister must have made it clear back then that, in the unlikely event of her daughter's seducer having survived and one day returning, he would not be welcome. 'Forget her and get on with your life,' the wing commander told him. From his friends in the barracks he got the same message. Leave well alone. One said Auriol had a new man in her life and would be upset if he turned up. She wouldn't want to know him. Maybe, as single men will in such circumstances, they also told him with a wink and a nod that he'd had a lucky escape from the responsibilities of fatherhood, make the most of it.

Joe Sankey listened to these siren voices instead of seizing the moment and going to claim the woman who had inspired him as he made his 'home run'. On 8 September 1943 Auriol, convinced Joe was dead, gave birth to a daughter and named her Joanna – Joey, for short – after him. As the little girl grew up she asked about her father and was told by everyone – mother, relations, friends – that he had died in the war.

My uncle told me my dad was in the air force. When I asked my gran she said: 'I don't know anything more than that, lass.' My mother eventually married and I had a step-dad, but it kept preying on my mind who my real father was. But it wasn't until 2000, when she was getting old and in ill health and I was afraid she would take the secret to the grave, that I finally asked her for his service number and anything I could trace him by. She just looked at me with a stony face and said she was very hurt that I should want to know. Later she did give me his full name and an old address but stressed she did not want me to pursue the matter. She didn't want the past raked up. She said she thought I would be ashamed of her and what she had done and that I was illegitimate. But I just wanted to find out about my dad and to look for his grave and put some flowers on it.

I wrote to the Ministry of Defence and to every organization I could think of. Then I went on a television programme about tracking down people in the war and after that a chap rang me from Canada to say he had Joe Sankey's medals. He had bought them from somebody who bought them from Dad *after* the war. After the war! So Dad had survived. To hear this was such a shock, I dropped the phone. So then I started tracing anyone with the name of Sankey and wrote them all letters.

One morning I was doing the ironing when the phone rang and it was the matron of a nursing home in Blackpool, who said, 'I've got your father standing here. Do you want to talk to him?' I wasn't sure. I felt so flustered. In the background I could hear someone muttering to her and then she asked me my date of birth. I told her, and she repeated it at her end and I could hear him say, 'Yes, that fits.' I asked if I could come and see him, and the matron said to come any time.

I put down the phone and carried on ironing. Then I thought: 'What the hell are you doing? Drop the ironing, get in the car and go!' Three hours later I was sitting in the car outside this big nursing home, shaking like mad and thinking: 'My dad's in there.' Eventually I went inside and sat in the matron's office drinking tea and preparing myself. Then she took me to see him, and he was such a small person, very tiny. And I thought: 'This is my dad!'

It was so emotional. All the staff were crying, so was I, so was he. The nurses kept coming and looking at us and then bursting into tears. I was overjoyed that I'd found him. 'Your dad is one of life's gentlemen,' the matron told me, and I knew what she meant. He was very shy, very articulate, a gentleman. He told me he'd been wondering all those years what had happened to me. He said somebody had told him that my mother had had a baby called Joey and all his life he thought I was a boy. Then he grabbed my hand and said: 'You're not angry with me, are you?' And I said: 'Why would I be?' I was just so happy.

But in old age Joe had clearly come to hate himself for his lack of faith and resolve and he told the long-lost daughter who had finally tracked him down: 'I regret to my dying day that I took notice of what other people told me to do.' She believes he felt sad about it for the rest of his life.

He never told anybody anything at all about himself. He got married after the war in 1950 and had a son, but his wife and child knew nothing at all [about me]. I find it amazing to think that if all those years ago he had gone to Mum's house first, everything would have been different. Why didn't he? He'd come so far to get home, to do the right thing, taken so many risks to get back to me and my mother. He only had to go those extra five miles . . .

And although Joanna had finally found the father she was searching for, this story does not have the happy ending it deserves; such is life, such is the aftermath of war. There was no reunion of her star-crossed parents, no teary greeting after sixty years of misunderstanding, no tango steps retraced. The dance of time was to a more sombre tune.

After meeting Dad, I told him I was going to see my mother. 'Please tell her I'm sorry,' he said, though in my eyes he had nothing to apologize for because there was nothing else he could have done. When I got to her house I didn't tell her straight away. We chatted away as normal, my step-dad went to bed and then I said to her: 'Do you know where I've been today? I've been talking to my dad.' I thought she was going to faint. She put her hand to her mouth and she said, 'How can that be? He's dead.' And I said, 'No he's not, he's alive.' It was a massive shock for her. If I had ever doubted it, the look on her face now convinced me she had spent her whole life believing he had been killed.

The flood gates opened and I thought she was going to pass out. It was very difficult for her to try to come to terms with. She'd lived her life thinking he was dead. She sat up all night and was still up the next morning, walking around like a zombie. She refused to meet him. He asked me to ask her but she wouldn't, and I had to be very careful what I said to her so as not to cause her distress. He told me to tell her how sorry he was, and that he would always regret listening to other people.

He and I formed a close bond. I was just so happy to have found him. My only sadness was that I couldn't get back his DFM [Distinguished Flying Medal] and his other medals, which he had sold for £400 to a chap in a pub when he was short of money. However, I did manage to buy some copies from the War Office and he was so chuffed when I gave them to him. He said he remembered when the king pinned his original ones on his jacket at Buckingham Palace.

He had been a widower for thirty years when we met and had lived on his own until he had a slight stroke in 1995 and moved into the home where I found him. I would drive up to see him as often as I could, and my husband and I would take him to his local for a pint. He was so keen to see me he would stand outside the home and wait for my car. He would tell everyone: 'She's coming today.' In many ways it was the end of his wartime journey to be reunited with me.

She had just ten months with her father before he had another stroke and died at Christmas 2001. Just over two years later, her mother died too. It was St Valentine's Day, just as it had been when his plane went missing in 1943. Sixty-one years had passed but finally this sad, unfulfilled romance was laid to rest.

★

The conditions were, of course, ripe with the possibilities of love and sexual intrigue. Young libidinous men thrown into the sort of adventures they would have only ever expected to experience vicariously in films or books. On the run, in disguise, living in foreign places, hopping in and out of strange beds, frightened yet alive – here was a brew of excitement, adrenalin and hormones. Mixed in too was mind-numbing boredom, hours, days and weeks of nothing to do, locked up, desperate for company and fun. Theirs was not generally a promiscuous generation – as one airman put it, 'in those days we took good behaviour for granted'.[3] But it was no wonder that many evaders fell with a passion for the women helping and sheltering them. There were so many French, Belgian, Dutch girls on the way home – couriers and guides for the escape lines, daughters, sisters and wives in safe houses. Early on in the war, 24-year-old Gordon Instone – captured at Calais, twice escaped from German custody – was hidden on a farm in the dark one night, bedded down behind bales of straw in the hayloft. His breakfast, he recalled, was brought by Yvonne, 'a tall, long-legged girl of about 19 with a fresh complexion sprinkled with freckles, large grey eyes and a mass of honey-coloured hair. Where her cotton dress opened at the neck, her throat showed strong and sun-tanned.'[4] He himself was a sight to behold – gingerish beard, long matted hair, filthy clothes, rank smell. She thought he was an old man until he cleaned himself up and put on a new shirt. Then she told him, '*Tu es jeune et vraiment beau*' ('You are young and really handsome'), and he blushed red. He stayed on at the farm for a considerable time, joining in the chores, becoming one of the family. It was an entirely new life for a city boy like him but 'Yvonne helped and advised me, cheered me when I felt down. She always seemed to be there with a bottle of wine when my thirst was becoming intolerable as we worked the fields with the full heat of the summer sun beating upon our backs.'

She darned his socks and gently corrected his French when he got his tenses and genders mixed up. He helped her bake bread, fold the ironing, fetch water from the well. She was no backward peasant girl, as he quickly discovered. She had been convent educated and was well up on the present political situation. One night they heard the roar of planes overhead and looked out to see German bombers heading in the direction of England, then suffering under the Luftwaffe's Blitz. 'With a heavy heart I watched them disappearing on their mission of destruction. Then I felt a hand in mine and Yvonne was looking up at me with sympathy and understanding in her eyes. I smiled and squeezed her hand. She knew what I was feeling.' Little feminine touches began to appear in his attic room – some curtains on the window, matting by his bed, a jam jar of fresh wild flowers. When they went for an evening stroll she had a trace of lipstick and her hair, normally bunched in a net at the back, had been brushed out to fall in waves on her shoulders. The blue woollen dress she wore clung to her curves. That night, as she held his arm tightly down by the river, he confessed that he had a fiancée back in England. 'Is she pretty?' Yvonne asked and he said yes. 'And will she wait for you?' the girl went on, and he said he did not know.

The sun was sinking in a red glow, a delicious smell pervaded the air and a few sleepy birds twittered in a tree above our heads. I felt very close to Yvonne at that moment and England seemed very far away, and my life there as unreal as if I had dreamed it all. She sat down by the water's edge and pulled me to her. This was reality and I did not want to let go. I put my arm around her and she looked at me searchingly and said, 'I wish you would stay here for always, darling.' Then she threw her arms around my neck and kissed me passionately on the lips. 'I love you,' she said, 'and I think you love me a little too.'

I returned her kisses – for I was not made of ice – but my conscience smote me. I might be infatuated but I did not love her enough to stay. I should never have allowed this situation to develop. I tried to tell her that, fond as I had grown of her, I was still in love with Elizabeth, my girl in England, and one day I intended to go back and marry her if she still wanted me. 'And even if there were no Elizabeth,' I added as gently as I could, for I could not bear to appear utterly heartless, 'you know there could not be anything permanent between us. Your parents would not hear of it and after all they've done for me at the risk of their lives, I could never do anything against their wishes.'

'No, no,' she cried, burying her head in my shoulder, 'Mother and Father like you very much. We have all grown fond of you. And you say you have come to love the life here in the country. Why go back then? We could be happy together, I know. And one day Papa would give you part of the farm.'

Instone told her he was worried that, by staying, he was endangering their lives. 'I am a marked man as far as the Germans are concerned.' And anyway, he had escaped from the enemy in order to get home and he had to do so.

But she was not persuaded, and conscious of her closeness, I began to feel less convinced of my idealistic intentions. 'If you stayed,' she went on eagerly, 'you would be safe, whereas if you leave you may be shot by the Germans or sent to Germany for slave labour if you're mistaken for a Frenchman or Belgian. Even if you succeed in getting to the coast [which was his plan] and getting a boat, you may be drowned in the Channel or die of exposure before you're picked up! What good would you be to your Elizabeth then?'

'Nevertheless, I have to go,' he said, but the thought and the words were a struggle for him.

And that was not the only struggle I was having to contend with either! For we were alone and the evening was beautiful and England was very far away. I looked at her face and marvelled for the hundredth time at her perfect complexion, as flawless as a child's. I ran my fingers through her hair, and told myself that I was a fool. Then I said: 'I'm sorry. It isn't that I want to go, I would far rather stay here. But I *must* go. If only I could make you understand.' I kissed her softly and then heard myself saying: 'The trouble with you is you're too darned attractive.' And I kissed her again much less gently. Later on I got up, pulled her to her feet and said with a determination I did not feel: 'Come on, it's high time I took you home. Your mother will be wondering what has happened to you.'

But Yvonne was not about to give him up so easily.

For the next day or two, she and I seemed to be constantly together. My attraction to her was something I had not bargained for and I was torn in two directions at once. I began to wonder if perhaps I was in love with her after all, so happy was I to be with her. Meanwhile she did everything in her power to make me stay, and I was in a fine state of perplexity.

Events solved his dilemma. He was introduced to another evader hiding in the area, an RAF fighter pilot, and together they planned their journey home. When he told Yvonne, she sobbed and ran to her room. He made his preparations to go, and on his last night the family held a feast in his honour. Two farmyard chickens went in the pot. The best wine was poured and everyone one drank '*à bas les Boches!*' ('Down with the Germans!'). Afterwards he sat in the garden with Yvonne and she pleaded with him not to go.

I took her hand. 'I must go, Yvonne, and you know I cannot take you with me.' She sighed, realizing that my mind was made up. 'I suppose I've known all along that this had to happen,' she said. 'So kiss me goodbye properly now and promise me to take care of yourself!' I put my hand on her shoulders and did as she asked. As I kissed her tenderly, her cheeks were wet with tears. '*Bonne chance,*' she said, and went inside and closed the door. I made my way to my room, with very confused emotions. Sadness and disgust with my own selfishness vied with the excitement and anticipation of the adventure before me. I could hardly wait to be on my way.

Setting off in the morning with his RAF companion, Instone stopped at the top of the lane to look back at the farm. 'I waved to Yvonne, a small solitary figure in a yellow dress standing outside the houses in the valley below me.' Then he turned the corner and was gone. He didn't expect to see her again, not before the end of the war at least, but he was back within days. There were no boats at the Channel coast to escape in. Instead the Germans were everywhere and he limped back to the farm, in agony from the blisters and sores on his feet. He was welcomed in but the free-and-easy atmosphere had gone. An RAF bomber had come down nearby and the Germans were flooding the area hunting for the crew, taking hostages and threatening reprisals. Patrols could be at the door at any minute. It was as if the war, which before he had found so easy to forget, had suddenly gone up a gear, turned more dangerous than ever. He was put in his old room but warned to be prepared to make a run for it. The roar of motorcycles in the yard brought him out of his bed and to his feet. *Les Boches!* He climbed out of the window, down a ladder left there for that purpose, and dashed for the shelter of some trees on the hillside. There he watched and waited until he saw the German soldiers leave. He went back. But it had been a close call, and that night the house was on edge with nervousness. Lying in his bed he heard a noise. Rats? Or Germans? It was neither.

I saw the dim light of a lamp and a figure in something pale and flowing coming towards me. Yvonne's bare feet padded softly on the boards of my uncarpeted room. She knelt by the bed and put her arms round my neck. 'You were so unhappy tonight,' she whispered. 'I couldn't sleep, thinking of it. I had to come.' The shawl around her shoulders fell to the ground as my arm encircled her. Her skin felt cold and she was trembling. I put out my hand and extinguished the flickering light of the lamp.

But if Yvonne believed she had him back for good she was wrong. Once again, events made a nonsense of human hopes. A day or so later Instone went to a nearby village and sat in the café listening to the local chat, trying to pick up on what was happening. A German officer came in, a private soldier by his side. They grabbed him. They were rounding up men of military age for forced labour in Germany. He protested that he was a farm labourer and needed to work his family's land but they just laughed. He was marched to a cell and, as he lay down to sleep on bare wooden boards, he knew there would be no more nights with Yvonne in his bed. Ahead lay slavery in a coal mine or a munitions factory in Germany. Home and Elizabeth seemed a long, long way away.

*

Intimacy was a shock. In domestic matters, this was a generation brought up on prudery that still echoed Victorian times. The sexes did not always mix that comfortably. But for evaders and their helpers, reserve and embarrassment had to be overcome as circumstances crashed them together, though it was not always easy. In family homes, adolescent daughters were likely to get a crush on the handsome and mysterious young men who had suddenly invaded their lives. Harry Levy, a bullet in his chest from the air battle in which he had been shot down, was visited in bed by a sweet 14-year-old, daughter of the doctor tending and hiding him. She came, she said, to practise her English, and sat beside him, perhaps a little closer than necessary, her hands resting on the counterpane, touching his.

She looked up and, meeting my eye, turned a delicate pink from her neck to the roots of her hair. 'You're blushing!' I said teasing her. 'Blushing? What eez blushing?' she asked, forehead and nose wrinkling. 'Red. Your face is red . . . *rouge*.' 'No, no, my face eez not . . . red . . . not blushing,' she said, covering it with both hands. Then she took my hand and smacked it and said: 'You are bad, naughty, stupeed . . . Engleesh boy.'[5]

Such flirtations were a pleasant diversion for the boys, a reminder of better times, and, as long as too many teenage hearts weren't badly broken, harmless. Sometimes, however, infatuations and affairs could get out of hand and prove dangerous to the security of everyone involved. One reason why 21-year-old Private Peter Janes, a veteran of the surrender at St Valéry-en-Caux in 1940, stayed on in a coal-mining community in northern France rather than try and make it to Spain was because the local Resistance was arranging for a plane to come and pick up him and other evaders in the area. But another reason was the plethora of local girls he fancied – 'my multitudinous lady friends in the *Nord*', as he put it in his diary.[6] There was Mathilde, his host's teenage daughter, and Gilberte and the 'breathtakingly lovely' Hélène[7] – and that was just for starters, because after them came Louisa and Jeanne, the mayor's 'exquisite' daughter Bernadette and the young woman in the baker's in the next village whose soldier husband had escaped to England. The Germans had denuded this part of France of young men, taking the soldiers away as prisoners of war and the civilians for forced labour. Janes and his friends filled the gap. His diary jottings read like Casanova or Frank Harris:

*12 June*: Jeanne came in during the morning and stayed most of the day. She is a handsome girl, big and tall and has a peculiar stateliness. To my great surprise she let me get in bed with her on Monday morning for an hour and also all the other mornings too. Not that she is particularly amorous but it is a great satisfaction. I think that she is the loveliest girl I have made love to yet.

The well-named Aimée has been in every day and I am in trouble because she says there is a young married woman who badly wants what they call here '*un morceau de viande, vendé sans ticket*'[8] from me and does not hesitate to ask for it. She has already sent me a letter that should never have been written in any language, never mind the highly coloured French.

*15 June*: Have had Aimée in three times today and together we kept up a really disgusting conversation. She is the most highly sensual girl I have ever met and that is really saying something in France. There is another young woman who badly wants me to have a go at her and Aimée finds it highly amusing that we can't fix it up.

*25 June*: Gazelle Eyes came to see me this morning, a tall, graceful, beautifully fresh creature. I can't imagine her as a participant in a violently passionate love scene but should like to be the other half of it if she ever did.

It could not last. Someone was going to get hurt, and a woman scorned or a wronged husband might want revenge and drop a word in the wrong place.

In the end it was not Janes but one of his fellow evaders in the area who went too far. He was lodging with a married woman and mother of two whose husband was away. All was well until he got her pregnant. An abortion was arranged but the whole town seemed to know. It was a messy business in a Catholic country, the woman was very ill and suddenly the atmosphere turned against the Englishmen. In his diary Janes now wrote:

*26 August*: We have been warned to get out of here because things are going to blow up in two or three days.

Fortunately, he had had a visit a few weeks earlier from a red-haired man who identified himself as a British secret service agent and said he could arrange to move him into unoccupied France and then home. Now Janes got back in touch with the man, and Harry Cole, for it was he, spirited the two Englishmen away.⁹ There was barely time for farewells and certainly not to all his conquests. But after all that had happened it was better to be gone. Out in the open, travelling among the Germans, risking spot checks and with a guide who turned out to be a traitor – all that seemed considerably safer than staying in a village where so much love had soured.

Bert Spiller trod more carefully with the woman who became part of his life. In Paris he had put himself in the hands of a priest, who introduced him to one of his parishioners, a spinster in her mid-thirties, dressed all in black and with a sombre nature. Her name was Marguerite and he was to stay hidden at her parents' flat while plans were made for his departure. As she led him there through the crowded streets of the capital, past cafés and bars full of boisterous German soldiers and their girlfriends, she slipped her arm through his to make them look more like a couple, less like a pair of fugitives. 'I gave her full marks for her astuteness, and as we looked at each other and smiled I could see that her face had lost some of its sadness and gained an air of defiance as if she was enjoying the moment of deception in front of the Germans.' At the flat the arm was withdrawn and she showed him to a camp bed in the kitchen and wished him goodnight. He admired her bravery. Her parents were absent, they were alone and she had no certainty he wouldn't try to take advantage of the situation. Then again, he told himself, if he did force himself on her, his chances of getting any more help from the Resistance would be slim. 'I made a mental pledge to be a good boy.'[10]

It was a wise policy but one not always straightforward to implement. One evader remembered showing too much eagerness to help the woman of a house he was sheltering in with the washing up. He was only being polite but he abandoned the pots and pans after realizing he was in danger of transgressing one of the cardinal rules of escaping – 'never do anything which might make a husband jealous'.[11] Another, an American, recalled being housed in an empty flat with two of his crew and food being brought to them twice a day by a girl named Paulette, beautiful, blonde, buxom and married. She used to linger over lunch, talking to them, making them feel at home, until the day she brought the food and left immediately. Her husband didn't like her being so friendly with them, and since he was 'Captain Jacques', the local communist Resistance leader responsible for their welfare as well as 'the roughest looking man I had ever seen in my life', they decided not to argue.[12]

Jealousy didn't apply in Bert Spiller's situation, but the principle of being on his best behaviour was the same. He and Marguerite shared the flat for several days and nights in increasing intimacy, and she would bustle round the kitchen making soup while he lay in bed or got dressed in front of her. Conversation picked up despite the language barrier, 'and a smile reminiscent of the *Mona Lisa* even came over her face'. They slipped into comfortable domesticity, like a couple.

Marguerite would go out early to work each morning, leaving me something for breakfast and lunch. In return I cleaned the flat, as silently as I could to avoid alerting the neighbours. I also read everything I could find, including the labels on the packets of food in the kitchen, which wasn't a long task, as she hadn't much. In the evenings we would get a good fire going and spend happy hours teaching each other our mother tongues. It was cosy and very innocent and I came to look forward to her return. In other circumstances it could, I suppose, have led to an indiscretion, but the overshadowing presence of propriety and the possible repercussions if anything dishonourable came to the attention of the Resistance group, happily prevented me from losing my head.

But it very nearly happened one night when I was shaken from sleep by gunfire in the distance and the reverberation of bombs. I drew the curtains to see several searchlight cones, heavy flak and the distant ground flashes of bombs. As I watched I felt a touch on my shoulder. It was Marguerite in her dressing gown looking like a startled rabbit and shaking visibly. I naturally pulled her towards me and we clung together during the whole of the raid, until the noise had died down and her trembling had ceased. I kissed her forehead and she gave me a smile. It was an affectionate moment when things could have got out of hand, but it passed.

But perhaps it was just as well that two days afterwards, word came that I was to leave for the south with a party of evaders. That night our evening language exchange lacked enthusiasm and we just stared into the fire, knowing that our brief acquaintance was coming to an end. The next day she took me to the Gare de l'Est railway station. On the way there on the Métro she openly held my hand to throw off any suspecting onlookers. Then, after introducing me to my courier, she struggled to keep her composure before holding my face and kissing me fully on the lips. '*Adieu*,' she whispered and walked off. I never saw her again.

Hélène de Champlain, a teenager working for the Resistance, also walked away but she found it hard. Her passions were stirring for one young American airman in a party she had to guide from Avignon in Provence to the Spanish border. In her work she often used her sexuality to her advantage. She flirted with an SS captain on the train, agreeing to have lunch with him, hinting at the possibility of something more, in order to distract him from the men in her charge. She had him so ensnared he even carried her suitcase, full of incriminating maps and documents, past a luggage inspection. But she knew not to get emotionally involved, to keep her distance – until Stan the US airman unlocked sexual feelings she had suppressed for the sake of survival. He was a Latin type with black hair and a dark complexion and when he took her to the door of her room in the house they were staying in and mumbled 'boon swouir' in an appalling accent she was tempted. She resisted but it was a struggle.

I gave him a kiss and quietly closed the door. Inside, I sat on the bed to undress. Then I looked at myself in the long *armoire* mirror and approved. My waist was trim, my legs and thighs slim and long and my breasts firm and round. I allowed my imagination to wander. I brooded over the strange situation I was in for a girl of my age. I found myself among young men most of the time, and yet no ideas of sex ever seemed to work their way into our relationships! But Stan was very attractive and he seemed to like me. I turned off the light and stretched out on the bed but I couldn't sleep. I was restless. Annoyed, I told myself, 'They'll be gone tomorrow!' But I didn't sleep a wink that night.

The next day I handed them over to a guide to take them over the mountains. Stan took me by the shoulders, bent slightly toward my ear and whispered: 'See you, girl, and watch those Krauts!' His eyes were a little watery and he gave me a long kiss on the lips while holding me tight. I did not understand the meaning of the words but I certainly liked his kiss. I handed him his bag, he gave a last goodbye and I watched him make his first steps towards what I hoped would be freedom. I turned round and walked away, feeling romantic and dreamy after his kiss . . .[13]

Her wish was to go back to being a normal young woman – to take some time to think about the lovely period she had just spent with such an attractive man, 'to feel alive'. The daydream was quickly shattered by bad news. Alerted by the SS captain she had duped, the police were coming for her, and she had to go into hiding. Even a little flirting was dangerous in these troubled times.

★

Gordon Instone did *not* end up in Germany. That was where the German officer sent him after rounding him up for a forced labour battalion, and the English soldier, keeping up his pretence as a French peasant, was in the back of a lorry on the first stage of the journey to the border when he dived for freedom. He grabbed a wheel jack, slugged the two guards and, as the vehicle slowed for a corner, dropped over the tailboard. For the third time he was on the run but now with the possibility of being charged with a serious offence, murder even, if he was caught. As before, he miraculously fell into helpful hands. He was in trouble from the fall, shoulder dislocated, knees and elbows lacerated. An elderly French couple took pity on him, sheltered him, clicked the shoulder bone back into place, let him rest, then sent him on his way. He set out thankful that his luck had held again. A dozen kilometres down the road, he walked into a small village, went into the bar and ordered some soup.

The *patron* was a stocky man in his mid-fifties, unshaven with a ruddy complexion and hair parted down the middle. 'He was in shirt sleeves and braces and spoke French in an unusual accent, which I couldn't place, though it seemed curiously familiar.' It took a while for Instone to catch on. When he did, he said to the man: 'You're no Frenchman. You've got a cockney accent!' The man thrust out his hand. 'And you'd have to be English to know it,' he said. 'Wotcha, cock! And I bet you're a Tommy!' He walked to the kitchen and called out in French: 'Marie. Bring some cognac. The good stuff, and hurry.'

A dark-haired, buxom girl of about 18, wearing a very short, tight cotton dress that she had obviously out-grown, brought the bottle and he poured me a drink. 'Now, my boy,' he said, 'tell me what you're doing here.' I told him of being captured at Calais and how I had got away and stayed at a farm but I said nothing about my latest escape and the two Germans I had been forced to kill. He slapped me on the back and filled up my glass and said how good it was to talk to someone British again.

His host, he discovered, was a deserter, but not from this world war.

He told me he'd been in France 'since the first little packet of trouble in 1916. I was stationed near 'ere and got very friendly with the daughter of the bloke that owned this café. One day we were moved up to the front line and I didn't fancy me chances much in all the mud and blood so I cleared out and come back 'ere. The girl's dad let me stay, so I did and after the war I couldn't very well go back to England. Me and the girl got married – I didn't tell them I already had a wife in England – and when the old boy kicked the bucket he left us the business. The wife and two daughters do most of the work but at the moment she's away with the youngest one visiting a relation. That was me other daughter you just saw. Growing up into a real woman she is now. I'm going to 'ave to keep me eye on 'er!' And he winked at me.

As the brandies slipped down and the confessions slipped out, Instone found himself being reeled in like a fish on a line. 'You don't want to go back to England,' his increasingly genial host proclaimed. 'What's the point? You've done your whack! Why don't you stay 'ere for a while and enjoy yourself? Nice bit of quiet. Nice bit of wine and good grub. And the Germans don't trouble us. And me daughter don't get a chance to meet any young fellers round 'ere. It's a shame. She'd take to a well set-up young chap like you and she's a good-looking girl, my Marie! Nice bit to cuddle!'

The girl stood there while he elucidated her charms in English, as if she were a champion cow. Luckily she spoke only French and did not understand precisely what her father was saying, but she must have guessed the drift. She fingered her apron shyly and smiled at Instone from under her eyelashes.

I addressed a few friendly words to Marie in French and begged her not to stop whatever she was doing, and she disappeared into the kitchen again, looking, I thought, rather relieved. 'What's the matter with yer, boy?' said her fond father in an indignant and almost hurt voice. 'She's a nice girl, ain't she? And she likes you, I can see that! Why don't you stay 'ere for a while and get to know her better.' Grinning at him in spite of myself, I replied, 'Thanks very much, pal. I'd love to stay but no thanks.' He said, 'Just as you like, boy! But you're a bloody fool. You'll only go and get your silly young 'ead blown 'orf or a bullet through yer gizzard! And for wot? Look at me. I stayed 'ere and I'm all right.'

The cockney bar owner let Instone wash up and stay the night in an outhouse. He refused all payment and shook hands with the airman as he left next day. 'You're a silly young fool,' was his parting shot. 'We'd have got on well together, you and I. But never mind! Goodbye.' Instone could see genuine regret in the older man's eye but he himself felt as if he had just notched up yet another escape. He walked away, rounded the corner out of sight 'and allowed myself the luxury of a good hearty laugh'. Twice he had had the temptation of a safe berth in France, twice he had refused. Now, as he journeyed to Paris and then down through France, the thought of getting home to his fiancée Elizabeth was the real temptation. His duty as a soldier and a patriot was driving him homewards, but so was his love for her. He had one more brush with the Germans, caught in a railway station, chased by soldiers and shepherded to safety behind the voluminous skirts of a crowd of peasant women on their way to market.[14] And he had one more brush with love. He made it to Marseilles, largely on foot, and now hoped to find a boat to take him out of France. The prospects looked poor and he sat down disconsolately on a park bench. A middle-aged woman and her daughter struck up a conversation. He thought they looked sympathetic and told them all about himself. They were refugees themselves, from Strasbourg, now living in rooms in a small hotel. They offered help.

I declined but the daughter, whose name was Simone, put a hand on my arm. She was small and plump with fair hair and penetrating and vivacious grey eyes. She gave me the impression of being a very practical and determined young woman. 'Come and have a meal with us?' she said, and before long I found myself in a small, old-fashioned hotel bedroom, sitting in a comfortable chair, while Simone and her mother prepared an omelette and coffee on the gas ring. I had only known them for two hours. I felt intensely grateful as I stretched out my legs – which had not stopped aching for a month – and relaxed in unaccustomed luxury.

One thing led to another. He stayed the night, in a single bed, while Simone joined her mother in a *grand lit*. And another. The next day he and Simone strolled through Marseilles, soaking in its sights. 'I felt at ease with her, as if I had known her for years. She was gay and cheerful, full of vitality and with a wonderful sense of humour, and I became very fond of her.' His determination to find a ship bound for North Africa waned. 'It was not easy to break away from the warmth of her friendship and the comparative safety and comfort of the hotel rooms, in order to face once again the loneliness, hardships and uncertainty of the future, especially in the middle of a winter which every day became colder.'

There was even less incentive to leave when Simone's mother went away for a few days.

That evening, when we had eaten, we settled down in front of the fire in her bedroom and were soon absorbed in an animated conversation. Time passed quickly. I glanced at my watch and saw that it was past 11. A sudden silence fell between us as we realized we were alone together in the quiet privacy of her room. I took her in my arms and kissed her. She relaxed, her cheeks warm and a mischievous light shining from her grey eyes. 'The minute mother's back is turned . . .' she began, but I stopped her there. 'Your mother has been gone a good 12 hours,' I said, 'and if I were a Frenchman I would be considered slow, wouldn't I? Luckily for you I'm English and you're safe. You've only to say stop and I will – or you can slap my face.'

She kissed me deliberately, drawing my face nearer with her hand on the back of my head. I told her: 'In England you would be considered a very bad girl and I would be considered to have taken advantage of your mother's absence to seduce you.' She said: 'I am, and you have.' I pulled her onto my lap and said: 'We will hurt no one by snatching a little happiness while we can.' Then I began to make love to her, and her passionate response awakened in me a heady intoxication I had never experienced before.

For a week they had the hotel rooms to themselves.

We were engrossed in each other and lived only for the present. So far as the brief, futureless nature of our affair allowed, we were happy. We got up late, went for long walks. We would buy bacon or sausages and eggs and take them back to the hotel to cook, drawing the curtains early to shut out the bleak winter evening and going to bed early.

And when her mother returned and seemed happy to accept their relationship, the affair continued – but not for long. One day Instone was stopped by a French policeman and taken away to internment in Fort St Jean. He visited Simone whenever he was allowed out but things were never the same. Inside the fort he was among other Englishmen and all the talk was of getting home. A break-out was planned. He had one last night with Simone, made his farewells, 'thanked her for all she had done for me'. And then the fugitive was gone. His love on the run had run its course. He ran for home and Elizabeth, the fiancée waiting for him.

*

In the intense atmosphere of a fugitive existence, thrown into the sort of close companionship and high-pressure dependency rare in ordinary life, emotions ran high. Jack Newton was a married man but the feelings he developed for the Comet Line's Dédée de Jongh in the few days he was with her crossing the Pyrenees were indistinguishable from love. He even got to sleep with her, though chastely and along with the other four evaders in the party when they had arrived exhausted at 'Tante Go' de Greef's house in Anglet.

The bed was huge, with decorative brass knobs and an inviting mattress, but what were we going to do with Dédée, the only woman among us? Should we men sleep on the floor and let her have the bed all to herself? She wouldn't hear of it. 'We will all sleep on the bed,' she told us. 'But, I will sleep in the middle, the two married men – Jack and Gerard – will sleep either side of me, and the two single men, Larry and Jurek, on the outside.' So all five of us piled on the bed, fully dressed.[15]

For whatever reason, Newton, married for just three months before he was shot down, did not sleep well that night. Perhaps he felt a little troubled. On the train from Paris he had found himself glancing at Dédée, noting her slim, delicate figure and angelic, elfin face. He couldn't help feeling a special bond with her. It could just be the realization that she had his life in her hands. 'When you are thrown together in such a life-threatening situation, you become very protective towards each other.' But equally he thought there was something extra in her eyes when she looked at him. She had shown him no particular affection, though he had been electrified by the occasional brush of her arm or pat on his back. Were they purely accidental or a hint that he was a little bit special to her too? Not that he was going to do anything about it. 'I wouldn't have done anything to compromise my marriage to Mary.' Nonetheless he had to admit she was 'a most attractive and gentle young girl, and I became very fond of her in my own sort of way'. She, in her turn, loved teasing him and singled him out as 'my brave young airman'.

While they waited to make that trip over the mountains he got to know her better, though finding out anything about her was not easy. She encouraged him to chat about himself and his wife and home but, in her charming way, would reveal little about herself. She was one of those people who delight in letting others talk while holding themselves back. She was open about her loathing of the Germans for overrunning her country and her fears for her father but was a closed book on everything else. Newton was overwhelmed with growing admiration for her and, as his biographer suggests, probably something more – 'perhaps it was love for someone who had put everything on the line, including her own life, to try and save him from the tyranny of Nazi occupation'.[16] And he was her first, of course. Newton was, as he himself proudly put it, 'her first English airman to be passed through the organization, so this must have counted for something in her eyes. And she always looked at me so deeply as though into my very soul. It was quite extraordinary. That was how I knew I was special to her.'

Once the journey was over, the mountains and river crossed, and he was safe in Spain he had time to reflect. She had gone back to France and he missed her.

We had been through so much together. Her bravery had such an incredible effect on me that, now she was no longer by my side, it was unsettling. I would turn to her to say something, and she wasn't there. But her sweet face, her funny little ways, her gutsy determination and dedication to what she was doing, were etched in my mind from that day forever.

It remained that way sixty years later.

I only have to close my eyes and I can see her as clearly as if it were yesterday. As are memories of my wife, Mary. How many men can truly say they have two eternal loves in their lifetime? For me, two women have made that life so complete, in two very different ways. I have always remained true to Mary and to Dédée, to whom I owe my life. It will be that way until I die.

★

In the Breton town in which she lived, pretty 22-year-old Janine Jouanjean developed a loathing for the Germans. Her first memory of seeing one of the invaders was when she was out walking her pet spaniel and a German soldier picked it up to pat it. 'I was so cross and angry, I just grabbed it back. How dare he!'[17] So when her brother Georges – known to all as 'Geo' – joined the Resistance, though well aware of the dangers, she was eager to help. He brought home British airmen on the run and she was called on to help when one of them had to be moved to a different house. His name was Gordon, and her job was to cycle along with him and her brother. It always helped to have a girl around at times like this. Two young men on their own might attract unwelcome attention, especially now. The collaborationist Vichy government had just signed a decree ordering all Frenchmen over twenty to report for *service du travail obligatoire* – compulsory factory labour in

Germany.[18] A girl with them made it seem more natural. At the very least she would distract the soldiers. Janine glanced at Gordon as they rode along. He was younger than her, just nineteen, but not bad looking, she thought, in fact, quite handsome, though his shabby clothes let him down. Otherwise he was just another in a long line of evaders, easy come, easy go.

She had no idea that, although a navigator in the RAF, Gordon Carter was in fact of French origin. He had been born in Paris to English parents and lived in the suburbs there until he was thirteen. Then the family moved to the United States and for three influential years of adolescence he grew up an all-American boy, deep into baseball and the like. But in his heart he saw himself as English. When war broke out in Europe he decided to cut short his studies at Dartmouth College in New Hampshire and, aged eighteen, went to Canada and joined up. Captivated by a description of aircrew as 'gentlemen of the skies and minions of the moon', he plumped for the air force. His first commanding officer considered him 'calm and confident, very mature for his age, intelligent, deep thinker, dependable, responsible, serious, very good background' and a commission followed. Then it was across the ocean to England. In a teashop in Bournemouth he listened intently to two Free French pilots at the next table discussing how to escape if they were shot down in France. 'I wondered if I would one day find myself in such a predicament . . .'[19]

In the autumn of 1942 he was assigned to the Pathfinders, the elite force newly set up to lead the waves of bombers into action and mark the way to the target. His fourteenth trip, on 13 February 1943, was the unlucky one. The target was the German submarine pens at the port of Lorient on the west Brittany coast. Heavy flak destroyed the Halifax's port inner engine and Carter led the bale-out. He landed literally in the arms of a French youth.

As I neared the ground I heard a voice calling out and I plunged into the outstretched arms of a lad, whose immediate words were: '*Tu es mon frère*' ['You are my brother']. I felt confident. I spoke French and, having lived in France for thirteen years, it was no great problem for me to behave like a Frenchman. I was in a unique position really. If anyone was meant to be an evader it was me. I had no real concerns about what the future might hold. Of course you could never be absolutely sure whom to trust, but it never really crossed my mind that I would be dealing with people who would let me down.

With the mid-upper gunner, who landed nearby, Carter began walking south-east, plotting a course for Spain on the Michelin map he had wisely brought with him. He was convinced their best bet was to pass themselves off as French and he buried his escape kit so as not to have anything incriminating on him if searched. A family took them in – though only because they said they were Canadian. If they had been British – blamed even now, more than two years on, for the sinking of the French navy – they would have been sent packing. The airmen ate *crêpes* and bathed their blistered feet while three eligible daughters giggled over Carter's good looks and wavy hair.[20]

They next fell in with a local Resistance leader who had a wireless link to London and a plan was made for them to be picked up by submarine on the northern coast of the Brittany peninsula. The trip there was an adventure, full of scrapes with German sentries and French policemen. Finally, they reached the beach and crouched behind rocks waiting for a signal from the sea. One flash came . . . but that was all. Hours later they crept away. 'We felt pretty disheartened. Our exit from hostile territory had failed and we were back to stage one again. Our prospects didn't look too good.'

For the next week they stayed hidden in a Cistercian monastery, drinking plum liqueur. Then Geo, Janine's brother, newly recruited as the Brittany end of the Pat Line, came to guide them to Paris. But the French capital was not safe. A flat he wanted to take them to had Gestapo soldiers at the door and Geo had to run for his life down the stairs and along the street as gunfire was loosed at him. The way south was now all but impassable, with Pat O'Leary under arrest and many other Pat Line helpers also in German hands. There was no alternative but to return to Brittany

– and it was there that he was now taking his bicycle ride with
Janine. 'She was blonde and very attractive. I was immediately
attracted to her.' He fixed her chain when it slipped, and she took
note of him too. He was lodged at the house of Geo and Janine's
married sister Lucette, but cycled back to see Janine every day – a
dangerous thing to do along roads patrolled by Germans.

Over the next fortnight the pair went for long walks together
in the countryside and watched water spiders skimming across the
surface of a spring. They laughed over books, tended a small potted
love-apple plant with orange berries, went to the cinema. He
washed her hair for her. Sitting in a field, Gordon dared to ask for
a kiss, and she agreed. He recalled:

I was falling in love. Here I was, an evader in occupied France spending
wonderful time with a beautiful lady, and some people might think it
was madness. But what was happening was happening and you just got
on with it. That was life.

It was mutual. Janine was swept away by her handsome airman,
though they had known each other for just a few days. She was
enchanted when he asked if he could kiss her:

It was such a gentlemanly thing to do and not something I'd experienced
before! I think I was falling in love with him then. It seemed perfectly
natural. We went out together. We were a normal courting couple who
just happened to be in occupied France!

If others saw what was happening, they didn't let it stop the
primary objective, which was to get Carter back to England. Geo
had a plan to hijack a new type of German motor torpedo boat
which was undergoing sea trials off the Brittany coast and drive it
to England. He asked Carter to join him. The airman was troubled.
He thought the idea pretty preposterous but decided to chance it.
'I had to grab any opportunity to relieve my helpers of my presence
and get back home.' But what about Janine and his increasingly
serious feelings for her? She could come with him, they would

flee together, he decided excitedly. But then he talked to her, and cool heads prevailed. There would be danger. She was better staying with her family for the time being. But he had to go. Their last meeting was sad but Janine did not cry. 'As we said goodbye we didn't make any promises. None of us knew what the future might hold. I felt terrible. He was sitting in a car and as it pulled away he was looking back at me. I remember his face. I didn't know if I would ever see him again.' Carter couldn't take his eyes off her as he drove away. 'She was leaning out of the window of the house, a wistful look on her face. I didn't know if I would ever see her again but I told myself that I would. I would do my best to see out the war and then make my way back to France to be with her.'

Carter was taken to Tréboul, a small port near the tip of Brittany. The plan to steal a German motor torpedo boat had been abandoned. Instead he joined a party of a dozen Frenchmen trying to get to England to join the war. Their vessel would be an old fishing boat tied up against the harbour wall. It would be no easy departure. The Germans had sealed every port along the coast. Every shipping movement was strictly controlled. But there were ways. In the dark the men quietly filed down the hill to where the 40-foot sardine boat was squatting on the mud. Armed German sentries were patrolling the quay, but as each turned his back and tramped in the other direction, an escaper dashed from the dark, dropped to the harbour floor and then clambered up on board. One by one they filled the tiny hold below deck until it was impossible to move. They sat in the dark, absolutely silent, until the sun came up and with it the tide that floated the little boat off the mud. Then the captain, a local fisherman, and his two-man crew went on top and began to make her ready for sea.

They left on the turning tide, the engine chugging into life, casting off under the eyes of the Germans, pulling away from the harbour wall, slowly out towards the harbour entrance. Before that point, the harbour narrowed between rocks on the port bow and a German guardhouse on the wall to starboard. Boats had to stop there for a final check. Sometimes the sentries insisted on coming aboard for an inspection, which would have been fatal on this occasion. Down below, hearts stopped, breath was held, as the captain swung her in, idled the engine but left a big enough gap of water to deter a suspicious guard from leaping on board to conduct a search. Just at that moment two Resistance members walked into the guardhouse to create a diversion. One claimed to be a workman with urgent repairs to carry out and the other complained about his car being tampered with. An argument broke out, and in the clamour the German guards waved the fishing boat on its way.

It was a long chug out through a deep bay where German boats and sea planes patrolled but finally they made the open sea where the Bay of Biscay meets the English Channel. The elderly engine strained through the rolling waters as they passed German destroyers lying up at Brest. As darkness fell a force 9 wind blew up and the boat was tossed mercilessly through the night. In the hold, the fourteen passengers clung on, vomiting violently into the filthy mix of salt water and diesel that sloshed over them. The one consolation was that the storm must have grounded any German aircraft sent to find them when they failed to return to port. By the time the tempest calmed, they were far enough from the French coast to feel safe.

We ran up a French tricolour with a cross of Lorraine, the emblem of the Free French, on it. We had water to drink but no food. After a fine day riding the swell, without as much as sighting a ship or plane, we sprang a leak which no amount of bailing could contain. The seamen among us managed to stretch a large piece of sail under the hull, and we were thus able to continue on our way. That night we ran into a thick fog bank. When dawn broke, our third day out of Tréboul, we sighted a coastline on the horizon ahead of us. As we slowly put-putted towards it, a small fishing craft approached. English? Irish? French? We stood off, waiting either to welcome it or fight. It turned out to be a Cornish crabber. It guided us through a minefield (we hadn't even thought of that hazard!) to the lifeboat slipway on Lizard Point. We made fast alongside the ramp and I told the bobby and the few locals who had gathered who we were. Tea and sandwiches were brought and then we were escorted by two naval vessels to Newlyn. I was incredibly relieved to be home and very happy to be safe again.

But home was not where his heart was. Janine haunted Carter's thoughts from the moment he landed.

What had I left behind? God only knew how long it would be before I was in touch with her. And she and her family and all those people who had helped me were in danger every day. There was always the risk of someone denouncing them, whether out of jealousy, to settle an old score or the lure of a reward – a flood of such anonymous letters reached the German authorities every day. And then they faced a firing squad or deportation to concentration camps, often after a long spell of torture.

He resolved to be optimistic. Back at his squadron he told everyone of the girl he had left behind, the one to whom he was 'engaged' – an exaggeration but forgivable. His return had made him a bit of a hero, and his whirlwind romance added mystery and glamour. He pencilled her name above his bunk and, when he went back on operations, he had '*Pour Janine*' painted on a 1,000lb bomb loaded on his plane for a raid. Colleagues noticed the dreamy look that came into his eye as his mind returned, as it constantly did, to 'his beloved France'. On a training course in Lyme Regis in Dorset, he lodged with a retired major with three daughters. He enjoyed their company but kept his distance.

I never forgot that I was spoken for. Indeed, my thoughts were always with her. I visualized her beyond the horizon when I gazed across the sea from the cliff or the pier and I dreamed of her every night . . . a fleeting vision in which I was searching for her and never quite catching up.

★

Gordon Instone was home. He had left Simone in Marseilles, put all those other French girls out of his mind too. A train took him to Perpignan and then he and his party hired a taxi to get within a mile of the Spanish frontier. Twenty-four hours later they were in Spain. He endured an unpleasant time in Spanish hands but was eventually repatriated through Gibraltar. On the Rock, 'my thoughts dwelt with happiness and anticipation upon my family and on Elizabeth'. And then it was back to London and that first exciting phone call to his mother. 'Everyone was well and waiting for me.' At home, all his civilian clothes were cleaned, pressed and hanging neatly in his cupboard. His mother had never believed the official telegram saying he had been killed in Calais. She knew her Gordon would come home and had everything ready for him. She showed him the pile of letters of commiseration that had arrived following his 'death'.

He glanced at the local paper and there was a photograph . . . of Elizabeth! She was all in white and on the arm of an army lieutenant. He had been away, presumed dead, for a year. The fiancée he had fought heaven and earth to get back to had married someone else. It didn't seem fair. But, as the old saying went, nothing ever was, in love and in war.

## 7. Rule Britannia

In dirty seaman's overalls, RAF sergeant Bert Spiller lurched along the quayside, clinging on to the deckhands on either side of him, and broke out into a raucous tavern ditty. Behind him came his pals, Smitty and Mac, in a similarly inebriated state and similarly supported. As they approached the coaster tied up against the wall, the captain hurled abuse at them from the bridge, complaining loudly about his crew returning off their heads on cheap Rioja and rum. The Spanish policemen patrolling the river port at Seville laughed out loud as Spiller stumbled up the gangplank onto the deck and was slapped hard across the ear by the skipper. Then he was ordered below. He reeled down through a hatch and then, instantly sober, made his way through a succession of doors and along catwalks to the propeller-shaft locker, a bolt-hole in the bulkhead where the airmen would hide while the ship and its cargo of oranges were searched before departure for Gibraltar. The drunken charade – aided, it must be said, by a glass or two of real wine – was another ruse to get evaders out of neutral Spain, and was preferable to the normal masquerade as sightseeing students because it did not require the production of papers. Here in Seville there was no need for the lengthy wrangling about identities that held up the phoney coach parties at La Linea, the Spain–Gibraltar border. As long as a man could do a passable imitation of a drunken sailor – and which airman couldn't? – he was on his way.

Spiller, Smitty and Mac sat crammed into the tiny locker for two hours, not daring to move, especially once the ship's engine started up and the propeller shaft was turning inches away from their noses. But then the rusty door swung open and they went up on deck to breathe in some fresh Atlantic air as the ship nosed out of the Guadalquivir estuary and turned south, past Jerez and Cadiz, towards Gibraltar. At some stage in their journey home, most evaders took to the sea. There was always risk involved. Even on the 100-mile coastal cruise that Spiller and his friends took, the lookout was watching for enemy submarines in the straits that separated Europe and Africa. And the last stage, the week-long Atlantic slog in a troopship from the Rock to Britain, in convoy and shepherded by destroyers, was frequently interrupted by enemy dive-bombers and submarines. Back in 1941, soldier Derrick Peterson got more danger than he bargained for when the Royal Navy warship on which he hitched a ride home from Gibraltar was diverted to join the hunt for the *Bismarck*. The German battle-ship was sunk before they got to the scene but the Admiralty then sent them to find her supply ships, and he was at sea for seven weeks. It was a great satisfaction for him, a survivor of the ill-fated BEF, to stand guard with rifle and fixed bayonet over captured German sailors.

These same North Atlantic waters that provided a passage home were not always benign. The 'moat' kept island Britain free from invasion but was also the last ditch in the obstacle course aircrew had to negotiate on their way back from bombing missions to the continent. Ron Scales was a tail gunner in a 'special duties' squadron flying Halifaxes out of Tempsford in Bedfordshire on solo missions dropping supplies of arms and equipment to Resist-ance groups and secret agents in occupied Europe. Flying low on moonlit nights, often following the snaking course of a river below or along a long, straight poplar-lined French road was exciting stuff. Once, helping a passenger don his parachute, 'my scalp tingled as he told me he was on his way to assassinate someone'.[1] The airman stared at the long commando knife strapped to the man's leg and imagined it in use. On another occasion a woman agent, young and blonde, sat silent and apprehensive in the dimly lit fuselage, then flung her arms round him and kissed him just before she jumped. For all the daredevil element of their smash-and-grab operations, he felt secure enough. He wasn't the one disappearing through the hatch into the unknown. Until the night of 19 September 1943, his twenty-second birthday. His mother had sent him a cake with a note that said, 'I hope they won't make you fly on your birthday, dear.' But they did – two drops in Holland, both quickly accomplished, along with a special scattering of V-shaped bars of chocolate for the civilians below, each marked: 'With the compliments of the RAF'. Then it was a dash for home.

Approaching the coast north of Amsterdam, about to leave enemy territory behind, the sky was suddenly filled with tracer bullets and flak. A fighter plane was on their tail, half a mile behind and closing fast. In the rear turret, Scales let rip with the Browning and saw his bullets smash into the German cockpit. The satisfaction was brief as shells from the Ju-88 shot under his feet, inches away from flesh, and the bomber began to lurch and yaw all over the sky. The enemy fighter flashed past, in a steep dive, and Scales tipped the turret to pour more gunfire into it, driving it into the sea, where it blew up. But the Halifax was in deep trouble too. The port fin and rudder had been blown away, and the skipper was having to fight to keep her level. They were now out over the North Sea, fingers crossed that they would make it to the East Anglian coast. It was not to be. The controls to the reserve fuel tanks were shattered. The engines were about to run dry. They would have to ditch. The crew braced themselves against the rear spar as the skipper nursed the crippled machine down towards a dark and empty sea.

There was a shuddering crunch as we hit the water, followed by another, and another, and then miraculously we slewed to a stop. We left the ditched aircraft in the strict rotation we had rehearsed so often. I was second and went swiftly up the short rope ladder to the rear escape hatch in the top of the fuselage, then out into a cold, wet and very unfriendly night. I slid from the fuselage onto the wing, then off into the sea and struck out for the dinghy that I could see bobbing a few yards away. Thank God it had released properly from its housing in the wing, thank God everything had worked as it should. But as I reached the dinghy, I became conscious that the sea had suddenly emptied and the big black shape of the Halifax was no longer there. The plane had sunk.

Scales hauled himself into the dinghy, then pulled in the four other crewmen who had exited with him through the rear hatch. As they huddled exhausted, tossing in the heaving sea, they realized the captain and bomb aimer were missing.

We began to shout their names as we paddled around in the darkness, calling, whistling and listening but there was only the sound of the wind and the waves. Finally it dawned on us that they had gone down with the aircraft. They were supposed to have come out of the front hatch above their seats in the cockpit but the speed with which the aircraft sank was too quick for them.

Dejected by the loss of their comrades, cold and wet, they sat as dawn broke around them. The meagre light from a remorselessly clouded sky revealed nothing but grey sea in all directions. 'The day passed interminably slowly, we bailed out the excess water with our hands and a flying boot and shivered and dozed, alone in an empty sea.' Then, as evening approached, they heard aircraft engines in the distance. They fired a flare and watched excitedly as the red light curled upwards into the sky.

A Stirling bomber swung towards us out of the grey. They had seen us. We stood up and waved wildly at its familiar shape and could see the faces in the cockpit and the gunners waggling their guns. It circled us and an Aldis lamp started to flash Morse. They were going to drop us another dinghy with dry clothes and rations. They came in over us, the bomb doors opened and out came the dinghy. We groaned with frustration as it fell several hundred yards away, too far for us to reach. All we could do was to watch it as it slowly disappeared from view among the waves. The Stirling circled us and flashed us that it was returning to base and would send out an air-sea rescue launch.

Rescue seemed imminent. They would be home soon. But their spirits sank again as night set in and then dawn rose with still no sign of the launch. They poured yellow dye into the sea around them to make themselves more visible. 'We bailed, we dozed, we shivered, it rained.' Another day went by, another night. Thirst now replaced sea-sickness as their principal concern. There should have been ample tins of water in the dinghy but someone either had forgotten to load them or had stolen them. Through cracked and salt-encrusted lips they cursed whoever was to blame. The next day they drifted, barely able to lift their heads above the dinghy's sides to scan the empty sea. But then one of them did peer out and saw a smudge on the horizon. Land!

It was the wrong land. They heard an aircraft and looked up, but instead of the comforting shape of a Stirling saw a German fighter. The current had hauled them back to Fortress Europe again. The landing was horrendous. Rollers picked them up and tossed them towards the beach and the dinghy turned over in the raging surf. Only four of them struggled to the shore. The mid-upper gunner did not make it. 'We spotted him outside the surf, briefly saw his yellow Mae West and his arm raised. Then he'd gone and we saw him no more.'

They were hardly in any shape to evade capture, though they tried. Scales went looking for help from locals in what they presumed (rightly) to be Holland. He ran into a German patrol.

Suddenly we were bathed in the harsh glare of a searchlight. Instinctively I ran but bullets were flashing past and so I stopped and raised my arms. There was a babble of guttural voices, then we were surrounded by German soldiers and searched while much discussion took place about our uniforms and our aircrew badges. I heard the comment, '*Englischer Flieger!*' and we were marched off.

Steaming hot tea revived them. They were prisoners of war and the unpleasant aspect of that particular ordeal was about to begin with the arrival of four SS men in a black Mercedes. But the ordeal of the cruel sea was over. Meanwhile, over in London, discussions were beginning on whether the sea that had washed Scales and his comrades back to occupied Europe might also provide a quick and easy passage out of it.

★

The men of Room 900 were in deep trouble. Traitors and infiltrators had all but smashed the Pat and Comet escape lines and closed the exit routes over the Pyrenees. 'The escape movement seemed to falter and lose confidence,' Airey Neave recalled.[2] His masters in intelligence were displeased, returning to their old theme that escape work jeopardized spying and sabotage. He and Jimmy Langley retorted that a bomber pilot's life could be as important as blowing up a bridge but found that this then put them in hock to their other Whitehall masters, the Air Ministry. Since the number of evaders getting home had now dropped away, the Ministry had some searching questions. Where were the trained replacements for those agents and helpers caught by the Germans and why weren't embryo organizations in place ready to take over from compromised lines? 'In other words,' as Jimmy Langley put it, 'what the hell had we been doing all the time?'[3] It was an unjust accusation given the Air Ministry's lukewarm support for MI9's activities in general and IS9(d) in particular, starving it of men, resources and money.

Once again the organization was caught up in the pointless whirl of Whitehall politics as the RAF made a bid to take over the entire evasion business and oust Crockatt as its head. The brigadier stood his ground against those trying to chip away at his tiny fiefdom, but the battle in the corridors of power was a bitter one and it appalled Neave. 'I was aghast at the belief that airmen shot down by the enemy were of minor importance to other Intelligence branches. We had to fight every inch of the way to rebuild the escape lines.' It was rumoured that the issue of who should run them went to the War Cabinet and that Churchill – ever one to take the wind out of the sails of his service chiefs in favour of smaller, maverick units – reined in the RAF. He had probably had Dansey whispering in his ear as well, but, whatever the mechanism, Room 900 was reprieved. 'We were ordered to redouble our efforts and at last promised all the moral and material support we needed.' Work was put into rekindling the smouldering ashes of Pat and Comet. But the main focus of attention switched from southern France and Spain to the north and the setting up of a new evacuation route across the sea from Brittany.

Gordon Carter had just got back that way and MI9 had taken a great interest in his story, asking if he would go back to France and help organize things there. He decided not to. If he went he would not be able to stay away from Janine, the girl he had fallen in love with, and that would put her in great danger. Recruitment for a Brittany mission went ahead without him. But finding the right people for this delicate mission requiring tact as well as nerve was hard. Langley sent in two Free French agents but one was betrayed and the other shot by a German officer in a brawl over a woman. Then he alighted on Vladimir Bouryschkine, the extraordinary Russian-born, American-bred basketball champion who, while official coach to the Principality of Monaco basketball team, had been recruited as one of Pat O'Leary's lieutenants in the south of France.[4] He had fled when things became too hot for him there, and was now training with the intelligence services to go back.

'Val' Bouryschkine had been lifted from a beach near the Spanish border by the Q-ship *Tarana*, a 200-ton armed trawler with a British naval crew, which carried out clandestine missions in the Mediterranean from her base in Gibraltar. She flew under whatever flag suited the situation – Moroccan on some occasions, Portuguese on others. Fishing tackle was strewn over her deck and the crew wore Portuguese fishermen's tartan shirts (bought in bulk in Lisbon by Donald Darling!). At sea they would often repaint her battleship-grey hull and superstructure in different colours as a disguise. She was part of a special 'navy' run by the intelligence service, known officially as the Coast Watching Flotilla (CWF) and used chiefly for dropping agents and supplies on foreign shores. There was no reason these trips should be a one-way passage, and she and other ships in the flotilla made several trips to Canet-Plage, a pre-war pleasure resort near Perpignan, to take off evaders in Operation Bluebottle, a plan conceived by O'Leary, Darling ('Sunday') and Langley at a meeting in Gibraltar.

In the months before his arrest by the Germans, O'Leary rented a seaside villa where up to fifty evaders gathered. It was a risky business getting that number of men to rendezvous there and the very first attempt was a flop. The men were ready but the ship failed to appear. They waited on the beach, with O'Leary flashing his torch expectantly into the dark night, but no boats came. At least, not to the right place. The captain of the *Tarana* was furious, heading back to Gibraltar after a wasted trip and complaining there hadn't been 'a single bloody pongo on the beach'[5] he had sent his dinghies to. The evaders trooped sullenly back to the villa and waited again. Conditions were terrible. Sleeping bodies occupied every flat surface – on and under the beds, on and under tables. Cigarette smoke clouded every room. The lavatories were out of operation. Locals began asking questions and the risk of being caught soared. They tried again, traipsing down to the beach only to traipse back to the stinking villa when the *Tarana* failed to appear yet again. The atmosphere there was rank in every sense. 'Many had lost faith in the escape organization,' Langley wrote later. On the third attempt, they made it – just. The *Tarana*'s launch hit the beach a quarter of a mile from the agreed point and in the dark it was only just spotted. But contact was made, and thirty-five evaders were taken off. Four days later, after a slow slog the length of the Spanish coast, they were landed at Gibraltar.

One of those brought home this way was Wing Commander Whitney Straight. He was a pre-war international racing driver, a Battle of Britain fighter ace, hugely wealthy and very well connected. He had been shot down in northern France while beating up German torpedo boats in the Channel and successfully evaded all the way to the Spanish border before being caught by gendarmes, in true playboy style, having a final meal in France before crossing over. Interned in the Vichy detention centre at St Hippolyte-du-Fort at Nîmes, he had put his name forward as eligible for repatriation on the same swap scheme for the wounded under which Jimmy Langley had gone home. With a fractured skull, a bullet in his flesh and damaged eardrums (plus the connivance of Dr Rodocanachi of the Pat Line, who was on the medical panel which examined him[6]), he was accepted and was on his way home with eight other wounded officers – actually at Perpignan, the last stop before the border – when Vichy (on the orders of Hitler, it is said) cancelled the humanitarian agreement as a reprisal for an RAF raid on the Renault tank factory in Paris.

Straight sent a personal message to Winston Churchill in London demanding that something be done to get him home, and a place was found for him on the *Tarana*. Some at MI9 disliked this string-pulling and queue-jumping. Why should one evader merit more attention and more risks than another, one of the team queried. But Crockatt knew that bringing home a celebrity like him with influence in high places would do wonders for MI9's reputation. He put pressure on Langley day after day, demanding to know what he was doing to get Straight home. When he finally stepped off the *Tarana* at Gibraltar, it was a welcome feather in everyone's cap. For Langley and Neave, however, a more important passenger on board was Val Bouryschkine. He had experience of working with an escape line on the ground, he now knew about beach rescues. He was ideal, they thought, for Operation Oaktree, their emerging – and increasingly urgent – plan for a sea rescue route across the English Channel from Brittany.

Langley had talked to the navy – their involvement a positive outcome of that high-level command to pull their fingers out. There had been much poring over charts and sucking on pipes before Anse Cochat, a cove near the village of Plouha on the eastern coast of Brittany, was selected as the ideal spot. Though the cliff above it had a German gun battery and searchlights, there was a steep path down to the sea and a cave where evaders could hide while waiting to be taken off. And then it would be a 120-mile trip across the Channel to the Devon coast. Val was to be dropped in France to set up a new chain of safe houses in Paris and a way of bringing men across country to the beach.

His mission started badly. Nine times a plane took him over to France and each time the pilot failed to find the dropping zone. When he finally went, he was out of contact for a fortnight. Langley and Neave nearly went mad waiting for a radio call. He eventually got through to say he had things moving in Paris and was now in Brittany, where he had found what he called 'a whole regiment' of Allied airmen holed up in a château owned by Comtesse Betty de Mauduit, an American. A hurried trial run to take off Val and a few of these men failed in the absence of proper wireless communication. It was also summer and the nights were not long enough for the operation to be completed under cover of darkness. Shortly afterwards he was arrested by the Germans as he tried to shepherd them south to take the old mountain route into Spain. The Comtesse was arrested too, betrayed by Roger le Neveu, now operating for the Gestapo from Rennes, the Breton capital, though her birds had fortunately flown in time, also down that difficult line to Spain. But its deficiencies were ever more glaring. The sea run across the Channel now became even more of a necessity.

Fortunately, MI9 had found the right man to make it happen. His name was Lucien Dumais and he was a Canadian commando, a sergeant-major who had fought in the disastrous Allied raid on Dieppe in August 1942, been stranded and then made his way back down the Pat Line. He too had been taken off Canet-Plage by boat. Now he was to organize similar missions from Brittany. They didn't come any tougher than the 38-year-old Dumais, compact and stocky with an aggressively short fuse that over the years he had controlled and converted into the discipline of the perfect fighting man. At Dieppe, the Allies' first sortie to the German-occupied European mainland, he had stormed ashore from a landing craft as the sea around him turned red with the blood of comrades. The beach was a killing field as German forces poured relentless fire from every direction onto a 200-yard strip of sand. Somehow he made it to the promenade and the shelter of the casino. There he fought to hold ground, but of the forty-five men under his command he had just a handful left at his side. The rest were scattered in the pandemonium of battle or dead. He watched helpless as machine-gun bullets carved into a soldier in his platoon, splitting open his belly and spilling out his guts. Hopelessly out-numbered and with retreat the only option, he escaped back to the beach and into the waves. A boat was leaving, he grabbed a rope dangling over the side and tried to haul himself on board.

The pack on his back filled with water and dragged him down. Exhausted, he let go – of life itself, or so it seemed to him at the time.

The tide pushed him ashore, and from the beach he watched the last of the Royal Navy ships disappear, taking the remnants of a badly battered battalion home. For those left behind, the choice was either to go down in a futile gesture of defiance or surrender. Sickened at having to do so, he tied his handkerchief to the end of a rifle and raised it in the air. The Germans took 1,500 prisoners that day, all now marched away from the coast. The sight of that long line of captives nearly broke Dumais's heart. 'I knew things had gone badly but had never dreamed it was on such a large scale,' he recorded.[7] His spirits were battered but not broken. Before embarking on the raid, he and his men had been briefed on the escape lines. Not names and addresses but just that such organizations existed. That was enough for him to tell himself there was a way home. He was going to try. After clawing a way out of the cattle truck speeding him and the others by train to Germany, he jumped. He did not find the escape line as such but plenty of helpers popped up to shelter him on his way – 'as if a whole conspiracy had been formed to help me'. In one house gendarmes knocked at the door in the small hours and he scrambled away across the roof. They hadn't been after him. Looking down, he saw a Jewish woman and her seven-year-old son being dragged screaming into the night. France was meekly surrendering its Jews to the German gas chambers. His problems seemed trivial by comparison.

It was not until he got to Marseilles that he linked into the Pat Line. His first call was at the American consulate, from where he was directed to Dr Rodocanachi's surgery. There he was interrogated by O'Leary himself before being taken to the station and put on a train. Dumais was slow to catch on as

I was ushered into a compartment full of men. They did not look like normal travellers and when Pat started to introduce me to them, *in English*, I wondered what crazy company I had fallen into. Then the penny dropped: all these chaps were in the same situation as me. Several were English and a particularly tough-looking one turned out to be a Scot who had been on the run since Dunkirk, two years or more. I had been lucky. After only six weeks I was on my way to England.

But now he was going back. At first he had refused any such mission. A 'one-armed major' asked him to think about it, but 'I had had my fill of being lost behind enemy lines. I was in no mood to resume such a tense and hunted life.' He took up a liaison position with the British First Army in North Africa, until a new and pompous CO set him on edge and he got in touch with the major again. On a bench in St James's Park on a glorious summer's morning, MI9's Langley spelt out the dangers to him. 'You do realize, sergeant major, that if things go wrong and you're caught, you will be shot, but only after the Gestapo have finished with you.' It seemed to Dumais an incongruous subject to be discussing on such a lovely day in the centre of London. Langley went on, 'And there will be nothing we can do for you. As far as we are concerned, you will have ceased to exist.' Dumais nodded. '"I understand," I said, and suddenly it seemed as if the day had grown chilly. "I'm ready to go."' From that moment Dumais ceased to be a Canadian soldier. Indeed, now listed as missing, he ceased to exist officially at all. His new identity would be as Lucien Desbiens, a Parisian funeral director. In training over the next few weeks, he became that person. Total immersion in his new personality would be his only defence if he was ever caught.

Meanwhile, down in Devon, crews of the 15th Motor Gunboat Flotilla were put on standby at their base in Dartmouth harbour for what was now officially designated Operation Shelburne. The flotilla of four boats had been established the previous year to run agents and supplies to the Resistance in France. They too were in training, learning signals and practising night landings for the high-speed dash the 120 miles over the Channel to 'Bonaparte', codeword for the beach at Anse Cochat.

Dumais and his wireless operator were landed in northern France by Lysander in October 1943. In their pockets were old Métro tickets and false French army demob papers. They also had the usual evasion paraphernalia of compasses and maps, plus a few new tricks from MI9's department of technical surprises – fountain pens containing tear gas and escape rope built into the soles of their slippers. In money belts were stashed 750,000 francs. 'Don't be stingy,' he was told. 'Spend as much as you see fit. You can always have more if you need it.' Clearly the atmosphere in MI9 had changed considerably for the better. They took the train to Paris, where their initial task was to rebuild the fractured network of helpers and safe houses in the capital. It was difficult work in untrusting times when so many were languishing in Gestapo cells. Could any escape line be secure? Was anyone safe from infiltrators? There were other worries too. Christine, the first agent he met, was in desperate straits. She had run up debts of 40,000 francs feeding and clothing evaders. She had been sending her 'parcels' south not knowing what became of them. 'We've had so much trouble,' she told him. She sobbed with relief as he handed over money and told her he was preparing a new route which would take its first shipment in a few weeks' time.

His main work was with Paul, a middle-aged Corsican lawyer, an experienced escape-line agent but now extremely jittery. Dumais persuaded him to re-establish his connections and safe houses. They agreed on new, strict security rules. Meetings were to be fewer, social contacts between helpers banned, guides were never to meet. Above all, every airman was to be thoroughly interrogated and investigated the moment he came under the network's control. 'The rules were intended to impress on members of the network the idea that they were professional and were not therefore at liberty to gab as they pleased,' Dumais recorded. 'Stopping careless talk was not easy where the French were concerned. They liked to tell people they were doing some-thing for their country; and then it only needed one friend to say something in front of an acquaintance who was a collaborator.' But his new rules took root, and one evader was to be most impressed at the way the system handed him on without his guides ever meeting, even in an emergency. He was left waiting outside a Paris station by a guide who decided there were too many German security men around and it was not safe to go inside.

He said, 'Wait here and someone will pick you up,' then he went away and we never saw him again. We stood there for some time, as if in limbo, and then a young girl in a black fur coat with a man on her arm came right up, took my arm and said in English: 'You will come with me.' It was amazing the way they were able to set up alternatives at short notice. Their communications and intelligence network under the most trying conditions was outstanding.[8]

With a system starting up again in Paris, Dumais now made his way to Brittany to liaise with sympathizers there. His initial contacts were not encouraging. The first man he told about the evacuation plan from 'Bonaparte' went away from the meeting and told his brother – and was then most indignant at the suggestion that his brother might not be able to keep a secret either! But then he found a Resistance leader named le Cornec he could rely on, and the plans advanced once more. Soon, Dumais decided, the time had come to trigger the first operation. A moonless night in mid-December 1943 was pencilled in, and in Paris fifteen 'parcels' were put on the express train for Brest, each one carrying forged papers allowing him to enter the forbidden coastal zone. They were met at the town of St Brieuc and taken to Plouha and other local villages to be hidden until the morning. Overnight a gale blew up and a message was sent from London via the BBC postponing the operation for twenty-four hours. They waited nine days but the foul winter weather did not relent. Everyone was stood down.

It was the end of January before a window in the weather offered itself. The BBC news at 7.30 and 9 o'clock carried the message *'Bonjour tout le monde à la maison d'Alphonse'* ('Hello to everyone at Alphonse's house'). It was on. Dumais heard it in a café and had to restrain himself from leaping in the air with excitement. He and le Cornec raised their glasses to 'a busy season'.

The *maison* in the message was a stone cottage a mile from the top of the cliff path down to the cove. Here the first batch of evaders assembled on the night of 29 January 1944. Conditions were tense. A curfew was in operation and soldiers patrolled the villages. Dumais tucked a revolver into his belt. 'We had a very good chance of being shot or ambushed,' he recalled. In the cottage he addressed the fifteen 'parcels', plus two others recently delivered. All were understandably nervous after a month cooped up since the postponement. 'This is the last lap of a long journey,' he told them. 'If everything goes well, you'll be aboard a British warship in two hours and in England by nine o'clock tomorrow morning.' But it might not be a picnic: 'If we're attacked, you are all expected to fight. If you have a knife, use it. If not, use your feet, your teeth, anything. If you get your hands on a German, show what you can do.'

One of those listening and taking in every word was B-17 pilot Lieutenant Dick Smith. He had been shot down just a month earlier while returning from a raid on Mannheim and been lucky to drop straight into the hands of the Resistance. He welcomed in the new year of 1944 drinking Calvados and partying in a safe house before being moved to Paris. There he was chosen to join the evaders already in Plouha for the first Shelburne mission. A teenage girl came for him and put him on the train at Montparnasse. In his pocket were papers identifying him as a geologist and another set saying he was to report to Germany for work in sixty days' time. He was given a French newspaper to read and ordered to speak to no one. At St Brieuc he waited in the square, feeling conspicuous in a long black coat and a grey fedora. Certainly the other evaders also waiting there noticed him. In that garb they thought he was a Gestapo agent! He then got on the local train to Plouha and, as instructed, got off when a girl in knee-high rubber boots walked down the aisle and opened the door. 'To my amazement five other young men in various modes of clothing got up along with me and followed her off the train and back down the side of the railway track. It must have been an odd sight.'⁹ She said her name was Germaine and she took them to her house where they stayed for a couple of nights. There he was told her real name was Marie-Thérèse le Calvez and she was a much respected

Resistance worker. And now she was one of the people in the cottage at Dumais's side that night as they waited for the boat trip home.

The *maison* was now alive with activity as the men lined up to leave. Jackets were turned inside out so the black lining was outermost, socks pulled over shoes to deaden footsteps, contents of pockets secured. They were even made to jump up and down to ensure they didn't 'rattle'. 'Hold on to the coat tails of the man in front,' Dumais ordered. 'There's no moon and otherwise you'll lose sight of him. When you get to the coast, you'll have to go down a steep cliff. Lie on your backs and slide. When you get to the bottom you will be told where to sit. There will be no smoking, talking or coughing, either on the way or on the beach.' The senior ranking officer among the men was given a wrapped bottle of cognac to give to the first British security officer he met on the other side. If he was in danger of being caught he was to ditch it in the sea. The next in rank was handed a small piece of folded paper with similar instructions, and told to swallow it if he had to. The cognac was Dumais's little joke. It was simply a gift for Room 900. But the paper it was wrapped in was his 30-page report on everything he had set up in France in the past few weeks. It was in code. The small piece of notepaper held the key.

In London an anxious Airey Neave sat by his phone. He had applied to go to France himself on the first boat but was refused permission. There was too much secret intelligence in his head to risk capture. He was alone. Days before, Langley had permanently switched to other duties, leaving Neave in sole charge, overseeing a distant operation that had every chance of going wrong. His superiors were expecting a failure. After all, pretty well everything else had failed so far. In the ranks above him, the official verdict on Shelburne was that it was 'extremely risky'.

At Anse Cochat, the lights of the cottage were turned out on the dot of midnight and the group filed out into a pitch-black night. The march to the cliff went smoothly, though Smith thought it longer than he expected. 'We wound through the night on a really circuitous route. We even went through some pigsties whose smell would dull the noses of the dogs that the Germans patrolled with. All the time we could hear the sound of the surf somewhere ahead of us.' The slide down to 'Bonaparte' was fine too and they collected in the cave on the beach to wait nervously. From the cliff top, a French volunteer flashed out the letter 'B' in Morse on a torch straight out into the sea. Another light shone from the beach. A mile and a half offshore, out of reach of the German searchlights, Royal Navy gunboat 503 heaved to in the swell as the crew spotted the lights. The anchor was dropped on a rope rather than a chain, and a rating stood by ready to sever it with an axe in case of trouble. A few hours earlier the boat had slipped out of Dartmouth, the captain having just been briefed on the German navy's recognition signals of the day, a service provided unknowingly by the Germans themselves via the Enigma intercepts at the Bletchley Park decoding centre. Arriving in French coastal waters she had cruised quietly with minimum wash until the flash from the beach was seen. Then four rubber boats were dropped over the side and sailors and commandos clambered in and rowed with muffled oars for the shore. There, Dumais was staring out anxiously.

Five hundred yards away to right and left of us were German listening posts; but with the darkness and the noise of the sea, it was unlikely they would spot us. Ten miles away, on the Pointe de Guilben, there was a radar installation and a battery of medium guns, but they were the navy's worry, not ours. At about 1.15 a.m., we saw dark spots on the sea. We watched them intently. They were not an illusion, they were moving slowly towards the shore. I waded out to the centre one, flanked by two Resistance fighters, pistols drawn, ready to fire. A figure jumped off the bows and came closer. I called out the password: 'Dinan.' The reply came: 'St Brieuc.'

It was the Royal Navy. I put away my pistol and waved my arms to the operators. They quickly unloaded the incoming supplies [arms, a wireless, whisky, cash], and then brought the men out and saw them into the boats. In twelve minutes the sailors were rowing back to their parent ship, taking some very happy 'parcels' with them.

Smith remembered it slightly differently. The first boat that came ashore unloaded supplies but no money, and the Resistance were not going to let a single evader off the shore until they had seen its colour. 'Some way to fight a war – no faith even between Allies!' Smith said to himself as the boat went back for the cash. Only when it returned did the loading begin. He was called from the cave and was so cold as he waded out to the dinghy that as soon as they were off he grabbed an oar and rowed to warm himself up. They came alongside 503 and he hauled himself up the ladder on board and then down into the hold. There he lay as the engines roared into life and they bounced away on a choppy sea, England-bound. 'At times you could hear the screw come out of the water and feel the tremendous slam of the bow as a wave crashed over it. We ate salty bean soup and were then shown to triple bunks and told to hang on. It got really rough, and the others were hanging out of their bunks retching and trying to hit a bucket sliding up and down the middle of the floor. It was not a nice sight and an absolutely horrible smell.'

At 9 a.m. the next morning Neave got through to the duty officer at Dartmouth to be told that the gunboat was back. She had pulled in alongside the paddle steamer *Westward-Ho!*, which served as a depot ship, and discharged nineteen passengers – seventeen of them Allied airmen. Also on board was Val Bouryschkine. He had been held by the Gestapo, beaten and threatened with execution but then escaped from Rennes prison during an air raid. Despite breaking a leg jumping the wall, he and a Russian companion had got to Paris and linked up with the organization he had set up and which Dumais had taken over. The journey to Brittany had been a nightmare for him and he had been carried down the cliff path on a stretcher. His arrival home was bittersweet. He was banned from further operations in France, theoretically because he was too well known to the Germans by now. The harsher truth was that Dansey didn't trust his story. He had been in Gestapo hands and then got away. There was too much treachery in this business already to risk any more. It was probably the right call. Better safe than sorry.

Back in Brittany, Dumais was doling out the supplies that had arrived on the boat. There were Colt .45s and ammunition for the Resistance fighters and whisky and cigarettes for the guides and helpers. Most important of all was a case containing bundles of used 10,000-franc notes – 4 million francs' worth! He handed some of it round, then shut the case tightly. Too much money could be as risky as too little.

I had discussed with le Cornec how much he would give each person, and he paid them accordingly; but seeing all this money, they imagined I was going to dish it out by the fistful. I could not pretend they were getting paid adequately for the risks they were taking; those were beyond computation. But we did not want anybody working purely for money. We paid a good wage, plus expenses, and to overpay had its own dangers. Some people lose their heads when they get a bit of money, start drinking heavily, and then start talking. In addition, if a number of people in a small town suddenly appeared flush, the word would quickly get around and suspicions might be aroused.

The first Shelburne operation over, a contented Dumais took the train back to Paris. He mused that what he had just done repaid some of the debt he owed to those who had helped him escape from France. Arriving in the capital brought him back down to earth as in one moment the entire operation faced ruin. A snap police search outside the Métro, and in his hand a case containing millions of francs. It was too late to run. He edged towards a young gendarme in the inspection party and tried to bluff his way through. 'Open the case,' the policeman insisted. Dumais tried a threat – 'If I do, you're a dead man,' he hissed. 'Open up,' came the response. Dumais went for honesty – 'Are you with me or against me?' he asked. The gendarme recognized the coded question. 'We're searching for food,' he said, 'but I'll have to look because the German inspectors are watching.' He poked through the contents, examined a shirt, saw the money. 'It's Resistance money,' Dumais whispered. 'Go on, clear out,' the policeman said as he snapped the case shut.

In London, Dumais's close call was unrecorded as plans went
ahead for the next operation across the sea, and then another one
after that. Evaders were still piling up in Paris and they were
wanted out as quickly as possible on what was now dubbed the
'Cross-Channel Ferry Service'. The only problems were on land
rather than at sea. Moving large bodies of men through the French
countryside was difficult, as Resistance worker André Hue recalled.
'They were too conspicuous in places where everyone knew
everyone else. No matter how loyal the locals might have been,
tongues wagged and the Milice listened.'[10] Fortunately the course
of the war was now moving the Allies' way, and that had an
important side effect, as twenty evaders discovered when they
were stuck out in the open with curfew approaching one evening.
The lorry taking them from the train to the beach was caught
on the spikes of an unfinished German army tank-trap in the road.
They piled out of the back and were bodily lifting the lorry
off the spikes when two gendarmes appeared. Like Dumais in
Paris, the Breton guide came clean. At this point in the spring of
1944, France – indeed, the entire world – could whisper of nothing
but the Second Front. The Allies were coming, and soon. Hence
the German tank-traps and increased security on the coast. The
beneficial result was that French policemen who once might have
veered towards Vichy and Germany in their loyalty were now
looking to the future. The two gendarmes let the lorry and its
occupants go.

American flight engineer George Buckner would travel in that
same lorry in March 1944 when he went on the Shelburne exit
route. During his stay in France he did everything he could to act
like a local. He taught himself to smoke like a Frenchman, the
cigarette stuck to his lower lip even when talking and allowed to
burn right to the end. Throwing a butt away with any tobacco left
on it was a certain way of attracting attention. He also learned to
urinate openly. When a train he was on was stopped by a bombing
raid and everyone milled around on the track he headed off for
privacy between the carriages. 'Just in time I remembered it's the
little things that give you away. In France do as the French and,

battling all my inhibitions, I relieved myself in full view of everyone.' He was dangerously fascinated by the German soldiers. He
couldn't get over their normality. Through the lace curtains of one
safe house he watched a group of them fixing their bicycles and
chatting and smoking. 'You somehow think the enemy is different,
like some alien creature. But the difference was only their uniforms.'
Out in the country, from another safe-house window he saw a
man fly-fishing on a mill pond, 'so peaceful and so incompatible'.
Was there really a war on? But there was and it was the reason he
was now getting down from that lorry in a dark lane and being led
by the 17-year-old Marie-Thérèse le Calvez past a café filled with
drunken German soldiers to her mother's house. There he and his
crew mate, gunner David Warner, were digging in to soup and
bread when a pale-looking Marie came into the room, held a
finger to her mouth and whispered: '*Les Boches!*'

Her mother opened the door and we feared the worst. We thought we
had been caught. We heard talking, then silence and the door closing.
Her mother's head appeared. Apparently one of the soldiers at the café
had a flat tyre on his bicycle and wanted a pump. Marie smiled a huge
smile and patted her breast in a gesture of relief.

   That night Marie led the two Americans down lanes and tracks
to a shed in the shadow of a large stone house.[11] Inside, in the light
cast by a dim lantern, they saw a short man in a black hat and coat.
'Stand against that wall and be quiet,' Dumais said in perfect
English.[12] Then three more men arrived and were given the same
treatment. One of them turned towards Buckner. It was a face he
knew! A guy from his squadron whose plane had gone down a
month before theirs and who was thought to be dead. They stared
at each other. 'My God! You guys too,' the resurrected airman
said. More men arrived until there were eighteen in all, trickling
in from various safe houses in the area. It was only then that they
were told they were about to be taken back to England by boat.
'You could hear the gasps,' Buckner recalled. 'We hadn't the
faintest idea we were anywhere near the sea.'

Their instructions from Dumais now had an extra note of caution. German sappers had recently mined the top of the cliff – an anti-invasion measure. But as they did so, from behind bushes Marie-Thérèse and other Resistance fighters had plotted every booby trap and ancient shell buried in the ground. A path was marked through the deadly field with white cloth. 'Don't wander out of line,' the evaders were warned. Down on 'Bonaparte' beach, Buckner could easily have been left behind. The tide was out, leaving a vast swathe of sand against a black sea and sky, and when the small boats appeared, 'out of thin air', all he could make out were dim figures in the distance running towards them. With his shoes and socks tied round his neck – he had taken them off expecting to have to go in the water – he and Warner raced to take their places. They were the last to get there and had to wade waist deep into the sea to push the boat off the bottom before they could pile in over the sides, squeezing past the rowers to find somewhere to sit. On board the gunboat, all the evaders packed into the tiny mess below decks, and there were more surprises. They recognized even more of their companions – seven men in all from the 92nd Bomb Group. It was an emotional moment for Buckner when the boat tied up against the *Westward-Ho!* in Dartmouth. 'My odyssey was over.' He had been away for forty days and he knew it had been 'the most profound experience of my life. I saw the heights to which the human spirit is capable of rising when there is a belief in a cause.'

Security was intense for the returning airmen. They had to hand over all possessions, souvenirs, false papers and so on. Even their clothes were taken away and replaced with British battledress. They were taken to London in a special railway carriage with military policemen at the door. Dick Smith had been through the same sort of drill when he got back. 'We weren't allowed to speak to anyone other than British security or our own group. In London we were intensively interrogated. We had to take an oath of secrecy for fifty years about our experiences. We could only tell people we had been shot down.' No one resented the caution. Lives were still at stake over the water. It was the least those in safety could do for those who weren't. Shelburne would go on to bring around 140 evaders home before it was wound up in August 1944. It had been a 'splendid exploit', as Neave put it, a triumph of cooperation between Room 900, the Royal Navy and French patriots and partisans.

★

One of the reasons for the success of the Shelburne 'boat train', as Neave called it, was that the activities of MI9 had the full support of the Americans. The Eighth Air Force's build-up in Britain had been slow and it was not until 1943 that it began hitting Germany in any numbers or with any regularity. And when it did, it found the Germans hitting back. B-17 Fortresses did not always live up to their name. Messerschmitt fighter pilots who dared to come at them head-on out of the sun found it surprisingly easy to break into the tight formations and cause havoc. It would be another year before the Eighth found the answer with its own long-distance fighter-plane packs to defend the bombers. Until then, it was sustaining massive casualties. On one raid in October 1943, to the heavily defended ball-bearing factory at Schweinfurt in southern Germany, sixty B-17s, more than a quarter of the force sent that day, were shot down. Morale among the crews was ebbing fast. On some missions as many as a fifth of the planes taking off returned before reaching the target as frightened men seized on any technical fault as an excuse to turn back. Showing them that, even if they were shot down, they had a good chance of survival was increasingly vital.

The Americans – though they had their own Washington-based department, MIS-X, specializing in evasion[13] – were happy to let MI9's experts take the lead. Langley quickly discovered that Americans were very good at making things happen. When he asked his US liaison officer if he could get his hands on some Colt .32 automatic pistols, not a regulation service weapon but much favoured by agents in the field, he got a positive answer. 'Sure, captain.' A month later, the American produced twenty of them, plus ammunition, and a promise of another 300 if he needed them.

How had he done it? 'Easy,' he told Langley. 'The War Department asked the Mayor of Chicago to put out an appeal to the gangsters.' Then, when in conversation with a US Air Force general he raised the question of airmen having civilian clothes to change into, he was staggered to hear him instruct his staff officer to get on to Washington and have every one of them issued with a pair of grey flannel trousers. Under his breath, Langley muttered: 'My God, this is going to be a different war now.'

Handling American evaders brought new problems as well. For example many of the men had German names, a result of the US's immigrant history and 'melting pot' culture. Their loyalty was never in doubt, even among those who were so newly American that their grandparents were German-born. But a name – an Otto, a Muller or a Buckholtz – could easily unsettle the French, Belgian and Dutch people they would depend on. The helpers needed helping over this hurdle. They also had to be issued with a different set of questions to establish a man's identity. It was no good asking an American about 'Jane', the striptease cartoon character in the *Daily Mirror* who was a wartime obsession of every red-blooded British serviceman. Baseball was a surer bet.

Out in the field they could certainly cause unexpected problems. RAF evader Kenneth Skidmore found himself travelling incognito with two Americans he thought stood out 'like the proverbial sore thumbs'.[14] They were tall with USAAF-regulation cropped hair and just too healthy looking to pass as undernourished war-weary Europeans. Their names were Pitner and Plishke, one a pilot from Kansas, the other a navigator from Wisconsin, and being of German descent, on trains and buses they liked to talk very loudly in what they considered fluent German. This only served to make other travellers uneasy – they assumed the two men were Gestapo. Gordon Carter had the opposite problem. The American airman he was with in France wouldn't stop asking him in English – *sotto voce* but not *sotto* enough – what was going on.

Fortunately none of this applied to pilot Jim Armstrong. He was one of those young Americans arriving in England when casualty figures were at their worst. The 384th Bomb Group he joined was losing a dozen bombers and a hundred airmen each month. Aged twenty, his chances of making twenty-one looked pretty slim. The colonel urged them to fly tighter formations but some men had other ideas on self-preservation. Armstrong's radio operator had a breakdown, sobbed and said he could not go on. He was relieved of duties. Then, on missions, the co-pilot began carrying an extra bag containing socks, underwear and a toothbrush. Armstrong took the hint. 'I began to review the French phrase sheet we had been given and carried it everywhere in my shirt pocket.'[15] On the way back from bombing Stuttgart and flying into a strong headwind that cut their speed to 90 mph, an engine stopped and they slowed even more. Then flak pierced a fuel tank and a German fighter was on their tail. Armstrong sent his crew out first and then jumped himself. With burns on his hands and face and a twisted ankle when he landed, he doubted if the French phrase book would be of much use. In his condition he would be easy meat for the Germans. His next home would be a POW camp. An old Frenchman, a veteran of Verdun, saved him from that fate, bringing him food as he lay up in a wood. When he was able to walk, he moved on. Some people he met were afraid and told him to go but most let him show them his phrase sheet and point to its first sentence – *'Je suis un aviateur américain.'* It was usually enough to get a meal and a bed.

Eventually he landed up in the home of an Englishwoman with Resistance connections. His way back to Britain was arranged in Paris, where he teamed up with other members of his crew. They were to go from Brittany, though via a different route from Shelburne. He was sent to Quimper on the opposite coast from 'Bonaparte' beach. A French fishing boat would take him out into the Atlantic to rendezvous with an English warship, he was told. It was all arranged, 'a piece of cake'. But then came a knock on the door, a cry of 'The gendarmes are here' – and he and nine other airmen crawled through a window, out into a courtyard and then into a back alley. There was a dash through the streets to a new safe house, where they waited for five days before being told the way out by sea was not possible. They would have to return to Paris.

They were in the capital for a month before a new escape plan was made, to the Pyrenees this time. As their train pulled into Toulouse on a mid-December day, snow was falling and by the time they alighted at Carcassonne it was six inches deep on the ground. Armstrong froze, not with cold but at the sight of German soldiers manning the ticket barrier. He couldn't very well show them his phrase sheet. 'The game's up,' he thought. 'One look at my false ID card, a few questions and I'm on my way to a POW camp. There's no escape!' But there was. Their guide led them to the lavatory on the platform and there they stayed nervously for an hour. Then the guide returned and took them back outside. There was no one at the barrier. The German soldiers had gone. Their exit was free. But the way over the mountains was not. Too much snow made them impassable, and so it was back to Paris. And then, on Christmas Eve, it was off by train again, this time back to Brittany.

The seemingly endless journey continued and they arrived at Tréboul, the same west-coast fishing harbour from which Gordon Carter had left eight months earlier. On Christmas night some thirty excited men were assembled in a house in the town. They ducked through the streets after curfew, narrowly avoiding a German bicycle patrol, and down to the waterfront. There they took off shoes and socks, and waded out to a boat lodged on the mud. 'I was about to climb on when a voice from on board hissed: "Go back, the escape is off." I couldn't believe it. Another aborted mission! Would I ever get to England? If this is a joke, it is in poor taste!'

It was no joke. Apparently the diesel on board had been stowed away and no one could break the lock to get at it without making a noise that would have woken the whole neighbourhood. Thirty disconsolate souls filed back to the house from which they had started, the end of a very un-merry Christmas Day. The next day the 'packets' were scattered to different safe houses in the area and there they stayed for the next four weeks, fighting boredom and impatience.

Armstrong never let these emotions get the better of him. He had been lodged in so many different places by now that he knew the drill, and he had always been the perfect guest, constantly aware of his hosts' kindness and the risks they were taking on his behalf. Not all of his countrymen were as thoughtful. Some, the products of small-town America in mind if not place, found it impossible to grasp that they were in a different culture. A few never understood why the locals didn't speak English and thought they were just being difficult. The lack of real coffee had others bewildered and bereft. In Belgium, Anne Brusselmans had a Canadian 'guest' who was slow to appreciate the land he was in and the people who were protecting his life. Her daughter recalled: 'He preferred the girls back home; houses were nicer in Canada, drinks were better and available, and the trains were definitely more comfortable. When my mother heard this she told me: "Let's get him home to Canada as soon as possible!"'[16]

Nadine Dumon remembered escorting one American on a train who complained that the wooden seats in the deliberately chosen third-class compartment were not what he was used to. That same young man with his wealthy background also misunderstood her. 'How much are you being paid to work in the Resistance?' he asked. 'I was very angry,' she recalled, 'because I received nothing at all! I did everything as a volunteer, no payment.'[17] He grumbled too when the shops were closed on a public holiday and, in the safe house they had fled to in an emergency, there were only biscuits to eat. The fact that much of Europe was on subsistence rations or below failed to register with many from the land of plenty. One Dutch family gave some bacon and bacon fat as a special treat to the airmen they were hiding in a shed behind their house and then watched in dismay as they dumped it from the frying pan into the garden. Old World people could be offended by New World manners. A rather genteel Dutch woman hid evaders on her country estate and complained:

It is easier to have 30 Frenchmen than three Americans. They are terribly spoiled and know little about Europe and the hardships we have had to suffer. They are not very civilized, always lying around with their legs propped up on a chair. They are also constantly burping. In the beginning they made no excuse but later they learned to say 'Pardon me'. The entire day they read and smoke cigarettes. All my own tobacco is gone, and now they are starting to hoard it themselves. The temperature in the room has to be 70°F or the 'gentlemen' are too cold. They don't have much to say themselves. And we are so stupid, perhaps out of gratitude towards America, as to spoil them. The house is peaceful again now that they have gone.[18]

She would have had no complaints against Armstrong, though he was as anxious to be gone as she was to see the back of her troublesome Americans. As he sat in a room overlooking the sea at Tréboul, he imagined himself home in Florida gazing across the warm waters of Tampa Bay.

The open window let in the refreshing scent of salt water and I tried to keep my thoughts positive. Soon I will be on a boat heading for freedom. England is just a short distance away. The days of that January 1944 dragged on and some feelings of scepticism about getting another boat began to creep into my thoughts. Each day we heard cannon fire from the big German guns. Was it target practice? Or a warning to the French to stay in line? Was it for the Germans' morale in face of the impending invasion? No matter the reason, it did nothing for *our* morale.

Patience was rewarded and on 21 January it was action stations again. They walked to a fishing boat moored by a dock and were settled in the stern hold. Standing or even sitting was impossible. The ceiling was so low they had to lie like sardines, a dozen of them in all, quietly waiting in the pitch dark for the voyage to England. The waiting dragged into hours, six at least, maybe more. Finally, there were footsteps on the deck above and bangs and crashes as the side boards which kept the boat upright at low tide were stowed away. Ropes were untied and there was the wonderful sensation of movement. Armstrong tried to shift position and was told sharply to be still. 'We're on our way,' a voice said. 'We're drifting out with the tide but you have to be quiet.'

The plan was to try to get past the German sentries manning the checkpoint at the mouth of the harbour before starting the engines. At the stern a fisherman was steering the boat with a long oar, keeping her in the channel. Armstrong took another gulp of the fetid air, looked at the sea water sloshing around his head and feet and prayed that he would neither suffocate nor drown.

Suddenly, a piercing cry broke the silence. 'Halt!' Frozen with fear, I visualized a German guard with his automatic high-powered rifle aimed at us, about to fire if we did not stop. We were sitting ducks and I unconsciously braced myself for the blast. A light went on and then off . . . and then the engine started. The Germans had switched on their searchlight but saboteurs onshore had cut the power. We were making a run for it. The engine hit full throttle. We were not turning back to surrender. It was full speed ahead now! Now all we had to worry about were the big guns on the cliff and German patrol boats out in the bay!

But two hours went by without incident. They were now out in the full swell of the Atlantic. A storm kicked up and the hatch covers which had been taken off to allow air into the packed hold were slammed back on. The men below retched in the darkness and Armstrong thought of Jonah in the belly of the whale. He prayed for a similar deliverance. Water was seeping in, which the bilge pump was failing to hold. A sailor came below and cleared away the handkerchieves, bread, biscuits, and chocolate that had floated from the airmen's pockets and were blocking the sump.

They sailed for eighteen hours until finally the hatch was opened and they saw the dawn of a new day.

The sea was calm and we scrambled out on deck to breathe fresh air and stretch legs, arms, back, and all the numb parts of our bodies. In the distance I could make out some islands. After almost five months in enemy-occupied land, the first glimpse of jolly old England filled me with indescribable joy. At last, through trials, troubles, and tribulations, freedom was at hand.

A patrol boat came out to escort them in and within the hour they were entering Falmouth harbour.

When at last we set our feet on land, some kissed the ground, others jumped with joy, and all of us, each in his own way, thanked Almighty God for our freedom.

Not all the boat people were as lucky as Jim Armstrong. Lieutenant Roy Davidson was another young American who joined the fight in Europe at the toughest time of the war for the Eighth Air Force. He went on that fateful mission to Schweinfurt in October 1943, the day marked in American aviation history as Black Thursday. His B-17 was in the middle of the formation, usually the safest place to be. But that day the enemy fighters streamed straight into the heart of the pack rather than chipping away at the edges and he found himself in what seemed to him to be 'the greatest air battle the world had ever known. It felt as if the whole German air force was coming at us from all directions. And they had two cracks at us. They hit us on our flight to the target, then refuelled and were ready for us again on our return flight.'[19] It was on this leg that his B-17 was caught by a Messerschmitt. 'The flaps and the elevator trim tabs were knocked out and the plane was trying to do a loop.' He and the co-pilot struggled with the controls to keep the plane level, then ducked down into cloud cover, hoping to limp home. Two engines were out, and then a third began to stutter.

A big four-engine bird won't fly on one engine, so we had to set her down somewhere fast, but where? Everywhere we looked there were only hills and trees. Then we spotted a little clearing and I headed for it. The closer we got, the smaller it looked. We were flying at 200 mph as we dipped over the last treetop for a belly landing in a field of cows. By kicking the rudder I was able to manoeuvre the plane so no cattle came through the cabin. If they had, we would all have perished. The wings hit half a dozen of them with a dull thud. Apparently there was a lot of beef on the black market in that area of France the next day.

When the crew was clear of the plane, Davidson detonated a fire bomb on the fuel tank. Then they scattered in small groups as they had been instructed to do. He felt that aching fear and loneliness so many airmen experienced as the truth of their situation hit home.

You are not an aviator any more. You're down on the ground in a country where you don't speak the language and you don't know anybody or where to go. Just here in this big old world by yourself – and what are you going to do about it?

And then, after being taken in by a French family and passed down an escape channel, he had that first, spine-tingling brush against a German, a rub of the shoulders on a train and a realization that 'this is the enemy, the one I had been killing from afar and now was standing next to. I held my breath when they checked my false ID card, sure they would arrest me. Had they spoken to me it would have been all over. I would have been caught.' In his fear was a premonition of what lay ahead.

His helpers, he discovered, were in a state of anxiety. There in Epernay, east of Paris, the Germans had devastated the local Resistance groups and all contact with the next links in his escape had been lost. He felt utterly alone, desperate to be back among his own kind but with no idea how to get there. In the house he was lodged in, he was hidden from the children. Then one of them spotted him and explanations had to be made and stern warnings issued. What a temptation for the little ones to tell their friends they had an American flyer staying at home. He watched the parents lecture them '*jamais, jamais, jamais*' to say a word, 'or else the Boche will take your mother and father away and you will never see them again'. The risk he was placing them in was another burden on his troubled soul.

For three months he waited, never able to relax, living on his nerves, praying for a miracle to take him home. And eventually it came. He was sent to Quimper in Brittany with the promise of a fishing boat out into the Channel and a high-seas rendezvous with a British warship. His spirits soared. He even allowed himself the luxury of thinking about his sweetheart, Betty. Perhaps he would get to see her again after all. In his despair he had begun to think it unlikely. It was a pretty tenuous relationship anyway. They had had just one date before he went overseas and he had been pushy, asking her to be his girl, to wait for him. It was a scene repeated among young people in every country at war, a sign of the times. She didn't say yes, no promises at all, but then again she hadn't said no, so she was the one he had poured his heart out to in letters from England. It was a correspondence he longed to take up again.

And the chance was coming. Over the BBC radio came the coded message that the operation was on. 'In a few hours we would all be back in England. I felt excited. The end was in sight. I could taste freedom.' That night he joined others, mainly Frenchmen, in a lorry to the beach. Then a guide took them out across the sands, single file, stepping carefully in the tracks of the man in front, snaking through a German minefield. At the water's edge there were rowing boats to ferry them out to a fishing boat. They climbed on board, the engine kicked into life and they were off out to sea.

At first the ride was smooth and everything was deathly quiet out there on the Atlantic. But then the waves got bigger and we began to roll and bob like a cork. All thirty of us were soon sea-sick. But worse was to follow. It was 3 a.m., just three hours before our rendezvous time, when the engines stopped running and the captain announced that the boat had sprung a leak and the engine room was flooded. As we drifted on the waves, I was very scared. I really felt we were going to drown. It was well below freezing and the cold Atlantic wind went right through you. Most of the Frenchmen gave up. There were some spies among them and they threw their secret papers overboard. Everyone else got

on their knees and started praying. A British pilot and I also prayed but
we were bailing water at the same time.

The wind and current took them back to the French shore.
They narrowly missed the jagged rocks that dotted the Breton
coastline before smashing onto land beneath steep cliffs. 'We
climbed to the top and started walking, trying to get as far away as
we could from the wreck and then hide. Three of us were on a
little country dirt road, soaking wet and freezing cold, when a
German soldier stopped us. I knew that was it, the end of my
freedom, but, after what we'd been through on the sea, I was just
happy to be alive.' It was an emotion that was not going to last
because everything he had ever feared about the Germans was
about to overwhelm him. He was as helpless to resist it as the
fishing boat had been out on the Atlantic waves.

We were taken to Gestapo headquarters at Rennes, where I refused to
give anything other than my name, rank and serial number. A German
major pointed to a leather strap with nails in it, hanging on the wall.
'You'll talk,' he said. I thought he was bluffing. I was a POW. I had my
dog tags to prove it, and I was entitled to be treated according to the
Geneva Convention. But then I heard them using the strap on a Frenchman and knew it could be my turn next. I have never heard such
screaming in my life. Just listening to it was an awful, hideous, terrifying
experience. I didn't want to betray all those French people who had
hidden me. I knew I would have to make up some sort of story.

Which he did, concocting an account of who had sheltered him
that was vague, described stereotypical people and apartments and
gave no names or addresses. It fooled no one, and his next destination was Fresnes, the notorious German military prison in Paris.

We were put in small cages that were too short to stand in and too small
to sit down. Here I saw the names of several US airmen scratched in the
paint. I was worried. It didn't seem I was heading for a POW camp as
I had hoped. Almost every day I heard Frenchmen yell, '*Au revoir, mes*

*amis; vive la France*', as they were taken off to execution. I could hear them being shot in the courtyard, and I realized this could easily happen to me and no one would ever know. I was completely at their mercy. I began to think I would never get out of there alive. Not only would my family never see me again, they would never discover what happened to me. I started to chisel my name and serial number on the cell wall, just in case. I found a nail and with it I etched deep in the plaster: 'Lt. Roy G. Davidson, Jr., USAAC 798452, 1944.'

If the worst happened, it would be all that remained of him, another evader who had tried to do his duty and had fallen on the battlefield. Meanwhile a bigger battle, the decisive one of the war, was about to begin. The likes of Roy Davidson would not be alone and stranded on the European mainland for much longer. Millions of their comrades-in-arms were standing by to liberate that benighted continent. From across the English Channel, rescue was on the way.

## 8. Digging In

It was every evader's dream to be whisked home by plane. In their mind's eye, they would be crouching down in a field suddenly lit by torches and then a Lysander would wheel in out of the darkness, touch down and wait, its props still turning, as supplies for the Resistance were unloaded. Then it would be a dash for the door, hauled inside as the plane was already moving, up and away for a low-level swoop back over the Channel and, in no time at all, a pint of beer and the safe-and-sound companionship of old friends again. No mountain slog, no stinking hold in a fishing boat, no sweat. And it *did* happen. After five weeks in hiding Fred Gardiner was told a plane was coming in with arms for the local Resistance group and there would be room for him on the return trip. He very nearly missed the connection as he tramped four miles across countryside and had to break into a run to get to the designated field as the aircraft circled noisily overhead, flashing an identification light. The only thought in his head was that every German soldier for miles must also have seen and heard it. He prayed nothing would go wrong.

We reached the landing field and I was alarmed to see that most of it was ploughed, leaving only a strip of grass with a haystack at the end. Would this be long enough? The Resistance men set out sticks as markers for the pilot, and I flashed the letter 'R' with a torch, the 'safe to land' signal. The aircraft came in over the haystack and landed with a considerable bounce a few yards in front of us, then quickly came to a stop and taxied back. The engine sounded deafening – and I half expected the enemy to rush out from all sides.[1]

With two others – one a fellow airman and the other a secret agent codenamed Grand Pierre – he climbed quickly on board, huddling on the floor as the cabin door was slammed shut.

I noticed there were no parachutes – no room for them – and realized with a jolt that we were still in extreme danger. We flew back in bright moonlight at 5,000 feet. There was no cloud and the ground was clear below us. At the coast there were a few searchlights but they made no attempt to pick us up. In the distance I could make out Brighton and soon we were coming in for a smooth landing at RAF Tangmere on the south coast of England. I felt very emotional, certainly thankful and quietly satisfied, but very relieved to be safe at last.[2]

But such rescue flights were rare. From the beginning the Air Ministry had ruled that Lysanders were not to be used to pick up RAF stragglers, a view encouraged by Dansey at MI6 with his usual obsession about not mixing intelligence and escape operations. But where it mattered, hearts sometimes overruled heads, and those actually running operations would do their best to bring back unscheduled passengers if they could. If an evader was lucky enough to be in the right place at the right time he might just get a surprise flight home.

But by now, with the escape lines shot to pieces, getting back to Britain was an increasing problem for everyone. Joe Purvis of the Royal Northumberland Fusiliers, a prisoner of war since the surrender back in 1940 on the north French coast, had escaped from a salt mine in eastern Germany by hiding on a goods train. He got to Switzerland where he was kept for a year before trying to get home via southern France. He was given an address in Toulouse to go to but when he got there he found the escape line over the mountains had ceased operating. He bedded down with the local Resistance.[3] More and more downed aircrew were also settling in with the communities who hid them. They were then drawn into the growing fight against the German occupiers.

The Resistance was swelling. It wasn't just because the course of the war had swung in the Allies' favour. The Germans' 1943 order conscripting all men in occupied countries over the age of twenty for forced labour in Germany was a shot in their own foot. It turned a sullen but subservient population into an actively defiant one. It was no longer possible to stand aloof from the occupation.

In every family, fathers and sons had to choose – to obey and be exiled to the Third Reich or to resist. Tens of thousands of young men went underground. If they were going to die, better to do so in defence of their country than meekly worked into the ground in the conqueror's factories and fields. It was into a France at last showing more of its mettle that Lancaster bomb aimer Denys Teare dropped in late 1943. He was full of optimism despite the trauma of the bale-out. 'Perhaps a few weeks' cross-country running would bring me to the Spanish border and eventually to the British Embassy in Madrid,' he told himself.[4] He was not to know that this route was now hopelessly compromised. What he *was* aware of after a night of walking in his flying boots was that his feet were a mangled mess of blisters. He would have to seek help. Lorries full of soldiers clearly hunting him and the rest of his crew settled the matter.

He approached two farm labourers, who fell over themselves to help him. In clothes they dug out from home, a beret on his head and a fishing rod under his arm, he was transformed into a peasant out for a stroll along the canal, bent on a little angling. He was given a place to hide and he told his hosts of his plan to get to Spain. They shrugged their shoulders and told him it was impossible. He would never make it. He would be caught and shot as a spy. He protested that he would keep his RAF shirt as proof of his military status under the Geneva Convention and they shrugged again and laughed. 'Perhaps people in England believe that international laws are kept,' one of his newfound friends said, 'but we French people have been under the Germans for three years now and know their cruel and dishonourable methods.' And so an overnight stay turned into days and days into weeks. 'They said it would be safer to stay with them and so I did. The intelligence lectures at the squadron had emphasized that we should always do what our helpers said because they knew more about the local circumstances than we did, but that didn't stop me being impatient. I was desperate to get home.'

He passed the time in domestic chores during the day and card games at night. Each evening activity halted for the BBC.

We crowded round the receiver, tuned to a whisper, and listened to the news from London. In between items, popular patriotic songs, forbidden by the Germans, were played and affected me as much as they did the rest of the household. I wanted to march down the street singing the 'Marseillaise'. Then would come a sadder tune and the news of poor French prisoners, the slave workers and the heroes dying in concentration camps. Someone would say quietly, '*Pauvre France*,' and, glancing round the room at the tear-filled eyes, I began to realize what the years of occupation had meant to these people.

All the plans for his evacuation seemed to falter. He was told that his way out would be by boat from the coast, and he awaited the arrival of a false ID card and a courier. Neither came, though he stood by the door and watched for a fortnight. Instead there was news of arrests and executions of Resistance workers in Paris. Nobody was moving; there was danger everywhere. Best stay put. But his presence was causing conflict in the household. There was talk of rewards at the end of the war for sheltering the likes of him. The British were going to pay out thousands of francs when the time came – and everyone fell to bickering over who should get the lion's share. He benefited from this unpleasantness in that everyone vied with each other to be extra kind to him, but it saddened him that he should be the cause of squabbling between people who were all taking huge risks on his behalf, and had done so long before there was any thought of money. He would have left but he was aware of increasing danger outside the haven he was in. He watched a dogfight in the sky as Allied bombers passed over on their way to Germany. Fighter planes downed a Flying Fortress and its crew parachuted towards safety, only to be machine-gunned in mid-air. On the ground German soldiers raced to find the bodies of the airmen, roped them to a motorcycle and dragged them along the ground. Clearly the war was entering an even more barbaric phase. Once again, he was better off staying put.

It was not until the first week of January 1944 that Resistance fighters came for him and he at last left the farm that had been his home for more than three months. His new lodgings were in the town of Bar-le-Duc, where German soldiers regularly patrolled the streets and he was even more confined than he had been out in the country. At least there he could get fresh air and exercise. Now he could not even go out into the backyard to feed the rabbits – essential sustenance in many wartime French homes – in case he was spotted by neighbours. As more weeks passed he tuned in to radio broadcasts from London. Increasingly the news was of Allied successes – the British maintaining their advance up through Italy, the Russians chasing the German panzers back into Poland. Overhead, the American Eighth Air Force, its Mustang fighters now fitted with extra fuel tanks and providing protection for the fleets of bombers all the way to and from their targets, was at last getting the better of the Luftwaffe. To those who dared to be optimistic, Hitler was on the defensive, on the run even. But just beyond the door, the Nazi hold was as fierce as ever. The Germans caught a local Resistance fighter, a father of five small children, as he operated the group's wireless transmitter. He had known all about Teare's presence in the town. How long would he be able to resist the inevitable flogging and torture? News also came of arrests back in the village where he had first hidden. It was time to leave the town, and quickly. 'I considered myself extremely fortunate to be getting out alive.'

He was smuggled to another town ten miles away and told once again that he would be on his way home soon, this time by Lysander. He was excited by the prospect of home in just a few days' time. 'I saw myself opening the garden gate, running down the path and bursting through the front door to tell my family I was alive and well.' But again he was disappointed. In the house where he was now lodging he slept in a downstairs room with a rifle by his side. It was an ancient weapon with a short barrel, clogged with dirt and unused since the First World War. He had never held a gun before but told himself he would fire it if he had to, knowing full well that such an action would cross a threshold and invalidate any claim he might have for POW status if he was caught. His helpers now were two brothers and 'I decided that if trouble arose I was not going to raise my hand, shout "*Kamerad*" and end up behind barbed wire as a prisoner of war while they were executed for helping me. I was prepared to take the same risk as them and to shoot our way out of trouble side by side.'

He felt himself veering from an evader to being a partisan, a far cry from the bank clerk he had been in civilian life. It was a conscious choice: 'I still wanted to get home to my family but I felt a growing affection for these people who were risking their lives for me. They were like my own brothers. I began to realize I could be of use to the Resistance. I forgot my dreams of England.'

The local maquis – Resistance fighters – were preparing for guerrilla warfare to back up the anticipated invasion. They were assured of arms drops when the time came for the acts of sabotage they planned, but until then they were to build up secret stocks of food and other supplies to draw on for the fight. At home, he and the brothers also made elaborate escape plans in case the house came under attack. They cut a concealed hatch in the roof of the loft from which they could get away in an emergency and plotted a route across the fields to the woods. But Teare knew the chances of escape were slim.

I would make a desperate run and be shot down. I would rather die a quick death than be captured. After being in hiding so long and having passed through so many links in the Resistance chain, I knew too much and didn't rate my chances of standing up to torture if the Nazis wanted that information out of me. I knew I would weaken and talk.

He thought himself incapable of suicide, even in extremis. There was one member of the Resistance group – a fireman who had gone underground rather than be conscripted to Germany to fight fires in bombed-out cities – who carried a razor blade sewn into his trouser turn-ups and had resolved to cut his wrists if caught. There was a story too of a British agent in Gestapo hands who bit through his own veins to die. Teare knew he did not have the willpower for that.

The times were dangerous; knowing whom to trust was a grow-ing problem. From conquerors confident of their control, the

Germans had become nervous occupiers, sensing the coming invasion, aware that every Frenchman was an enemy in waiting. The story was told of a pair of local gendarmes who came across five dirty, unshaven men on a country road. They identified themselves as Russian POWs on the run, and one of the gendarmes, a patriot at heart, wanted to let them go. But he did not know his colleagues' political leanings and so he said nothing. He helped round up the strangers at gunpoint and took them in. At the police station, the leader of the gang produced papers showing he was a Gestapo officer. They all were, on a mission to infiltrate the Resistance and flush out sympathizers. This was going to be a very dirty war.

Meanwhile, in Belgium, RAF bomb aimer Tom Wingham was being recruited into the Armée Blanche, the White Army, which was resisting the German occupied forces there. He landed in Holland after his Halifax was shot down in April on its way to bomb Düsseldorf and had been shunted south in the general direction of Spain before it became clear that the route to the mountains was no longer tenable. It wasn't just the German assault on the escape lines that was causing this. Allied bombers were pulverizing the French railway network as a preamble to Operation Overlord, the long-awaited invasion of northern Europe, hoping to slow the movement of German reinforcements to the landing beaches when the time came. The lines to the south on which hundreds of evaders had journeyed were now primary targets. The order was for those on the run to stop and dig in, probably for the duration. Wingham was sheltering in the house of a miner, though the man himself did not know. His wife and 21-year-old daughter had taken in the English airman and dared not tell the head of the house in case he turned him away. Wingham stayed in a locked bedroom, quiet as a mouse ('I did not snore in those days,' he recalled in old age), and was let out when the miner was at work on the 2–10 p.m. shift every day. Then he would have the freedom of the small house and while away the day, sometimes clearing the kitchen table for a game of ping-pong with Mady, the daughter, while her little dog snapped at his feet.

It was unreal – in occupied territory, the enemy all around and playing table tennis watched by a Pekinese. I almost forgot who I was and what I was doing there. Was this normality? But then normal for me had become sleeping at night with a bloke in the room next door not knowing I was there. When I asked the woman what would happen if her husband found me in the house, she said, 'He would tell you to leave.' But would he report me to the Germans? I asked. She didn't think so. 'You see,' she said, 'he is neither for the Germans nor against the Germans. He is neither for the English nor against the English. He's a miner. He would simply want you to go.'[5]

That she could keep the secret of her Resistance activities from her husband astounded Wingham. They clearly held polar opposite views on which way the war was going and this extraordinary gulf between them left Wingham uneasy about his safety. An approach to become a Resistance fighter himself offered him a way out. A visitor came in great secrecy to recruit him for a planned mini-army to harass the Germans in the Ardennes mountains. Wingham was in two minds.

I was aircrew trained, and crawling around in the forest with a .303 rifle was not really my style. Then again, I was dying to get back into the war. You feel so out of it as an evader. I also felt that, if there was going to be fighting, I would prefer to be out in the open rather than cooped up in a house with street fighting going on around me. So I agreed to go in the last resort. I said if things got bad, he could call on me to join his band.

He went sooner than expected. He was in the house on his own one evening, crouched by the radio to listen to the BBC, when from outside there was a squeal of tyres, slamming car doors and heavy footsteps running.

There was a crash on the door, and shouts to 'open up'. I tore upstairs to climb out through the bedroom window but Gestapo officers were already on the roof battering at the shutters to get in. I was trapped!

Instinct took over. I ran back down the stairs and into the cellar. I had never been down there before and it was dark with just a glimmer of daylight coming through a small grating. Apart from a few beer crates it was empty. Above me I could hear the smashing of windows and the pounding of footsteps.

I went to the darkest corner and by chance found a cavity in the wall. I tucked myself inside and pulled the crates across in front of me. I was just in time. Two Gestapo men were coming down the stairs and ferreting around. As I peered through the beer crates, hardly daring to breathe, they struck matches and walked towards me. My heart was thumping. Surely they must have seen me. They were so close I could smell them . . . And then they turned round and went back upstairs. I waited down there, wondering what to do. I didn't dare go back up in case someone was still there. At the very least, surely they would have left a guard on the door? I decided to stay where I was until the morning.

The raid was no chance affair. The visitor who just a day or two earlier had recruited him to the Armée Blanche had been arrested after a mistress he dumped denounced him. He yielded under torture. Wingham found out years later that, when the Germans arrived, the woman sheltering him had been just across the road in a shop. Seeing what was happening, she tried to rush back to save him. Friends restrained her to prevent her from being arrested. But she had returned when the Englishman finally plucked up the courage to leave the cellar the next day. 'She was in the bedroom collecting a few personal belongings. She was overjoyed to see me, for my "disappearance" had been a mystery. She and Mady were going into hiding, and I was to do the same.'

He was taken to the farm of a family involved in Resistance activities. One son would disappear at night to blow up electricity pylons, and everyone was involved when the railway line to and from Germany was raided. With the connivance of the level-crossing keepers, goods trains would be brought to a halt and wagon doors forced open for the locals to swarm on board and 'liberate' the stocks of potatoes and coal the Germans had stolen for themselves. It was training for the bigger liberation they dared hope for soon.

The Resistance members, however, were a mixed bunch, and falling in with them could be disconcerting, if not downright scary. 'A. B.' Smith, an air gunner shot down in May 1944, was one of three American airmen well settled on a farm in Belgium when a lorry pulled into the yard with a dozen hard-looking characters on the back.

They were a maquis band, unshaven, wearing rough rumpled clothing and heavily armed. They had pistols, ranging from World War I Lugers to Walther P-38s, hand grenades, rifles and Sten guns. They swaggered inside, to be met by the farmer's wife with politeness but not warmth. They needed somewhere to hide. She was resigned to having them there. Their leader was a beefy former sergeant in the Belgian army known as Commandant André, who kept a semblance of military discipline. But they handled explosives and firearms in a careless manner. When they told stories of dynamiting bridges and killing Germans, they would show off by waving their guns around or playing with the pin of a grenade. Some even put pistols to their head and pulled the trigger.[6]

Their wildness was demonstrated when they raided a farm nearby on the dubious grounds that its owner was pro-German. Like rustlers in a Western film, they returned with booty, including two pigs, one of which was slaughtered with a burst from a Sten gun. The Americans were appalled at what in their eyes was 'an act of outright robbery'. It reminded one of them of the stories his grandpa had told him about outlaws in the American Civil War. Their spirits sank further when the gang – for that was what they resembled – turned on one of their own members. He was physically the weediest of them, and André grabbed him and thrust a cocked revolver into his stomach as he bullied and berated him. The dressing down went on for a quarter of an hour as the horrified Americans watched, expecting the trigger to be pulled at any moment. The little man pleaded, denying whatever treachery or dereliction of duty he was being accused of, and finally tempers calmed and the gun was put back in its holster. What concerned the airmen even more was that they suspected this demonstration of machismo had been put on for their benefit. But worse was to come.

The next morning, the Americans were watching from an upstairs window when a stranger appeared in the yard on a bicycle. They had been warned about him. His name was Charles; he was a member of the group but he was attempting to wrest the leadership from André. The issue was about to be sorted. Charles walked in through the front door of the house, down the tiled hall and then opened the back door. A semi-circle of maquis stood facing him, Sten guns levelled. The Americans suddenly grasped that they were about to witness an execution.

There was no command. The executioners simply opened fire. Charles stumbled forward, making a desperate dash to escape, like a drunken sailor performing the hornpipe. Then he collapsed face down in a pile of manure, ringed by the people who just moments before he thought were his friends. Then there was more firing into his body before everything went quiet.

Charles had arrived with two of his men and they too were gunned down – an accident apparently. No harm had been intended to them but they had panicked when the first shots were fired, pulled out their guns to defend themselves and been mown down. It was a pity, the Americans were told, but *c'est la guerre*.

It was not, however, war as the airmen knew it or wanted to experience it. The Resistance in Europe was always riven by internal conflicts, whether personal (as appears to have been the case here) or political (with communists and nationalists at each other's throats over who would gain the post-war ascendancy). This was a private war into which evaders had no wish to be drawn. Smith and his friends moved to a different hiding place to await the arrival of the Allied armies.

★

The invasion was coming. Everyone knew that. As British, American and Canadian forces gathered for intensive training in southern England and the Supreme Allied Commander, General Dwight Eisenhower, drew up plans for the biggest ever sea-to-land assault in history, only the date of D-Day was in doubt. The urgency was greater for some than for others. In a safe house in Brussels, Flight Lieutenant Terry Bolter was deeply moved by a conversation with Jean, a middle-aged man working for the Resistance. The Belgian knew how close he came to death every day.

We are just a few men against the powerful organization of the Germans. No one is infallible. Sooner or later you make a mistake and bang . . . you are dead! It is so easy for people in England exhorting us on the BBC to be brave and to carry on the fight. But it is an uphill battle over here. Sometimes I wonder how many brave Belgians will die before the Boches are beaten. If the British don't come soon, it will be too late.[7]

Outside the window came the heavy tramp of a German patrol in the street, and knuckles went white as hands gripped the arms of the chairs until the enemy soldiers had passed by. Bolter wondered how much longer the Resistance could carry on in such conditions.

There was also the not insignificant question of whether or not Operation Overlord would *succeed*. The outcome was not to be taken for granted. Hitler's Atlantic Wall was a tough obstacle. The one great advantage the Allies had was that they could choose where along the 1,500 miles of northern-European coastline to mount the assault. The Germans were jittery. They didn't know where to concentrate their defences so everywhere north and west of Paris was on high alert. In Room 900 in the War Office in London, Airey Neave pondered what all this meant for him. His ferry service from Brittany would have to stop – the last one (for now) was in March. And the bombing of the French railways to hamper the movement of German troops was already making the journey south to Spain a risk too far. But that meant some 400 to 500 evaders being stuck where they had landed up – in countryside and in cities that would very soon be fierce battlefields. Nobody could expect the Allied military, embarked on a campaign that would decide the outcome of the war, to hold their fire to protect the lives of those marooned in the middle. They would also get short shrift if caught by an enemy on the defensive and possibly on the run. Neave took it on himself to try to find a way to protect them.

The easiest option was to tell them to keep their heads down and hope for the best. There was precedent for this. Six months earlier the Italians had surrendered and the order had gone from London to the British men in the POW camps in Italy to 'stand fast'. The army did not want tens of thousands of freed prisoners on the loose, possibly on the rampage, and getting in the way of the fighting that still had to be done against the Germans. In some camps, the men disobeyed. As soon as their Italian guards had gone, they scarpered too, heading for the hills and the coasts, linking up with partisans, tasting freedom. But in most camps the men stayed put as ordered, waiting to be officially liberated, processed by the powers-that-be and sent home. Their patience and their obedience cost them their liberty. Within forty-eight hours German soldiers had replaced the Italian guards in the goon-towers. Within weeks, the 50,000 POWs who stayed were on their way to camps in Germany and another year and a half of captivity.

Their sad fate never seemed to worry the military hierarchy, and it seems unlikely that Neave would have run into much trouble if he had just let matters take their course. But he wasn't that sort of man. Unlike those he worked for, he had seen the inside of German POW camps and knew the dreadful longueurs of life behind barbed wire. He also knew from first-hand experience the risks taken by local people who hid fugitives, 'the strained white faces in the lamplight of the kitchen, the knock at the door and the quick fear in their eyes'.[8] He conceived a plan to establish secret forest camps where evaders could congregate, be supplied with food from the air and, if necessary, be defended.

He hit a lot of opposition.

At MI9, my plan was considered imaginative but 'too risky'. It was argued over many meetings that the men would be safer staying hidden in Paris, Brussels and other large towns. But I felt that not only would food be scarce, but it was too much to ask individual families to run the risk of hiding the men until the Allied armies arrived. No one could foresee what progress they would make, nor was it possible to tell whether the Germans would defend Paris and Brussels. I also expected an outburst of SS and Gestapo activity against our agents.

Over everything hung the fear that if the Germans knew they were losing the war they would turn to brutal methods and spare no one. There was a danger that Allied airmen with false identity papers in civilian clothes would not in the future be treated as prisoners-of-war. Panic-stricken German troops might shoot them out of hand, along with those who helped them. Airmen might also take up arms and join Resistance groups as the Allies drew near, thereby running every chance of massacre by the SS.

For all these reasons I was sure the safest plan was to evacuate the men, especially from Paris and Brussels, and hide them as far as possible away from German troop concentrations. I knew that it was fraught with risk, but it was the best chance of saving these men from capture or summary execution as partisans.[9]

He prevailed, but only after overcoming very strong objections from Crockatt over the dangers of setting up what the brigadier called 'private armies'. What finally swayed him were his fears of a massacre if no precautions were taken. Neave now began recruiting agents to drop into France and Belgium to find sites for his camps. He received unexpected support from the Air Ministry for once, finally aware that the bulk of men in hiding were trained aircrew whose lives were in the balance. There was a new willingness to help with supply missions and parachute drops. In Brussels and Paris attempts were made to breathe life into the remnants of the Comet Line, now largely run by Michou Dumon, Nadine's 20-year-old sister. She continued the work even though the rest of her family, as well as Dédée de Jongh and hers, had been arrested and were in German concentration camps. But traitors – now led by a mysterious character with a finger missing on one hand – were still infiltrating the network and there was never any let-up in the betrayals and the arrests.

In London, Neave had first considered the idea of a chain of camps all the way down to the Spanish border, with evaders carried between them by lorry and bicycle. But with so many German troops now forced onto the roads because of the bombing of the railways, this seemed to involve too many risks. One camp was better, and Neave sat with a map of France and put his finger on the Fréteval forest, 200 square miles of thick woodland 100 miles south of Paris. It was dense but surrounded by open spaces ideal for parachute operations. He gave it the appropriate codename of 'Sherwood'. The route there from Paris was easy enough – train to the town of Châteaudun and then a ten-mile hike down country roads. Also in its favour was that the Resistance was very strong in the area. The only possible drawback was that it might become a battlefield itself if and when the Germans were forced back towards the Loire. Other camps were mooted, one near Rennes in Brittany for evaders stranded by the ending of the boat evacuation and another in the Ardennes for those in Belgium. But 'Sherwood' quickly became everyone's favourite. The officer in charge was to be a Comet Line veteran, Jean de Blommaert, known as 'the Fox'. He was parachuted into France and made his way to Paris to begin arrangements there.

The Paris escape network was in tatters. Michou Dumon had reluctantly fled to Spain as the Gestapo began tracking her, and de Blommaert was very nearly betrayed by a double agent as soon as he arrived. He geared up a Comet Line helper, Philippe d'Albert-Lake, to make arrangements for assembling and transporting evaders and then went south himself to set up the camp that would be their destination. In the little town of Cloyes he found farmers willing to supply the secret camp with fresh meat, vegetables, butter and eggs. It was no mean feat, given the severity of rationing then gripping France. Then, with the help of locals, he went out into the woods and chose a site among the trees. It had a spring of pure water and, despite having a road nearby, it was well concealed in the undergrowth. A slight slope provided easy surveillance of the approach and he reckoned the Germans would only find it if they actually walked right into it. He was joined by Lucien Boussa, an RAF squadron leader, whose job would be to marshal the men and keep them under control. Neave reckoned the biggest problem in the camp would be keeping order and preventing the men from trying to escape on their own, whether from boredom or claustrophobia. The squadron leader would keep them in line.

But a firm decision was taken that the men would not be armed. Guns and ammunition were dropped for the Resistance fighters who would protect the camp but were to be denied to the evaders so as not to jeopardize their status under the Geneva Convention. On 20 May the first evaders were brought by train from Paris and hidden in houses in the area. In the forest, a couple of tents bought on the black market were pitched, parachutes slung over branches as covers and supplies hidden. The bare bones of a camp were there, nothing more. Along the nearby road, Wehrmacht lorries and armoured cars pounded day and night. Was this site really so safe after all? It was too late for such thoughts. Everyone was on tenterhooks for the long-awaited invasion, and the signal that would bring Sherwood to life.

Meanwhile Terry Bolter had fled Brussels. Among the group hiding him arrests were coming thick and fast. He was almost taken himself. The Germans were jumpy, and when a sabotage bomb went off, he was stopped in the street by a patrol, made to put his hands in the air and frisked for weapons. The Germans let him go without questioning him, but it was a sure sign to leave. His friends took him to another house where eight American flyers were crowded into the living room. With Comet Line escorts they went by train to Paris. The organization had been infiltrated and undermined but it seemed to Bolter to be working with remarkable efficiency as they were picked up by new escorts in the French capital and taken to safe houses. Philippe d'Albert-Lake had quickly taken the line in hand, and he and his wife Virginia were putting together this very last trip south to the Pyrenees before concentrating their efforts on the Fréteval forest. Bolter spent a blissful few weeks at the Lakes' country house outside Paris. There were peaceful walks and parties with dancing, and he could have stayed. 'But I didn't want to wait for liberation in the camps. I had been an evader for nearly six months and if there was an opportunity of getting home sooner rather than later I wanted to take it, even if it meant a greater risk.'

His decision was all the braver because he would be travelling on his own. In Paris, a courier saw him onto the midnight train to Bordeaux and at the other end he was to be met by a girl trailing a green scarf. She wasn't there, so he set off on foot to an address he had been given. A cyclist came past, looked him over and then flashed a green scarf at him. She asked where he had been heading and when he told her she said, 'Everyone living there was arrested yesterday. There are Germans in the house now! There is nowhere else you can stay so you will have to wander about Bordeaux all day and then catch the last train to Bayonne. Here is your ticket. Don't go into cafés or into places of amusement. The Germans have doubled their patrols.' He did as he was told and was in Bayonne the next day. But there was now none of the practised drill there had been in the days of Dédée de Jongh. A well-dressed man whose name he never knew met him.

He told me that he had arranged for a band of smugglers to get me across the frontier into Spain. Very soon one of them would be arriving and would bring a bicycle for me. He then shook me by the hand, wished me '*Bonne chance*', and departed. It was not until I reached England that I learned he personally paid the thousands of francs to secure my safe passage into Spain.

The journey up the mountains in the mild spring weather, with lush grass underfoot and cloudless sky above, went well. Then it was into a chilling mist before ascent turned into descent and the twinkling lights of Spain came into view. They waded the river, silently skirting the German sentries on the bank, and suddenly it was all over. He reported to the Spanish police and told them the requisite lie that he was an escaped prisoner of war, not an evader.

It was 4 June 1944. The last trip of the Comet Line was completed, the final 'package' promised by Dédée de Jongh to the British consul in Bilbao three years ago had been delivered.

★

Less than forty-eight hours later, the world changed. Lancaster flight engineer Ray Worrall was crossing back over the English Channel at dawn after a bombing mission and from 6,000 feet looked down on an historic sight.

As far as the eye could see there were boats of every shape and size all going in one direction. The water behind them was streaked by the zig-zag wakes of the ships taking evasive action as they reached the danger zone. Flak was bursting and there were gun flashes from the French coast. I looked up to the sky. Not a German fighter to be seen, but hundreds of Allied aircraft, like the boats, all going in one direction.[10]

The news electrified Europe. In eastern France, Denys Teare crouched near the wireless on 6 June 1944 listening to every bulletin from London. Landing craft were swarming onto the Normandy beaches, paratroops and soldiers on gliders were already behind the German lines, bombers were devastating the coastal defences, a toehold had been secured. Tanks were now going ashore too. He listened in awe but also in dread. 'I hardly dared think what would happen if the invasion was beaten back. Perhaps the Allies would not be able to mount another for two or three years. That would be terrible for me and for the millions of people in Europe who were waiting to be freed.' Outside on the streets of Bar-le-Duc, the Germans were putting up a smokescreen of nonchalance, denying anything extraordinary was happening while stopping every vehicle they came across and searching it. Tension was high.

Down in the Fréteval area, the invasion was the signal for the thirty Allied airmen hidden in houses to move into their new forest home. It was more primitive than Neave had intended. A young girl delivered fresh bread every day on a horse-drawn cart and there was hot food from fires made of charcoal so as not to give off any smoke. It was shelter that was the problem, and it was to be another month before a successful parachute drop was made bringing tents, medicine and clothes. Communications were dreadful, with the wireless often out of operation. In Room 900 Neave tore his hair out, unable to find out what was happening. But numbers were pouring in and by the middle of August 150 evaders were camped under the greenwood trees like a band of latter-day Merry Men. RAF pilot Cliff Hallett was among them. He had been shot down just a couple of days before D-Day attacking railway sidings in Paris. The rest of his crew were either killed or captured – three of them caught hiding in a brothel in Paris and sent to Buchenwald concentration camp, this extreme measure an indication of how jumpy the Germans now were and how vindictive they could be towards Allied airmen who fell into their hands. He had wanted to go to Paris too but the Resistance fighter sheltering him ordered him south.

I was in this old Fiat being driven with two other airmen, an Australian and an American, and had no idea where we were being taken. We were passed from person to person until on the edge of a wood we met a man who interrogated us to make sure we were not German spies. He was carrying a huge stick with a knob on the end of it and I have no doubt that if he thought someone was an infiltrator he would use it to kill them.[11]

This man was one of the armed Resistance guards ringing the camp. He gave the nod to Hallett and pointed him into the forest.

We walked in and it was an amazing sight. There were tables and chairs all roughly hewn out of tree trunks and branches, pots, pans and cooking fires, and makeshift tents. I couldn't stop thinking of the teddy bears' picnic and the Boy Scouts. We were instructed not to make any noise so as not to give ourselves away. We talked in whispers. One night a Welshman who could speak French went off to visit some local farmers, drank too much Calvados and came back singing and shouting. He got into real trouble.

They slept on beds of straw, and the first task every morning at 6 a.m. was to cover the tents and equipment with fresh branches so that the camp could not be seen from the air. This was a protection not just against German spotter planes but also against marauding Allied fighters intent on beating up anything remotely military. Sentries were then chosen to lie up under cover and keep watch for anyone approaching. After that, each day was likely to drag. The weather was fine for sunbathing and recreations were devised, including chess with improvised pieces and golf with ersatz clubs and balls. For a while there was a large poker school, which ended when Hallett scooped the entire cash pot, around £600, and Squadron Leader Boussa, in charge of the camp, put a stop to gambling for fear that it would sour relations between the men. According to Hallett,

Boredom was the real enemy. Occasionally we got a glimpse of the pretty farmer's daughter, who came to get water at the well at the edge of the woods. Her sister looked after sheep in a meadow and men would ogle her too, though we didn't have any direct contact with them. They gave us something to talk about, however. A barber came once a week to cut our hair, and we got regular visits from a doctor. I was put on a special diet because I had internal injuries from my parachute drop.

The main topic of conversation was the progress of the war. The wireless operator posted news bulletins on a tree in the middle of the camp known as Hyde Park Corner, though none ever answered the question every man asked himself and his comrades constantly – when will we get out of here? And the news from Normandy was not cheering. The Allies had expected to gain a foothold and then storm through the French countryside. But the Germans dug in at towns like Caen and then the narrow country lanes bottled up the tanks and made progress slow. For those bedded down beneath the trees 125 miles away, the wait seemed interminable. Stopping men from breaking out through sheer impatience and nerves was a major problem for Boussa.

More evaders were now arriving all the time. They came by

bicycle, car and horse but most walked. Resistance volunteers would escort them down country lanes and back roads. Often they were given pitchforks and hoes to carry like authentic farm labourers. In an emergency they could slip into a field and pretend to be at work. With numbers swelling, a decision was made to split the camp. If the original was allowed to grow, so would the risk of discovery and once the first camp reached a total of twenty-five tents, a second one was set up a few miles away. Jean de Blommaert took command of this. Hallett believes there was another reason for the second site – animosity between the British and American contingents. 'We all had the same objective, the same hope of freedom and victory, but we could not stand each other.' He said the RAF boys disliked American braggadocio – 'everything in the US was twice as big, twice as nice as in England. They said only they could win the war and they did not like it when we told them they had not wanted to know about the events in Europe till Pearl Harbor and Hitler's declaration of war forced them to take up arms.' For the sake of peace, Boussa decided to separate the Allies before things got out of hand.[12]

One new arrival was Ray Worrall, who had been so awed by the sight of the D-Day invasion fleet. Seven weeks later he was unexpectedly in France himself, brought down by bombs dropped accidentally from another Lancaster above his in the formation. The tail sheered off and they went into a fatal dive. He was frozen by fear on the edge of the escape hatch, unable to believe this was really happening to him, and only a shove into space from the man behind saved his life. He tumbled through the air like Alice in Wonderland, he recalled. 'Down, down, down. Would the fall never end?' And then, when he hit the ground, he collected himself and ran off like the White Rabbit. He was alone in a country of huge uncertainties. It was a battlefield, or about to become one. It was a bad time to surrender. 'I thought the Germans wouldn't bother to take me prisoner. They would just take me into a field and shoot me.' But if he evaded, whom could he trust? Who would trust him? He was loath to seek help. His only thought was to head for the Allied army, now in Caen, so far as he knew. As he walked westward he trembled with fear when a car containing four German soldiers approached . . . and to his relief drove on past. Then a small boy on a bicycle came up to him and called out: 'Are you Ray?' When an astonished Worrall nodded, the boy went off and came back later in a car.

The driver was a tall man who spoke good English and I felt from the start that I could trust him. He gave me a civilian overcoat to put on and told me to get in the back of the car, and we drove off. It was wonderful after nearly three days of walking alone along French roads. He told me he was the local doctor and that his wife was English. We came to a farm and he took me into the kitchen and introduced me to the farmer and his wife. Then the doctor left and I never saw him or the boy again.

In a bedroom asleep he found his wireless operator, Ken – which was why the boy had known his name – and a Canadian air gunner from another plane. 'It was a great comfort to be with friends and not alone any more.' That night they drank champagne, bottle after bottle. Apparently a train taking supplies to German army headquarters in Paris had been bombed by the RAF, and the locals took their pickings from the wreckage. The next morning two more RAF evaders arrived, along with some Frenchmen.

We were told we were going on a long walk. By mid-afternoon, footsore and weary, we approached a large forest covered in thick foliage. Our French friends left us and we continued along a path and there was this amazing camp in the woods. The skipper [from his plane] was there, and we all shook hands amid cries of, 'Fancy you bloody fellas turning up again.'

It was almost like being back in a RAF community again, except that everyone was in scruffy civilian suits and unwashed and unshaven. It was great to have so many people around, though I realized we were still in plenty of danger, with Germans all around us. There was still a long way to go before we'd get home.

Worrall thought life in the forest 'boring, rough and dangerous'. The spring proved inadequate for so many men and most just went filthy rather than go through the trouble of washing either themselves or their clothes. Lice became a problem. Food was meagre – coffee and a slice of bread for breakfast, beans for lunch with a little rabbit meat, bread for supper. Occasionally there was fish, which locals caught and brought from the River Loire. Another Sherwood 'outlaw', Flight Lieutenant Alex Campbell, recalled green apples as the main diet. He also became adept at making ersatz coffee from roasted barley seeds. And chocolate bars could be melted into a bedtime drink. 'We would enjoy this while listening to the BBC news and often the Vichy version as well. Then we would compare the two reports and come up with a fairly accurate picture of the approaching Allied forces.'[13]

The two things the men had in abundance were cash from their escape kits – but nowhere to spend it – and wasps. The trees were riddled with nests and they were stung constantly, a dozen times in one day in Worrall's case. But he was cheered when, a few days after his arrival, his radio operator, navigator, bomb aimer and rear gunner turned up. The gunner was hobbling with the aid of a stick, having literally shot himself in the foot. Against regulations, he had taken to carrying an RAF-issue revolver with him on operations and had been showing it off to one of his guides, bragging about its power compared with the ancient pistol the Frenchman packed, when it went off. The bullet put a hole in his ankle. Of Worrall's seven-man crew, six survived and were brought to the forest. When they returned home it was only the tail gunner who got the DFC, for his ankle wound!

On a number of fraught occasions, the Fréteval camp came close to discovery. Cliff Hallett recalled the night when a unit of 300 German soldiers set up camp less than 100 yards away. The evaders went into emergency mode, dousing the fires and not even daring to whisper.

That night we had nothing to eat and couldn't speak. It was quite terrifying. Boussa said that if anything happened it was every man for himself. This was particularly worrying for me because I was injured and still on a stretcher at that point.[14] He said they wouldn't be able to carry me so I would have to be left. The Germans would get me and all he asked was that I keep my trap shut for twenty-four hours to give everyone a chance to get as far away as possible. 'Then you can tell them whatever you like,' he said. It was a pretty nasty prospect, given what the Germans were capable of.

Fortunately the unit pulled out the next morning, unaware that they had been sleeping within a stone's throw of scores of fugitive Allied airmen. 'It was a huge relief in every sense,' Hallett said. 'It meant we could have breakfast!' Incredibly, the local German forces kept away from the forest. They would from time to time fire volleys into the undergrowth but never ventured in. The only outsider to penetrate the camp was a scruffy man who wandered too close and was brought in by the sentries. He spoke a language no one knew and was thought to be a Russian deserter or an escaped prisoner of war. He could not be allowed to leave in case he was picked up by the Germans, so he stayed, and paid for his keep by doing all the unpleasant menial jobs. But the disaster those in the camp always feared came frighteningly close one day – and was averted only by one woman's outstanding courage.

★

Virginia d'Albert-Lake was an American in her mid-thirties from Dayton, Ohio, who had come to France in 1936 and a year later married Philippe. They were Resistance workers, using their flat in Paris and their isolated house in the country twenty-five miles from the capital to hide Allied airmen on the run. Virginia found the work exhilarating as she escorted evaders through the French capital, arm in arm and chatting intimately like lovers to allay suspicions. One day she was hailed by a family friend and simply kept on walking, preferring the reputation of an unfaithful wife to dangerous explanations. Her job had been to deliver men to the trains taking them south to the Pyrenees, but then had come the new instructions to send them to Fréteval. A backlog of men was already building up. She and Philippe had eight crammed into the Paris flat and feeding them became a major problem. Food had to come from the black market and in quantities that might raise eyebrows. Once when cycling home with a basketful she fell and tin cans rolled everywhere, but luckily no one saw. She cooked on a two-ring stove as best she could, given that there was gas for only an hour or two a day. After picking up evaders from other Paris safe houses, it was a party of a dozen that finally set off for the camp, some of them reluctantly when they were told the possible dangers ahead. They took the train as far as they could, which in the post-D-Day transport chaos was the town of Dourdan, a good sixty miles from the forest.

Over the next two days the men and their girl escorts walked to Châteaudun, sometimes in small groups of two and three, at others bunched up and very conspicuous on the country roads. Virginia and Philippe rode back and forth between them on bicycles, encouraging them on. It was hard on bodies unfit because of weeks of inactivity while in hiding. Blisters and fatigue slowed the pace. In villages they passed the people were unreceptive, cowed by a recent sweep by German troops and the arrest of those found sheltering fugitives. There were other dangers too. Allied fighter planes were buzzing around, shooting up anything that moved at speed on the open roads. They passed a lorry on its side riddled with bullets and then watched an attack on a German munitions train in the distance. At Châteaudun, there were Resistance friends waiting and a place to stay despite a heavy presence of German soldiers in the town. The final leg of the journey lay ahead and for the foot-weary evaders it was made easier by the acquisition of a horse and covered cart. Philippe went ahead to the forest to warn that they were coming and Virginia on her bicycle led the strung-out procession that now wended its way the last few miles to Fréteval. She recalled:

I was up front with Al, one of the American airmen. We were on our last stretch of road, with which I was already familiar, so I put away the map. We had ridden too far in advance of the cart, so stopped to wait.

It was hot and Al took off his coat and put it in my bicycle basket. Then, with a happy smile, he said: 'Isn't it wonderful that we're nearly there! To think that we hesitated about making the trip and nothing has happened at all! I do admire your courage!' I said: 'Thanks, Al, but don't say such things. We're not there yet.'

Just then the cart hove into sight around the bend behind us, and we mounted our bikes and rode on. A stranger joined us, pedalling in from a side road and we continued this way for about a kilometre, the three of us in single file, the wagon about fifty yards behind.[15]

They were approaching a main road, from which a large black car unexpectedly turned and headed in their direction.

I felt nervous. What was such a car doing on a desolate side road like this? I pulled to the side to let it pass, but instead it stopped. There were three men in it – German police! One of them ordered us to get off our bicycles and then they came over and asked for our identity papers.

As she wrote down this account many years later, Virginia trembled when the entire scene came back to her 'in frightening vividness'.

I handed over my identity card, which stated that I was born an American citizen. I had never pretended otherwise, as it would have been impossible considering the strong accent with which I spoke French. The Nazi glanced at my card. 'What are you doing in this region when your identity card states that you live in Paris?' he asked gruffly in perfect French. 'We have been searching the farms for fruit and eggs,' I lied.

He glanced at Al and the stranger and asked: 'Are you with these two men?' I said: 'No, we were riding together quite by accident. They joined me from a side road further back.' As I said it I was conscious of Al's coat in my basket, and obviously a match for the trousers he was wearing. I wondered if they had noticed it.

I tried to appear unconcerned and prepared to mount my bicycle, but I was tense and trembling. I knew that this moment was a crossroads in my life. I pushed down on the pedal but the Nazi roared: 'Not so fast.' Something broke inside me. I knew it was all over. The sun that only a few minutes ago was so bright and warm, now seemed eclipsed by a grey fog of fear. Sweat started in my armpits and my scalp tingled as I stood there in the dusty road, gripped my handle bars and waited.

It was indeed over. The Germans questioned the stranger, his papers were in order and they let him go. That left Al.

He looked tense and wretched as he handed over his ID card, which stated that he was French. But he could not speak the language. He tried bluffing at first with a '*oui*' or a '*non*' but made no sense. 'You're an American, aren't you?' the German said.

Virginia had been right about Al's coat in her basket. The German had noticed it and it was her lie about them being strangers that had alerted him, he told her. Now all she could hope for was that the others in the party would not be taken too, and she glanced behind to see the cart stopping about thirty yards away and the men sneaking out of the back and disappearing into the under-growth. The Germans saw nothing. 'I was so grateful.' She was very scared. Though she kept her composure, 'inside a heavy misery was clutching at me and dragging me down'. This was compounded when she realized she was carrying on her a list of Resistance members in Châteaudun that Philippe had written out for her: 'A feeling of guilt came over me which was worse than anything I had yet suffered. All the people I had met in Châteaudun, the grocer and his toddler, the farmer and his family, they all rose up before my eyes. I was miserable.'

In this alone she was lucky. One of the Germans searched her bag, found a map, then the note. He turned it over in his hand, and then put it back along with the rest of the contents and returned the bag to her. While he wasn't looking, she slipped her hand inside the bag, surreptitiously tore the note to shreds and slipped the pieces into her pocket. Later, at the German police headquarters, she crammed them into her mouth, chewed and swallowed them. She had saved others. She could do nothing to save herself. A guard nonchalantly told her, 'You will probably be shot tomorrow morning. We haven't time to judge people since the invasion.'

He was sitting on a desk, his legs dangling. I was standing in front of him, quite weak at the knees. But I thought, if they shoot me, they shoot me, but I won't talk. No matter how frightened, I would not give him the satisfaction of showing it. So I remained erect, confidently smiling. 'Aren't you frightened?' he asked. 'Don't you realize you'll soon be in the hands of the Gestapo?' I did not answer.

Al and I were driven to Chartres. It was dark when we arrived but I glimpsed the beautiful spires of the cathedral before we stopped outside the great heavy door of the city prison. It opened and I was led along shadowy corridors and down an echoing stone stairway to an underground cell. My guide indicated a straw mattress on the dirt floor, and threw me a smelly blanket. I heard him close the door, turn the key in the lock and slide a heavy bolt into place. Then his footsteps died away. There was complete silence and utter darkness. I was in a dungeon.

A living nightmare was about to begin.

The news of her arrest, brought by the airmen on the horse and cart who eventually found their way there, caused consternation in the Fréteval camp. Extra sentries were posted and Boussa put the men on alert to flee at any sign of a German attack. 'They could come at any time,' he told an assembly at Hyde Park Corner. A forester with a cottage at the edge of the wood laid a fire in the grate to light as a signal if he saw troops approaching. It was the only warning they would get and if they saw smoke from his chimney they should run like blazes. The fire was never lit. Virginia kept her silence – at terrible cost, as we will see.[16]

Elsewhere in occupied Europe, others were hearing the slam of prison doors in those difficult days following the D-Day invasion. Welsh airman Jim Davies had successfully stayed hidden in Friesland in the north of the Netherlands for four months, living in ordinary homes. There the Resistance was involved less in armed activities and sabotage and more in hiding anyone the Germans sought – Jews, young men required for labour in the Third Reich and Allied airmen. There were no formal escape lines and no network of British agents. Holland was MI6's greatest wartime failure. All its secret operations there were compromised from the very beginning. There were some attempts to get evaders to the coast and home by submarine. A few were ushered north in the direction of Scandinavia. But the best bet for an evader like Davies was to bed himself in. And this he did until the invasion. Allied troops were on European soil but it would be a long time before they reached Holland. He felt inspired to go south and be liberated sooner rather than later. With false papers as a businessman, he travelled first class by train, sharing a compartment with a German officer, to Arnhem and then on to Nijmegen and Tilburg, from where he crossed over into Belgium. There he was taken up by the Belgian Resistance in the shape of a girl named Anna. She was attractive and neatly dressed and encouraged him to walk beside her rather than follow at a distance as was the case with some couriers. Together they took the tram into Antwerp and then strolled arm in arm to a safe house. He stayed there a week until Anna came to fetch him.

She said she was taking me to meet the head of the Resistance in Antwerp who would help me on my way to the Allied armies in France. It was a glorious Sunday morning in early August 1944 and I was excited, convinced I was only a day's journey away from freedom. Anna handed me over as promised and I went with this man to his office. He told me that he would provide me with a French passport and take me by car to a little French village near the front line, where I would wait for the Allied advance.

Then he interrogated me about the RAF and followed that with questions about my journey from Friesland. He said the Resistance wanted to compensate all the good patriots who had helped me and asked for a list of names.[17]

For a reason he was never quite sure of, Davies was cagey.

I told him they had all given false names – which wasn't the case – and I would be delighted to let him know after the war when they got in touch with me. Then we got in a car, to go to France, or so I thought. Instead we drove to Antwerp jail. There the so-called Resistance leader announced, 'I am a Gestapo officer', and with a click of his heels he left. I had been betrayed. The diarrhoeal truth hit me. I was angry, helpless and afraid.

Later he would learn that Anna was a traitor working for the man with the missing finger: Prosper de Zitter, a Belgian collaborator who with his agents systematically infiltrated the escape line between Holland and Belgium, causing hundreds of arrests and many deaths. Davies was just one of many victims – and in civilian clothes with two forged passports and a Belgian work card and no longer in possession of his RAF identity disc, his prospects did not seem good.

I was thrown into a filthy little cell, 8 ft by 4 ft, bare except for a bucket in one corner, a straw mattress alive with bugs on the stone floor and a picture of Hitler on the wall. I was not the first airman to enter it. A previous occupant had written in English above the door: 'Abandon hope all ye who enter here.'

For others, though, the arrival of Allied forces on German-occupied soil was a chance to hit back. Sergeant John Vallely had been evading in France ever since Dunkirk, living in Normandy and working with the Resistance. The struggle for the landing beaches was still going on when a German fighter plane crash-landed near his village. 'I was a soldier, still fighting a war, and I realized that this pilot was about to return to his base, pick up another plane and start attacking the invasion forces again. He had to die.' The German was shot. Four years of humiliating occupation was paid for. 'You would have to experience it to understand,' Vallely said in defence of this action.[18]

Walter Farmer, an RAF air gunner, went into action against the Germans too after D-Day. He had been shot down ten weeks earlier over Belgium. His was a miracle escape from a burning bomber. He had been clambering towards the escape hatch as the wing broke off and the plane lurched drunkenly. He reached out to grab something . . . which proved to be the door handle. The door opened and he just fell. He remembered nothing before regaining consciousness on a forest floor, his parachute stretched out alongside him. He had headed into France and it was there that he wandered into a band of guerrilla fighters in a forest.

The man in charge was a Free French major, his second-in-command an English SAS captain. There was also an American lieutenant. They were well supplied with arms, ammunition and explosives, all dropped by planes. The silk from the parachutes was used to make tents, so we had comfortable quarters. Everything was fine at first and morale was high because our numbers were growing. Six more French officers parachuted in and after the news of the invasion local recruits were coming in to join up all the time.[19]

This proved their undoing. One of the new boys went home to see his wife and was captured by the Germans. They made him talk and then launched an all-out assault on the camp. Soldiers swarmed into the forest and in their first attack shot and captured the SAS captain. A furious firefight broke out in the thick woodland as the Resistance mounted a rearguard action, pulling back but giving (and suffering) large numbers of casualties as they retreated tree by tree.

The Germans could not advance without a lot of noise as they broke their way through the undergrowth. We would lie still with our Sten guns and wait until they got near before ambushing them. But then they brought up their artillery and shelled us all night long. We took a lot of casualties. It was a terrible time, the worst I ever encountered in my life. I felt sure I was going to die.

They were forced back into a gradually closing pocket in the woods.

We were caught in a triangle. One side was the River Meuse, another a road and the third a railway. The major decided we would have to break out, and we split up into three groups to go out in different directions. The group I was in went for the road, which the Germans were patrolling with tanks and armoured trucks. We waited for a gap and ran across at high speed, down the high bank on one side and up the bank on the other. Bullets were flying everywhere. I remember one of our men charged at the Germans, a Bren gun on his hip, firing furiously at them. He had just heard that his brother had died in Germany and he wanted revenge. They got him but his selfless action saved many lives on our side as we beat a retreat under his covering fire.

The maquis scattered into even denser forest where tanks and trucks could not follow. Farmer had survived but the unit was smashed. He hid in the forest for three days with nothing to eat but a piece of old mouldy cheese and some grass. Liberation might be close as the Allied armies finally fought their way out of the Normandy bottleneck and swept into the French hinterland but staying alive until then was a completely different matter.

*

Gordon Carter was pottering around the dusty garden outside his hut in Stalag Luft III at Sagan in Poland when the news of the D-Day landings reached him. A huge shout went up. 'They've landed!' In the bleakness of this far-flung prisoner-of-war camp, devastated just two months earlier by the murder of fifty RAF officers who had tunnelled out in the so-called Great Escape, this was a moment of profound happiness. It was a joy to know that prisoners (and evaders, of course) were no longer the only Allied servicemen with their feet on European soil. The landing beaches might be a thousand miles away but Act One of the drama that would eventually release them from a barbarous captivity had begun. Carter should not, of course, have been anywhere near German-occupied territory. He had been shot down back in 1943 and made his way home by fishing boat from Brittany in one of the very first cross-Channel escapes. MI9 had tried to recruit him for a role in the Shelburne escape line but he had declined. He chose to get back into the air. Most RAF evaders who got home were kept away from front-line service on their return. The reasoning was that, if they were shot down again and if the Germans identified them, they would be tortured for details of their escape and those who had helped them. It was sound thinking – and ignored in his case on the dubious grounds that, since he had never at any time been in German hands, his name was unknown to them.[20]

After getting home he was deemed by the squadron doctor to be suffering from 'strain of escaping enemy territory' and sent on two weeks' sick leave. Then it was back in the air. On reflection, he thinks it was unwise to let him go. It definitely would not have happened if he had been in the American air force. Its evaders who made it to Britain were invariably ferried back to the US almost immediately. 'But at the time I had no problem. I just said I am going back to my Pathfinder squadron and they said here's the ticket. I didn't have to argue with anybody, and I was pleased to be back.'[21]

In the US he was something of a hero because of his exploits. He was awarded a DFC, which was enthusiastically reported by the press in the town in which he had spent his teenage years. The *Bronxville Review-Press* had been following his RAF career with huge interest. It had written about his return and now, with his medal for heroism, it repeated the story, as it did again when he received his medal from King George VI at Buckingham Palace. It was fame, however fleeting, that he would later come to rue. For now, though, he was back in the air, his log book filling with impressive operations such as Hamburg and the German flying-bomb research centre at Peenemünde. And, when off-duty, he wrote long and loving letters to Janine, the girl he had met all too briefly in Brittany but to whom he felt drawn for ever.

Years later he would remember these jottings as rather matter-of-fact, about his squadron life and his family. In fact they were outpourings of deep love and longing. '*Je pense à toi toute la journée. Non seulement celle-ci mais celle d'hier, d'avant hier et ainsi. Je t'aime beaucoup.*' ('I think of you all day long, not just this day but

yesterday and the day before that and so on. I love you very
much.')²² He longed to hold her close, to have her in his arms at
night. He tried to picture her hair, her eyes, her face, her mouth,
but none of his efforts could quite capture *vraiment* the real her.
These were letters written into a void. They could not be sent.
There was no postal service into occupied France. Each lovingly
composed letter, in immaculate French, was sealed in an envelope
and sent to Carter's Aunt Dot in Haslemere, Surrey. She had
instructions to send them to Janine once France was liberated if he
himself 'should happen to be out of the picture by then'. He
contemplated his death – a 15 per cent chance, as he told Janine in
one of those letters – and becoming a prisoner of war – 45 per cent.
His chance of seeing out the war unscathed he put at 30 per cent.

And that being the case, he decided to prepare himself to evade
again, should it be necessary. He was encouraged in this by the
new pilot he teamed up with, Squadron Leader Julian Sale, also an
experienced evader. He had come down in Holland in 1943 and
made a remarkable return home via Belgium, France and Spain
without the help of any escape organization. He walked and cycled
most of the 800 miles. RAF historian Air Commodore Graham
Pitchfork rates him as 'one of the great air force evaders' and the
citation for the DSO for his epic journey declared 'his unconquerable spirit of determination, great gallantry and fortitude have set
an example beyond praise'.²³ Carter and Sale both knew better
than anyone what lay out there in a Europe under the Nazi heel.
Physical fitness could be the difference between captivity and
freedom, life and death.

Julian and I would get up at 4 a.m. and go for long runs around the
airfield. We also practised penetrating the perimeter fence and attacking
parked aircraft. We had two organized exercises where we were taken
out in a lorry at night and dumped in the middle of nowhere to get
ourselves back to base without being picked up by the police. We took
them so seriously we even set fire to the odd haystack to divert attention
from where we were actually going.

He and I also took to carrying civilian clothes with us on operations in specially made lightweight packs on our backs underneath the Mae West and the parachute harness. I'd also bought a revolver in the local town. This was all because I felt pretty sure I would eventually be shot down again.

In fact it was a mechanical fault that next got him. They were returning from a wasted trip to Frankfurt. Low cloud made it pointless dropping the flares they carried to mark the target for the bomber stream coming in behind them and they went home with the fireworks intact. At 1,200 feet and coming in to land, a flare went off in the bomb bay and the Halifax filled with smoke and fire. Navigator Carter baled out and landed in a field but Sale, having given the order, noticed the mid-upper gunner's parachute had gone up in flames and stayed at the controls to land the burning ship. He got a bar to his DSO for that piece of raw courage. The incident took its toll on Carter. Though outwardly he was having a fine social time, visiting friends in London, lunching at the Savoy, basking in the glory of the three stripes he carried on his arm as a squadron leader, inside he was suffering. The stress of close on fifty operations was getting to him and he badly wanted a respite – hardly unreasonable given all he had been through. Only the greater fear of being declared LMF (lacking moral fibre) stopped him, though he admitted, 'I was at the end of my tether. I wasn't afraid of being shot down or even dying. But my capacity to do my job properly was diminishing. I knew I wasn't far off becoming flak-happy, where you begin to do stupid things.'

His problem was solved by the enemy. On a flight to distant Leipzig in February 1944, German fighters were waiting over Holland. It was one of Bomber Command's worst nights with seventy-nine aircraft lost. Sale corkscrewed, yawing to port and starboard, nose up and nose down, trying to throw off the attackers but a Ju-88 got underneath and took out the innards of the Halifax with its upward-slanting guns. It burst into flames.

Julian immediately gave the order to bale out, and after what seemed like ages fighting the centrifugal force flattening me against the fuselage as the kite started to spin out of control, I went through the hatch. I felt immense relief at finding myself alive and on the end of a chute, albeit over Germany. I knew this had saved me from the ignominy of having to ask to be taken off ops.

It was a long, cold, oxygen-starved descent from four miles up, falling for some twenty minutes through the thick of the 800-strong bomber stream following behind the Pathfinders. 'I could see the shapes roaring past me.' He thought himself very lucky not to have been hit by a wing or have his parachute collapse as someone's slipstream stole his air. In his head was the thought of getting away. He guessed he was in Germany this time, a different kettle of fish from France, where he had landed before. But he fully expected to get home 'if I just put one foot in front of the other westwards'. He landed in snow, buried his parachute and followed a track to a road. A sign pointed to Celle, a town between Hamburg and Hanover. As the sun rose he muttered '*Guten Tag*' to people he passed. He had already discarded his revolver, realizing it would probably draw more hostility than help. Now he ditched his distinctive RAF Omega watch. He also put on the civilian suit he had brought with him. In his head he had a vision of crossing the border into Holland and sinking a welcome jug of Dutch beer. To anyone he met he pretended to be a foreign worker, and the ruse worked until he met some children. Trained to report any strangers, they ran off to tell a sailor shooting crows in a field, who turned his shotgun on Carter and marched him off. He had lasted three days and travelled forty miles. 'I was bitterly disappointed I hadn't got any further.'

He was treated well enough by the local officials he was taken to and was soon handed over into the custody of the Luftwaffe. Just north of Frankfurt was Oberursel, the Luftwaffe's interrogation centre for downed Allied airmen, and it was here that he was processed into the POW system. The routine questioning began to take a sinister turn when he got hints that they knew he had been an evader once before. He began to worry. He told them he had stolen the civilian suit he was wearing when captured, except that the photographs of himself he had in his pocket – for use on forged papers and obviously taken in England – had him wearing it. Had they noticed the discrepancy in his story? What was more, the suit was one he had acquired in Brittany. Here were clues that an astute investigator might put together to reveal his secret.

I sat there waiting for the fateful moment when he would let on knowing about my 1943 evasion or question me about the photograph. I must assume to this day that he was completely unaware of this, for otherwise I would have been passed to the Gestapo.

But the fear of the Germans discovering he had been a fugitive before and torturing him to extract the name of Janine and all the others who had helped him last time hung over him throughout his time behind barbed wire. She was a worry but also a consolation. 'My thoughts were always with her and the hope that I was going to see her again.' For him, freedom was a long cold winter and a dangerous spring away. On the other side of Europe, however, liberation was coming closer every day.

# 9. *Libération!*

The hundreds of thousands of Allied ground troops now pouring onto the European continent were fortified with an MI9 lecture on what to do if they found themselves cut off behind enemy lines. It was delivered by intelligence officers with the sternest injunction not to be caught. 'Your job is to fight, and only through wounds, lack of ammunition or food should you ever allow yourself to be captured.'[1] And if captured, a soldier's duty was to escape and get back to his lines 'at the earliest opportunity. We want back every possible man with his arms and equipment.' In the meantime he was encouraged to be as great a nuisance as possible to his captors. 'Every German soldier occupied in guarding you or searching the countryside for you is one less in Germany's war machine.' What followed was the familiar advice developed by Brigadier Crockatt and his men over three years of monitoring mainly RAF evaders – approach farmers, priests, doctors and teachers for help, and only do so when the person was alone, never in a crowd. 'With all these people be honest, answer their questions (unless in regard to military operations). Remember they do not know that you are genuine and they have to be careful.' Then that 'earliest opportunity' point was made again, with an added threat.

Remain hidden with your host as long as may seem desirable. But don't overdo it, no matter how attractive the daughter may be! Keep in mind your job is to get back to your own lines. One evader in France found life very comfortable staying with a farmer. The daughter was attractive. He married her. The old man is dead and he now owns the farm and has two children. But we have that man 'taped' and he will find he will have to answer some very awkward questions at his court martial!

For those who were left without shelter and help, there were also detailed survival tips on everything from changing your socks to how to skin and cook rodents (ten minutes for a well-done rat, five for a mouse) and boil up stinging nettles for their nutrition. Dead dogs found in the road should only be eaten if still warm. 'It is possible that your bowels will not move regularly,' another tip offered, an unsurprising observation in the circumstances. 'Do not let this alarm you.'[2]

How many soldiers ever put such advice into practice is unknown, though the battling in Normandy that summer was intense and the Allies had it far from their own way. The Germans fought hard to contain the invasion to a pocket by the beaches, and it was not until the middle of August that they were forced out of Normandy. Then and only then did the rest of France lie wide open to the advancing British and American forces. They were nervous times until then, and it was into this uncertain maelstrom that airmen were still falling in considerable numbers. There had been no let-up in the air war. Bomber Command and the Eighth Air Force had been diverted to invasion-linked targets in the run-up to D-Day but, with that work done, they returned to strategic bombing of Germany.

Nineteen-year-old Jetty Cook from West Texas was scrambling back in a shot-up B-17 from a run to an aircraft factory in eastern Germany. As the plane lost height, the crew threw overboard guns, equipment, anything weighty they could lay their hands on, to try to keep her in the air long enough to cross out of German airspace. At 1,000 feet, it was time for the crew to go, and top-turret gunner Cook was happy to be floating on the end of his parachute – until bullets fizzed passed him in the air. To his horror he saw German soldiers on the ground lining them up as targets. He was lucky to escape but as soon as he landed he heard vehicles coming his way. Then he saw them – half a dozen soldiers with dogs, now surrounding his radio operator and pummelling him with their rifle butts, then turning to fire at the fleeing figure of his co-pilot, who slumped to the ground. Cook kept out of sight and when the soldiers had gone he walked westward and found shelter at a farm. To his relief he was in Belgium and his rescuers were active in the Resistance. They gave him a choice – turn himself in to the Germans and go to a POW camp or join them in the fight. He decided to stay and found himself welcomed wholeheartedly because he could drive a car, unlike many Belgians of his age.

His skill was quickly put to good use . . . on a bank raid.

We had three cars with four Belgians in each, all heavily armed with pistols and sub-machine guns. I stopped just past the bank, while three of the fellows went in, guns drawn, and came out with two German soldiers chasing. The guys in one of the other cars took care of them and we all raced away.[3]

In a trice he had gone from air gunner to Jesse James, though the booty was not money but food coupons. The group was harbouring so many Allied airmen, they were short of rations. But this was a brutal war he had joined. In Liège he was boarded with a family: a husband and wife and an eight-year-old girl.

Jack, a Canadian officer, and I were with them just three days when the Resistance came and hurried us away. We grabbed our personal effects, just toothbrush, razor and spare shirt collar, and ran to a waiting car, one of those wood-burning contraptions they had because there was no petrol. As we were crossing a bridge we saw German soldiers cutting off the road behind us and three SS cars drive up to the building we had just been in. Somebody must have tipped them off that we were there. The man, woman and their daughter were dragged out, and I heard a couple of days later that they were executed, the little girl too.

His next refuge was a bordello thronged with German customers. 'It was a very safe place. All the girls were members of the Resistance and they picked up useful information from their work. We weren't allowed to touch any of the wares but from the attic we could hear jackboots up and down the stairs all night long.' For contrast he was then moved to a convent, where he found more than forty Allied evaders like himself hiding. From there another Resistance operation beckoned.

Jack and I drove to a forest about fifteen or twenty miles south of Liège. There were fifteen to twenty Belgians there and our mission was to blow up a railway bridge The four-man team I was with had the job of taking out a German guardhouse. We approached it around 2 a.m. and I saw a soldier sitting with his back to me, smoking a cigarette. I slipped a piece of piano wire over his head and garrotted him. His helmet came off in the struggle and the noise alerted the other guards so we took care of them too.

Ten minutes later we heard a train coming. Two Belgians had floated down the river on a raft and set explosives underneath the bridge. As the train reached the middle, they hit the detonator and blew it up. There were a dozen carriages full of German soldiers heading for the front in France. Most of them went into the river, and we had men on both sides machine-gunning them.

Cook estimated that several hundred German soldiers were killed that night. It was some revenge for the little girl and her brave mother and father.

The dangers local helpers faced could never be underestimated. RAF wireless operator Frank Haslam was also in Belgium and hurried away from the first house he was welcomed into when he counted eleven barefoot children coming down the stairs to stare at him. They watched wide-eyed as he drank a cup of milk, ate some cake and then accepted a gift of some hand-rolled cigarettes from their father before setting out again into the night. He knew the invasion had changed the game for men on the run, for better and for worse. They had somewhere to run to now – their own lines. But equally the enemy would be on high alert and nervy. He picked up some silvery paper he saw strewn around him. It was 'window', the metal-coated strips of chaff jettisoned by bombers like his to confuse the German radar. He turned it over in his hand, 'a little bit of England', and that led to thoughts of home.

I tried to picture Mum and Dad. What would their immediate reactions be to the news that I was missing in action? Each time I had said my farewells I had seen fear in Mum's eyes. Dad knew there was an even chance of me not coming back but outwardly always appeared cheerful. Mum would need a whole lot of condolence and she had not been in good health in recent years.

I had always told them that if anything did happen they must never give up hope until the worst had been confirmed. I could of course give myself up now and they would be informed in due course that I was a POW. No. I had to have a go at getting home. I had to live with myself for the rest of my life and I had never been a quitter.[4]

Now a new family appeared to take care of him. He spent some time observing a particular house on the outskirts of a village in the Flemish part of Belgium. It was dark before he plucked up the courage to knock on the door and was greeted like a long-lost relation.

A young man pounced on me and hugged and kissed me on the cheeks time after time, crying 'Engels, Engels'. I was not used to such emotion and felt embarrassed as he held me at arm's length and took a long look at me. Then photographs were produced of a good-looking fellow – 'Mijn broeder, en Engleand' – and then of a younger man, 'Ook mijn broeder – Gestapo kaput.'

It turned out his brother Gaston had been shot by the Germans a few months earlier for Resistance activities. The other brother, Michel, had escaped to England to join the Free Belgian Forces. They brought me Gaston's dark pinstriped two-piece double-breasted suit to replace my RAF uniform.

That night he lay snug in a bed, looking out through the window at the stars. Home still beckoned. There was a girl in Skegness, near his base, who would be wondering where he was, and another in Manchester he had met on basic training in Blackpool and whom he visited when on leave. 'She was a very pretty girl but I got the feeling she had other boyfriends. I did not blame her.

There were no ties, couldn't be until the war was over. But I did wonder if she would shed a tear for me.' The next day the family brought him news of the war. The Allies were still caught up around Caen in Normandy but in the east the Soviet army was pushing onwards in East Prussia. The squeeze on the Third Reich from west and east was beginning, though there was a long, long time and a lot more dying to come before the end would be in sight. In the air above he saw a Messerschmitt fighter swoop low, the black crosses on its wings clearly visible. The Luftwaffe was taking a hammering from the joint offensive of the British and American air forces but still its planes flew the skies. Its presence unsettled Haslam. Time hung heavy, and as the days dragged by he felt lonely. He could not converse with his hosts. All they could do was make signs to each other, an unsatisfactory form of communication. The days alone in the house while everyone was out working seemed interminable. He longed to be on the move, heading for the Allied front line – though all the news indicated that the front line was barely moving. Be patient, he was told after three weeks in limbo. More weeks stretched ahead.

I played all kinds of patience. I peeled potatoes, swept floors and made cheese from goat's milk. I spent hours looking and listening out of the bedroom windows when aircraft flew over. I walked from room to room keeping watch when I was alone in the house, but kept quiet when people knocked at the door. I heard the Allies had broken out of Normandy. My hair was getting longer.

His boredom was eventually relieved, though not in a way he would have wished.

I was alone in the house when I heard a vehicle and looked out to see a military car approaching. I gave the room a quick scan to see if there was anything incriminating and then I sped up into the loft and got under the hay. There were knocks at the door and German voices. Dogs began to bark, large ones by the sound of them.

But then the jeep went away. He breathed a sigh of relief – only for another vehicle to roar up to the front door. Frantically he hid again, this time in an old bakehouse attached to the building, and then watched in horror as a German officer walked towards it. Haslam hauled himself inside the old brick oven and knelt there as the German cast his eye around.

He stood with his back to me, so close I could almost make out the initials on his signet ring on the hand dangling behind him. Oh God! Don't let him bend down and see me.

The German had other thoughts on his mind. The fields around were being seized for an emergency airstrip. From Haslam's host family he was demanding immediate use of the bakehouse as a control room. The officer left to make preparations and now somewhere new had to be found for the fugitive. There was no time to ferry him to another safe house, even if one could be found at such short notice.

There was no other choice. It had to be the cellar under the bakehouse, which was entered by a hole in the floor. I was to get into a sack and hide among the sacks of potatoes stored down there. I remembered to relieve myself first, then took a slice of bread and jam and went to earth.

By now the Germans had returned, equipment was being brought in, furniture moved into the room above me. Outside, planes were coming in to land. I lay there with pins and needles, moving whenever I dared to try and alleviate the discomfort. I dreaded what would happen if I fell asleep and snored. Someone switched on a wireless and there was music.

He came out only when the Germans left for the night. After that ordeal he stayed concealed in an upstairs bedroom, ready to leap inside a wardrobe if anyone rattled the door knob. Days passed before the Germans departed. Equipment was bundled into a lorry, the planes flew off eastward towards the Fatherland, the temporary airfield was abandoned. 'Goodbye, Luftwaffe! We were ecstatic and hugged one another in joy and relief.'

Meanwhile, Denys Teare, bedded down with the Resistance in north-eastern France and waiting for his chance to strike a blow at the enemy, was under attack – by his own side. The town of Revigny was a railway junction with sidings where German ammunition trains parked. One night in late July, RAF bombers struck. The house Teare and his friends were in backed on to the sidings and as soon as they heard the drone of the Lancasters overhead, they fled for their lives.

Suddenly white flares started dropping and the whole town was lit up and trembling with the roar of the engines. Men, women and children were running, heading for a dried-up canal to shelter in. I suddenly became aware of a uniformed figure at my side. I turned and saw it was a German soldier. But he was far too intent on getting away to worry about me.

Bright green markers floated down, followed by the horrible whistling sound of the first bombs. A 4,000-pounder dropped right on the ammunition train and in the enormous sheet of orange flame I could see the wagons blown 50 feet into the air. I tried to keep as flat as possible, wishing I could burrow into the ground like a rabbit. I knew all too well that a bomb aimer had only to make a small error of judgement and we would all be dead.[5]

The junction was destroyed and ammunition and reinforcements denied to the German forces in Normandy. Three days later the British Second Army broke out of the Caen pocket, a giant step forward in the battle for France. The Revigny action had contributed in some small way to that advance but at a huge cost in RAF lives. Those German fighters whose continuing presence had so disturbed Frank Haslam had a good night over Revigny, downing 24 of the 110 bombers that had set out from England. Bomb aimer John 'Ginger' Brown was in one of them, caught by cannon fire from a Messerschmitt in the very moment he released the bomb load. The fuel tank in the starboard wing caught fire, the wing broke off and the plane flipped on its back. Brown lay pinned to the floor of the spinning fuselage and knew his life was over. What worried him was the effect his death would have on his parents. And then he saw stars, the real things, shining in the night. He was out. The Lancaster had blown apart and sent him with it. By some almost impossible accident of chance, he was in one piece. He pulled his ripcord and the parachute opened. He drifted down into fields a few miles from Revigny. His flight engineer Bill Johnson landed close by and they made plans. Remembering their evasion lectures, they took out their escape maps and plotted a route south to Spain. 'The RAF hadn't told us the escape lines had ceased to operate since D-Day. They probably didn't want to tell us anything that might diminish our morale. And it worked in that Bill and I really believed we could get to Spain, even though I had broken my left foot on landing.'[6]

Two days later, instead of journeying south, they were sitting with Denys Teare – and wondering if he was a German in disguise. The Resistance had found Brown and Johnson and taken them to Teare's house in Revigny. Teare had been on the run for ten months by now, speaking nothing but French. His English was faltering. 'He could hardly string two words together,' Brown recalled. 'If I had voiced my suspicions the Resistance might have shot him. They certainly looked capable of such an action.' It did not come to that. Brown soon realized Teare was on the level. From him he learned too that the escape lines had closed, which was why they were holed up here along with a growing number of other Allied evaders. There were now eight in all in this one house (along with a dozen French Resistance fighters) and their presence in a small town was becoming too conspicuous. Food was a problem too, their meagre ration of potatoes stretched ever more thinly. One night they dined on the head of a horse that had collapsed in the street. It needed a circular saw to cut it up.

Teare was also becoming wearied by some of his companions. An air drop of ammunition and arms to the Resistance was expected and the British airmen were asked to help collect the containers and hide them in a wood. Teare was shocked by their reluctance to volunteer. One argued that he was a married man with responsibilities and shouldn't be asked to take the risk. Others

refused outright. He was ashamed. The Resistance men risked
their lives every day to bring food to the airmen. In the end Brown
and another of his compatriots went with him, but the mission
was a failure. No plane came, no arms were dropped. But Teare
still felt shamed by his comrades-in-arms. They were also getting
careless, wandering about the house whistling loudly and openly
sunbathing in the garden while chatting away in English that could
easily be heard from the street. One Canadian idiot had even gone
outside to ask a German soldier for a light, just for the hell of it. It
was even more foolish because the cigarette he lit had its Lucky
Strike brand-name on the side. Luckily the German didn't notice.
Teare grew increasingly fearful of discovery and disaster just as the
end – and survival – might actually be in sight. He decided it was
time to leave the town, still swarming with Germans, whose 'Lili
Marlene' marching song often filled the night, and with a couple
of others headed deeper into the countryside for safety.

*

Airey Neave was determined to get back into the war. He had
wanted to slip aboard the motor torpedo boats plying to Brittany
but his MI9 bosses had said no. But after D-Day no one was going
to stop him getting to France. Sections of MI9 had gone over,
under Jimmy Langley and an American counterpart, to set up a
joint Allied unit at Bayeux to debrief men returning from behind
enemy lines. But everyone seemed to have forgotten about the
encampments at Fréteval and elsewhere. Setting these up was as
far as the planning had gone. No one had given much thought to
how they would be liberated. The action man in Neave, too long
behind a desk, saw his opportunity. He left Donald Darling in
charge of the phones in Room 900 and crossed to Normandy.

His first plan was to send French and Belgian agents in civilian
clothes through the German lines to bring out the men hidden in
the forest south of Paris. But this proved impracticable because of
the heavy fighting in the Normandy countryside. It would take a
proper military unit to get through, and the top brass in 21 Army
Group showed no interest in a special mission. It was a job really

for the Commandos or the SAS, but they were otherwise engaged. Neave would have to ignore all the rumblings about 'private armies' and assemble his own armed snatch squad. He was spurred on by fears about what might happen – what might already *have* happened – to those in his charge. He could get no information. Wireless links were down. He had heard nothing from Brussels for weeks. He sat impotent outside Caen, on the wrong side of the front line, listening to the pounding of artillery and tanks day and night. 'I was determined that as soon as a breakthrough occurred on any part of the Allied front, I would make a dash to them.'[7]

Then, at the start of August, came the vital cracking of the German line at St Lô, followed by another breakthrough at Avranches, opening the way for the Allied forces into Brittany. He packed his jeep and drove towards Rennes, site of a camp for evaders who had been turned back from Lucien Dumais's Shelburne operation.

The road was a terrible mêlée of German dead and broken transport, the corpses of mules and horses blocking the way. We drove through villages, narrowly avoiding ambush by the retreating enemy, and we were often cut off from American forces. The exhilaration was unforgettable. The smell of pursuit was in the air.

But by the time he got to Rennes, his birds had flown. They were moving up to the coast, where Dumais was back in business with his cross-Channel escape route. Neave tagged on behind the spearhead led by US General George Patton into central France. He reached Le Mans on 10 August, confident that Patton would continue his thrust due east, on a line that would take the American forces close to Fréteval, now just fifty miles away. But Patton swung north instead, to Alençon and Argentan, closing the Falaise gap through which the German forces were retreating and trapping tens of thousands of enemy troops west of the Seine. It was a strategic triumph, which sealed the Allied victory in Normandy. But it left Neave and his 150 campers isolated.

It was a serious position for me. I had counted on tanks and armoured cars to help me recover the airmen. I did not possess sufficient firepower to deal with any large body of Germans. I had only half a dozen jeeps and a few automatic weapons to effect their rescue from enemy-held territory. Nor did I have any direct communication with the camp.

Here was a hopeless situation. Ahead lay nothing but unknown German forces and unknown risks. He should have stopped there and then. But the atmosphere in liberated Le Mans was feverish. The main square was packed with excited war correspondents and Free French forces, all intoxicated by a heady mix of freedom and cheap white wine. He had to keep the momentum going.

I was worried and alarmed. I feared a tragedy if we waited any longer. There was a strong possibility that, hearing the sounds of battle, some of the men in the forest would break away and join Resistance forces in civilian clothes. The Germans were in a mood of panic. They were harassed in their retreat by the French underground who mined the roads, threw petrol bombs at tanks and sniped at them. We had heard grim stories of massacre by the SS and seen evidence of it on our way. Whole families had been shot and their houses burned.

I sat in the dining room of the Hôtel Moderne studying the route to Fréteval. If what I was planning went wrong, I would be responsible for a terrible tragedy. Nonetheless, I began to search around for transport and armed protection.

He presented himself to the local American corps commander, told him half the men in the forest were US airmen and requested a few trucks and armoured cars. The American turned him away. He was under orders not to move and would spare neither troops nor transport. He thought the rescue impossible with anything less than tanks.

We returned to Le Mans greatly depressed, but in the courtyard of the hotel found a large number of armed jeeps. Standing by them were troops in maroon berets. They were an SAS squadron of four officers and 34 men who had just completed a mission in Brittany and were awaiting orders. This was a remarkable piece of luck.

In high spirits, I hurried into the hotel and found their commander, Captain Anthony Greville-Bell, in the lounge. He was a dashing young officer, ideally suited to 'private warfare', and no respecter of red tape. I could not have found a more suitable person to help me in this adventure.

The SAS captain radioed London for permission, which was granted. Now the only problem was transport. The local Resistance men scoured Le Mans and found a fleet of grey-painted Citroën coaches, abandoned by the retreating Germans. They ran on charcoal in the absence of petrol, were mechanically unreliable and there was every chance of them breaking down on the way to the forest or, even worse, on the way back, fleeing with the fugitives and the Germans on their tail. But there was no alternative. And the urgency of the mission suddenly became apparent when an excited Lucien Boussa, the squadron leader in command of the Fréteval camp, arrived. He had heard the Allies were in Le Mans and had driven there to say the Germans *seemed* to have gone, but the relief column should come soon because otherwise the men would begin to drift away. 'We're having trouble keeping them calm. Already some have left, and are in surrounding villages,' he told Neave. 'Many of the local people are already showing the French flag. It will be dangerous if the Germans come back and take reprisals.'

For all Neave's eagerness to get underway, delay was forced on him. The coaches were still being worked on and would not be ready for another twenty-four hours. He sent a small detachment of SAS troops back to the forest with Boussa to tell the men to wait. On the way they ran into a German patrol and shots were exchanged. It was clear that a rearguard of the enemy remained. There was still some fighting to do before the rescue was complete. A disaster could not be ruled out.

Inside the forest camp there was certainly consternation about what to do. Ray Worrall recalled the rising tension as it became known that the Allied army was moving their way. The initial sign was RAF planes attacking German ammunition dumps in nearby woods. 'It was very frightening. After all we had been through, we did not want to be killed by our own airmen.'[8] The next sign of the war coming closer was the columns of German infantry that now trudged along the road at the edge of the forest. Canadian pilot Flight Lieutenant Alex Campbell of 514 Squadron hid in the trees on sentry duty one evening and watched 'a confusion of men heading in an easterly direction. They left no doubt they were the survivors of an army in retreat.' To his delight, an American B-26 Marauder swept low over the road and raked the enemy line with heavy-calibre machine-gun fire.[9]

The temptation for the men in the forest now to leave and head west in the hope of meeting the advancing Allies was almost irresistible. But resist it they had to, according to Worrall:

The orders from Lucien Boussa were that we must stay put and not try to get away on our own. If we did, he warned, and we were caught, then everyone would be in danger. The retreating Germans would be at the forest in no time to shoot the lot of us. But it was very difficult just waiting.

The sound of nearby gunfire set nerves even more on edge and ten men left on two American tanks that happened on the forest encampment. The majority stayed, following orders, but amid growing fears of discovery. 'We would be sitting ducks,' Worrall said. Then, while Boussa was away making contact with Neave in Le Mans, there was a panic that the Gestapo were closing in. Worrall scattered with some of his friends for a nearby village.

The locals had had no idea we were in their forest and were astonished to find themselves confronted by people speaking English. But a girl got some eggs and made omelettes which we washed down with red wine. The French were excited and kept patting us on the back and giving us more wine. Then a farmer took us to his barn and we slept in the hay. The next day we walked back to camp. Boussa had returned from Le

Mans and told us an armoured convoy was on its way but there were difficulties and that it would be some time before we were rescued.

Back in Le Mans Neave was increasingly frustrated by those difficulties. He looked longingly at the fleets of US trucks standing around doing nothing. But the American commander remained unmoved by fresh pleas. It probably did not help his cause that Neave was dressed in corduroy trousers and looked like a privateer. And then the Resistance transport was finally ready. Neave was called to the main square in Le Mans where, decked with flowers and French flags and guarded by civilians with rifles, were sixteen coaches and trucks. 'I was assured they were all in working order and though the operation seemed comic, I decided that we could wait no longer. We would leave the next morning.'

Joined by twenty-three Belgian SAS troopers who were at a loose end, they set off on a fine sunny day, a ragbag of soldiery, some in uniform, others wearing civilian clothes and sporting Free French armbands. There were 100 in all hanging on to the carbon-fuelled buses as they spluttered down the country roads, the oddest convoy ever to go to war, more like a seaside outing, as Neave observed from his jeep. It was 13 August 1944, D-Day plus 68. At every village they passed through, girls ran out with cakes and wine and French tricolours appeared at the windows.

Cautiously we approached the forest. Then at a clearing beside the road, there was a loud yell of delight and tattered figures ran from trees and jumped up on our transport. The airmen were lean, bronzed and dressed in rough French working clothes. Some were angry and impatient. A few had disappeared. I could only apologize for our failure to arrive earlier.

Cliff Hallett never forgot the tension of waiting for the buses and then the sight of them chugging into the clearing. He didn't recall a great deal of cheering, just a sense of relief and a wish to get out of there as quickly as possible.

Most of the newcomers were speaking French but there was a chap walking round speaking English, so I went across to him and asked: who might you be? He said: 'My name's Airey Neave.' He told me he was always determined that he would be there when we came out.[10]

Neave was annoyed, however, that American tanks had already whisked away some of the campers, given how reluctant the US military in Le Mans had been to help him. His convoy now headed out of the forest and back behind the official Allied front line. On the way the SAS picked up some German stragglers, whom they pushed into the coaches beside the airmen. It was hard to believe but Operation Sherwood was over. And none too soon. The next day German soldiers were back in the forest. If the delay had been any longer, there would have been a battle and possibly the bloodbath Neave had feared. Ray Worrall certainly believed they would all have been shot if they had not left when they did.[11] As it was, Neave used the SAS radio to tell Darling in London that 132 men had been brought out from Fréteval. Later, in a sad footnote, Neave would record that nearly all went back on flying operations and thirty-eight of them were killed in action before the end of the war.

★

With the Germans on the retreat from Normandy and their lines strung out, there was now a chance for individual evaders to make their way through the front lines. It was an incredibly risky thing to do, as RAF Mustang pilot George Pyle discovered. His Mustang had crash landed four days after D-Day while dive-bombing enemy tanks and trucks bringing reinforcements to the beachhead. Locals had hidden him and moved him progressively away from the front line. Then, along with those locals, he became a refugee as they were forced from their homes by the Germans and pushed south, away from the fighting. As he got further from his own lines, he decided to stop this 'nomadic existence' and take his chances crossing no-man's-land. He persuaded a Resistance stalwart named Yvette to guide him and as they trekked over fields they found themselves in a silent battlefield.

There were shell craters, and dead beasts lay bloated in the hot sun. Occasionally the smell of death drifted across to us. For all we knew we could have been in a minefield. At one stage I saw some Germans in a hedgerow. Later Yvette told me she had seen a partially concealed tank and a German machine gun set behind a haystack. We reached a road and walked for a while until we saw a village ahead, shrouded in smoke and apparently burning from end to end.[12]

Here Pyle was handed over to a new guide while the brave Yvette made her way back to her own village. He was the local baker, his shop on the German side of the front and the farmhouse he lived in with his family a mile or so away on the Allied side. He had been crossing back and forth for days, he told the airman breezily. It would be no problem.

We climbed over a damaged bridge, walked a mile along a road and then came to a fork. A German tank was parked under a tree and a trooper in the turret ordered us to stop. The baker explained that we were going to his home but the German just pointed ahead, shook his head and said 'Tommy!' He refused to let us pass. But then the baker asked if we could take the other fork in the road and the German agreed. We hurried away before he changed his mind.

But even down this road there were soldiers everywhere, under hedges and lying in the long grass beneath camouflage covers, their machine guns pointing in the direction the two men wanted to go. A German officer stepped out from behind a tree and ordered them back the way they had come. Instead, once out of sight, the baker led the way into a wood and they crossed over fields and through deserted farmyards until they came to another road. They crossed it with extra care – German machine gunners were known to sweep it – and then crawled under a hedge, narrowly avoiding the fins and tail cone of an unexploded mortar bomb.

And then we were at his farm. With a wide triumphant smile on his face, the baker declared: 'You are free!' But it didn't feel like it and I asked him where the Americans were. He pointed across the field. 'Over there.' We walked to the end of a narrow lane and turned into another field. In the centre was a tree and underneath it was a small field gun encircled by a single strand of barbed wire. An American soldier in a filthy uniform was leaning wearily against the tree, his rifle hanging down from his shoulder. 'Am I glad to see you,' I said.

Pyle's war was over as he was shunted back along the American line in a jeep on a beautiful summer's evening. He passed groups of captured German soldiers squatting with their hands on their heads, guarded by GIs. In the other direction an endless stream of lorries and equipment kicked up immense clouds of dust, feeding the Allied thrust as it headed relentlessly eastward.

One hundred miles away, Paris was a city of rumours and lies, patriotism and denunciation. Nervous German soldiers marched its streets. The Resistance lay low, waiting for its chance to strike, anxious not to move too soon. Earlier that month the partisans of Warsaw had risen against the German occupiers, but prematurely. Even now the brave Poles were being slowly slaughtered as the Nazi soldiers took back the city street by flaming street and block by bloody block (while Stalin's Red Army, in an act of the direst political cynicism, waited on the other side of the River Vistula and refused to intervene). This was a time for extreme caution if Paris was not to suffer a similar holocaust. Joe Murphy, an American bombardier, had been in the French capital since Easter. For months since being shot down in November 1943, he had been hidden in the Channel port of Le Havre. He had then moved to Paris as the first leg of a journey south to the Pyrenees, and here he had stayed as the escape line ground to a halt. His host believed the boys in her charge should not grow unfit and stale so, rather than keep them battened down in her flat, she took them on the tourist trail. He visited Sacré Coeur, Notre Dame, Napoleon's Tomb, rubbing shoulders with German soldiers on leave. There were trips to the zoo, the race course, even a nightclub to ogle the can-can girls.

But the city's normality was a façade, and a crumbling one at that. In cinemas the Germans took to stopping the film, turning up the lights and checking papers. Young men dodging the labour draft would be hauled out and taken away in lorries. After D-Day, with tension mounting, a man in Murphy's position had to decide whether to wait in a city that, as far as anyone knew, the Germans would fight to defend, or try to make the Allied lines. He had somehow missed the move others had made to Fréteval forest but now, with a group of fellow evaders, he began the trek to Normandy. They went by train as far as they could, until there was no more serviceable track ahead. Then they walked. After four long and weary days on the road, a farmer gave them shelter, and they lay in his hayloft for close on a fortnight, waiting for the Allied front line to creep towards them. It finally arrived. American GIs swept into the square of the nearest village. It was all over, almost an anti-climax in the end, without fighting and without fanfare.

RAF bomb aimer Bill Knaggs was also on the road trying to meet up with that advancing front line. He was coming from the north, having been shot down while attacking a German rocket site in a forest twenty miles inland from Dieppe. He wandered through an area thick with Wehrmacht reinforcements, got to the Seine and found he could go no further. Resistance forces he fell in with sent him to Paris. He arrived in a city in suspense. Food was in short supply. The streets had lost their usual bustle. Army patrols manned every major crossroads and there were frequent raids on homes. The people seemed tired and nervous and trusted no one. He was passed from safe house to safe house until he reached the northern suburbs, where he was lodged in a flat belonging to Jacqueline, an English-speaking secretary and a Resistance activist. He posed as her cousin and fiancé. From the radio, he plotted the Allied thrust towards Paris. Outside the streets were increasingly filled with German military traffic leaving the city. 'There was an air of expectation, tempered by a feeling that over-confidence could lead to carelessness.'[13] He and Jacqueline were walking along one day, arm in arm and chatting away in English when a German soldier stared hard at them. It was a reminder of how precarious existence still was. From Paris came news of a local man's teenage son who had attended a Resistance meeting in a cellar. The Gestapo had got wind of it and rolled in grenades that killed everyone.

But very soon Paris was free. Tragedies like the one in the cellar apart, the Resistance chose its moment to show its face. On 18 August barriers blocked the streets; snipers pinned down enemy soldiers. The police prefecture and the town hall were seized. Meanwhile, American troops raced to the outskirts, stepping aside to allow a Free French division to be the first liberators on its historic boulevards. Airey Neave was in the vanguard and forced to wait anxiously outside Paris for the French to arrive to lead the *libération*. He had made his way from Fréteval as far up in the advance as the American field commanders would allow a man they tended to think of as, at best, an irregular and, at worst, a 'bandit'. He still had some of his SAS escort and they relieved smaller camps of evaders in farmhouses and barns near Beauvais and Mantes. But it was the fate of those who remained in the capital city and the network of helpers that was his biggest concern. Should he send in couriers in plain clothes? He had lists of addresses of Comet and Shelburne helpers and was anxious to get to them before a last-ditch Gestapo sweep uncovered them. A delay of just hours could be vital, one of days fatal. He jumped the gun a little, leaving the French division to fight its way through German opposition while he sped in his jeep through back streets to the Champs Elysées. He then toured a city crackling with sniper fire – to find most of his agents safe and well.

Paris proved as impossible to defend in 1944 as it had been in 1940, and on 25 August the German commander surrendered, having refused to implement Hitler's 'scorched-earth' orders to demolish the city, its bridges and its finery. In the wake of the French division, exultant Allied troops poured in from the south and west. Out in the northern suburbs, Knaggs watched the Resistance take openly to the streets and begin to attack the retreating German convoys. The locals were lightly armed and no match for the Germans. The fighting was bitter and bloody, and one-sided in the Germans' favour – until the Americans came to join in.

Their shells drove the enemy off and early the next morning we were awakened by the sound of tanks. Down in the street a slow-moving armoured column stretched out in both directions. I went down and jumped aboard a tank, and told an American lieutenant who I was. 'Come with us and chase the Jerries,' he urged me but the idea of continuing the war in a tank had no appeal to me. Jacqueline and I celebrated with friends. Their joy and relief at liberation were indescribable. Much wine flowed and luxuries tucked away for years for just this occasion were brought out.

Thirty miles to the north of the city, liberation was still awaited. Sergeant William Cupp, ball-turret gunner from a US B-24 Liberator of the Eighth Air Force, was in hiding on a farm, listening to the news about Paris and wondering when it would be his turn. He had been shot down six weeks earlier over Belgium and been passed south along a chain of safe houses until he and his navigator, Lieutenant Bob Donohue, were less than two hours' drive from the centre of Paris. For a week they had been dug in, feeling the war getting closer, and their freedom with it.

From the roof of a barn, we watched two American Thunderbolts attack a train less than a mile away. The wind from the south also carried the distant thunder of artillery fire. That night we huddled round the radio to hear General Charles de Gaulle urge all Frenchmen to rise and strike the German rattlesnake that was coiled round their country and loosen its hold forever. We all stood with glasses of Calvados and toasted him. As we retired to bed, I noticed one of the sons, clad entirely in black, slip out through the door, his rifle in his hand. The next day I heard that the Paris–Dieppe line had been blown up. Then a report came of fighting in the streets of Paris. Soon we had no more electricity, and the radio was stilled. Was this whole area about to become a battlefield?[14]

The two airmen discussed their chances of getting to Paris safely. Perhaps it had been liberated by now – they had no way of knowing. But would they ever get across the River Seine, which stood between them and the city, if the Germans had blown the bridges? They decided to go for it anyway.

It was easy at first as they walked down peaceful and deserted country roads. War? What war? They woke after a night spent in the open air and in the distance could hear shelling. Then they approached a village to refill their water bottles and were driven off by the sound of machine-gun fire.

We heard the whistle of an incoming shell and threw ourselves to the ground. It struck a short distance ahead of us, scattering dirt everywhere. We hurried on but had not gone fifty yards when another burst behind us. We took to the fields, hiding behind stoops of corn from the German sentry we could see on the road ahead.

In fact there were German soldiers everywhere – on bicycles on the road and in the village streets. If they were going to make any progress, they would have to brazen it out. They did, and got away with it, passing within fifteen yards of a knot of men in grey uniforms without a challenge. Occasionally a shell burst in woods to their right and left but most of the fire now seemed behind them. They were making good progress and quickly covered the next mile.

We were exposed on a sloping field of stubble, with the nearest protection in woods 500 yards away. But we weren't worried because we had not seen German soldiers, or anyone for that matter, for some time. Suddenly a shot rang out and a bullet kicked up dirt near our feet. We stopped in our tracks, raised our hands in the air and turned toward the sound of the shot. Three German soldiers were manning a machine-gun nest dug into the hillside.

They were marched up the hill. An officer appeared and questioned them. They flashed their fake identity cards and indicated they were farm workers whose native language was Flemish. They were going to visit their sick grandmother on the far side of Paris.

The officer did not accept the explanation, and even to me as I delivered it, it sounded thin. He accused us of being English airmen from an observation plane that had recently been downed by ground fire, which we vehemently denied. He forced us to kneel. 'No matter,' he said. 'No innocent person would be foolish enough to walk into a combat zone. If you are not military, then you must be civilians up to no good. You will be shot.'

Soldiers grabbed us and pushed us to the edge of a wood. We stood with our backs to the trees and a tall soldier with a Schmeisser machine pistol took position twenty feet in front of us. Another threw a camouflage tarpaulin over our heads and the officer called out in German: 'Ready, aim . . .' That's when I shouted, '*We're Americans!*'

The officer called '*Halt!*' and the tarpaulin was hauled off their heads. They were prisoners, yes, but alive. The tragedy was that they had stumbled into no-man's-land, as close to crossing into friendly territory as it was possible to get. The Americans, it turned out, were just 200 yards away over the next rise. Cupp and his fellow airman had made it to the Allied front line that had been their goal ever since being shot down a week after D-Day. But they were on the wrong side.

They were not treated well. An officer beat them up, and then there was a deadly game as they were made to cling to the front bumper of a captured American jeep while it was driven at high speed at various solid obstacles before the brakes were slammed on. They hung on for dear life as the driver tried to dislodge them, and riflemen stood by waiting to shoot them if they fell for trying to escape. Then they were driven to a village for interrogation and bundled inside a building from which flew the swastika flag.

I told them my name was Cupp, William L., serial number 17097098, and I was a sergeant in the United States Army Air Corps. The officer asking the questions informed me that any military person dressed in non-uniform fashion was to be defined as a spy and treated accordingly. He proclaimed that whether we were actually spies or the American airmen we claimed to be made no difference. 'We have not taken a captive alive for more than a month,' he said, Clearly, he did not expect us to be exceptions.

A firing squad of a dozen or so grey-uniformed soldiers began to assemble.

I tenaciously clung to the belief that somehow good fortune would not desert us even now, and that we would still be extricated from the doom promised us. I stood facing a wall, and tried to work out some way of escaping. Outside in the rear garden, a big gun boomed out every few minutes, shelling the opposite front line. But then came answering artillery fire. Shells were landing nearby. In my mind I saw us being shot . . . but then the Allies quickly advancing and finding our bodies bleeding but still alive. This improbable thought gave me a little courage to face what lay ahead. But in truth I was utterly shaken up. My mind went to all those friends and family I wanted to say goodbye to.

Then came the *whoosh!* of an incoming shell, and a mighty explosion rattled the windows. The firing squad ran for the door. Then came another *whoosh!* and a shell sent plaster and dust everywhere. A German officer was frantically packing up documents into a case as Cupp and Donohue sat at a table, watched by a single rifleman who had remained.

I reasoned that as long as Bob and I sat close together, the rifleman posed a threat. But if we were separated a bit, he couldn't point the weapon at both of us at the same time. Observing him, he seemed to handle his gun clumsily. I thought he might be much more at home with a type-writer than with a rifle. Bob must have had the same thought because slowly we sidled apart. A little bit to begin with, then some more. A few more inches and we would be able to jump him from both sides.

All of a sudden, the door crashed open, a soldier came in and, with pistol drawn, motioned the two Americans into the back of a car waiting outside. As it drove them away, Cupp wondered if they were going on a one-way trip. But then the driver spoke. He had once lived and worked in Chicago. Did either of them come from there? Cupp, a farmer's boy from Iowa, eagerly laid claim to being from the Windy City. The tension eased – until the car drew into a clearing in some woodland and there stood a group of soldiers in black uniforms. The colour meant only one thing to the Americans – Gestapo.

To their relief, they were now to learn that black was also the uniform of the German tank corps. A panzer officer offered them food – '*Essen?*' Cupp misunderstood. He shook his head and tried to explain that his squadron had never bombed Essen, the German city in the Ruhr, only French targets. The German looked puzzled and ignored the answer.

He strode to a little trailer attached to a truck parked nearby. Raising the lid, he revealed soup thick with noodles. It smelled good, and we accepted a portion gratefully. A young soldier was assigned to guard us as we made short work of the soup. Others lounged around the trucks parked among the trees, playing cards or dozing. They seemed a bored and weary troop.

Some came over to chat and were surprisingly friendly. They had no animosity to the American flyers for what the Allied air forces had done to Germany.

They looked upon us as brothers under the skin. One told us we were lucky to be POWs. He said: 'You will be taken to Germany and placed in a wonderful camp with comfortable quarters, good food, tennis, and swimming. And there will be parties, with girls to dance with. You will like it very much.' The fellow had tears in his eyes, comparing those prospects with his own situation – dirty, damp and in the middle of battle.

Suddenly there was action stations. A staff car skidded into the wood and an officer shouted that the enemy was advancing fast. Everyone was to get out at once. The Americans were loaded onto a truck. Motors revved. Loud commands were issued, and the convoy moved out, heading north-east, away from the front, away from freedom. That freedom was tantalizingly close even now as the speed of the Allied advance through France took the Germans by surprise. At one stage the lorry nearly ran into an American tank blocking the road ahead. A high-speed U-turn, and the driver raced away, with Cupp and Donohue in the back grateful that their fellow countryman in the Sherman had chosen not to fire, though disappointed they had missed an opportunity to be released. More retreating German soldiers hauled themselves onto the lorry, clinging to the running board and the sides as they fled the Allies. And so the two one-time evaders went into captivity in Germany as their lorry joined the mass retreat. They looked out on a scene reminiscent of 1940 – but in the opposite direction. Vehicles of all sorts clogged the road through Cambrai into Belgium, then Brussels and onto the border of the Fatherland. In the ditches and fields alongside, throngs of German foot soldiers plodded, anxious to stay ahead of the Allied tanks pursuing them. 'There must have been more than 100,000 men moving on that road,' Cupp recalled. 'The line extended as far as the eye could see.' That meant there was no chance of escape. To have tried to slip over the tailboard and run would have been certain death, and, as all evaders knew in their hearts, the uncertainties of a Stalag were preferable to that.

★

All over France, evaders luckier than Cupp and Donohue were coming out of hiding, but not before some dangerous moments when lives could still be lost. Tucked away in a remote country chalet not far from Revigny in north-eastern France, 'Ginger' Brown was caught in crossfire as American and German big guns exchanged fire. 'Shells whistled over our heads far too close for comfort. Fortunately it was not long before the Germans had had enough and their gunfire ceased as they hastily retreated eastwards. The ensuing silence was truly golden.' He and his companions made for the nearest town in jubilant mood, to find the fleeing Germans had left a final legacy of barbarity. From a departing troop carrier, a soldier had tossed a grenade into a crowd of women and children who had come to see them go. There were many casualties – 'a dreadful end, typical of what the Germans were capable of. And of how we had to be on our guard.' Tanks and armoured carriers from the American Third Army were soon speeding through on the enemy's tail, with no time to stop and acknowledge the flags and the warm welcome on offer to them. The towns-people celebrated their freedom with a special thanksgiving mass in the church. Then they let rip, hugging and kissing and crying tears of joy. Champagne concealed from the Germans for four years flowed freely. Brown sat quietly among the ecstatic throng.

It was exciting to witness such a unique occasion. But it was also sad for us because we had lost good friends. Three crewmates were killed when our blazing Lancaster bomber blew up. They were Australian and now lay buried in a French churchyard, thousands of miles from their homes and grieving families. We remembered also our navigator, who had been captured and was behind barbed wire. There was a strong bond of comradeship between the members of a bomber crew because we were so dependent upon each other when flying. It was just luck that you survived and they didn't. Nothing could explain why that happened. I don't think I ever felt guilty but sometimes I would wonder why I got away with it and they didn't.

His reflections were cut short by another cruel aspect of war now being enacted before his eyes – retribution.

A group of women – the so-called 'Jerry-bags' – were forcibly paraded in front of the town hall to have their hair cut and heads shaved as a mark of shame for having consorted with German troops during the occupation. I found it difficult to watch. But the French felt very deeply about what these women had done. They had received presents, clothing and extra food from the German troops as reward for their favours and then flaunted these benefits in front of their neighbours. Now they were being made to pay.

In these moments of instant revenge, no one was safe from denunciation or misunderstanding. A truck full of evaders rescued from the secret camp in Fréteval forest stopped in one town centre and was suddenly surrounded by angry armed locals baying for their blood. They mistook the scruffy Allied airmen in their tattered clothes for German soldiers captured in battle and were all for settling some scores. The mood changed when one airman produced his RAF badge and the crowd cottoned on, and now there were wine and cigarettes on offer instead of bullets in the head and ropes round the neck. But as one of the evaders noted wryly: 'Fancy getting this far and then being lynched by our friends.'[15]

For 'Ginger' Brown it was his enemies he still had to worry about because, as he and his companions celebrated liberation in their town square, a terrible rumour halted the party. The German troops were apparently on their way back. 'There was a real sense of panic. We had thought it was over but perhaps we were still in danger. Was it never going to end?' All the flags and bunting were torn down, and the men were ordered to report to the town hall. There they were each given a Resistance armband and sent to man hastily assembled barricades. He found himself with a group of middle-aged Frenchmen carrying old rifles and gingerly trying to load them. Fortunately they had some professional help too. One American tank had remained in the town. Its crew made sure their armour was between them and the town's excitable defenders, now waving their guns around and threatening all sorts of terrible fates on any Germans who dared come back. 'But I had seen what a German Tiger tank could do, and my enthusiasm was somewhat less than theirs.'

The evening passed with no sign of a German counter-attack. Sentries were posted and everyone else stood down from the barricades to get some sleep. Brown borrowed a sleeping bag from the American tank crew and bedded down under a tree. He woke in the morning ice cold and covered in dew, and his first confused thought was that he was a captive. 'Then I spotted the American tank and all was well.' Even the breakfast cup of bitter acorn coffee proffered by a beaming French woman tasted good. Nothing had happened during the night and the Germans had indeed gone, but the situation was still considered fluid and it was decided to keep the barricades manned. As the day passed – the first full one of liberation – Brown discovered precisely what it meant to the French. An old man approached him and the American tank commander and, through an interpreter, said his wife was very ill in bed and close to dying. Her last wish was to see a soldier of the liberating army.

The old man's face lit up as he led us down the road to his cottage. As we went in, the American released the safety catch on his rifle. We were a little nervous, wondering, as you did at these still uncertain times, if we could trust him or if we were being lured into an ambush. But there in the bedroom lay the frail old lady. The American put the back of his hand to her cheek and she bravely gave him a weak smile. He gave her a little kiss on the cheek and, though she didn't speak, she had a satisfied look on her face, happy to know that her home town had been liberated. It was a very special moment.

Such a relatively peaceful ending to years of occupation was not always the case. Denys Teare, who had shared a house of refuge with 'Ginger' Brown at one stage, was hiding on a farm deep in the French countryside, working side by side with the French family sheltering him and almost removed from the realities of war.

Sometimes, we almost forgot the daily danger in which we lived. There were no military objectives in the vicinity, so the Allied bombers which were almost continually droning overhead did not trouble us. Often we would pause for a few seconds, listening to the heavy crump of bombs in the distance, or to watch a group of Mustangs go streaking across the fields at low level looking for something worth destroying, but there was not even a railway line at the little village. It seemed as though we were living apart from all the horrors of modern warfare which were raging on either side.

Such detachment could not last. Wounded German soldiers began appearing. A medical centre for them was set up in the village and ambulances parked beside the farm. He and Australian airman Fred White kept their heads down, knowing that even at this late stage in the war, discovery would have meant death for the family protecting them. Then the Resistance brought news of hundreds of British paratroops landing twenty miles away and the two evaders decided the time had come to seek liberation rather than just wait for it. With a maquis to guide them they set off towards the distant rumbling of artillery, little realizing that what lay ahead would be more dangerous than anything they had encountered in the war so far.

The main road was packed with retreating Germans on bicycles, motor-cycles, in trucks and any conveyance they could find. Some were tattered and torn, with dirty, unshaven faces, and their one thought was to get to Germany. They paid no attention to the old car we were in, chugging along at a steady 15 mph in the opposite direction.

They came to a forest and there in a clearing was a group of evaders like them – three Americans, five Australians and six Englishmen. They were just lounging about and had disappointing news to convey. The paratroop landing had been exaggerated and, in truth, was nothing more than a handful of SAS soldiers who wanted no help from a bedraggled band of lost airmen. They had taken off on their sabotage mission and left the evaders behind, unarmed and in the path of a beaten German army, whose mood had become very ugly.

The most appalling accounts of atrocities were circulating. Then a young Frenchman staggered through the bushes into the clearing, his face terror-stricken and his whole body trembling. He was the sole survivor of a Maquis camp which the Germans had surrounded. Every man had been shot. Staying in the forest was clearly unsafe. We dispersed in twos and threes.

Teare and White chose to go to a village where they knew there was a doctor. Teare was a sick man. Months of under-nourishment and over-anxiety suddenly overwhelmed him with an outbreak of scabies; the sores turned septic and abscesses covered his body. They got to the village and took shelter in the house of a Resistance worker named Adolphe. The doctor was visiting patients elsewhere but would be back. Across the field they could see lines of German soldiers marching eastward on the main road, detonating bridges behind them as they went. That was not all they were using their explosives for, and news came of them hurling grenades into shops in the square of a small town nearby. Thirteen people were dead, one of them the doctor, shot in the head by a soldier in the last departing lorry.

We listened in silence. Back home we had read of atrocities on the Russian front and imagined that a certain amount of exaggeration would have to be allowed for. Now we were almost face to face with the ghastly truth, and did not know if during the next few days we also might become victims ourselves.

They had every reason to fear for their lives. Across the field came the sound of gunfire. Later they discovered that what they had heard was the machine-gunning of men and boys from a village in the forest.

A German column had arrived as if from nowhere and rounded up fifty male inhabitants – just boys and old men, the only ones left – ostensibly to put them to work. The soldiers then ransacked houses for whatever valuables they could find and set them alight. When one man broke free and ran to his burning home he was shot in the back. This was a signal for wholesale slaughter, Teare recorded in his memoirs.

The prisoners were lined up in threes at the side of the railway. A woman approached the officer in charge and asked if she could give some food to her husband before they took him away. The soldiers laughed and said, 'He won't need any food where he's going.' Then they counted the prisoners . . . and their own ammunition. 'Have we got enough cartridges?' a soldier demanded, watched by fifty pairs of petrified eyes.

A captain ordered three machine guns to be placed in position. Realizing what was about to happen, the women pleaded for mercy, but he announced, 'An officer and three men have been killed by partisans, and this village is going to pay the penalty.'[16] He turned to his men and said, 'Let's get on with this. The Americans will be here tomorrow.' Then he barked out an order and the machine guns mowed down the defenceless men.

The reprisals did not stop there. Three other villages were torched and twenty-four people murdered. Two old men were too weak to leave their homes to be shot and were burnt alive in their beds. Teare was shocked to the core.

Sometimes during the previous twelve months I had had a feeling of self-satisfaction at successfully evading capture for so long. It had seemed quite a romantic situation and I thought of the pleasure I would get when I told friends of the exciting times I had played hide and seek behind the enemy lines. But now I was seeing warfare at its absolute worst.

That night he and White sat in Adolphe's house gripping shotguns and prepared to fight if the Germans tried to repeat their retribution in his village. 'We knew our liberators were only a few miles away. The question was whether we would be alive to meet them.' Outside they could see through the curtains Germans moving on all sides of the house. Grenades were thrown into the post office and bridges were blown up.

At dawn, the village was as silent as a graveyard, and the anxious faces peering through the blinds could not see a single Nazi in sight. The sun rose and birds began to sing. It was a glorious summer morning, but nobody left the houses; they were all watching and waiting. Fred and I peered across the field towards the main road. At last came the sight for which we had waited so long. Two mud-bespattered American tanks came nosing their way cautiously along the highway.

Teare was safe at last, but he was to discover more tragedy and atrocity before he finally left French soil. He made his way back to Bar-le-Duc, the town in which he had spent a lot of time during his years as an evader and made many friends among the Resistance. Some had fallen into the hands of the Germans, who, before retreating, took them from their prison cells, drove them into the woods and shot them. Thoughts of them filled his head as he was driven to Paris and then boarded an aeroplane for England.

Skimming over the Channel in a Dakota, I realized how extremely lucky I had been. I owed my life to the loyalty, courage and kindness of so many everyday French people. These people had risked everything to protect me; I owed them a debt of gratitude which I would never forget.

\*

Belgium was the next country to be freed. Two weeks after Paris was liberated, Brussels was *en fête* too. Pilot Officer George Fernyhough and his pilot, Squadron Leader Jack Trobe, had only recently arrived from Holland, to learn from their hosts that all SS men had deserted the city and the rest of the German military were preparing to leave too. The two men decided to see for themselves and strolled the streets to witness this piece of history.

A fleet of 'Red Cross' vehicles was lined up outside the German HQ and all sorts of documents were being loaded into them. The vehicles were really ordinary staff cars with a convenient red cross painted on the roof. There weren't even injured German soldiers inside, just high-ranking German officers and their belongings. The German troops were leaving on bicycles and horse-drawn carts with no sign of order.[17]

Their stroll almost ended in disaster. A German officer called them over to him. His car was stuck in a ditch and he demanded their help to haul it out. All three grabbed the rear bumper and hauled away. 'I was scared,' Fernyhough recalled. 'I suddenly realized it could all go wrong. But in fact it was the German who was panicking, not us, because he was so anxious to get out of Brussels. Nonetheless, if he had found out who we were, there was a real chance he would have shot us.' The German's anger rose as the car resolutely refused to budge, for all their huffing and puffing. Eventually he gave up and walked away, and the two English airmen scarpered smartly in the opposite direction. In more than four months on the run, it was the closest they had ever got to being caught, and for it to have happened then would have been appalling. Two days later the British Guards Armoured Division rolled into the centre of Brussels, unopposed, not a German in sight. 'It was wonderful, the thrill of a lifetime,' Fernyhough recalled.

At Liège, seventy miles closer to the German frontier, Tom Wingham had just a few more days to wait for liberation. By now the Germans were in full retreat and the Allied spearhead moving so fast that the city changed hands with very little destruction. There had been time, however, for barbarity. Wingham was taken to see the bodies of five Belgian teenagers shot by a retreating SS unit. 'They lay in open coffins with appalling wounds caused by dum-dum bullets and I undertook to report the SS commander to the appropriate authorities.'[18]

Frank Haslam put on his RAF uniform to step out of hiding and go and greet the Americans. 'It was a little shabby, damp and full of creases. What the hell – I put it on.' He marched proudly down the road, away from the farmhouse where not so long ago he had hidden in the oven of the bakehouse praying a German officer would not look his way. On the way to the nearest village he stopped to share tears and kisses with the locals. There were cries of '*Vive le Tommy!*' In the square, all eyes were on a column of American troops, their progress temporarily halted by trees felled across the main road to the border by the retreating Germans. The crowd made way for him to get to the stationary American vehicles and he introduced himself to a helmeted officer. GIs thrust packs of cigarettes and chocolate into his tunic.

But he must have looked an odd sight, his hair long, his English stilted after so long and interspersed with words in German-sounding Flemish, his RAF uniform suspiciously close in colour to Wehrmacht grey. That was a confusion that no one wanted in these heady times. This was demonstrated when the word went out among the villagers that a German soldier had stayed behind and was sitting in a nearby house.

I was dragooned into dealing with him. We found him in the kitchen with his hold-all on his lap and his rifle and ammunition lying on the table. He said he had stayed behind because he didn't want to fight any more. He had ageing parents back in Germany who would have no one to look after them if he was killed. We handed him over to the Americans, who interrogated him and then sent him back down the line to 'the cage', as they called it.

I felt sorry for the man, for as he walked away some of the GIs spat their gum at him and made derogatory remarks. I suppose that these forward troops had seen their friends die and had good reason for their behaviour, but I put myself in his place. The boot could so easily have been on the other foot in my case.

The next day Haslam made his way back through the lines until he came across some British soldiers and was directed to their field headquarters. There he was telling his story to a major and a captain when he realized they did not believe him. The odd word of Flemish still creeping into his vocabulary was again suspicious. Then they told him he would be detained for further inquiries. It was not the reception an evader would ever have expected.

I could see myself being locked up with some of the enemy. I blew up and told them to find someone who had lived in the places in England where I had been brought up and stationed. Some discussion took place and the captain left the room, returning with a corporal who came from Doncaster.

I told him the addresses where I had lived, the schools I had attended, the places where I had learned to dance and where I had worked. He asked me about Doncaster High Street, who played for Doncaster Rovers and so on. In the end he said if I was not genuine, he would eat his beret!

And now, but only now, it was all smiles. A whisky bottle was opened and explanations offered by the officers about how – rightly – they had to be sure.

US airman Jetty Cook also had a problem proving his identity. It almost cost him his life. He was hiding in a village just south of Liège with the tail gunner from his plane and ventured out onto the streets as columns of German tanks laden with trucks were trundling through on their way to the border at Aachen, twenty-five miles away.

We were walking around a little shopping area when suddenly three cars pulled up and out jumped a dozen Belgian youths carrying pistols and bandoliers. They accused us of being Germans. I kept saying, 'No, American, American,' but they wouldn't have any of it. They took two ropes out of the car and put them around our necks and started dragging us to a lamp post. They were going to lynch us! As the rope got tighter around my neck, I kept insisting they call the family who were sheltering us. Finally one of them, a girl, recognized the name and knew they were hiding an American. She convinced them to wait, then rang the family and cleared us. But it was a close call.

That night, the boot was on the other foot as Cook went out on patrol with a local policeman – the man who had been hiding him – to round up collaborators.

We were in a pre-war Ford and had already taken two lots to the school gym, which was being used as a detention centre, when one of the policemen recognized two Gestapo agents. We cornered them in a cul-de-sac and put them in the car, one in the front seat, the other in the back. As we were driving along at 45 mph, the one in the front seat with me grabbed at the steering wheel. The Belgian sitting behind me blew his brains all over the windscreen. At the gymnasium, the other

Gestapo agent spat in my face when I told him I was American, and one of the Belgians grabbed him by the neck and snapped it.

By the morning, the streets were filled with tanks and trucks again – American ones this time. Cook was in the throng on the pavement and dancing in the road, laughing and cheering at the freedom he had never been sure he would live to see.

★

Liberation had come to Brittany too. As the Allied armies had broken out of Normandy and raced east towards Paris, one spearhead had gone east into the Brest peninsula. In the town of Carhaix, Janine Jouanjean greeted the freedom of her country with joy but also anxiety. What had happened to that adorable English flyer who had so briefly lit up her life that wonderful spring a year and a half ago? She knew he had got back to England. A cryptic message on the BBC news confirmed that. But what now? He had promised to come back to her. Something inside compelled her to believe him, against all the odds, all the vagaries of a vicious and unpredictable war. Then, one day in August 1944, the postman arrived with a huge bundle of letters from Gordon Carter, full of love and hope. He had written them many months before and now, with the postal service between Britain and France restored, his aunt had sent them on. Janine sat and read them all at one sitting, one after the other, the story of his life since he had taken the rough sea crossing home, the declaration of his undoubted and undying love. 'Reading them made me so happy,' she recalled. 'The hope was there again. Now I knew for sure we would see each other some time. It was wonderful.'[19] And then, a while later, came disappointment. Another letter arrived from England, from Gordon's aunt, with the news that he had been shot down again and was a prisoner of war in Germany. 'It was a devastating shock. I went from that joy of his letters to concern and worry for him.'

He was not the only man missing in her life. Her brother Geo, a Resistance worker through whom she had first met Gordon, had been arrested by the Nazis two months after the Englishman had left. She had no idea whether he was alive or dead. He had been taken to Germany, that was all she knew. For his patriotism, for defying the Germans and for helping evaders to escape, he was paying a terrible price. And there were thousands like him in Nazi hands, men and women, young and old, for whom the liberation of their country came too late.

# 10. Paying the Price

Just ten days before Allied troops entered Paris in August 1944, Len Bareham, a 23-year-old RAF airman from East Barnet, was in a crowd of ragged, wretched, half-starved prisoners at a siding in the Gare de l'Est station. Heavily armed German soldiers stood facing them; guard dogs snarled and strained on their leashes. There was a crash as the doors of the cattle trucks beside them slid open, and the line of soldiers and dogs harried the men and women up and into the bare-boarded wagons that would be their mobile home for the next five days. They struggled aboard to shouts of 'Schnell! Schnell!', eighty in each truck – no room to sit or lie down, just stand passively, shoulder to shoulder, crushed together like so many old suits in a closet. The crowding was even greater than usual. Trains fleeing the French capital for Germany were precious. But in Nazi-occupied Europe, even in a crisis of evacuation, room could always be made for Jews, enemies and those the state wanted to punish. 'We were mostly RAF in our truck,' Bareham remembered,[1] an indication of just how successful the Gestapo had been in rounding up evaders in recent months. He had been on a bombing raid to limestone caves just north of Paris, an underground store for the V-1 flying bombs – Hitler's revenge weapon – which had been unleashed on southern England after D-Day. His plane was hit by flak and shortly after baling out he made contact with the Resistance. For four weeks a small village was his home, and then he was picked up by car to be taken, he was told, to a field where a plane would take him home to England. He was uneasy as, with another evader, they raced along country lanes at high speed before pulling into the drive of a large house. Another car was waiting there, and they were bundled in the back – where a German officer sat, a gun in his hand. They had been betrayed.

That night they arrived at a Gestapo building in northern Paris and were dumped into separate cells after being told, ominously, that, since they were in civilian clothes, they were assumed to be spies. After a sleepless night they were then taken by van to Fresnes prison. Here Bareham was put in a grim cell with a high window through which he could just see the tops of trees and the sky. 'It was cramped, very hot and stuffy. The palliasse to sleep on was full of fleas and bed-bugs.' But there was a good spirit among the prisoners.

There were clearly a good many RAF and Americans in the prison and we shouted to each other through the windows and ventilators. We also tapped out Morse messages on the pipes. We could hear bombing by Allied planes outside and the general feeling was that the Americans would be here very soon and the war would be over in two months.

But then came a buzz of rumours that they were to be moved from under the very noses of their liberators. To their dismay, these were true. On the morning of 15 August the cell doors were flung open and all the British and American prisoners herded together on the ground floor. Bareham was astonished to see close on 200 around him, including his flight engineer, bomb aimer and rear gunner. Along with the other inmates – around 2,000 in all – they were loaded into trucks and taken to the station and now they were packed together as the wagon doors were slammed shut and bolted and the train pulled them slowly away from any hope of a quick release. Where it was going no one knew, except that the direction was east – into Germany. Looking around him, he felt lucky. He had been in custody for just a week. There had been little time to make him suffer. But others who had been in Fresnes longer than him showed signs of the terrible beatings they had taken.

The train's progress was slow along tracks patrolled by Allied fighter planes. For hours it was stopped in a tunnel, and the prisoners were left to cook in the stifling summer heat. As the train moved on, in Bareham's wagon some of the French set to work heaving up the wooden floorboards and once they had made a big enough hole the daring dropped through onto the track as the train moved. When their escape was discovered, the guards forced all those remaining to strip naked. Nervous and trigger-happy, they then threw a French teenager off and, as he ran, shot him in the back 'while trying to escape'. Their mood lightened only after the train crossed out of France and into Germany. Bareham and his fellow RAF men now calculated they were heading for Frankfurt and Dulag Luft, the main interrogation centre for captured aircrew. 'We were sure this must be our immediate destination.' But the comfort that thought gave them was erased as the train kept going east for another 150 miles. On Sunday 20 August it passed through the town of Weimar, home to Bach, Goethe and Schiller, a monument to Germany's cultural heights. Five miles further on it stopped at a place that plumbed that same nation's depths of depravity – Buchenwald. It was a final destination in every sense.

We disembarked at midday and were hurried through the main gates, above which were emblazoned in large letters *KONZENTRATIONS-LAGER BUCHENWALD*. Inside there were machine-gun posts everywhere. We were kept waiting in a courtyard before the arrival procedure began. This consisted of a shower and delousing.

We had heard stories that the showers were often a disguise for the gas chambers and were very apprehensive at being shoved into a large building and the doors closed behind us. It was a relief when the sinister-looking apertures in the ceiling issued hot water after all.

We were then shaved completely from head to foot and given our clothing – ragged trousers, a shirt and vest, but no socks or shoes. Thus equipped we were marched barefoot over sharp stones and rocky ground to our 'quarters', which were no more than an area of cobblestones without any shelter from the elements.

The regime that now ruled their lives was unbearably harsh. Partly the camp ran on whim. Bareham listened aghast as he was told of the Kommandant's wife, who admired a Russian's tattooed back and thought it would make a nice lampshade. He was shot and duly skinned. But it was also run on routine brutality, often dished out during the daily assembly of all prisoners for counting, the *Appell*. The shortest of these lasted several hours, the inmates standing without shelter or relief, threatened and abused. On one notorious occasion, he was told, it had gone on for thirty-six hours in harsh winter conditions, snow a foot deep. Prisoners were beaten for trying to help comrades who collapsed.

We had very little food. Our daily ration was a quarter of a loaf of rye bread, margarine, potatoes and a bowl of thin soup. At night we lay on the cobbles, without blankets to begin with, then with a very thin one each. It was late summer and the nights were cold. We slept as best we could huddled together in small groups.

After some three weeks in the open we moved into one of the huts, still with one blanket each. These billets were terribly overcrowded and held 500 or more men. We were kept in shelves about six feet deep and no more than two feet high, and so closely packed that movement was virtually impossible. The hut was overrun with fleas, bed-bugs and lice.

Worse still was the constant fear. 'We were all out of uniform with only our dog tags to identify us and we were told that we could expect to be treated as spies. None of us expected to survive.' But they did. The RAF evaders were held in Buchenwald for two months, then they were released to the custody of the Luftwaffe and taken away to air-force POW camps. Only after the war did Bareham learn how lucky they were to get out alive.

It became clear later that once we had left Fresnes we were all to be executed. In fact at one time, our mass execution was only days away. But somehow the British officers in the camp smuggled out a letter to the Luftwaffe, informing them that aircrew were being held illegally in a concentration camp. Apparently it reached Hermann Goering[2] himself, who exerted his pressure to obtain our immediate transfer to Luftwaffe control.

**18**. George Fernyhough in 2005.

**17**. George Fernyhough in 1944 after the presentation of his Distinguished Flying Cross in 'recognition of gallantry displayed in flying operations against the enemy' – a term regularly used to disguise the actions of evaders.

**19**. George Fernyhough's fake Belgian identity card naming him as Theodore Jonkers.

**20**. Evaders hiding in the Fréteval forest shortly before liberation in 1944.

**21**. Spring 1943 in Paris. Three evaders *(bottom right)* are secretly pictured at the Trocadero walking behind a German naval officer and towards some German soldiers.

**22**. Pat O'Leary (Albert-Marie Guérisse) caught on camera by a street photographer in Marseille.

**23**. Andrée de Jongh (Dedée), in London to receive her George Medal, is presented with an RAF clock in recognition of her incredible efforts to help evaders.

These
measure
$1\frac{5}{8}'' \times 1\frac{5}{8}''$
or
4cms × 4cms
**ALWAYS
CARRY
3**

Fig. 1

Fig. 2

# GOOD

# BAD

Fig. 3

Fig. 4

**24.** RAF units received instructions detailing the correct style of photo to be carried by aircrew in case they were needed for false papers.

**25**. Joanna Jones is reunited with her father Joseph Sankey in Blackpool in 2001. He had been shot down in 1943 and Joanna – and her mother – believed he had been killed.

**26**. Evader Tom Wingham, shot down in 1943, at the Escape Lines Memorial Society reunion in York, 2005.

TELEPHONE:
GERRARD 9234
Extn.............

Any communications on the
subject of this letter should
be addressed to :—

THE
UNDER SECRETARY
OF STATE,
and the following number
quoted :—

Your Ref. .... P.408419/3/P.4.(B.6.)

AIR MINISTRY

(Casualty Branch),

73, OXFORD STREET,

W.1.

4th March 1944

Sir,

With reference to the letter from
this department dated the 24th January 1944,
I am directed to inform you, with great regret,
that in view of the lapse of time and the
absence of any news concerning your son,
1438430 Sergeant T. D. G. Teare, since he
was reported missing, it is now proposed to
take action to presume his death for official
purposes.

I am accordingly to ask that you
will be good enough formally to confirm that
you have received no further evidence or news
regarding him.

I am,
Sir,
Your obedient Servant,

for Director of Personal Services.

J. G. Teare Esq.,
268 Higher Road,
Halewood,
LIVERPOOL.

**27.** The letter to Denys Teare's parents telling them he was now presumed dead.
In reality he was fighting with the Resistance in France.

**BUCKINGHAM PALACE**

*May 3rd 1944.*

The Queen and I offer you our heartfelt sympathy in your great sorrow.

We pray that your country's gratitude for a life so nobly given in its service may bring you some measure of consolation.

*George R.I.*

J. G. Teare, Esq.

**28**. And the letter from the King offering commiserations to Denys's father.

**29.** The Pyrenees – many evaders had to cross this unforgiving landscape on their final leg to freedom.

**30.** Families and friends of evaders retrace the escape routes over the Pyrenees in 2001. It is incredible to think that many evaders had to make this journey with no protective clothing and shoes made of rope.

The majority of Allied evaders caught by the Germans did indeed end up in proper POW camps, though often after an ordeal in which at some point or other they felt sure they would die. RAF airman Harry Levy was Jewish and afraid he would be singled out for anti-Semitic treatment. Locked in a cell in St Gilles prison in Brussels with a Star of David on a yellow card pinned to the door, he would lie awake at night and hear names being called out along the corridor. Then there would be the clatter of cell doors opening, the tread of feet on the tiled floor as men marched away, the heavy clang as the iron grille at the end of the corridor shut behind them. 'I listened, shivering with cold but drawn by a fearful fascination.'³ He told himself reassuring stories – that those whose names had been called were going on a work detachment. But the more likely truth kept seeping into his brain. 'Were they being taken out to be shot? I found it hard to believe. The condemned men, too, perhaps, found it hard to believe, right up until the last moment, when, tied to posts, or backs against a wall, the squad of German soldiers in front of them levelled their rifles.' He wondered when they would come for him. They never did, though the mental torture he suffered was immense as his time in St Gilles dragged on. He was promised a transfer to a POW camp, delivered personally by a seemingly sympathetic Luftwaffe officer. 'Soon. Two or three days, no longer,' he was told. No one came for him.

Disappointment grew into despair, and despair deepened as the days stretched into weeks. The German's words, then, had been lies, his kindness part of some softening-up process, to what end I couldn't imagine. My hair and beard grew, and, with my pallid gaunt face, I began to resemble those others, the thousands, the millions of Jews trapped in Hitler's prisons and concentration camps.

Drained of energy, tired of inventing ways of killing time, I would pace the cell from one side of the bed to the other – eleven strides, past the door, along the wall with the cupboard, under the window, and back to the other side of the bed. I struggled with fear and depression. I felt completely at the mercy of these people and the hatred that possessed them, symbolized by the yellow card on my door.

Prayer saved his sanity.

I entered my inner world, and gradually a deep pool of calm and peace arose in me, as when a small child recovering from illness, I had lain weak but safe and warm in the comfort of my mother's bed. I accepted my condition.

The next morning, a Luftwaffe officer arrived and, after ten weeks in solitary confinement, Levy was at last on his way to a camp. He was thin to the point of being a shadow. Catching a reflection of himself, he could only wonder who the ghost staring back at him really was. But at least Levy and Bareham and other evaders had been taken out of the living hell of the Third Reich's penal system. In POW camps they were largely free from the merciless rule of the Gestapo and the SS. But many of those who had helped them while they were free remained crushed under the heels of sadists and savages. Could they possibly live to tell the tale? Or would they pay the ultimate price?

★

Donald Darling, MI9 liaison man in Gibraltar and then Neave's successor manning Room 900 after D-Day, knew more than anyone about the men and women who risked everything to hide, comfort and courier Allied evaders in occupied Europe. As he debriefed those men who made it home, he built a mental picture and a filed record of the individuals who had opened their doors, closed their curtains, defied all common sense in order to give those on the run a fighting chance of staying free. After the war he flew over Europe and thought 'of those cramped city flats and outlying farm buildings down below which had sheltered so many clandestine travellers'.[4] The occupants who put their lives at risk were young and old, rich and poor, professional and peasant. An evader was as likely to find himself in a château or a smart city apartment as on a farm or in a miner's cottage. In this democracy of danger there were barons and barmen, rich countesses as well as the family in Paris – attested to by four separate evaders – so poor they dined on rats, yet still did what they could for 'guests'. There were nuns who smuggled men into their convents, as well as the stripper who called at hideouts to 'entertain' the boys. Eight times Darling was shown identical souvenir photographs of this lady, naked except for high-heeled shoes and a pearl necklace. A husband-and-wife team without children was considered the safest combination. It was also helpful to have neighbours who would ignore comings and goings at strange hours of the day and night and not report unusual noises, faces and extra food to the police. Teenage girls were a useful distraction when ferrying evaders through city streets but boys of the same age were a danger. They were liable to be rounded up for forced labour.

Darling was astonished by the reserves of inventiveness and quick thinking quite ordinary people could draw on in an emergency. One woman, a very new recruit to the business, feigned an epileptic fit at the platform barrier at the Gare d'Austerlitz in Paris when guards began questioning her airman. She pulled the same trick at another station on another occasion. 'She was attractive, which helped matters,' Darling commented. But for all their ingenuity, for each escape-line helper it was a race against time to stay ahead of the Gestapo and the military police. And they knew full well that, once caught, they could expect no mercy. Their fate would be the very worst that the Nazi state, inventive in its cruelty, could devise.

One arrest often triggered others, which was the case with the Maréchal family – mother Elsie, father Georges and 18-year-old daughter, also Elsie – captured by German officers who came to their home in Brussels posing as American airmen seeking shelter. In St Gilles prison they suffered many vicious beatings before being put on trial. They were taken in front of a military tribunal of heel-clicking Luftwaffe officers in full uniform with sticks in their hands. The proceedings were in German, which the Maréchals barely understood. They had never met their defending officer, and his plea lasted just five minutes. They were sentenced to death for 'acting in support of the enemy'. Back in St Gilles, mother and daughter shared a condemned cell. The younger Elsie recalled:

Every evening at 5 p.m. we had to put our coats, dresses and shoes outside the cell to make sure we would not escape. All night long the light was left burning, and guards did the round regularly looking in through the spy-hole to check on us. But we were allowed to receive parcels of food and visits from our relatives, which made a big difference. Others told us we had a good chance of being reprieved and so our morale stayed high despite all the insults, threats and punishments we received.[5]

Son Robert – who had escaped the round-up only by pretending to be slow-witted – was allowed in to collect their laundry, and he would find messages written in tiny handwriting on cigarette paper sewn into the hems of garments. He also smuggled in paper, ink, coloured pencils and other implements so that, with a little ingenuity, the prisoners could enjoy the forbidden pleasures of embroidery, crochet and playing cards. But despite these amusements, time hung heavily, as did their sentences. 'Every Friday a number of prisoners were called out for deportation to Germany the next day, and every week we wondered if it was our turn next.' Then, though they did not know it, their pleas for clemency were turned down. It was autumn 1943 and Berlin had just taken a particularly accurate pasting from Bomber Command. A furious Goering was not in the mood for mercy. There was a last meeting – though, again, at the time they did not know it. The two Elsies were surprised when Georges was brought to a little room near their cell. They had not seen him since the trial, and they spent some quite unexpected family time together. 'We left each other in a happy and hopeful mood.' But that night Georges's name rang out down the corridor along with those of ten others, seven of them Comet Line workers and organizers. They were taken from their cells to a holding pen for the night. There a Roman Catholic priest waited with them and a mass was said. Paper and pen were produced for final letters. 'Tomorrow I shall make the great journey, and you can be proud of me,' Eric de Menten wrote to his family. 'I regret nothing. I die for the ideal we have all shared. Keep smiling.'[6] At dawn on a wet and windy autumn morning they were taken to the Tir National, Brussels' rifle range. Eric apparently smoked a last cigarette and chatted with the soldiers about to execute him. Facing the firing squad, witnesses said, they sang patriotic songs and called out 'Long live Belgium! Long live England! Long live Liberty!' All refused blindfolds. They looked their enemy in the eye right to the very end.

Wife and daughter did not know of Georges's death for a week. Then three officers came into their cell and one read out the notification of his execution. Daughter Elsie recalled: 'I saw Mummy standing very straight, pale, with her lips trembling and I felt as if I had been knocked on the head. When the three men had gone, I took her in my arms and she sobbed. There was nothing to do but cry together. Maybe our turn would come soon, but we were just indifferent. What worse could happen to us now?' They did not die a quick and defiant death. Their fate was a slow torture, which began when their names were called out on New Year's Day, 1944. Mother Elsie scribbled a note which was smuggled out to her son.

My very dear Bob,
A little word to say au revoir to you because I believe that we are going to leave soon. I am so sad, Bob, that Daddy has gone away before us. I would have so liked to stay together until the end. It is possible that Elsie and I leave next Saturday, but naturally one never knows in advance. Continue to study hard for it is very important for you. I am so happy to see you have become a man. Good courage and see you soon.

At the railway station they were among eleven men and eleven women herded onto a prison truck coupled onto the normal passenger train going east. With the sort of above-the-parapet courage that set helpers apart, Robert managed to get on board the train and travel as far as the city of Namur, where it stopped for just a minute or two. There he got out and ran the length of the platform to try and give them a parcel of food and clothes. He was not fast enough and the train pulled out before he could get to them. But they saw him and his selflessness was an inspiration. 'I still see it,' Elsie recalled. 'My brother running as hard as he could and the train was going and he couldn't see us. But we could see him. It was the last image we were to keep of Belgium.' They needed every last iota of hope they could muster to deal with what lay ahead in the grim SS-run network of labour, concentration and extermination camps. And for them there was an extra refinement of misery. They were classified as '*Nacht und Nebel*' ('night and fog'), condemned to be lost in the darkest parts of the empire, shunted from prison to prison, Gestapo cellar to Gestapo cellar, horror camp to horror camp, until all trace of them had disappeared. It was a specific punishment for opponents of the Nazis in occupied countries and intended to intimidate local populations into submission by denying the families and friends of *les disparus* all knowledge of what had happened to them.

The Maréchal women's first stop was the prison at Aachen, where faces stared out through the wire gratings of cells to which daylight never penetrated. Then they were moved again – packed seven at a time into cells meant for two on the prison train.

Thirsty, perspiring and panting for air, we slept on hard floors. A bucket was all we had for sanitation. The air stank horribly. From the stations we arrived at, we were escorted through the streets by Gestapo officers and fierce dogs to wherever we were to be held.

There was a fresh indignity at every place they stepped.

In Cologne we joined 160 women stark naked in an enormous shower-bath hall, then passed into another large hall to dry without towels. All the time, soldiers passed in and out. In Frankfurt we saw a man wedged in a cage in which he could neither stand nor sit. He was covered in blood. In Nuremberg the lack of air in our cell sent us staggering backwards.

Finally they came to Waldheim, near Dresden.

This was like stepping into the Middle Ages. It was an old dilapidated building, cold and musty with the silence of the tomb. An inmate we recognized whispered, 'It's hell here.' Our hair was cut with clippers to the nakedness of a billiard ball and we were given a convict costume of a thin cotton dress, wooden sandals and a triangular black headcloth. It was January and freezing. We were put to work on munitions, sewing and mending, making nets, cutting leather or sorting rags.

Winter and summer we rose at 5 a.m., dressed, stripped to the waist and washed in cold water very quickly. Then it was work – *Arbeit, Arbeit* – in silence all day long for twelve hours with at most a twenty-minute break for a scant meal. The place was ruled by iron discipline.

All we possessed was comb, toothbrush, spoon, mug, towel, and our daily bread ration, which we carried constantly with us in a small linen bag. Woe betide anyone who left theirs unguarded, for the bread vanished like magic. We mixed with thieves and murderers. One had killed her baby by putting it in the oven. Another had killed her child and fed it to the pigs. Then there was the woman serving four years for listening in to the radio from London.

Young Elsie developed terrible abscesses on her back from the beatings she had been given back in St Gilles. She was also working in a Siemens factory where her job inserting copper coils into metal cases aggravated her wounds. When she collapsed, a prison doctor lanced the abscesses without anaesthetic. Four prisoners held her down. Her skin peeled and she became very thin, but after three months' illness she rejoined her mother. The threat of the death penalty being carried out always hung over them. Prisoners would be called out for a one-way trip to the guillotine at Dresden. But for the Maréchals there was more travelling – to Leipzig to be packed, standing-room only, into a small, stifling cell on a hot summer's night; to Potsdam to sleep on a bare floor. Some prisons, the one at Lübeck, for example, were almost decent with clean, running water and a real bathroom, but others, like Stettin, were hellholes. Here the SS chief made them sing Nazi songs. 'We heard stories of Polish prisoners being given the choice either to hang their companions, or else to be hanged themselves.'

The constant disruption and travelling and never knowing what lay ahead left them increasingly exhausted. Elsie saw her mother beginning to bend under the strain. She cried for the first time. They knew of the Allied landings in Europe, that Germany was under siege and the war was closer now to ending than it had ever been. But victory might come too late. Young Elsie urged her mother not to give in. 'Don't let the Germans win,' she told her.

News of the liberation of Paris and Brussels had the prisoners singing and dancing in their cells – for which they were punished with three days without soup or exercise. Facing defeat, the SS determined on revenge while they still could. The *Nacht und Nebel* caravan was to end in an extermination camp. Young Elsie could not believe what she was seeing as she walked through the gates at Ravensbruck, the concentration camp exclusively for women. 'An open cart was being pulled along and piled inside were bodies, naked, thin – just bones – with the limbs dangling everywhere, with mouths and eyes wide open, abandoned in a miserable death.' They were told this picked up the bodies of those who died at night and were deposited outside each block every morning to be taken to the crematorium.

The new arrivals were herded into a large tent already bursting with 1,600 Jewish women lying on the ground.

The awful spectacle of this tent is engraved on our minds for ever. Some were ill or dying, others sleeping in pools of water. Pails, jugs, cans were the lavatories. We spent the night walking up and down trying to keep warm, but in the end were forced to lie on the damp ground and sleep for an hour or so.

The next day they were showered, deloused and allocated to a hut filled with three-storey bunk beds. It was three to a bed. 'We slept fully clothed with our meagre possessions under our heads to prevent them from being stolen.'

*Appell* was at 5 a.m. each morning, the women, blue with cold, standing strictly to attention in lines for hours.

The SS arrived, arrogant, superior, boots stamping. They counted us time and time again, and if it was not right we had to wait without moving for hours in spite of freezing fog, beating rain, wind, freezing snow, storm. We wondered if it was possible to be colder, more hungry. Of course it was possible because human resistance is unbelievable.

The work they were then set to was hard and unremitting. They dug trenches, carried coal, chopped wood, unloaded railway trucks. But it was the hunger and cold that broke the spirit more than the labour. And the dysentery. It struck newcomers almost immediately, and the stench it generated – along with that from bodies burning in the crematorium – was the abiding, awful smell of Ravensbruck, which, according to Elsie Maréchal, no film or book could ever properly capture. 'It must be lived to be realized.'

What particularly appalled young Elsie was the treatment of old women, their age and modesty a reason for extra brutality rather than respect. They had to strip naked alongside the younger ones to be run to the showers, 'their poor fleshless bodies trembling with cold and fear'. She recorded the death of one of them, who stopped her as she rushed from her top-tier bunk to *Appell* one morning:

She was lying in a lower bed, very old with completely white hair. She wanted to say something and so I put my ear to her mouth. She asked me to tell her son that *Maman* was dying bravely for France, that she loved him above everything and that he must keep on trying to be a good boy. I tried to hear her name but I couldn't. Then I was hit with a truncheon by the guard in charge of our block and was forced outside. When I came back, her bed was empty, her body gone. Sadly I never knew who she was, so I could never pass on her message.

Even worse was when a friend's 80-year-old mother died and she helped her carry the corpse to the pile.

I took her by the feet and she took her by the shoulders and I thought, 'That's your mother, your dear mother, and there's not a tear, not a sign of sadness in your face, nothing. That's what we've become – without emotion for anything.' We simply took her down, and that was that.

If they didn't collapse and die, the old were weeded out like dead heads on a flower bush. In a long queue, the women had to shuffle naked in front of a doctor who selected the unfit for what, with malicious humour, was called the *Jugend Lager*, the youth camp, a few miles away. Here they were starved and left out in the cold without blankets. Any who survived this were then marked for 'the black transport' to the gas chambers. One day Elsie senior was selected for the *Jugend Lager*, the first step to extermination. She was rescued by a fellow inmate, a Jewish doctor, an old friend from St Gilles, who quietly changed the mark of death the German doctor had just put on her card. It was a brave act of defiance, the light of goodness and mercy flickering, however faintly, in the black abyss, a snowball in hell. But was it too little too late?

*

What kept the spark of life going? Nadine Dumon, another member of the Comet Line, was also in Ravensbruck but, through all its horrors, there was only one time she wished to give up, to die.

I was always determined to survive and to get home but once we were being taken to a different camp and after five days and four nights in cattle trucks I was in a very bad state, freezing and bleeding from the ear. We were being marched through the snow and I thought how nice it would be just to lie down and go to sleep. The guards would shoot me, and it would all be over.

Then I saw in my head someone telling my mother that I was dead and decided I could not let that happen to her. I told myself I had to get back for her sake. She had had too many worries and sadness already and I didn't want her to have more.[7]

And not for a moment did she regret her work hiding evaders, even though it took her to hell and back. 'I was fighting the Germans. No regrets.' But in her sad eyes live on the memories of those who shared her cause and did not return – her own father, a doctor and Resistance activist, dead in a concentration camp; Frédéric de Jongh, the teacher who recruited her, shot by firing squad. 'That's a terrible, terrible price to pay for what we did.' There were 154 other organizers and helpers of the Comet Line who died for the cause, 73 of them a slow, lingering death in concentration camps. Scores were shot and executed in other ways. A dozen were simply never traced. With the 'NN' for *Nacht und Nebel* against their names they disappeared into the 'night and fog' of Germany and were never seen again. In each arrest and death there was a family tragedy. Baron Jean Greindl, alias 'Nemo', whose identity young Elsie Maréchal had taken endless beatings to protect, was eventually cornered by the Gestapo. Agents also seized his wife and took her to headquarters. There she saw her husband and for a brief moment they held hands. Almost imperceptibly he shook his head from side to side, indicating that his position was hopeless. It was over. She handed him a rosary but before he could take it he was seized and dragged away.[8]

When she next saw him several months later he had been sentenced to death by the same military tribunal that had condemned the Maréchals. She was allowed to visit him for just a few minutes at Gestapo headquarters, after which he was taken back to the special quarters in which he was being held. Greindl was considered a prize capture. The Germans still failed to grasp that the young Dédée de Jongh was the inspirational leader of the Comet Line they had now so successfully broken up. They saw the count as the top figure and kept him locked up in solitary confinement under constant watch at a Belgian army barracks from which rescue was impossible. There he died in an Allied air raid in September 1943. It is said that the 105 American B-17 bombers that attacked Brussels that night passed over the baron's country home on their way to the capital and his five-year-old daughter, little Claire, looked out from her window and said, 'Don't let them bomb Papa!'[9] A stray single bomb did just that. His wife arrived at the barracks the next day to find a ruin. The following day she was told her husband was dead. He was said to have died instantly in the blast, and the marks on his body once it was dug from the rubble seemed to confirm this. If so, it was a better and quicker end than many of his comrades suffered.

It can be hard for those of us living six decades after such events in a peaceful democratic society to comprehend fully the barbarity that humans inflicted on others in Nazi-occupied Europe. There is often a tendency to soften that past (deny it, even) rather than stare unflinchingly into its true awfulness. The likes of Geo Jouanjean could not avert his eyes. The unspeakable, the unimaginable, was actually happening to him – Resistance fighter Geo, the brother of Janine, whose RAF boyfriend Gordon Carter he helped to return to England by boat from Brittany. Betrayed by a traitor, he was arrested and lodged in prison in Rennes. There he was beaten, held down in a bath until he nearly drowned and chained in the punishment cell. This was a cage little more than four feet high and four feet wide. He slumped inside like a trapped animal. Years later he did his best to describe the indescribable:

You cannot sit down nor stand up. You are attached to bars by handcuffs. The light goes out and you are in the dark. You don't know if it is morning or evening, day or night. Something to eat every three days, in principle, when one arm is freed and you have three or four minutes to gulp it down. Unshaven, unwashed, and as for the rest of it . . .

As to how long I spent in that cage, that I cannot say. Seconds turn into hours, hours into days, days into months. Time no longer means anything. Nightmares then and always. But time does pass, the endless minutes drone by. Fear gets to me more and more, fear of dying, fear of losing my legs, fear of being a thing of pity, not a coward. I know that my last hours are coming.

When the doors of the cell open, death will come. Bullets go straight through you, they burn and tear your body. I can imagine them, but my face, my mouth, my eyes. What pain. Already I can hear the noise of the screaming bullets.[10]

He thought about his mother, who had also been arrested and was in the same prison. The Gestapo had severely beaten her in front of him. 'I think a lot about her, alone in a cell, my poor mother, so small yet so brave. Surely she would hear the salvo of the guns at my execution, then the coup de grâce. She would know – everything gets known in a prison.' Suddenly the light in his cell went on, and he turned away from its blinding glare. Hands seized him. He thought the moment had come. Be brave, he told himself. 'Mother!' his soul screamed out. He was wrong. He was taken to another French prison, then another. Then, after a year, all of it in solitary, he was on a cattle truck to Germany. He never understood why he hadn't been shot. Perhaps what he now faced was worse than death.

First stop was Birkenau, part of the Auschwitz extermination camp and the actual site of its gas chambers.

The doors of the wagon open wide. The SS shout and yell at us. We help those of our friends who are too weak to climb down and carry out those who have died. We are beaten into line, then counted. The Germans kill a few of the weak ones. Some who have gone mad in the wagons are clubbed to death. We are counted again, and beaten again.

But arriving here was an administrative mistake far from unusual in the bureaucratic Nazi state. Others were meant to die here in their hundreds of thousands, especially Jews and gypsies. But not him.

The group I was with only got as far as the quarantine camp. The SS realized we were not Jewish and that there had been a mistake. Some German official must have put the wrong code on the movement label showing the destination of our convoy. The SS kept us together to be sent somewhere else. However, we were tattooed. On my left arm I have the number 185795 in indelible ink.

Two or three months later he was transferred to Buchenwald. This too was to be a short stay, and then he was sent to Flossenburg concentration camp. To him it was 'a charnel house, your welcome to death'. If he had retained any idea of human goodness and civilization, it died here as he witnessed scenes that made a mockery of the words 'of generals, cardinals, magistrates, wise men, intellectuals, etc. What a joke, what a farce!' Typhus was rampant in his block. Men lay about naked and covered in vermin, filthy, repugnant, dying in agony.

Here we have a new type of being, neither human nor animal. Some have to go around on [all fours], some crawl, some can move only an arm, which points desperately but towards whom? A leg dangles and shakes, others can only open and close their eyelids. Others stare with great shining eyes, already understanding the mysteries of death. Their flesh is split, they are covered in filth and yellow sores giving out the stench of disease.

Those not killed by contagion died by the bullet. Geo recorded how he peered through a hole in the wall that surrounded Flossenburg's punishment block – 'a very secret place, entry to which was prohibited'.

I saw a naked man come out of the main door into the yard, followed by an SS guard holding a revolver. The naked man is now walking with the SS man in his steps like a shadow, the revolver held very near the back of his neck. A shot, muffled by the noise of the camp, and the body slides down a short ramp towards the ovens. Three minutes go by. The door opens again, a naked man comes out, the SS guard behind pushes him brutally, the man walks more quickly, a shot and a shape wavers and falls, slides down the ramp.

He watched as twenty-seven men were dispatched in this way before another morning at Flossenburg came to an end.

Just one victim showed some hesitation, but he was kicked savagely and beaten with the revolver butt towards his death. Your eye, appalled and horrified, counts each step in this weird ballet – fifty-two steps with the black barrel of the revolver just an inch or two from the back of your neck. And then the last noise you hear before you die.

Pierre d'Harcourt, deported to Germany for helping evaders, found his courage deserting him in Buchenwald.

Often I stood on parade waiting for *Appell*, with all my resources gone. At these moments I was on the point of deliberately collapsing on to the ground to let the SS haul me to the experimental block or finish me off with a pistol there and then.[11]

An old and exhausted Russian man on his work detail complained that he had had enough, and the SS officer in charge sent for a rope and hanged him on the spot. Harcourt found it difficult to decide whether this was an act of sadism or a humane one to put a suffering creature out of its misery. In this culture of death, it took a strong will to carry on, but even this was not a certain key to survival.

Luck, simple serendipity, probably decided who lived and who died in that lottery of the damned. Mary Lindell would one day walk out of Ravensbruck only because she was recognized as a trained Red Cross nurse just when such a vacancy arose in the camp hospital. She also, it must be said, had the sort of imperious personality that seemed to rise above every act of bullying, every kick and punch, the Gestapo and the SS aimed at her. She was the English-born wife of a French count, and as the Comtesse de Milleville yielded position to no one. If she was frightened as she and her family helped British Army evaders in the early days of the war and then RAF airmen, she never showed it. (Well, perhaps just the once when she thought the Germans had executed her son.)

Mary Lindell was a woman of the English upper classes, brought up to speak her mind, stand her corner and take no nonsense from anyone. She was a figure tailor-made for one of those pukka, village-green propaganda films the wartime British loved to watch. Such indomitability might seem a ridiculous weapon to bring to bear against the most brutal and tyrannical regime in modern history, but her record shows it was surprisingly effective. She served nine months in Fresnes prison in Paris for assisting the escape of British officers, a surprisingly puny sentence considering she called the German military court officials 'swine'. Even more surprisingly, her judges stood at the end to salute her.

After serving her time she escaped to England, was recruited by Airey Neave and Jimmy Langley and sent back as an agent to try to restore the broken escape lines across the Pyrenees. As 'Marie-Claire', she was on every wanted list when she was arrested at Pau station. 'At last we meet,' the Gestapo officer said as he seized her arm. The Germans so prized her capture they wanted to send her to Berlin for a show trial. Instead she was taken to Ravensbruck. On arrival, she instantly organized the women around her, grabbed extra blankets, refused to give them back. Once again, for whatever reason, authority backed down in the face of her steady gaze. But the harsh regime would soon dull that gleam. She was a middle-aged woman who had twice suffered bad falls, most recently from the Paris train when trying to escape. On that occasion she had also taken a bullet in the cheek and another in the skull. She would have died if a German surgeon had not patched her up.

And now she was going to die for certain. Another long *Appell* in the bitter cold, perhaps two more if she was strong, and then the pneumonia she had suffered many times before would return. And how could she be strong on the pitiful food rations? Spirits slumped around her. She determined not to give in, but the choice was rapidly becoming no longer hers. The calling out of her name saved her. Normally in Ravensbruck, to hear your name was a death sentence, a summons to one of the 'black transports'. Not for Lindell. She was wanted to work in the infirmary. Her biographer has no doubt it saved her life.[12] The position also meant she could save the lives of others. She now had a bed to herself, clean blankets – and that vital reprieve from *Appell*. As the German matron, a martinet who terrified most inmates, told her: 'With luck, you may get home one day.'

★

All those who fell into the enemy's hands had to learn to handle their fear, otherwise the nightmare they were in would send them mad. Virginia d'Albert-Lake, the American-born woman caught while ferrying airmen to the forest camp at Fréteval, remembered how on her first night locked in a dungeon at Chartres she was awoken by the screaming and wailing of a woman in an adjoining cell who had lost her mind. 'The mad talk went on and on in the dark and I could only lie still and listen. It was horrifying.'[13] Then, transferred to Fresnes prison in Paris, she was put in with a woman who groaned and wept with pain. 'She told me she had been at Gestapo headquarters and suspended for hours from the ceiling by an arm and a leg. She was trembling and had a burning fever. I shivered too, in anticipation. The next morning she was taken away and I never saw her again.' For Lake, her loss of freedom was torture enough. At Fresnes there were exercise courtyards where for twenty minutes twice a week the prisoners could walk. 'I would look out from there through the bars to some grass and trees but I could never stay long. Tears soon blinded me.'

She herself was not tortured, for reasons she never totally understood though she was grateful nonetheless. The Gestapo officer who interrogated her told her he intended to treat her with respect 'as a woman and a patriot'. Perhaps it was because she was an American and he knew which way the wind of war was blowing. He kept to his word, though she was always aware he could change his mind on a whim. Waiting in a communal cell, her heart ached for the men beside her who had just come from the torture chamber. 'They were handcuffed and bleeding, and in such misery they could not speak. I recall one whose whole body was throbbing with pain. Only groans escaped his swollen lips.'

Her way was eased too when she was transferred to a different prison in Paris, one lighter and airier than Fresnes and with rooms rather than cells. And it was here that she was held as the Allies neared Paris and each prisoner heard the news, felt the excitement and then struggled with its implications. Would it mean liberation, evacuation or massacre? Hopes rose and fell. On 15 August 1944, the same day as Fresnes was emptied, so was Lake's prison. The Germans were not about to surrender their prisoners. Hitler, in his unreason, had ordered his armies not to give up anything his Third Reich had conquered. They were now yielding swathes of land in western and eastern Europe every day but at least the SS could hang on to its human booty, its conquered humanity. As the prisoners assembled in the courtyard, they could hear Allied guns in the distance. They were less than forty miles away. 'We were nearly crazy with despair. How cruel it seemed.'

But there was no relenting. At the suburban Gare de Pantin, the cattle trucks were waiting, along with SS guards to whip them in. The women were warned that if anyone tried to escape, ten hostages from that wagon would be shot. On the slow and exhausting journey out of France and into the heart of Germany she learned one piece of cheering news from a woman she knew. Her husband Philippe, also a Resistance worker and 'helper', was alive and safe in England. 'I nearly danced with joy. As long as he was okay it was all right. I could take care of myself.' At Weimar, the train had stopped and women whose husbands were also on board were allowed one last meeting beside the track before the men were shunted along the line to Buchenwald. She was glad not to have had to endure such a farewell. 'I had always heard that women endured prison hardship better than men and I had more faith in my future than ever, now that I knew he was safe.'

But her optimism took a severe knock when the women arrived at their destination – Ravensbruck.

As our doors were pushed back we saw new, severe-looking guards with SS on their collars. Our old guards suddenly adopted the same swift brutal gestures, the same loud raucous voices as the new ones. The atmosphere had suddenly changed. I felt tense and unhappy.

At first the look of the place was reassuring – there were lawns, flower beds, a lake in the distance. It was the first glimpse of the inmates that chilled the heart – 'horrible-looking creatures, thin and haggard with huge festering sores, sinister, unreal, unbelievable'. All too soon they would be like this. Like Elsie Maréchal, Virginia d'Albert-Lake found the camp's early morning *Appell* the greatest trial of all. 'The weird, penetrating siren that woke us will be, for me, always the most terrifying of sounds.' Standing outside shivering in the pre-dawn, eyes were drawn to the glow not of the rising sun but of the chimneys of the crematorium. By this stage of the war, the camp was full to bursting, and women were being sent on work details. In Lake's case that meant a three-day train journey to a munitions factory in Torgau. The work was hard and dangerous but it was a relief just to be away from Ravensbruck. She was given a job in the kitchen – another of a number of concessions afforded her because she was American. (She had also been allowed to keep her hair, unlike all the others, whose heads were sheared.)

For eleven and a half hours a day we peeled potatoes. Our fingers, hands and arms ached, and then became numb with fatigue. But I won't complain because we were permitted to eat all the raw vegetables we wanted. We were forbidden to carry any back to camp, but we did it all the same, hiding as many as we could in our clothes to give to the factory girls, who needed vitamins even more than we did. We also stole tomatoes from the commandant's personal garden.

Life became almost acceptable. 'The weather was invigorating during those beautiful autumn days but I was never cold because I wore my blanket. I had a healthy colour. The SS girl who guarded us was not unkind. I felt good.' But the threat of being returned to Ravensbruck was ever present, and inevitably the day came. Passing through the camp's gates once more was not the shock it had been the first time. Now she knew what to expect. But when that awful siren sounded again her depression was deep. Autumn had also turned to the chill of winter.

Every morning, going out of the door into the cold was like diving from a high platform into icy water. It took the same courage. It seemed even more terrible because winter was only just beginning and the early morning sorties stretched out ahead endlessly into the future. There had been times we were convinced the war would end that year but now, as the weeks wore on, we nervously felt that only a spring offensive by the Allies would terminate our misery.

There was also the added horror of a new SS girl more hateful than any she had so far encountered.

She was young, perhaps twenty-five, but hard, mean and cruel. She beat us with her stick. She pulled our hair. She seized the miserable little sacks in which we kept our possessions, dumped their contents on the floor and then kicked us as we bent to pick them up. She stole our wedding rings from off our fingers. She threatened us. She punished us. She deprived us of what meagre rights we had as human beings. I wish today that I could find her. I would point at her and cry: 'There she is! Make her suffer! Strike her! Kick her! Starve her! That's all she can understand.'

But Lake knew her own heart was hardening too when coats were issued to the younger and fitter prisoners like her, the ones who could work.

It was frightful to see the older women standing and shivering at *Appell*. We should have unselfishly surrendered our coats to them but we knew we were fighting to sustain life. Survival of the fittest became something real, no longer a phrase in a science text. Were we sinking to bestiality? Perhaps. Unselfish gestures were becoming more and more rare. No one wanted to die, especially in Germany, and with the war nearly over. Until then our only aim was to resist the cold, the hunger, the deprivations.

Darwinian creed did her no good. Her coat was soon torn from her back by the bully in charge of her hut just at the point when she desperately needed its extra warmth.

Lake was now moved away from Ravensbruck for the second time, to a separate work detachment a train journey away to the north. The pleasure of leaving the main camp was dented when the truth of their new assignment sank in. With Russian and Polish prisoners of war – always given the worst jobs – they were to extend a military airfield, dig trenches, build roads, runways and barracks, almost with their bare hands. It was work that would have taxed healthy men. To starved, exhausted and sick women it was tantamount to a death sentence. They laboured away in water and mud, which turned to ice and snow as the winter, later recognized as the worst in central Europe for fifty years, began to bite. The women had no stockings, sweaters, coats or blankets. A fortnight after the first snow some extra clothing did arrive but never enough. As November turned to December they would step out in the mornings into at best driving rain, usually a blizzard of snow. Day by day the temperature dropped. The airfield was close to the Baltic, and the wind howled across the flatlands and pierced every garment. That and diminishing supplies of food took a dreadful toll. Lake watched a young and beautiful Swiss friend turn into a wrinkled, bent and haggard old lady in two months.

I have never seen such human suffering. *Appells* were heavy with misery. Women fell unconscious on the snow and one's first reaction was 'I can't help; I'm so weak, I must save the little strength I have, or I shall fall myself.' Then, there followed whispers of 'Who is it?' and, if it happened to be a friend, one struggled out of a state of lassitude to step forward and clutch at the dead weight which, after all, was a human being that demanded sympathy.

The camp director always allowed us to take them into the infirmary, but, before all the work groups had left the camp, she went round and screamed and beat at those who were regaining consciousness and forced them out to work.

Lake found another friend crouching behind a shelter and repeating desperately over and over again, 'I can't stand the cold any longer, I want to die.' She wondered how much more she herself could take.

We had ceased to look for the end of the war, because we couldn't know when it would be. Instead, we centred our hopes on the end of winter, because we could count on it. The war might last through the spring, summer, and into the autumn of 1945. We could wait . . . if only we could get through this winter.

Would she make it? For Lake, Elsie Maréchal, Nadine Dumon and the thousands of other helpers incarcerated in those hellish conditions, there was still much waiting, suffering and, of course, dying still to do.

*

There was a land where people were free, however hard it may have been to recall or to visualize among the grey-dead landscape of guard towers, gallows and crematoria. In newly liberated Paris, Airey Neave came across a legendary figure he had never expected to meet. That the Revd Donald Caskie, deep into the task of rescuing evaders before anyone else, had survived the war was more than surprising; it was a miracle. The French had hounded him out of Marseilles and shut down the Seamen's Mission where he had hidden so many British soldiers and airmen before directing them towards home. He took up residence in Grenoble, watched in all he did by the German Gestapo and the French paramilitary police, the Milice. His normal congregation of polite elderly ladies was bemused by the security cordons they had to pass through just to take tea with the pastor. 'Such rough men,' one told him, 'and they breathe so heavily!' Despite the surveillance, he continued his clandestine work. His refusal to kow-tow, his preaching against Nazism and his efforts to stop the deportation of Jews were finally too much for his enemies. He was arrested and thrown into a cell – literally thrown, his face badly bruised as he was hurled against the wall.

His jailers were the Italians, in joint occupation of southern France with the Germans at that time in April 1943.

They were not as efficient as the Germans but they were more cruel. They treat prisoners like vicious cats playing with mice, but they lack the final savagery of cats. They do not kill without orders. Their absent-minded vindictiveness degrades the prisoner.[14]

He was kept in darkness, sleeping on rancid straw, pacing out his days between the damp stone walls of his prison. His bible was taken from him. 'Fortunately I had it in my heart and head and it preserved my faith and sanity. When despair threatened to engulf my soul, the voice of Christian reason asserted itself and I was consoled. In the darkness my heart lifted and joy surged through me.' He needed that divine strength when he was taken to the Villa Lynwood in Nice, a large house once belonging to an English family. Now what had once been a joy-filled Riviera holiday home was an interrogation centre and house of torture.

The plastered walls of my cell were evidence that the villa had become a projection of hell upon earth. They were covered with the names of men and women who had halted there on the road to death or the camps. I found signatures of old comrades of mine who had disappeared.

From his cell door he now watched as a guard with a bayonet prodded a young inmate down the corridor. 'The dark face was gaunt and unshaven. He staggered as he walked.' At the end of the corridor the prisoner was forced back in the other direction, and the procession went on all day, back and forth, for four days. The man's shirt was soaked with blood but the torture was unending. When he fell he was kicked back into action. 'Then it suddenly stopped and I heard no more of the man who marched. For hours I sank in misery, praying for him, feeling miserably futile that I had been unable to help him.'

Caskie had just managed to settle his mind to sleep when a hideous scream rang through the villa. A Resistance worker was being interrogated for the names in his Maquis group.

He screamed and whimpered but they did not get a word from him, just great sobs rising to high pitch like a demented, diabolic violin as the guards applied their trade of cruelty to his body. They stopped after an hour and a half and, left alone, he began to weep helplessly and weirdly. But he was also trying to sing, and louder and louder the words came through his agony. He was intoning Bach's 'Passion Chorale'.

> 'O Sacred Head sore wounded
> With grief and shame weighed down
> O kingly head surrounded
> With thorns Thine only crown.'

Most amazingly of all, he was singing it in the original German: '*O Haupt voll Blud und Wunden*'.

In this little hell, secluded in a garden on the most beautiful coast that God has created for the joy of man, the chorale of the gentle Bach was giving heart to a victim of the musician's own race and their Italian ally. Over and over again, he sang until the voice died to a whisper, and we both slept. They must have taken him away early in the morning. Throughout the next day there was silence.

Caskie was to be physically tested himself when he was transferred from Nice to the medieval prison at San Remo, just across the border in Italy. He was taken there on a spring evening with the wind blowing freshly off the Mediterranean. But once inside its gates he was plunged into hell.

A mournful heritage of age-old cruelty gave the place an atmosphere of doom. For centuries there was no hope for those held in its black, remorseless bowels. It was a place Dante might have imagined. Water dripped from the four-feet thick cell walls. The dungeons were foul.

He was led stumbling down stairways and along dark passages until the light from a torch flashed on a narrow iron doorway, rusted into the stone. It was dragged open and he was pushed inside a medieval 'bottle' cell. Shaped like a man, it was big enough to contain one human being.

It tapers at the top so that the face is never more than two inches from the walls that encase your head. You cannot move your knees more than a few inches. If you rest on your shoulders, the strain on the legs becomes agonizing. There are no facilities for physical relief and your own stench fills your lungs. It is, I conjecture, the most vile instrument of torture ever devised by men.

A person's vomit simply ran back down his face. The same happened with his screams. The sound flew back off the iron door and into his brain. Caskie suffered in the bottle for twenty-four hours before being taken to an ordinary cell. He awoke feeling close to death. 'There seemed to be thin sand in my veins and life was draining away. There was no sound in the place, no light. I might have been entombed.' He was in solitary, and stayed that way for a month. He built a life in his head, went back to his childhood in Scotland and in those vivid memories found the courage to carry on.

The dungeon walls would disappear and I would see again my island of Islay, the Paps of Jura, the view across the water, the blue hills and green fields, the lapping water on the beach. I heard the voice of my mother call me and summoned her to San Remo to stay my spirit when it seemed to fail.

His ordeal lessened when he was given companions to share his cell but only really ended when he was handed over to the Germans. For some reason, the Gestapo officers he encountered treated him with dignity. His imprisonment now became, in his own words, more like a holiday camp than his stay with the Italians had been. He noticed that the ordinary German soldiers who escorted him while being taken to Marseilles and then to Paris had an air of defeat about them. They talked less of glorious victories for the Fatherland and more of Hitler's delusions of grandeur. The devastation of their cities by Allied bombers was shattering for them. They knew more retribution was on the way. And so, his spirits recovering, Caskie returned to Paris, the city he had fled from in 1940. In Fresnes, the prison walls around him and the tramp of jackboots in the corridors dampened some of that new-found élan. He realized that whereas the Villa Lynwood was a house of torture and San Remo a place where people were left to rot, Fresnes was a slaughterhouse. He was serene in the face of death, which he came to accept as inevitable in this place. The Allied armies were advancing but he felt certain the SS would butcher everyone behind bars before fleeing. Every morning hostages were shot; every day the hot news tapped down the cold water pipes from other inmates was of new executions.

They came for him at dawn one morning, and he was put into a police van with a thin-faced young man, who trembled with fear. 'They have told me I shall die today, monsieur,' he said to Caskie. 'Pray with me.' Then he talked about his wife and his little children 'and my heart ached for him and that girl and those babies'. The van stopped, and the young man got up to get out but was motioned back into his place by a guard. They were at the Gestapo headquarters in rue des Saussaies. 'The pastor dismounts here,' the guard announced. 'The other one,' he said, indicating the young man, 'is for Mont Valérien!' This was the execution site above the Bois de Boulogne. Caskie managed to have a last few minutes with the young man.

The pale face turned to me blankly. It was deadened by despair. I put my hands on his shoulders and spoke to him, telling him that his children would be safe, and soon the Allies would be here and peace would come. His children would be protected. Tears streamed down his cheeks.

I told him to remember the One who died on the Cross for love of him and for his children. 'He is with you now, *mon cher*. You die in His company.' The young face was at peace before he took my hand and I left him.

As the young man was driven off to face the firing squad, Caskie stepped inside the Gestapo building to face his judges. He was accused of being 'a spy, agitator and agent for escaping soldiers and prisoners-of-war'. He stated his case but was just harangued in return. He stuck to his defence. 'I have committed no crime. I have done what any patriotic man would have done in my place. Would a German have abandoned his fellow countrymen? Would you have me abandon my people? Before God I have only done what any true man would do for his country.' He was declared guilty and driven back to Fresnes. There he was told he had been sentenced to death.

For the next six weeks he sat in his cell expecting his name to be called each dawn and to follow the young man he had befriended in the van to Mont Valérien. Each day he would hear others being taken there. Then, thanks to the intervention of a Lutheran priest, he was reprieved. No longer a condemned man, he was moved to St Denis, a different prison in the city, where he would 'wait and pray for the tramp of friendly feet through the streets of Paris and the sight of the fleeing enemy'. In St Denis, he felt brought back to life.

And then it was all over. The Germans began their exodus from Paris. Other prisons were evacuated, as we have seen, their inmates forced into Germany and its evil empire of concentration camps. But St Denis was an exception.

One night as I lay in the big barrack-like cell I shared with thirteen others, I heard a far-off blessed noise. A bell was ringing, the sign of liberation. That first eager tinkle called more and more bell-ringers to their posts and it was drowned in the rising tide of sound. The bells of Notre Dame, St Sulpice and hundreds of other churches in the French metropolis were ringing out the glad news on that memorable August night in 1944 that the Allies had entered the city and that our captivity was at an end.

The prison erupted into a great roar of happiness. Doors opened. Men ran freely through the corridors. The German guards had disappeared. Outside in the streets of Paris, the Resistance had gone into battle. A young Frenchman carrying a tommy gun arrived to tell the inmates to stay where they were, for their own good. The fighting went on for several days and there were still snipers taking lives when Caskie chanced his arm on the streets of the capital city he had not trodden for four long years. He made his way to a little café on rue Bayard, a ten-minute walk from the Champs Elysées. Gaston, the proprietor, was clearing a table. He had the key to the kirk next door that Caskie had left with him in 1940 after delivering his final sermon denouncing the Nazis.

The key was stiff in the lock but it turned with a grinding click and I flung open the door. Dust lay heavily on the interior. Motes danced thickly in the sunshine that flooded into the porch. The sound of footsteps echoed in the emptiness. On a table by the doorway lay the sprig of white heather I had left behind me, withered but welcoming. I was home.

Caskie may have been 'home', but scattered across Europe, many evaders and their helpers anxiously awaited the advancing Allied armies.

# 11. Lost in the Garden

That autumn of 1944 there was among the Allies great anxiety to get the job finished. The D-Day landings had been consolidated much more slowly than the strategists at Supreme Headquarters had intended, but then had come the break-out from Normandy and the mad dash across northern France that liberated Paris and then Brussels. The Wehrmacht was on its toes, heading for the Fatherland in something approaching disarray. Allied supply lines were stretched but one bold stroke could be decisive. In this context, it is not difficult to understand the attraction of the plan of Field Marshal Bernard Montgomery to bypass the static defences of the Siegfried Line. Paratroopers and a force landed from gliders would get in behind the retreating Germans and grab vital bridges on the lower Rhine and other strategically important waterways in eastern Holland. Here would be a toehold from which to steal into Germany through the back door. The war would be over by Christmas.

That was the theory behind Operation Market Garden. The practice was the disaster of Arnhem. The mission floundered owing to poor detailing on the ground – airborne forces were dropped disastrously far from the targets they were supposed to capture and hold; the relief column from Monty's Second Army coming overland was bogged down and never arrived; radio communications did not work. There was also a serious under-estimation of the enemy. The Germans put up sterner and swifter resistance than anticipated. Seven thousand British and American soldiers, cut off from the promised reinforcements, were killed, wounded or captured. But hundreds went into hiding, hunkering down in whatever shelter they could find.

Paratrooper Tony Deane-Drummond, a major in the British 1st Airborne Division, was trapped in a forward position where the battle was fiercest and most desperate – on the wrong side of the Arnhem bridge, a precariously held position facing the tanks of an SS panzer division and merciless sniper fire. 'Street fighting is always a bloody business,' he would observe later,[1] a typically British understatement for what quickly developed into a deadly house-to-house and hand-to-hand encounter. He rallied a group of soldiers whose company commander had just been shot dead and, under constant rifle fire, led them at the run to take cover in houses near the river. Only twenty of them made it. But their relief at putting brick walls between themselves and the enemy was short lived. Their position was hopeless. The rest of the battalion was pinned down half a mile to the rear and could not have come to their rescue even if the major could have got a message to them, which, with radios out of operation, was impossible. They counted out their ammunition. Just 100 rounds between them.

We took up defensive positions. It was 4 p.m. We kept up a sniping action to keep the Germans from getting too close, but by nightfall nearly all our ammunition had gone. I reckoned the enemy would attack the following dawn, and unless we were relieved by then we would be in a sorry plight.

Deane-Drummond knew retreat was the only option if they wanted to live. He split the men into smaller groups to slip away under cover of darkness and swim the river if they had to. He led the way to a house a few yards from the water and broke in.

We were looking at the river from a window at the back when I heard a German crashing through the front door. We all dived into the lavatory and locked the door on the inside. But then to our dismay a section of about ten German soldiers came upstairs, and from the sounds of tile-removing and furniture-shifting, it was clear they were setting up a machine-gun to cover the street.

They were trapped, five of them, in a loo, for the next three nights and days. 'We took it in turns to sit on the seat,' the major recorded laconically. Surprisingly, German courtesy over calls of nature saved them from discovery. 'Often German soldiers would come and try the door, but on finding it engaged politely went away and tried elsewhere.' The sounds of the desperate battle still going on along the river and in the town drifted into the tiny room. Through a window they looked up at a night sky turned flame-red from burning buildings. They kept as quiet as mice, never forgetting there was an enemy machine-gun post in the attic above and two more on the pavement outside. And apparently dug in to stay.

With no sign of the enemy moving, the major decided he could not take another night of confinement. During a lull in the firing in the small hours of the morning, they crept out of the lavatory, down the stairs and nervously inched open the front door of the house. Outside, the German machine-gun nests lay unmanned, their operators asleep, and the five men stole into the street.

We dodged from shadow to shadow down to the Rhine. As we swam noiselessly out into the river, bursts of firing broke out around us, and the reflections of burning buildings in the water made me sure we would be spotted. Then the current took me and I lost contact with the others as I was swept downstream. The chimneys of a brick factory loomed above me and I was clambering up the slippery bank.

He allowed himself a lingering hope that the Second Army land force might by now have reached this far, even though they would have been three days behind schedule. Realistically, he knew he was still behind enemy lines. Head down, he crawled along the muddy bank, aiming for a bridge which he had agreed with the men would be their emergency rendezvous if they were separated. Firing was coming from ahead and from time to time star shells lit up the sky. There would be more light soon. It was less than an hour to dawn. With renewed urgency he launched himself towards the bridge – only to fall into a watery slit trench, right on top of a German soldier. 'The game was up.' The major, who had been a prisoner of the Italians for sixteen months earlier in the war until he escaped, was in the bag again. The adrenalin that had kept him going for so long drained from his body. 'No longer was I a free man. Every bone and muscle ached for rest.' He gagged on the unwelcome smell of captivity – 'the acrid stench of stale German tobacco smoke and seasoned sausage'.

A car took him back into Arnhem, 'over the main bridge for which so many lives had been sacrificed, threading our way in and out of shell holes and along deserted streets'. In a church he was corralled with other prisoners, all with 'the haggard and drawn look of soldiers who have seen their best friends die, not knowing when their own turn might come'. Among them were his other companions from the river. It was a weary reunion. There had been no escape for any of them. But he had not given up thoughts of freedom and when they were transported to a POW holding cage in a large house just outside Arnhem – improbably with monkey-puzzle trees on the front lawn – he began plotting his next escape. Now was the time to act, before they were sent to Germany. He urged his fellow officers to join him, though the naïve – or the frightened – among them demurred. The house was heavily guarded. Surely it would be better to wait until they were in a proper prison camp where escape would be 'laid on', they argued. 'I told everybody I saw that our one and only chance of getting away would be before we left Holland.'

Left to his own devices he decided that, paradoxically, his best way of getting out was to stay put. The prisoners were certain to be moved, and soon – within a couple of days, he reckoned. If in the meantime he could find a bolt-hole he would go to ground until everyone had left. He scoured the house, probing walls and floors for hidden spaces.

In a ground-floor room I discovered a cupboard with a flush fitting concealed door covered with the same wallpaper as the rest of the room and difficult to see except on close examination. It was four feet across, twelve inches deep, and about seven feet high. Once I took out the shelves I was able to stand inside in tolerable comfort.

He stocked it up with water and food for a couple of days – a pound of lard and half a loaf – and locked himself in, waiting for the house to empty. But the Germans were working to their own timetable, not his. He would be in there for the next thirteen days and nights, in agony and growing weak from hunger and thirst.

There was no room to sit down because the cupboard was too shallow. I stood first on one leg, then on the other; then I leaned on one shoulder and then on the other. Every bone in my body ached. I managed to sleep, although occasionally my knees would give way and would drop forward against the door, making a hammer-like noise.

This could have been disastrous because the room outside was now in almost constant use by the Germans. Worse still they were interrogating the British prisoners there. As he strove to stay silent, he could hear every word of every interview – and was shocked.

We were supposed to give the enemy only our name, rank and number but I was surprised how few of our men stuck rigidly to this. Almost everybody gave a little additional harmless information, such as the address of their parents or wives, or whether they were regular soldiers or had been in the Territorial Army before the war.

Two actually supplied military information. One officer talked so much I nearly burst out of the cupboard on several occasions to stop the wretch saying any more. I would have done if he had started to divulge anything serious but luckily he did not know much. But the Germans found him such a promising source that they gave him lunch just in front of my cupboard. What agonies of mind and tummy to smell what seemed to be a delicious meal only a few yards from my hiding place!

To add to Deane-Drummond's anguish, when the day's questioning was over, the Germans used the room as sleeping quarters. He was now well and truly stuck.

I had no chances to get out at all, but I resolved to try to remain a little longer. My luck must come to my rescue. It had always done so up till now. By now I was automatically shifting my weight from one leg to the other, and leaning alternately on my right shoulder and then my left. It no longer required any thought or even consciousness. Little by little I eked out my rations – four mouthfuls of water every five hours and just a bite or two of bread. After ten days I couldn't eat any more bread because my mouth was so dry. I continued to pass water in spite of drinking practically nothing. I was able to direct my urine through a paper funnel into a corner of the cupboard where there was a gap in the floorboards to allow some pipes to pass down to the cellar. I did not feel the need to do anything more solid during the whole time, perhaps because there was nothing in my tummy.[2]

By day thirteen he was in serious trouble, racked by muscle cramp and his water virtually gone. 'Patience and caution were now finished. I told myself I would have to make an attempt to escape that evening or fail in the effort.' At dusk, there was usually a thirty-minute gap between the end of interrogation and the arrival of the off-duty guards to sleep. He gambled on this as his window of opportunity.

The minutes slowly crept by while I waited anxiously, my ears taut for the sound of the Germans leaving the room. Quietly I pulled on my boots and gathered my equipment, a work of art in that confined space.

But, unusually, some of the Germans stayed behind for a nap. He could hear them snoring loudly.

Then two of them woke up and stumbled out of the room. I was fairly certain there were one or two left. Eventually, by their grunts and the bumping of boots on the floor, I could tell that they too were getting up. I heard them go out, talking about a *Fräulein*. Cautiously I unlocked my door, opened it an inch, had a quick look round.

His calculation was wrong.

Damnation! There, not six feet away, was a solitary German soldier sleeping with his hands crossed over his tummy and his mouth wide open. I would be bound to wake him as I walked across the squeaky floor and opened the French windows to the garden. I decided to give him another half-hour.

Just then more troops came clattering into the building, some giggling local girls in tow, and went upstairs. A party began. A gramophone blared out, there were shouts and screams of excitement. Woken by the noise, the soldier got up and walked out.

I gently pushed the door open again. This time, the room was empty. I crept to the window and opened it. Outside, eight or ten guards were idly leaning against the garden fence a few yards away, discussing their sweethearts at home. But just then a lorry went by on the road, and the noise it made covered me as I dropped into the shrubbery and covered myself in dead leaves.

As it gradually got dark, the Germans left the fence one by one and retreated inside the house. When the coast was clear I climbed into an adjoining garden, feasted hungrily on some beetroots growing there, and then climbed through another fence into an orchard, where I munched my way through half a dozen apples. I felt the strength and vitality seeping back into my veins and I stretched my arms and legs with the joy of freedom and relief from that terrible cupboard.

But his chances of getting away completely were negligible without help. And with the town swarming with German troops, pumped up by their success in rebuffing the Allied attack and ruthless in their determination to capture those raiders still at liberty, there was a key question to which the major did not know the answer. Were the people of Arnhem brave enough to defy the dangers and shelter him?

\*

What is outstanding about the drama that took place in Holland in the autumn of 1944 was that it was played out on such a small stage. For several weeks from the middle of September, every noble aspect of the evasion story – courage, self-sacrifice, loyalty, defiance – was enacted in Arnhem, its suburbs and a few nearby towns and villages. In this restricted area, hunters and hunted were cheek by jowl. As British soldiers hid behind thin walls and under floorboards, literally inches from the enemy, the Dutch were magnificent. Despite the intense German presence on their doorsteps, local men and women took in the fugitives, ignoring the risks to themselves. With immense personal courage large numbers of them stared down the Nazi threats. One of those who escaped as a result movingly expressed his gratitude: 'Strangers gave me their beds, their food, their friendship, and risked their lives for my safety. What more could a man ask of a fellow human?'[3]

Dutch ingenuity was stunning. In desperation, five wounded paratroopers took refuge in a mental hospital, where a nurse they knew only as Mary told them to wrap themselves in blankets and join the throng of shrieking and howling inmates, disturbed beyond reason by the awful noise of the fighting around them. When the Germans came to requisition the building, she let the patients dance out into the street in a procession of the mad. The soldiers went too, capering and screaming along with the rest. By a small wood, she gave them the nod and they ran for the trees to make their escape.[4]

Dutch compassion was boundless. Lieutenant Colonel David Dobie of the 1st Parachute Battalion had watched his men being slaughtered by shells and machine-gun bullets before shrapnel in the eye and arm downed him too. Wounded, captured, he was marched off by the Germans to Arnhem's main hospital, the St Elisabeth. There he wandered through ward after ward, horrified by the number of British casualties. Outside, the lawn was a sea of soldiers lying on stretchers. He walked quietly past them, out of the gate and hid in an upstairs room in a partially destroyed house opposite. Down in the cellar, where they had been sheltering ever since the fighting began, were the owners, a doctor and his family. The doctor went upstairs the next morning, found the Englishman asleep . . . and, without a word, began to dress his wounds. In the back garden, just yards away, a German artillery battery was dug in. That night, right under the noses of the enemy gunners, the doctor smuggled Dobie along the street to another house nearby, where he was given civilian clothes and hidden for the next fortnight.[5]

It must be said that not everyone in Arnhem reacted in this way. Deane-Drummond, freed from his cupboard but alone and friendless, now had to make that initial contact with the locals himself – and ran into walls of fear. At the first house he came to he knocked gently on the door, called out that he was a British parachutist in need of help and was told to go away. 'My house is full. We have no food. Very dangerous to have you here,' the owner hissed through the bolted door. 'I walked away feeling rather depressed as I had fondly imagined that all the Dutch were pro-British and anti-Nazi.' It was the same at the next house he tried, and the one after that. Doors would not open for him. He huddled in the shadows as a German army truck swept by full of troops. Still starving, he fed himself from food scraps left out for cats and bedded down in a potting shed in a back garden to sleep.

The next morning his luck changed. The man of the house came to the shed for firewood and the major threw himself on his mercy.

I told him my story and he said he would do his best to help. He beckoned his wife to come from the kitchen out to the shed. She came, looking rather cross at being disturbed, saw me and let out a scream of terror. I must have looked a sight, with thirteen days' growth of ginger beard and in torn, dirty battledress trousers. Reassured by her husband, she recovered herself, went back into the house and returned with a plate of boiled potatoes and gravy. It was a banquet fit for a king!

The major set about finding a better hiding place for himself inside the shed. Up in the rafters were bales of straw. Too obvious, he thought, and instead fashioned loosely stacked seed boxes and apple trays scattered on the floor into a tunnel and crawled inside, pulling some sacks on top.

Hiding, always hiding! What a monotonous and horrible business! But I could not afford to walk about in daylight, unwashed since I left England, unshaven and dressed as I was.

He fell asleep, to be woken by the sound of angry German voices loudly accusing the Dutch family of sheltering a British officer. The man protested his innocence but the grey-uniformed intruders pushed him aside and began to search, marching upstairs and banging open doors and cupboards.

I was scared stiff and pulled the sacks closer, hoping against hope that they would ignore the shed. Then I heard them come out into the yard and straight towards me. A figure paused inside the doorway as his eyes got used to the gloom. He spotted the straw in the rafters and, muttering oaths and breathing heavily, he climbed up there. He threw down the bales, found nothing and left without bothering to look anywhere else. Once again my luck was in, and I was round another tight corner.

The close encounter was too much for the Dutch householder, however, and in a quivering voice he told the Englishman he must leave. But he sent him off well provisioned – with milk and sandwiches, more food than, in that time of desperate shortages for the Dutch people, he could spare. He pointed him towards a farmhouse a mile away in the country where he thought he might be safe. But here too terror of the Germans kept the doors firmly closed against him. His gentle 'V-for-victory' tap on the shutters was met with a curse to leave them alone. After several more failed, furtive attempts, it was a Catholic priest who finally took him in. His house and church were already crowded with a dozen evacuees and he even had some German troops billeted on him but he refused to turn the stranger away. Instead he was put in the charge of the caretaker, an elderly man who clearly welcomed this chance to do something for his country. 'I imagine his life must have been rather dull until now,' Deane-Drummond surmised, 'and he longed to take a more active part in the war.' The major was now 'his Tommy', his small cottage nearby his refuge. There he ate, drank, shaved off his beard and went to sleep for the next twelve hours in an attic bed between cool white sheets – 'What fantastic luxury! . . . The next morning the sun was streaming into the room and outside my window I could see a tree laden down with enormous red apples. I lay back, breathed in the beautiful fresh free air and thanked God that I was not a prisoner of war.'

The thought of his wife back home, six months pregnant with their first child, stirred him. 'Evie would be worried sick by hearing no news.' It was an incentive to get himself home.

★

In the century-old St Elisabeth hospital beside the river in Arnhem, another senior British officer was thinking of home too. By rights, Brigadier John Hackett, commander of the 4th Parachute Brigade, should have been dead. He had held out with his rapidly dimin- ishing force for a week, waiting for the relief force that never arrived. He was planning to lead his men in a fighting withdrawal back across the Rhine when a shell burst beside him and a splinter punctured his stomach. In the cobbled courtyard of the St Elisabeth an SS surgeon overseeing new arrivals glanced at his wound and told the British army doctor by his side (and now also a prisoner) not to bother operating. SS policy was to regard deep abdominal injuries as hopeless. A fatal shot of morphine was all that was required. The army doctor – in fact a South African by the name of Captain Alexander Lipmann-Kessel – ignored the instruction to kill off his commander. He was exhausted after performing dozens of operations already that day, but he pulled up his white mask and went to work, splitting his patient from breastbone to navel, fishing out the splinter and for three hours doing his best to repair the dozen holes in his lower intestine. German guards in jackboots wandered in and out during the operation, peering at the body on the table. The surgery was exemplary in the circumstances. Even so, when he came round, Hackett was a desperately sick man, though he refused to believe it. 'I did not doubt for one minute that I would get well,' he later wrote, 'and Kessel never hinted that there could be any other possible outcome than complete recovery.'⁶ Within days of going under the knife, though still unable to eat or drink, he was planning his escape. 'I took it completely for granted that I would get out as soon as it was possible.' He had not yet even managed to get out of bed.

A Catholic padre began to put together all he might need in a haversack – a clasp knife, a candle, some string, sticking plasters – while the brigadier engaged the nurses in conversation to learn a few useful phrases in Dutch. He wolfed down the thin soup, tea and Ovaltine he was now allowed (and slugs of cognac and a 1934 Nuits-St-Georges he was not) to build up his strength. He was touched by the loyalty of the locals. A nurse who was secretly hiding evaders at home was killed in a British bombing raid, but still the Dutch did not flinch. A man whose arm had been blown off in another RAF attack came to his bedside just to shake the hand of an Englishman. Then another visitor arrived offering more than friendship. His name was Piet and ostensibly he was from the Dutch Red Cross. In fact, he was a Resistance leader and his words were as welcome as the stew and potatoes Hackett had just graduated to. 'I can you get out of here,' the stranger promised and disappeared. He came back four days later, when the brigadier, though still desperately weak, was out of his bed for the first time and sitting in a chair.

Suddenly I became aware that Piet was standing in front of me. 'Can you walk a little?' he asked. 'I haven't tried yet,' I replied. 'I expect so.' He said, 'If you can walk out of the hospital in the next quarter of an hour, I can take you away. If not, I may not be able to get you out at all.'

It was now or never.

'Get hold of Captain Kessel,' I said, and when the doctor came I put it to him. 'Can I go?' I asked. 'You're the only judge,' he said. 'Do you think you can?' I thought for a brief moment and decided. 'Yes, I'll go,' I said. 'Let me have my stuff.'

A car with a Red Cross flag was waiting outside as Hackett, a mass of blood-soaked bandages and cotton wool wrapped round his head to make him appear even more badly wounded than he actually was, was lifted bodily from his chair and stumbled from the hospital, clinging to Piet's arm.

We went down a long passage, past rooms where British soldiers were lying sleepily on their beds, and suddenly we were in the open air. It was fresh and cool with a hint of rain. It was beautiful.

A young man was sweeping up leaves. He was always there, always sweeping. He was one of Piet's boys. We passed a red brick building, the mortuary. I knew this was where they had their arms hidden. Then we were through the gate and into a tree-lined urban street, scarred with slit trenches. Piet helped me into the car, the engine started, we were moving. Where we were going I did not know, nor did I much care. I was out and away.

They sped through Arnhem, a deserted city now as well as a battle-scarred one, its civilian inhabitants forced to leave by the Germans, young and old trudging out to the countryside while men of working age were conscripted at gunpoint into labour gangs to shore up the defences. A lone British evader who secretly watched the exodus was filled with pity at the sight of the dispossessed streaming away with the remnants of their lives in handcarts and prams – and with disgust as German soldiers moved in to plunder their homes.[7]

Hackett's destination was the town of Ede, ten miles away across the heath, where, he recalled as he peered out of the car window, he and his men had dropped just three weeks ago. The memory haunted him. He had been entranced by the descent – 'the air full of parachutes, like goose feathers blown in the wind or a legion of angels, both beautiful and terrifying' – and then been brought into focus by gunfire reaching up to him and the sight of a figure floating down beside him, 'a man from whom the entrails hung, swaying in a reciprocal rhythm. As the body moved one way the entrails swung the other.' It was a foretaste of the terrible slaughter to come. He shuddered at what had been – and then, as the car turned into a street of prosperous houses, each with a neat front garden and a flagpole, put the thought to one side. 'What had happened was irrelevant now. I had to think only of the present and how good it was to be free.'

That night he settled into his new home, with the de Nooij family, a brother and sister and three maiden aunts. They were novices, never having dared to take in evaders before. Now they did so enthusiastically, greeting him like an old friend and leading him to the room specially prepared for him upstairs. The exertion of his escape from hospital was taking its toll. Beneath his bandages, the wounds in his stomach were leaking. He was overtaken by fatigue. But he forced himself to climb the stairs unaided and then stepped into a tiny bedroom, 'all white and friendly, shining kindly in the light of an oil lamp. Everywhere about me was a feeling of goodwill.'

I turned to the trim white bed under a crochet counterpane. Above it hung a sampler, an embroidered picture of Sleeping Beauty and the words in Dutch: 'And she slept a deep sleep a hundred years long.' I climbed gratefully in, dead tired but in peace and complete content.

Such comfort, both physical and mental, was not the lot of all the Arnhem evaders. Another paratroop officer, Major Digby Tatham-Warter, slept in a damp, dug-out shelter underneath a wood pile in the backyard of the family hiding him. But at least he had a bed. Sergeant-Major Robert Grainger – who had danced his way out of the mental hospital with the deranged inmates – now lay in a grave-sized trench in the ground, an earth-covered lid over him to blend in with the field around him, while his Dutch helpers tried to find a better home for him. He was there for four days and nights, battling the terrors of claustrophobia, with just one small chink of light to keep him from once again joining the ranks of the mad, but this time genuinely. Every bone in his body and thought in his head screamed out for release. It came just in time. He was pulled from his hiding place, half-blinded, nerves shredded, and taken by horse and cart to a private house in Ede, where for days he roamed the tiny rooms, grateful for the space around him. At least in his 'tomb', Warrant Officer Fred Eastwood had company and conversation. Survivors of a glider shot down on its way to Arnhem, he and his platoon were taken in by a Dutch farmer who first hid them in a barn and then, with German soldiers combing the area, moved the ten of them to a specially built underground shelter. It was a concrete sewer pipe.

It was 18ft in length and less than 5ft in diameter. The entrance was a 2ft 6in hole at one end, through which we had to squeeze to get in. The other end was sealed. The entrance was covered with a wooden lid and this in turn by muddy straw and refuse. This camouflaged us from even close inspection but also obstructed most of the light and fresh air too. So impure was the air that when we lit matches it was impossible to keep them alight. We had straw, blankets and a single bucket for sanitary use.[8]

They were interred there for five 'long and dreary' days, the darkness relieved only by twice-daily visits from the farmer opening the lid to pass them bread, fruit, potatoes and milk. They could barely see or walk when they were allowed to stumble out into the fresh air again. The Germans had gone, they were told. They could relax again.

Hackett, on the other hand, though he was in a feather bed, was surrounded by his enemies. When he awoke on his first morning at the de Nooij home in Ede, he was astonished to find he was in a house in the very centre of what was, in effect, a German garrison town. There were an estimated 2,500 soldiers, on the streets outside, in barracks and billeted in virtually every other house but this one. Just thirty yards away from where Hackett lay in bed, on the other side of the garden, was a detachment of Feldgendarmerie, the German military police. He was hiding in the very middle of his enemies' camp.

The thought troubled him less and less as he was quickly caught up in the daily routines of this respectable, middle-class, solidly religious household. As he was nursed slowly back to health, he took tea in bed in the morning, a glass of wine with lunch. He read his bible, practised his Dutch. One by one the aunts would sit down with 'Mr Hackett', as they always called him, and talk. He would tell them about Palestine, where he had once been based, and they would thrill to his tales of the Holy Land. The Germans seemed to be part of a different world entirely. Occasionally other evading paratroopers would slip from their own places of hiding nearby to visit him but the family discouraged this. 'It would not do for the neighbours to see our house becoming an object of interest,' he was rightly told. His own safety lay in becoming utterly embedded with the de Nooijs. If a German search party came, he was to be explained away as an evacuee from a tuberculosis hospital. It was well known that German soldiers were paranoid about TB. A scarf soaked in strong disinfectant was kept at the ready to tie round his neck. Seeing that, none was likely to press an inquiry much further. His disguise was completed by a small badge indicating he was deaf. 'My role was just to look ill and not speak.'

And the fact was that, although Hackett would not admit it to himself, he was still a sick man. His stomach wounds were healing, but slowly. He was weak – so much so that when news came of a secret plan for a mass evacuation of the Arnhem evaders he had to concede defeat. They would have to go without him.

★

Airey Neave of MI9 was moving steadily north and east, in the vanguard of the Allied advance towards the frontiers of Germany. He had retrieved his band of Merry Men from the Fréteval forest in France, been among the first liberators on the streets of Paris and then followed through into Belgium until he stood on the border of occupied Holland. He already had agents inside the country, notably the artistically codenamed 'Frans Hals',[9] who had been in place for a year and had fed numerous airmen into the Comet Line via Brussels. Arnhem brought a new focus to the operation. Nijmegen on the River Waal, captured as part of Operation Market Garden, was now the furthest extent of the Allied advance, and in the watery no-man's-land between it and the Rhine American forces made regular furtive scouting sorties in canoes, engaging the enemy, taking prisoners but also coming back with extraordinary rumours they had heard about scores of Arnhem survivors holed up in houses and farms on the other side. Neave made a crucial discovery which confirmed this and made their rescue a real possibility.

Nijmegen's electricity power plant, it transpired, had a direct telephone line linked to a transformer station in Ede, twenty miles away in German-held territory. And it was working. The Dutch Resistance were using it to keep in touch with each other. The Allies could do the same to organize an evacuation of those men in hiding and in constant danger of discovery on the wrong side of the front line. Permission to use it was almost refused by Neave's nervous military bosses – what he described as 'the cold-feet department'. 'They regarded the idea of telephoning across the enemy lines as lunacy because the enemy would be tapping the line.'[10] But this was not so. 'It was simply a question of waiting each night for the telephone to ring at six o'clock and hearing a British officer's voice reading a long list of names.'

That officer – whom Neave knew then only as 'The Voice' – was Tatham-Warter, who, exhibiting exceptional bravery and brazenness, climbed out of his wood-pile refuge every morning, donned a white mackintosh and dark glasses and bicycled from safe house to safe house, barn to chicken coop or underground shelter, keeping contact with his fellow evaders, encouraging them, drawing up escape plans, liaising with members of the Dutch Resistance. His trips along cart tracks and obscure country lanes earned him the epithet of 'the wandering major' as, with complete disregard for the Germans, he turned up out of the blue to shepherd his growing flock.[11] His last call each day was to the electricity station to give his latest batch of names to Neave or to SAS Major Hugh Fraser, a new MI9 recruit (and, like Neave, a future Conservative Member of Parliament).[12]

A plan was formed for the Dutch Resistance secretly to assemble as many evaders as it could from the Ede area – at least 100 and possibly twice that number – and guide them eight miles through the German lines to a spot on the banks of the Rhine where Allied soldiers would bring them across to safety in assault boats. It was ambitious, even foolhardy in its conception. Could this army of fugitives, many of them weak and wounded, really be marshalled under the noses of the enemy and then make their way through hostile territory to a rendezvous on a blacked-out river bank without being discovered? But Operation Pegasus – 'the boldest of all the rescue operations we had undertaken', in Neave's words – was deemed a runner. For just once in the Second World War, the military powers decided to give priority to bringing evaders home. Lieutenant Colonel Robert Strayer of the 101st American Airborne Division, the officer commanding the Allied forces dug in closest to the Rhine, was given the task of organizing the rescue flotilla, though he was beset by doubts. He knew he could lay his hands on assault boats from a nearby detachment of Royal Canadian Engineers, that he could get his men in place, ferry them to the other side of the river, provide back-up and covering fire in abundance. When he called for volunteers, every man under his command stepped forward. But how could he or they be sure there would be *anyone* there to bring home, let alone the hundreds he was told to expect?

The apprehension was stilled by the unexpected arrival through the German lines of a lone figure – British paratroop colonel David Dobie. It was weeks since, wounded in the Arnhem fighting, he had walked out of hospital, been hidden in a house nearby by a doctor and then made his way south on his own, fully expecting at some point to meet the Allied front line advancing towards him. Instead he saw only German troops and, as he lay under cover in a rain-filled ditch, the hard truth hit him that the battle had stalled and his own lines were out of reach. He tramped away, passing battalions of fresh-looking and well-armed German infantry heading in the opposite direction to reinforce the Rhine. Fortunately he fell into friendly hands. A pretty Dutch girl guided him to Ede and soon he was joining Tatham-Warter and other officers in their clandestine meetings to plot a mass escape. Clearly they needed someone to carry their detailed plans ahead of them to their would-be rescuers. Dobie volunteered to go. The Resistance passed him from courier to courier in dreadful, stormy weather and through an area teeming with German patrols and danger. The houses of those suspected of helping escapers were in flames, their occupants shot or in prison awaiting deportation to concentration camps in Germany. Local men were being rounded up for forced labour. But he made it across the Waal in a wooden rowing boat with a single oar, and now was briefing Strayer – coincidentally an old friend – on what to expect.

They agreed that on the evening of Sunday 22 October an arc of ten red tracer shells would be fired from a Bofors gun on the Allied side of the river and repeated at hourly intervals. The evaders on the other side would respond with a V-for-victory torch flash and then hand-paddled assault craft, their flanks protected by riflemen, would set out to get them. Dobie told Strayer to have enough boats ready for the 140 men who would, he was confident, be waiting on the far shore.

★

Tony Deane-Drummond was even now preparing to make that escape. He had recovered from the ordeal of the cupboard, been passed into Resistance hands and hidden with a family of four in a two-bedroomed suburban house, along with two refugees, a Polish Jew and a Dutchman who had escaped from a concentration camp. At night the three runaways slept in a hideout under the floorboards. It was from his Resistance contact that he heard of the Rhine escape plan and was cautioned to be careful and patient. 'It would take at least fourteen days to organize. Everybody was to lie low and not excite too much attention.'

Meanwhile, Sergeant-Major Grainger was one of a small party who went out to reconnoitre a route to the river. The situation on the ground was not ideal. There were trails through the forest to follow but also numerous German machine-gun nests and patrols. How were so many men to slip past unnoticed? The odds did not look good. As one chronicler of the event noted later: 'It seemed preposterous that a column of more than company strength could walk right through heavily fortified German positions. On the surface it seemed suicidal.'[13] There were doubts too about whether the Bofors tracer would be a precise enough marker to follow. Measuring distance at night from a few red shells was neither easy nor accurate. The doubters reported their findings back to Tatham-Warter but he was undaunted. The Dutch had guns. So did some of the evaders.[14] If they had to fight their way through, then so be it. There was no going back.

Final arrangements were also falling into place on the other side of the Rhine, despite a last-minute panic when, three days before the start, a messenger came across the Waal with news that two of Neave's undercover agents had been spotted by a collaborator and were in the hands of the Gestapo. An SS detachment was in Ede. More Dutch civilians had been shot, homes burned. For twenty-four tension-filled hours there was serious talk of cancelling the mission. But too many people were in the know and on the move. Dozens of assault boats were already lined up on the Allied side of the river, while on the other young Resistance boys and girls were risking their lives to cycle from safe house to safe house to alert the evaders. Pegasus, for all its dangers, was on. Over the secret telephone line, Neave gave the go-ahead to Tatham-Warter, put down the receiver and then walked away from the power station 'with a feeling of optimism'.

Spirits were high elsewhere. On his last night in hiding, Deane-Drummond's Dutch hosts threw a party for him, inviting friends round with long-hoarded bottles of gin. A local baroness sent champagne for the 'poor British officer who is so thin'. Clearly his presence in the house was not the closely guarded secret he had presumed.

All the Dutch became exceedingly merry, and by the light of flickering candles they were soon singing patriotic songs at the tops of their voices. Then we heard an urgent tapping at the door, which went unnoticed at first because of all the noise. A voice said one word, '*Moffen*', which was the Dutch word for the Hun. The singing stopped, and smiles left every face. Apparently we had woken up a neighbour and he had come to warn us that the German billeted with him might wake up too.

But no Germans stirred, the danger passed and at dawn the next morning the major was dressed and waiting for the Red Cross lorry that would take him to the initial assembly point.

The lorry, driven by charcoal gas, wheezed, bumped and swayed through the streets of Arnhem and down the main road to Ede. Six civilians sat inside as I lay on the floor under some sacks, just in case we were stopped at a German checkpoint. I looked up and could see the sky and trees. I began to feel an elation that I had not had for weeks. At last I was on the move!

It gave him a boost too to catch sight of burnt-out German lorries, shot up and destroyed by RAF fighters.

Soon they were beyond the houses and out into the forest. The lorry halted, the passengers in the seats jumped out and signalled to Deane-Drummond. He crammed his battered felt hat on his head and followed.

We walked down a footpath, with the noise of the old Red Cross lorry getting fainter as it continued on its way to Ede, until we came to a small clearing with a tiny hut in the middle. To my astonishment it was surrounded by thirty or so British soldiers, busying themselves handing out equipment, boiling up water and exchanging tales of their wanderings. From the hut wafted a high old stench of unwashed bodies and when we looked inside there were another twenty men.

He was back among friends, many of whom he knew well. 'It was wonderful to hear up-to-date news again.' The gathering was not all paratroopers. There were a couple of Russians, a Dutch naval officer – and a lone RAF man with an extraordinary story to tell. Navigator Robert Lovegrove had directed his pilot low over Arnhem two days after the parachute landings, dropping fresh ammunition to the troops on the ground. Too low. A shell hit fuel containers and the plane went up in flames. He jumped from 1,000 feet, the chute opened at 100 feet and he fell onto the roof of a house in a village just outside the town. Helped and hidden by locals, he tried to link up with the airborne troops he presumed to be holding their ground in Arnhem. Instead of safety, he found himself in the heart of a military disaster. All around him were German tanks. From a garret where he lay hiding he looked over at enemy soldiers cooking food on fires in the garden. It was Lovegrove who witnessed the savage evacuation of Dutch civilians from Arnhem and its complete takeover by the German military. He decamped to a safer place and plotted with Resistance contacts on how he could get back to Allied lines. He tried to head south in an ancient ambulance, false papers in his pocket, a fake Red Cross armband on his arm, a white helmet on his head. But each mile he got nearer to the Rhine, he ran into more and more German forces. There was no way ahead – though he had certain proof that he was close to his own lines. British artillery were taking pot-shots at the village where he finally decided to stop. He trembled under the bombardment from his own side as the roof of a cottage fell down around him.

And then, when he was beginning to despair, came a message. His Resistance contact arrived in the ambulance with news that paratroopers were about to attempt a mass escape. 'Would I care to join them?' Strapped to a stretcher in the back of the ambulance, with bloodied bandages on his face and stomach (the gore from a cow killed in the latest Allied bombardment), he retraced his steps, back across ferries and German-held bridges, and now here he was in the middle of a forest with dozens of fellow countrymen, all delighted at the prospect of finally going back to Blighty. That afternoon the men cleared up the site of all their debris and any incriminating evidence and then waited in the undergrowth beside the road for lorries to pick them up. They were about to be taken to the next rendezvous, just three miles from the river, along the best route that Tatham-Warter's scouting parties could find to skirt the German troop position.

Deane-Drummond was impatient: 'Slowly the minutes dragged by to zero hour and the start of our last lap. Then at six sharp, three covered lorries rattled down the road, and we piled in, lying on the floor with empty sacks over us, like trucks full of potatoes.' If they were stopped, the drivers would try and bluff their way through. If that failed, they would shout out 'Kill 'em' and four soldiers would leap from the back and, in Lovegrove's words, 'deal with the Hun'. In the event, they came to two German checkpoints and were waved through both of them. 'They thought we were the rations convoy on their way to the regiments on the river,' according to Deane-Drummond.

As darkness fell the lorries stopped and the men jumped out. In a line they filed along a footpath, stumbling over tree trunks and brambles until they arrived at a house in a clearing not far from the village of Renkum. Other parties were already there, some having trekked on foot or on bicycle through fields and along tracks from as much as twenty miles away. There had been close calls along the way. One group had politely stood to one side on a narrow path as two heavily armed German troopers on bicycles furiously rang their bells and demanded right of way. Others had come in comparative comfort – in an ancient Model-T Ford, a Mercedes and a Chevrolet with solid tyres. Several dozen arrived in two small trucks, packed on top of each other in the back like layers of sardines. They crawled out, bruised, shaking and cursing – to the rapturous greetings of old friends. They were now 120 strong in all, which worried Deane-Drummond. 'However quiet each one might try to be, so many men moving through woods at night would sound like an army.'

Instructions went out. They were to group in platoon-sized units under the command of an officer or an NCO, don army uniform – or as much of a semblance of one as they could muster – and be ready to leave at 9 p.m. when the moon rose. This gave them plenty of time to cover the three miles to the river for the crossing, scheduled for 1 a.m. They should keep an eye out for the red tracer shells to guide them to the right spot. With an hour and a half to wait before the off, the major curled up in some leaves to sleep. 'All the more experienced among us did the same, but the younger ones were so overcome with excitement that sleep was the last thing they wanted.' The truth was that many of them were more nervous than excited. They had been inactive in confined and often unhealthy hiding places for a month and, as a result, were now unfit for the physical challenge they faced. They had also been warned they might have to fight their way through to the river. Were they up to a battle with the hardened, honed and well-fed German infantry who stood between them and home?

But, ready or not and rested or not, they were soon on their way. Like the master of a wagon train in a cowboy film, Tatham-Warter raised his hand, pointed the direction, and off they went along the narrowest of tracks through dense forest, led by Dutch guides. At the front marched a small contingent with arms; another group with Sten guns and rifles brought up the rear. In the middle were the majority, unarmed and defenceless. Lovegrove, as he wryly noted later, had nothing more than a toothbrush as a weapon.

They tiptoed (as far as army boots bound with sacking allowed) in single file through the darkness. Deane-Drummond recalled:

Sometimes the trees closed in over us like a tunnel, and the moonlight was completely shut off except for an occasional shaft of light through the branches. Each man was told to keep in sight of the one in front, and to be as quiet as possible.

But the noise they made was a problem from the start. Rabbits ran off at their approach. A deer bolted through the trees and the sudden crash brought them to a panicky halt. They thought they had bumped into a German patrol. As they moved off again, Lovegrove clung to the hand of the man in front of him so as not to get lost.

Across copses we went, frequently stopping and lying flat on our faces when the front of the queue saw something suspicious. At times the pace was that of a snail, then it would quicken until you had to run hard to catch up. A dry patch of undergrowth would crackle like gunshots under our feet and an officer would creep back along the line and whisper at us to cut out the racket or we would be discovered. It was the most thrilling journey I have ever made.

After two hours, the front of the column reached the edge of the forest and the men stared out apprehensively at the last obstacle – a mile of open fields between them and the river. The only cover was a 4-foot-deep drainage ditch. Deane-Drummond ducked down and set off.

We had to pass between two German heavy-mortar batteries, spaced about half a mile apart. They had been firing fitfully all night, and as we came closer the ear-splitting noise cut into the still night air and reminded us that caution was still vital.

They came level with the German positions just as, in the distance, the first burst of Bofors tracer went crashing into the air. As it hung there momentarily, like a bright necklace in the night sky, an audible sigh went down the column. They were on track and on time too. It was midnight. In just one hour they should be on those boats and away. But first there was a road to cross, along which, Tatham-Warter had warned everybody, German patrols were common. This was one brush with the enemy he had not been able to find a way round. Deane-Drummond crawled as close as possible and waited for fifteen minutes but there were no Germans to be seen. He led his men over the road and down the bank on the far side. Their luck was in.

But could it last? As the column crossed the road, the crash of more than a hundred pairs of boots on the hard surface sounded to Tatham-Warter like an elephant stampede. But somehow the noise went unheeded by the German sentries, positioned so close that the British evaders could hear snatches of their conversation. So too did the frantic sounds of men stumbling into each other in the dark, cursing and even shouting as the column, beginning to lose its discipline, snaked its way uncertainly towards its goal. As the escape neared its climax, he feared they were about to be exposed. Lantern lights flickered in the meadow behind them and he urgently sent out armed patrols to cover the flanks in case of a German ambush.

Now the river was only 300 yards away. Deane-Drummond followed a ditch down to its bank. He was one of the first to reach the water.

Nothing stirred on the river save the gurgle of flowing water, and a subdued swish from a nearby weir. A few marsh birds occasionally let out their plaintive cries. It was difficult to believe that we were in no-man's-land between Germans and Allies.

Through a mist swirling over the surface, he could glimpse the other side. The sight of safety so close was too much for some of his men and they began to chatter excitedly.

Suddenly a burst of German automatic fire sounded only fifty yards away. We all went flat on our tummies. Were we to be cheated of success at this stage? Would we have to swim for it? A thousand doubts went through my head as I wormed forward to see what was going on. But nobody was hit, and we could hear sounds of a small German patrol withdrawing hurriedly back across the fields. They must have been even more frightened than we were.

They had reached the agreed point – or so they thought. But there was no sign of life on the other side, no boats skimming across the water to their rescue, no response to the V-for-victory torch flash.

Fifteen minutes went by and nothing happened, except for the occasional weird, tearing screech of a German heavy mortar shell passing overhead. My imagination conjured up a hundred and one things that might have gone wrong.

In fact, the tracer shells had been misleading, as the doubters had feared. The head of the column was some distance from the designated crossing point. On the Allied-held bank, Captain Leo

Heaps, a Canadian-born officer in the 1st Parachute Battalion (and an Arnhem evader who had got back through enemy lines on his own a week earlier[15]), was waiting to order the assault boats into action. Everything was ready. Artillery batteries behind him were on standby to give covering fire if necessary. A line of white tape stretched from the bank to guide the evaders back to a first-aid post and a canteen stocked with hot drinks and food. Lorries were lined up to take the men to Nijmegen. There were stretchers for those who could not walk. Neave and Fraser stood nearby, wrapped in long greatcoats against the cold October night. Dobie paced nervously, casting his eyes across the river for the comrades he had so recently left behind and was now desperate to rescue. But on the other side there was no response, no sign of movement. Perhaps the men were huddled unseen beneath the bank. Perhaps they hadn't made it after all.

Then, quite by chance, Heaps glanced upstream.

I saw a tiny light flicker on and off, and raced down to Dobie to tell him. We watched together, and again saw a faint, red pinpoint of light several miles away from the prearranged rendezvous. We both ran to our boats. I shouted to the sappers to drag them along the shore as far as they could. Every yard would count. The closer we landed to the evaders the less distance they would have to walk. Ten minutes later all the boats were launched.[16]

On the far side, a relieved Deane-Drummond at last heard the rhythmic splash of paddles. Out of the mist the assault boats were nosing their way towards him and beaching on the mud. Machine-gunners piled out and took up defensive positions. The evaders splashed out through the shallows and climbed on board. 'Wotcher, mate,' a cockney voice whispered to Lovegrove. 'You've had it bloody rough out there, ain't yer?' The RAF man grabbed a paddle and dug it purposefully in the water.

Meanwhile Heaps's canoe had landed and he was creeping along the bank to search for passengers.

I headed towards the place I thought I had seen the red light. A flare shot up from behind the trees a few hundred yards away, illuminating the water. We stopped. Then in a few seconds, enveloped again by the darkness, we went on. After a little time I heard a strange sound like wind rustling through the meadow. But there was no wind. Instead, out of the grass came the sound of a multitude of shuffling feet. It started and stopped several times and then gradually became louder as a grey, amorphous column took shape. Here were our evaders. I rose with a shout and ran to them.

Heaps directed the line of tired men – 'it seemed to have no end' – to the waiting boats. 'The ragged file surged on, possessed with new energy.' By 1.30 a.m. the last of the stragglers had come in and been boarded. Heaps climbed into his boat and looked back into enemy territory. There was no sign of life. He noted that the Germans had not fired a single shot. What he would later dub 'the most amazing mass escape of World War II' was over without a single casualty. On the other side, Neave counted in the evaders – 138 in all, including several Dutchmen. Deane-Drummond was gleefully enjoying his first moments back on Allied-held territory. As he warmed his hands on a mug of hot tea, he reflected that this was his fourth Rhine crossing in six weeks. 'I had flown over it, I had swum it, I had been driven over it as a prisoner, and now I was carried across it in a boat. I preferred this last method.' The next day a concert was laid on in Nijmegen, and as he joined in the words of 'Abide With Me', Lovegrove was not the only man with a lump in his throat and tears coursing down his cheek. The fast-falling eventide and deepening darkness were behind them. They had survived.

★

News of the success of Pegasus was passed down the secret telephone line to Ede and soon reached John Hackett on his sickbed. He was pleased for those who had escaped but felt more lonely than ever before. He took comfort knowing that his family back home would now have been told he was alive, if not well or

entirely safe. Then he returned his thoughts to his other 'family',
the de Nooijs. As autumn turned to winter, they were his entire
life, 'my whole world'. This wasn't strictly true because they
brought him an abundance of books – Dickens, Shakespeare,
Thackeray, Wordsworth, Scott, Milton – and, like the Oxbridge
don he often resembled, he immersed himself in literature. From
time to time the real world intruded, and he looked up from his
books and out of the window at German soldiers strolling down
the street, 'generally unarmed and always untidy', as he noted.
Sometimes a platoon went by, singing marching songs, and he was
affronted by their 'barbaric' militarism. At night his rest, often
troubled anyway because of the pain from his injuries, was disturbed even more by a dog barking nearby. One of the aunts
discovered the animal belonged to the military police just over the
garden fence and, without a second thought, she went round to
ask them – indeed, *tell* them – to keep it under control. 'I have a
sick person in my house,' she informed its owner crossly, 'who
cannot sleep because of that dog of yours.' The German mumbled
his apologies. The canine howling ceased. Hackett slept. His health
improved and soon he was even taking a little light exercise. There
was fresh talk now of him making his escape back across the Rhine,
and an MI9 agent, a Dutchman codenamed 'Bat' (he had a radio
operator called 'Ball'), came secretly to say that a new mass rescue
attempt was to be made. 'It would mean some transportation being
found for me, but he saw no reason why I should not be taken
along,' a jubilant Hackett noted.

In Nijmegen, Neave was excitedly planning Pegasus II. The
first operation had been 'a striking and memorable performance',
but those who returned had come with reports of 150 other Allied
servicemen still behind the enemy lines, many paratroopers from
the Arnhem débâcle but also RAF and American air force evaders.
Surely they should be brought home too.[17] But that would mean
moving at top speed. It was already the last week in October and
winter rains would soon swell the Rhine and make it even more
difficult to cross. But communications with the other side were
excellent. The telephone line still worked and Neave also had

more agents such as Bat and Ball on the ground. A preliminary date – 16 November – was fixed, a new crossing point reconnoitred and selected and a dozen flat-bottomed boats with outboard engines procured so as not to have to rely on paddle-power against the faster-flowing current.

In Ede, Hackett was now living on hope, his mind set on England as fervently as, until then, it had been concentrated on his life in Holland. After the first visit by Bat, he had told himself he might be home for his thirty-fourth birthday, on 5 November. There would be a Guy Fawkes party, a bonfire and fireworks, just as in his childhood. He was disappointed still to be with the de Nooijs when the day came – though not with the special show they put on for him. At six in the morning he was woken in his bedroom with congratulations and birthday cards. Then the family assembled round the harmonium in the living room below and sang 'God Save the King', a dawn chorus that moved the brigadier to tears. They apologized for the early start, explaining that it would not have been wise to leave their singing until later, when German soldiers would have been out and about, and the strains of the British national anthem drifting out onto the street might have invited unwelcome attention. They gave him a blue and white Delft plate as a present and an apple cake (made with condemned pre-war flour!) topped with a Union Jack. Every member of what he now considered his very own family made a speech wishing him a swift recovery and many happy returns ... to England. That return now seemed increasingly possible and, as the tentative mid-November deadline approached, his army boots were brought out from their hiding place and he was taken for slow walks in the town, surreptitiously slipping through the streets in the dusk just before curfew, trying to build up his strength and speed.

His efforts were to no avail. German activity was intensifying in Ede and also in the area south to the river, which was now forbidden to civilians.

This meant it would be impossible to concentrate the escape party just a few miles from the crossing point [as had happened on Pegasus I].

There would therefore have to be a long approach march, of around fifteen miles and at night. This would be quite beyond my strength, and a stretcher party to carry me could hardly be considered.

Sadly Hackett had to accept that, once again, as other men were briefed for the journey home, he would not be going.

One who was being quietly rounded up for the evacuation was veteran RAF bomb aimer David Ward. He had been shocked to find himself a fugitive behind enemy lines after his Halifax got into trouble while circling a field near the Zuider Zee to drop supplies to the Resistance. As the crew strained their eyes through the dark sky for lights on the ground, the plane fell lower and lower, clipped a tree at 180 mph, went out of control and thundered along the ground on its belly. A terrified Ward watched branches slashing through the fuselage. Fire broke out.

When I felt the plane slowing down I stood up and undid the escape hatch in the astrodome. The others panicked and scrambled over me to get out, using me as a ladder. There was nothing I could do to stop them. They were bigger than me, and I had to wait.[18]

Outside, the men, lucky to be alive, dashed away as flames from their burning aircraft shot into the sky, a signal that would swiftly attract any German soldiers in the area. They were lucky again. Three men with Sten guns stepped from a wood. Dutch Resistance. 'They led us away into the darkness,' Ward recalled, 'and within two hours of crashing we were eating porridge in a farmhouse.' Their relief was tempered by the realization of just how dangerous a situation they had landed in. There were enemy patrols with tracker dogs out looking for them and Dutch SS living nearby. Just days earlier, they learned, the Resistance had ambushed a German staff car and the Germans had retaliated by arresting 600 men in the area for deportation to labour camps. 'It was unreal and scary, going from being an airman to someone hiding in occupied enemy territory. I found it almost too much to think about.' Later he would actually face the enemy, stopped by a soldier while cycling along a road. The man wanted a light for his cigarette. 'But it could have gone either way. I was in civilian clothes over my uniform. If he had asked for an ID card, it would have been all over for me.' The risks were brought home to him when the farmer in whose house they stayed was denounced by a German deserter he had also been sheltering – fortunately for the RAF men, a few days after they had been moved to another hiding place. He was shot by a firing squad and his body left to rot in the open for three days before the Germans allowed it to be buried. But now, after just six weeks under cover, they were going home. Ward vividly remembered the mounting excitement as he and his crew were taken to join other evaders. The numbers swelled along with the anticipation. 'Eventually there were 130 of us all gathered together in the middle of a wood, expecting to get home. This was damn good.'

'Good' was not the word that sprang to Neave's mind as Pegasus II, his brainchild, neared. His original enthusiasm was dampened by the rapidly rising waters of the Rhine, its 5-knot currents now possibly too strong even for powered boats, and by reports from scouting parties to the other side that the Germans were reinforcing their defences. It was clear the enemy had cottoned on to the Pegasus I escape and was on the alert for a repeat. The passage would be harder this time; it might even have to take place under fire. There was 'the serious possibility of serious casualties among men who were already wounded and who might be killed instead of spending the rest of the war in prison-camps'.

He was not the only person with reservations. Hackett had been excluded from the escape but what he knew of the plan made the experienced paratroop commander uneasy.

The party did not have the preponderance of fit, well-trained infantry, operating under officers they knew, as there had been on the first. They had also been in hiding several weeks longer. Very many of them, moreover, were not soldiers at all but RAF and had no idea how to carry out a difficult infantry operation at night through an area where

German patrols were active. What chance did they have, however keen they might be!

He expressed his doubts to Bat. 'What happens if they are dis-covered?' he asked. But the Dutchman was unfazed. 'They are a large party,' he replied. 'They are armed and will fight their way through.' Hackett went silent, aware of the gulf in experience between a military man like himself and an undercover agent. 'A tragic muddle seemed to me a virtual certainty.'

Hackett could only watch from the sidelines, increasingly full of dread. In the end, Pegasus II was not his call. It was Neave's, who now sent a message to Jimmy Langley, heading up the IS9(d) office in Brussels, expressing his fears that he was about to consign a large number of men to 'an extremely cold death'. But Neave took the chance. The news from Ede was that the new batch of evaders were already assembling. He ordered the operation to go ahead. 'The hopes of men who had waited so long could not be dashed,' he wrote in his memoirs. He and his support team would be in position on the southern bank of the Rhine at a village called Heteren at midnight on 22 November and wait there for the next three nights for the red torches to flash from the other side.

But even as the details were being radioed to his agents in-side Holland, events were turning against him. The Germans dis-covered the telephone line in the electricity power station and cut it. The direct link that had been so vital to the October success was severed. The Gestapo was also squeezing the Dutch Resistance and robbing the operation of much of its essential local back-up force. Then, with two days to go, a newspaper in England carried interviews with, among others, Deane-Drummond, about Pegasus I. The details were vague but there was enough for any astute German spy who picked up on it to deduce where that Rhine crossing had taken place and warn his masters in Berlin. It was not the only time that a newspaper report jeopardized lives. David Ward's parents were told in a letter from his son's squadron that he was behind enemy lines but not in enemy hands. His father informed the local newspaper, which had just reported Ward missing, and it printed the story under the headline 'Good news follows bad'. It could have been disastrous for a man on the run. 'It might really have given the game away,' Ward reflected later. 'Things like that could cost you your life.'

But the real problem with Pegasus II was not leaks but over-confidence, born of the overwhelming success of the first oper-ation. Nobody seemed to want to reflect on how close a call Pegasus I had actually been. Luck had been on the side of the evaders and their rescuers then. Now it seemed to desert them utterly. Not that David Ward, waiting in an empty poultry ware-house a dozen miles from the Rhine with 130 companions, had any such inkling. 'We were tense,' he recalled, 'but confident that this was the day we were going home. You don't think that it's going to go wrong.' But the omens were not good. As they set off on foot from that last shelter, it was pouring with rain and soon everyone was soaked to the skin. Towards the rear was Ray Kubly, an American air force navigator whose B-24 had been hit by flak on its way to Germany six weeks earlier. The Resistance had hidden him and now here he was, dressed in a British army uniform, a Sten gun on his shoulder and in the pitch dark, hanging on tightly to a cloth rope looped through the belt of the man in front of him in the column so as not to get lost. He was excited.

We'd been told we would be across the river by midnight and be drinking wine! I had a real sense that the end was in sight. This wasn't going to fail. I could almost smell freedom.[19]

The bedraggled column made it to a small wood and lay up until dusk before setting out on what should have been the last lap. It was now 2 a.m. and the river was just three miles away. But the men were finding it hard to stay together and the column began to stretch out and split up into smaller groups. Some found themselves wandering in circles. Out of the darkness, a startled David Ward heard a loud shout. '*Halt!*' They had stumbled on a German sentry.

I dropped down but the others scattered. There was panic with everybody running around. Many who had been in front of me disappeared and I found myself left in a small group in a wood. I can honestly say I was scared. But the sentry didn't shoot and so we set off again. I thought we still had a chance of getting away, of getting out of there.

But then another German stepped from behind a tree, right in front of me. There was a major from the King's Own Scottish Borderers beside me and he called out '*Freund!*' – which, of course, he was not. The German fired and killed him instantly. I could barely believe it. I saw the flames from the muzzle.

Bat had promised the men would fight – but with what? The unarmed Ward dropped to the ground and as he lay there, the German swung round and aimed directly at him. 'I saw another muzzle flash and a bullet hit me. My back arched as it went in.'

From dug-in enemy positions, machine-gun bullets raked the air. Kubly heard an anguished cry of 'Germans!' and the rat-a-tat-tat of automatic weapons ahead and decided 'to get the hell out of there'. He threw away his gun – 'I didn't want to be caught carrying a weapon; that would have been disastrous' – and ran back the way he had come, 'my thoughts of freedom rapidly receding'. Back in the wood, Ward lay wounded. He had taken two bullets, one between the shoulder blade and spine, and the other through his left heel. He lay there for two hours on the wet ground, thinking, 'I'm not going to die because I'm not spitting blood.' Eventually a British medic found him and gave him morphine.

I came to next morning with a couple of Germans carrying me into a castle they had requisitioned as a hospital. British doctors who were also POWs took the bullet out of my back and gave it to me as a souvenir. I was determined to get home with it. I put it in my pocket – to this day, I still have it.

Ray Kubly was still free but utterly dejected at being on the run again. And in circumstances more desperate than before. The weather was bitterly cold, he and his companion had no food or water, the Germans were close on their tail and they had lost contact with their helpers in the Resistance. 'We licked moisture from the trees to quench our thirst. We finally lay down under some big evergreen and gathered leaves and pine needles to make a dry and comfortable place.' He resorted to prayer, and found some consolation. 'I realized that things could be worse and that hopefully they would improve – and they did, eventually.' The next day they came across a house in the woods.

We approached cautiously as a dog came barking at us. An old farmer came out and we told him we were 'Tommies'. Could he give us something to eat and drink? He went back in and brought out some warm milk and hot porridge. Did that ever taste good! Then he showed us to a barn and we slept in the hay.

On the Allied side of the Rhine, Neave's reception party had waited in vain through the night of 22/23 November. The omens were bad for them too as their headquarters in the cellar of a small house on top of a dyke came under intense shellfire from German batteries. The weather was awful and the river itself was looking 'swift and treacherous'. They watched until dawn, worrying that, if there had been a signal from the opposite bank, they might well have missed it in the dark, the rain and the smoke from the guns. The vigil resumed the next night, and at 3 a.m. voices were heard calling across the water.

A storm boat was quickly launched and returned safely with three men, wet and shivering and barely able to speak. After they had drunk liberally from a jar of rum, they proved to be an RAF sergeant and two Dutchmen. They said their party had been challenged by the Germans, fired on and scattered. Several were killed and the rest taken prisoner. Only seven had escaped.

The disaster Neave had feared was now apparent, and he was deeply depressed. There was a lift in spirits when reports came in of more voices calling across the river. A boat set out, despite worsening weather and German flares illuminating the water, and the crew radioed back from the other side that they had found a British paratrooper and an airman and were bringing them back. The boat and the men failed to make it. Standing on the dyke, Leo Heaps heard their cries for help as the craft was swept away and overturned but he could do nothing to save them. Four more deaths were added to the Pegasus II toll.

Heaps never had any doubt where the responsibility lay for the whole sorry affair. After the war he wrote:

Neave's imaginative escape from Colditz two years earlier was the performance of an outstanding impresario. However, the planning of an intricately coordinated mass escape required different talents.

Heaps thought the whole MI9 and IS9(d) set-up too languorous, its officers brave, charming and sophisticated but dilettante and, as a result, even amateurish in their approach. There was an element of truth in this. Garrow, Darling, Langley, Neave – there had always been the air of the gentleman-adventurer, the privateer, about the British officers involved in undercover work to bring home soldiers and airmen on the run in occupied Europe. But this was hardly surprising, given the general indifference of the War Office to helping evaders. Under-resourced and under-rated, they had no choice but to resort to panache, bravado and sometimes, as with Pegasus II, wishful thinking.

*

In Ede, John Hackett felt the heat of the failed operation as the Germans followed up their capture of most of the would-be escapers with an intensive hunt for those few who had got away. A search of the de Nooijs' house was only narrowly avoided by the fiercest of the maiden aunts standing in the doorway and giving a piece of her mind to the three Germans who tried to force their way in. The arrest of Bat by the SS was another disaster. It was time for the brigadier to be moved. There was renewed talk of getting him home. Perhaps a Lysander could come for him, though the rain-soaked ground now made that unlikely. Or perhaps the Resistance could find a way to slip him across the Rhine in a boat. A plan was drawn up. If he could get close to the flooded area beside the river, on or around Christmas Day, a patrol of Allied troops would come over, penetrate the German lines and pick him up. It sounded good. A bicycle was found for the trip south and a safe hiding place identified just a couple of miles from the river where he could rest before the final foray. Hackett pored over maps, memorizing the route he would take. 'I tried to imagine what each bank, ditch, fence and path might look like. I had never prepared an operation more carefully.' He assembled his kit and began making his farewells to the family. They gave him a black silk cover for his luminous wristwatch. On Christmas Eve 1944 he sat waiting for a message from London to start.

It never came. The weather ruled out an escape. The winter nights were too bright and clear and the moon uncomfortably large. Yet again he would have to wait. Would it never end?

## 12. Fleeing the Ruins of the Reich

For most Allied airmen shot down over Germany itself, rather than the countries its armies occupied, the war was over virtually the moment their flying boots (if they hadn't been wrenched off when baling out, that is) touched the soil of the Fatherland. Capture was usually swift, whether by soldiers, police or civilians. 'No help is to be expected from Germans,' the official MI9 advice to British servicemen freely admitted. 'Evasion here is obviously more difficult.'[1] But have a go anyway, it went on, in a gung-ho spirit of adventure more suited to a Boy Scout camp than the realities of a country still in the grip of totalitarian rule, still in thrall to Hitler's evil genius, yet taking a terrible pounding from fleets of bombers dropping destruction and death day and night. 'There is a good chance of getting away,' would-be evaders were urged, 'and it would be well worth trying because of the nuisance caused to the enemy and the experience gained.' No mention was made of the countless well-documented occasions on which British and American airmen had been pitchforked, scythed and kicked to death by angry, vengeful crowds or hanged from city lamp posts and country-barn beams. Even those in the custody of armed Luftwaffe escorts and on their way to POW camps were not safe from the vengeance of the mob, incensed by the bombing of their towns and cities. In such circumstances, the advice to open negotiations with enemy civilians as if from a position of strength – 'Work on his fear of what will happen when the Allies arrive. In return for any help, give a chit stating what aid the German rendered. This may help to counteract his fear of the Gestapo' – seemed optimistic at best, and, at worst, to come from a different planet.

When he saw his first Germans after floating down into the middle of a vineyard in the Moselle valley, the instinct of wireless operator Sergeant Tony Johnson was not to tell them they were losing the war and try and do a deal with them but to run like hell in the opposite direction. Walking westward in what he vaguely thought was the direction of the French border, he had come upon a group of old men in a lane. They were standing and watching the flames and smoke rising from Mannheim, sixty miles away to the east, the city he had just bombed.

I was practically on top of them before I realized. We stood staring speechlessly at one another. Then they began to make hostile noises, and I turned on my heels and ran until I collapsed with exhaustion.[2]

As he rested, the reality of his situation came home to him.

I had a little light of hope that I might get away with this. But the fact was that I was trying to evade through Germany – and in RAF uniform! I still had on my brown leather flying jacket and blue air force trousers. I thought, I'm never really going to be successful with this escapade, am I?

He regretted having paid so little attention to the escape and evasion lectures back at the squadron. He was sorry too that he would miss his date with Joyce, the blue-eyed Land Girl with blonde wavy hair he had just met and fallen in love with. He hoped she would understand when he didn't turn up. Spurred on by the thought of her, he started off again, down another lane, round a bend, and right into more local people.

I decided to bluff things out this time. I sauntered past as casually as possible, praying they would not notice my uniform and flying boots in the early morning half-light. As we passed I was, surprisingly, greeted with a chorus of '*Guten Morgen*', and I thought I was in the clear.

Then a voice called out '*Halt!*' I broke into a sprint. There was a loud pistol shot. I stopped in my tracks. There was a real chance I could be killed here. I realized it was over, and I wasn't going to see Joyce for some time now. I was really going to miss her. I felt like bursting into tears.

Johnson turned, his hands in the air, to face a Heinrich Himmler lookalike with glasses and a moustache, 'a nasty face straight out of a propaganda film about the Gestapo'. He was brandishing a Luger pistol. 'Proclaiming his hatred for *Englanders* in general and *Terrorfliegers* in particular, he took running kicks at me to emphasize his disapproval.' The airman was shoved at gunpoint to the man's cottage but there an odd transformation came over the German. He politely introduced his wife and little daughters, who smiled and giggled, and the family photo album was brought out for show. Johnson proudly put his picture of Joyce on the table beside it. 'As we were getting on so well, I thought it the right thing to do.' The respite was brief. When the police came to take him away, he was escorted along the streets of a town through a gauntlet of snarling faces and shaking fists. At a railway station en route to a POW camp, a ferocious crowd closed in on him, kicking and punching. Just in time, military police came to his rescue. As he was hustled away to safety, the spittle of his enemies clung to his uniform.

In the first months of 1945 – as the bitterest winter in a century settled over Europe – the key question was how long Germany would continue to spit out the defiance and the aggression that Tony Johnson had experienced on its streets. Hitler's Reich was under siege. In the west, his Christmas counter-offensive through the forests of the Ardennes had been repelled, his order to send the Allies reeling back to the coast unfulfilled. British and American forces were on German soil and preparing to cross the next major obstacle in their way, the Rhine. And that was just one half of the pincer. In the east, the vast Soviet army was less than 100 miles from Berlin. The Führer expected his army and his people to fight for every inch of earth, to scorch what they could not hold and to die in the ashes. These were dangerous times for everyone. For men on the run behind the lines, there was an acute dilemma. Their own armies were temptingly within reach. But a chasm of hate and fear, vengeance and violence, stood between them and safety. Getting there would mean passing through a German population, both military and civilian, that might well be on the verge of blowing out not only its own brains (as its leader was to do just a few months later in his bunker) but also those of its enemies.

In such a volatile situation it was extraordinary, therefore, that Flying Officer Ron Carabine not only survived but managed to stay free inside Germany for more than a week. Escaping with his life when the Halifax he was piloting to bomb Dortmund on 20 February 1945 was shot down was miracle enough. Incendiary bullets from a Messerschmitt 410 started a blaze in the fuselage and he ordered the crew to jump as the plane began to spiral out of control. They never got the chance. Fire reached into the bomb bay and there was an almighty bang as the bomb load detonated in mid-air. 'The kite blew apart, and us with it,' Carabine wrote later.[3]

I remember being in my seat, hanging on to the control column, and the next thing I was in the open air with just quiet and nothingness all around me. My first thought was 'Oh God. I'm dead,' followed almost immediately by, 'No I'm not, I'm out of it. I'm falling.'

He was face down and spinning, with a clear view beneath him of the rest of his squadron homing in to attack Dortmund. He flapped his arms, pushed out his legs, managed to right himself, then pulled the ripcord on the parachute he couldn't even remember putting on. That was because he hadn't. Quite by chance he was wearing a new model, worn permanently rather than needing to be clipped on. He was testing it out. It even had the word 'experimental' printed on the surface. It made the suit bulky and uncomfortable and his crew had laughed at the sight of him in it. Now he was the one smiling.

I landed in some trees. I had two cuts on my head and one on my hand. Several of my joints seemed out of place. My left foot, left wrist, right thigh and right shoulder were all wrong, as was my left kneecap. I sat there for some considerable time until the full realization came to me – that I was alive and in a tree in the Third Reich!

The sound of voices sent him scurrying to the ground. He crawled into bushes and lay hidden as, for the next twenty-four hours, vehicles buzzed up and down a nearby road. He heard hounds baying. Clearly the hunt for him and his crew was on. Though his injuries made it difficult to walk, he set off westward by his compass, aiming for the Rhine. He avoided roads, sticking to open country, but the going was rough. He limped up snow-covered hills, 'at least once dragging myself along the ground pulling myself upward from tree to tree'.

I walked each night from dusk to dawn and stayed hidden in the woods each day. I took three Horlicks tablets per day, drank water from streams and ate occasional sugar beets and the hearts of cabbages.

Only twice did people speak to me. A woman came out of a house and said something to me. It sounded like a question so I answered 'Nein.' It seemed to satisfy her. The second occasion was when I met a chap coming towards me on a narrow path by the side of the railway. I wished him 'Guten Tag,' and that was that.

But, as the days passed, pain and exhaustion, not people, were his problems. He was still free but on the point of collapse. At dawn on his fifth day, he felt dreadful.

My leg was giving me trouble and I had not been able to find any drinkable water for the last thirty-six hours. I found a haystack and crawled in there and made myself really comfortable. I had the best night's sleep since leaving England.

He pressed on, reaching the Rhine near Cologne. It had to be crossed somehow. He tried one bridge, surprised that it was un-guarded, and set off, only to get half-way over and discover the rest had been blown out of the water by Allied bombers. He retraced his steps but his behaviour inevitably drew attention to him as a stranger. As he regained the bank, workers outside a factory shouted at him, a soldier ordered him to stop. 'I ignored him and pressed on. He continued to call after me for a while but he didn't pursue me or shoot and I managed to lose him in the dark.' And when he finally found an intact bridge and was about to cross, 'as happy as a dog with two tails', he walked straight into a line of sentries. He thought of turning round and running but reasoned that he would be shot for sure. So once again, he just kept going. In the dark, the German soldiers took no notice of the man in RAF battledress. 'They had stopped a car and were examining the driver's papers by torchlight. I don't think they saw me at all.'

Carabine was elated. He had come forty miles through the heartland of Germany and it was almost as if he was invisible to his enemies. Invisible and invincible. He could see no reason why he should not just keep walking until he reached his own lines. It was all too easy. At one point, he even tagged along behind a column of German infantry.

I was sneaking down a muddy path between the backs of two rows of houses. Ahead of me it joined a road and I could see this line of soldiers marching by. I turned around to go back the way I had come but some civilians were walking towards me. Either direction was dangerous but it seemed to me the military column was the better bet. I carried on towards it, slowed down at the end of the path and then joined in behind until I was able to sneak off down a side road.

It was nicely dusk by then but there were too many grey shapes around for comfort. I really could not believe this was happening to me. I had not joined the RAF for this sort of game. I was beginning to think my nerves could not stand much more of this.

It was his luck that run out. As he got nearer to the front line, there were more and more troops and fewer places to hide. He was sneaking past a large house when a voice ordered him to stop.

I walked on but it didn't work this time. An army NCO came running over to me, grabbed my arm and spoke to me in English. He hauled out a great pistol that looked as big as a cannon to me and told me to raise my hands. I surrendered.

He was locked in a cellar with an American fighter pilot, whose face was cut to pieces. 'He told me that, after crashing, a civilian with a whip had reached him before the military arrived.' Carabine was threatened. The guards made it clear that if he tried to escape he would be shot. During interrogation he was told he could be executed as a spy, run over by tanks, 'as we do to the Russians', or handed over to civilians for their rough rope justice. But none of this happened. He was spared the violent end he might have had from falling into enemy hands in this high-risk area of the war. On the contrary, as he was taken away to a POW camp, a Luftwaffe captain went out of his way to explain that he was in fact an Austrian, that he hated Germany and liked Englishmen very much. The iron mood, among some Germans at least, was softening. Survival for those on the run in the ruins of the Reich was a real possibility after all.[4]

American pilot Hal Naylor even stumbled on the semblance of an escape line in Germany as the country began to crumble into defeat. He jumped from his burning B-17 bomber and landed in a potato patch in the middle of a forest, alongside his navigator, Mac. Naylor's boots had gone, lost in the air, and his feet were soon icy from the snow on the ground. He lit a fire – flouting one of the basic escape-and-evasion instructions – and fashioned the fabric from his parachute into wraps for his feet. As he warmed up and mulled over his situation, he fixed his thoughts on his wife Jane back home in Atlanta, worried about her worrying about him when she was notified he was missing in action and told himself he would see her again one day. But he did not underestimate how hard it would be. 'I knew that hardly anybody got out of Germany after being shot down.'[5] He knew too that they had to be within 100 miles of the Allied lines, a few days' walking distance, a week at the most. They consulted the maps in their escape packs and took the first steps west along a dirt road.

It was around midnight of our second day in Germany when we came to the edge of a small town. It was eerily quiet as we walked up the street and came to a Catholic church. At briefings we had been told that priests hated the Nazis and might help us, so we went inside, crept across the creaking floor boards and hid between the pews.

We had both dozed off when the front door opened and a little old man in a clerical collar walked down the aisle to the altar. I decided to take a chance and slowly stood up with my hands over my head as if asking for mercy, which was exactly what I was doing. I said: '*Amerikaner Flieger, Amerikaner Flieger*', a term we had been taught. It was the only German I knew.

The priest lived up to the expectations of the US evasion instructors. He hurried the two men behind the altar, down some steps into a kitchen and locked them in the pantry while he went back up to the church to conduct early-morning mass for his parishioners. He came back carrying a pair of boots for Naylor. 'That's when I knew for sure we had done the right thing by letting our presence be known,' the American recalled. 'He was going to help us and not turn us in to the authorities.'

The priest had friends, who came for the two fugitives.

At night and in complete silence, we were led through rural areas only, never into any villages regardless of how small. It was far safer that way. We were never given civilian clothes to wear such as the evaders with the French, Belgium, and Dutch undergrounds were. Since we were in Germany proper, we stayed in uniform in case we were captured.

They were passed from house to house and had a new guide every night as, for the next few weeks, they hiked through the German countryside.

We did as we were told, asked no questions, had complete faith in our escorts. But, then, we didn't have much of an alternative. We could not have survived on our own. Mac and I would often talk about the hard conditions these people were living in, yet they were willing to share with us, the enemy who had been bombing them and their cities just a few days before. How they must have hated Hitler for what he was doing to their families, lives, and country!

I'd never heard of escape lines in Germany – at the time or since. I don't like to use the word 'underground' because I don't know if there really was one. I think we just happened to come across the right people who were there and able to help us at the right time, a huge big portion of luck.

Naylor got away, though his exit from the Reich was just as dramatic and mysterious as the trek itself. After six weeks their last guide took them to a field that, he explained, had once been a Luftwaffe training camp. They were to lie up in bushes in the dark, and be prepared to move swiftly into action. They hid, and then, in the night sky, heard the sound of an aircraft approaching. A blacked-out RAF Dakota transport plane came skimming in, touched down on the grass runway, throttled back, taxied to the end, then turned and, without stopping, came rolling back the other way. By now its rear cargo doors had swung open, a gaping invitation to the two men in the bushes. They jumped up and ran towards the moving plane – and were staggered to see a dozen other dark figures emerge from other hiding places and dash forward too. And more, and then more again, until twenty of them were pursuing the Dakota along the grass.

They were all downed flyers who, unbeknownst to us, had also been stashed very quietly behind other bushes by their guides. Obviously this was a well-planned operation between the German 'underground' and the RAF.

A panting Naylor needed help.

I was running alongside the open cargo door when a big Limey airman reached out, grabbed my arm, and yanked me aboard. He pulled others in too, and when the last man was on, he signalled the cockpit, the power of the engines came up, and we were airborne. We were up and away before any of us were able to catch our breath and get up off the floor and find a place to sit.

That night Mac and Naylor, exhausted but happy, slept in beds in the officers' mess in the Grosvenor House hotel on Park Lane, London. 'Life was so good!' They knew they owed theirs to good Germans, men and women whose names they never knew and whose help came as a complete surprise.

After the war, I regretted that I had not exchanged names and addresses with our hosts, but for their safety and ours, it was out of the question. I have often wished I could go back and thank them. I hope they all survived the war and enjoyed the new Germany that our Allied victory gave to them.

Was there really a German Resistance organization as such that had gone into action to save the airmen? It seems most unlikely. Defiance of the dictator had been systematically crushed out of the people in the dozen years since Hitler and the Nazis came to power and transformed the nation in their image. The communists, socialists and liberals were the first in the concentration camps – eradicated. The church and the army made their institutional accommodations with the state – disarmed. The potentially rebellious young were seduced into the Hitler Youth movement – absorbed. Dissent was ruthlessly dealt with by the secret police of the Gestapo and a compliant judiciary, violently and without mercy. Students in Munich formed a nascent opposition group – the Weisserose (White Rose) – but never got beyond handing out idealistic leaflets before their heads were chopped off and their protest died with them. They were denounced by their own teachers, a depressing sign of how deeply entrenched Nazi ideology had become in German life. That was in 1943. The following year, with the war going badly wrong, was the moment when opposition to Hitler might have thrived. But the failure of the July 1944 plot to blow him up and the vicious suppression of anyone remotely connected to it strangled any such hopes. In 1945, as the country plunged towards ruin, battalions of SS thugs enforced the party line by butchering deserters, defeatists and dissenters.

They could still win, the people were told. The British and

Americans would soon see sense, recognize Stalin as their real enemy and join Germany in a crusade against communism. Together they would push the Reds back to Moscow and beyond. It was a forlorn hope, flying in the face of the political and military realities, but, rather than turn on their Nazi masters, millions of Germans clung to it in those dog days of the war. Of course, individuals had always opposed Hitler but experience had taught them to do so quietly, in secret, among trusted friends. It must have been into the hands of a small band of like-minded people that Hal Naylor was lucky enough to fall. They did what they could. They protected his freedom and saved his life. The sadness for Germany was that there were never enough of them to make a real difference.

★

As the German army fell back into their homeland and the Allies punched their way eastwards over the Rhine, they left one country stranded in the rear, still under Nazi rule, its long-suffering people not merely denied their freedom but repressed, starved and terrorized more than ever before. The endgame of the war had come relatively easily to France and Belgium. In Holland, it was hell. Among those still waiting for liberation was Brigadier John Hackett, in hiding with the de Nooij family in the town of Ede. He saw the disappointment on the faces of his Dutch friends when radio reports made it clear that their country had been bypassed by the Allies in favour of a direct strike into Germany. They felt let down. And he felt his continued presence was putting them in increasing danger. The German occupiers were rapacious, scouring houses for food, clothes, blankets, bicycles, anything they could carry away. The threat of discovery was growing daily. The local Resistance workers were jumpy, and irritated too that, while they were putting their lives at risk, the British military seemed to be doing very little to get their own soldiers home. It was a fair point.

But the family remained loyal and reassuring, denying there was any pressure on him to leave. 'In good time, if God wishes, you will go,' these good people told him. 'Until then, this is your home.'[6] But their nervousness was all too obvious. He was also becoming a danger to himself as he began to venture on the streets in broad daylight. Just being out was an unnecessary risk. He could have been stopped for something trivial or, as a youngish man, now a rarity in Holland, swept up for a forced-labour gang. But he chanced his arm further and one day deliberately cannoned into a couple of German soldiers whose path he crossed, mumbled his apologies and went on his way. 'I badly wanted to touch them and speak to them,' he said later to explain this insanity. 'That was all. It was like being a little boy at the zoo.' Only later did he come to his senses and realize how stupid he had been. His capture could have led to reprisals, hostage taking, summary punishment for people he had grown to love and admire. He felt 'dreadful'. When a chance came to try for home, he grabbed at it, even though the risks were great.

There was, he learned from John de Nooij, the young man in the family and someone he trusted totally, a secret courier service running canoes twice a week through the marshes of the lower Waal with letters and intelligence for the Dutch government-in-exile. They didn't normally take 'tourist traffic' but an exception could be made for such a high-ranking officer. The MI9 agent Hackett was in touch with was horrified by the suggestion.[7] He knew nothing of this route. He suspected a trap. But this time Hackett would not be denied. Three times he had missed the boat home. Now he was fit and strong. He was going. Any doubts were overcome by a sudden security crackdown in Ede. Existing passes were declared invalid; new ones had to be obtained, signed by the Nazi mayor. Two de Nooij uncles were arrested and interrogated. They were released after a few days, heads shaved as a humiliation, but the dragnet was drawing too tight for comfort. 'I could no longer impose on them,' Hackett decided. He slept his last night in the bed under the embroidery sampler of the Sleeping Beauty, said prayers with the family around the breakfast table and then he and John set off on bicycles, south-west through the snow. A fifty-mile journey of great danger lay ahead, but the Englishman felt wind in his face for the first time in five months and was elated by this sense of freedom after so long under cover. 'My spirits soared like a kite.'

They passed through bleak countryside and threadbare villages, ravaged by war. Occasionally they came across bored bedraggled Germans, doing what soldiers spend most of their time doing, just hanging around, waiting, grumbling. No one even looked up as the two battled by in deepening snow until they came to a secluded house in a pine forest. Its warm and welcoming kitchen contained a wonderful surprise. Seated by the fire was the man who had saved Hackett's life – Captain Lipmann-Kessel, the British army surgeon who back in Arnhem all those months ago had refused an SS order to liquidate him and instead performed a miraculous operation on his stomach. He too was on the run, having tried and failed to get home on the abortive Pegasus II evacuation in November. The two men sat and talked, basking in the glow of renewed friendship and deep respect. The doctor then inspected his handiwork, tidied up the slightly festering stitches and pronounced himself satisfied with his patient's recovery.

After three days of rest and much-needed companionship, they went their separate ways, the doctor with another small group of evaders,[8] while Hackett continued with John, through the city of Utrecht and onto the Rhine Canal, which they crossed after bribing a boatman. The cost was two balls of darning wool John had brought from home, priceless in that hard winter and those even harder times. And finally he had come to the last stage, waiting in a town beside the waters of the Waal for a boat to come for him. He put on what he still had of his uniform, torn and stained with the blood of battle, his paratroop wings and medal ribbons faded. In the breast pocket he had his pink army ID card, the face of a polished British officer staring out from it, and his false Dutch papers, bearing the name of Johan van Dalen, the one he had assumed for what now seemed like a whole lifetime, this face old, drawn and sick. He felt in limbo, 'a sleeper about to awake. Something was over and something else was about to begin.'

A stranger rowed him across one stretch of river, silent except for the splash of an oar. In the dark and mist, 'we might have been on a boundless ocean'. He shivered in the cold, or was it from nerves? He comforted himself with the thought that it was just like playing smugglers as a boy, 'when the nursery fire gleamed on the brass fender and we children were being read to after tea'. Except that the men in jerseys and sea boots who hauled him out on the other side were real. And so were the Sten guns they carried, and the whisky they gave him to drink. Then he was off, following a guide across fields, over fences, past ponds and backwaters, until they came to a tree by a wide channel.

From a distance there was what sounded like the cry of a marsh bird and then silence. Then the cry came again, and again silence. I could almost hear my heart beating in the suspense. 'Curse that fellow! He's late again,' the guide said in a loud, gruff voice and lit up a cigarette. 'Is it safe to smoke?' I asked. 'Of course,' he said. 'There are no Germans for miles.' And we laughed.

A splash heralded the arrival of the canoe, and soon Hackett was out on the water again, languidly trailing his fingers over the side as it glided between reed beds, and then out into broader water. They stopped at a low bank, climbed over a dyke and waited while unseen hands humped the canoe across. Human shapes appeared out of the dark, seized Hackett's hand in friendship, wished him good luck. The River Waal stretched ahead, wide, deep and stirred by a strong wind. The canoe pushed off into rolling waves, lurching perilously until it finally settled in calmer water and they began to make progress. They zig-zagged to slip silently and unnoticed past German observation posts on either side of the river. Flares exploded in the sky but there was no gunfire. And then they were heading back into reeds, between islands and finally into a narrow channel that led to a small river port.

We came alongside some stone steps. People clambered down and helped me up. 'Hello, Shan [Hackett's nickname],' said a cheerful voice. 'We've been expecting you.' It was an old friend from the 11th Hussars, whose armoured cars were holding a stretch of the south bank of the lower Waal. I blinked in the bright lamplight. There was a haze of tobacco smoke, and around a stove were men in khaki battledress. I sat down surrounded once more by the familiar and comfortable jumble of the British army. I was among my own people again.

It was February 1945 when Hackett came home, but other evaders in Holland still had many weeks to wait. American airman Ray Kubly was one of the few to escape unscathed from the abortive Pegasus II evacuation and with a companion, Jack Murrell, managed to plug back in to the Resistance network of safe houses. They were lodged in the ice-cold attic of a country hotel, then in the much warmer home of a postmaster until German soldiers came to search it and they had to leave in a hurry. In another safe house they sat out the winter while in the distance they could just make out the air combat over the Ardennes as the Allies gradually won the Battle of the Bulge. On Christmas Day they thought of turkey and ham but dined on potatoes and cabbage. They longed to be out of the war zone. A little wine eased the pain.

Their escape came along the same route Hackett had taken a month earlier, though it took them more than one attempt. Their first foray ended in disaster when, cycling to the river, one of their group was stopped at a German checkpoint. Kubly was standing behind him, next in line.

He was made to take off his overalls to reveal his army uniform under-neath. When I saw what was happening I turned round to the others and said, 'Let's get the hell out of here.' We rode away on our bicycles. I expected the Germans to come after us but they didn't. It was an incredibly lucky escape.[9]

He made it on the next attempt, despite his understandable appre-hension.

Our hopes rose when we were told we would be free by midnight, but you cannot allow yourself to get too excited. We might run into a

German patrol and be shot. You are putting your life on the line. You want to believe everything will be fine and you will soon be out of this mess but you don't dare to be too optimistic.

Safety was a Canadian voice calling out from the dark river bank for them to halt. From the boat, Kubly sang out: 'Don't shoot – we are Americans!' They landed and climbed over a dyke, sensibly with their hands over their heads, just in case. After all they had been through, it wouldn't have done to be shot at the very last minute, and by your own side.

This, however, was what very nearly happened to RAF bomb aimer David Ward, another evader in Holland. Shot in the back by a German soldier during Pegasus II, he escaped from a military hospital with two other prisoners and sheltered in a pigsty until the Resistance found a permanent home for them, with an undertaker.

There were a lot of Germans around, and they came to the house a lot because it had a telephone. They would be downstairs on the phone while we were upstairs in the bedroom. It was unreal but there was nothing we could do except get on with it.[10]

After two months of being 'bored witless', they tried to reach the Allied lines and were stopped on the road by German soldiers. 'Machine guns were pointing at us. I was terrified. This was the second time for me, and I really did think this could be it, that my time was up.' But, by bluff and good luck, they managed to give the soldiers the slip and carried on to another house, where they waited a further month.

It was mid-April when we heard the rumble of artillery and next day saw tired and dirty enemy soldiers retreating past the house. That was a great boost. But then mortar shells came whistling in and we dived for cover. We were under fire from our own side. There was a crater four feet wide and a foot deep where we had just been standing. Can you imagine being taken out by your own side in the final minutes of your war, so near yet so far?

The next day the Germans had gone, and the men stepped outside the house, wondering what to do next. Just then two strangers approached.

Were they friend or foe? We had no idea. I was very nervous. But they turned out to be British SAS officers who had been told of our whereabouts and had come to collect us. We shook their hands. It was all over. Two days later we were flown in a Dakota back to England.

*

On the other side of Europe, in a rapidly shrinking Reich, millions of people were also on the move, but where and whether to life or death they could not know. Gordon Carter was one of a quarter of a million British and American prisoners of war ousted from their camps on Germany's eastern borders and force-marched west, away from the advancing Russians, their hopes of a quick liberation dashed. Long columns shuffled through snow and ice, faltering from exposure, exhaustion, sickness and hunger. Armed guards prodded them on. A rearguard of SS troops was rumoured to be disposing of those who could not continue.[11] They shared the crowded roads and tracks with a desperate civilian population, fleeing the fighting and the violent retribution of Stalin's now unstoppable hordes. In the past he had been an evader. Now Carter dismissed such an idea as 'crazy'. It would have been 'a piece of cake' to slip away. 'But where to?'[12] He knew how hard it was to survive out there when there were friends to help, as there had been for him in France two years earlier. In a hostile land, where every scrap of food and the simplest of shelters had to be fought for, his chances were slim. But he was in for a long haul. Having reached the other side of Germany, away from the Russians, he was then marched back in the opposite direction, this time away from the Allied armies pressing in from the west. For his family back in England, months passed without news. In Brittany, Janine, the girl he had sworn to return to and marry, could only wait and wonder if she would ever see him again. How would it end? Peacefully, or in a bloodbath, as the defeated Germans went down in a last blaze of defiance? As they trudged through the ruins of the Reich, the POWs could never be sure. One prisoner took hope from the sight of a German guard, also struggling through the snow, consoling himself with a bottle of schnapps and shouting 'Fuck Hitler' at the top of his voice.[13] With luck, there would be many more like him. With luck.

Others decided to make their own luck. For a week, RAF sergeant Tony Johnson stayed in the column marching from Stalag Luft IV, ahead of the Red Army. Then he decided he had had enough. If he could hide, he would soon be overrun by the Russians and liberated. It was dark as the POWs trudged down a farm track towards a barn to rest for the night. He saw a gap in a hedge and dived through it into a snowdrift. 'I was an evader in Germany again – for the first time in nearly two years. I was free, and it was a wonderful feeling.' As he waded through knee-deep snow, gasping for breath, the elation evaporated. What had he let himself in for? He came upon a pile of logs and lay down, 'somewhere in East Pomerania'. As he dozed, he dreamt of having his girlfriend Joyce in his arms again. 'It was set in my mind that I would get back to her as soon as possible and propose marriage. Hopefully, she was still waiting for me.' Then he walked, going east, a lone figure through a never-ending expanse of white, expecting to see Russians at any moment. 'Time and time again I would cock my ear and listen intently for the sound of gunfire, but all was frustratingly quiet.' In the bitter cold, struggling against a blizzard, his mind wandered as well as his feet.

I began to hallucinate. The first mirage was of a giant stack of Red Cross parcels towering in the snow before me. I was about to take a hefty bite out of a handsome luncheon meat sausage when it vanished. The reality was that I was on my own in the middle of nowhere and my body was letting me down. The chances of getting home were diminishing rapidly.

A hut came into view, the real thing, not a mirage. But nor was the German sentry inside, fumbling for his rifle and, in a panicky voice, demanding the password for entry to the snowbound airfield he was guarding.

I showed him my POW dog tags and explained that I had become separated from my column. I did not know whether to laugh or cry at being captured again but secretly I was relieved. There was a real chance I would have simply died out there and no one would ever have known. So much for that attempt to reach Uncle Joe's troops. So much for my attempt to reach freedom.

Johnson could well have been shot on the spot, particularly having been caught on the edge of a military installation. Instead he was treated with courtesy, warmed up, fed, allowed to sleep, and then driven to join the nearest POW column thirty miles down the road. 'I resumed the trek westwards, though my feet hurt terribly. I dared not take my boots off as I would never get them on again. I had to get used to being a cripple.'[14]

Two months later he escaped again. The column he joined had been deposited at Stalag XIB at Fallingbostel in north-west Germany, a charnel house of a camp, crammed to overflowing with 40,000 sick and starved POWs. When it too was evacuated, this time in an easterly direction, *away* from home rather than towards it, he concluded they were all walking to some murderous finale. He fled. It was easier to hide now, among the hordes of refugees and the growing number of Wehrmacht deserters living off the land, trying to survive Germany's imminent apocalypse. Above, Allied fighter planes had the skies at their command as they harassed the retreating Germans. In the distance he and another POW with whom he had escaped heard the unmistakable rumble of artillery fire. 'We were getting near our goal.' Near, but not near enough to be out of danger. Walking along a cart track over open heath, they came to a gate onto a cobblestoned road. Two German soldiers were coming the other way.

I was frightened, desperate not to be caught now, afraid they might be SS. But we were too near to about-turn without causing suspicion, so we strolled past them and in unison wished them a good night. We were walking away when the challenge came.

Over our shoulders we called out that we were Polish labourers, and quickened our pace. Then we threw ourselves into long grass beside the lane. And only just in time because now they were doubling along the lane to catch us up. We hugged the ground and dared not breathe as our pursuers hurried by only a few feet away.

Theirs was not the only confrontation with a beaten but still dangerous enemy in this uneasy no-man's-land. Ron Scales had waited until they were in western Germany and in the final stages of the forced march before, though stick-thin from malnutrition and utterly fatigued, he saw an opportunity to escape and took it.[15] The column had been called to halt for a rest but, while the others sat down wearily by the road, he and his buddy, Jim Perry, kept walking, aiming for a wood a few hundred yards away.

A guard shouted, '*Halt!*' and raised his rifle, so I said, '*Scheissen*', to indicate that we needed to relieve ourselves behind a bush. He grunted and watched as I began to unfasten my belt, then lost interest. Like a flash I was rolling down a slope deeper into the undergrowth.[16]

They hid in a disused quarry, from the rim of which they could see shelling in the distance away to the west. The front line was close. But so too was a village, and, as he climbed out of the crater one morning, Scales found himself face to face with a German civilian, clutching the hand of a little boy.

The man put his hand into his coat pocket and produced a large pistol which he pointed straight at my stomach. I raised my hands and said in my broken German '*Ich bin ein englischer Kriegsgefanganer*' [I am an English prisoner of war]. He said something I didn't understand and I just kept talking, desperately trying to take some of the tension out of a situation that could easily have resulted in a bullet in my chest.

Eventually he relaxed and put the gun away. We talked, as best we could, for quite a time. At one stage he said, '*Deutschland ist kaput. Alles ist kaput.*' I was careful only to nod sagely at this, and then quite suddenly he unbuttoned his jacket, pulled his shirt open and showed me a huge twisted scar across his stomach.

'*Russland?*' I said, thinking he'd been wounded on the eastern front. '*Nein*', he replied. '*Frankreich terrorist*', meaning the French Resistance. Apparently he had been ambushed at night in France by someone with a Sten gun. His injuries were so bad he was invalided out of the army.

I showed concern for his wound but all I could think of was what he would have said if he had known I had flown with a squadron that dropped arms, including Sten guns, to the Resistance. The gun that nearly killed him might well have reached France inside a container that I myself had dropped.

This bizarre *fin-de-guerre* encounter of two enemies, their lives so intimately linked by war and now by a desperation to survive after all they had endured, ended when the German looked up and spotted something in the distance. Bowling along a road a few miles away was, as the German pointed out, '*ein britannica Panzerwagen*' – a British armoured car. Scales's heart leapt. The other man, seeing defeat arriving on his doorstep, made to leave.

I fished in my pocket and brought out a tablet of soap from home that I had kept for trading. 'For your *Frau*,' I said. He took it, then the child's hand, and together they made their way down the hill until they were lost to my sight.

The next day, Scales and Perry waved down a British patrol and climbed aboard their armoured car, 'among friends again'. By now, Johnson was also back in the same fold after coming directly through the British and German front lines on Luneberg Heath. He was worried – and rightly so – about shells, bombs, mines, snipers, from both sides. They were in the middle of a furious firefight.

Our lads were having to struggle for every inch of German soil. Artillery fire came from behind us and the shells whined overhead. This was not a very healthy place to be. We edged nervously round a barn and in the shadows made out two khaki-clad soldiers in sleeveless leather jackets and tin helmets. We had made it. With cries of delight, my companion and I hugged each other and performed a silly waltz in the farmyard. Tears of joy streamed down our cheeks.

★

The outcome of those terrible marches in the last months of the war was a good one for the vast majority of British and American POWs. They survived. They went home. But what drove their Nazi captors to herd them across Germany like cattle is still unclear six decades later. Were they hostages? Did Berlin intend to have them all shot in revenge, like the fifty RAF officers who fled Stalag Luft III in the so-called Great Escape? Or was it just the result of an ingrained, totalitarian mindset? Their guards had no orders to release them so they clung on to them, in the face of all logic and humanity. It was a different scenario in the most terrifying parts of the Reich, the concentration camps. Here was the evil empire's darkest secret. Millions had already died in gas chambers, on gallows and from overwork. Those who had survived were witnesses to unspeakable crimes. They faced elimination. Among them were Nadine Dumon, Dédée de Jongh, Virginia d'Albert-Lake and hundreds of other French, Belgian and Dutch men and women who had been caught helping Allied evaders.

Even in the bleakness of Ravensbruck, where many of them were sent as political prisoners, the spirit that had brought succour to soldiers and airmen on the outside was undimmed. Nadine remained defiant. 'They didn't break me. I never waxed the SS guards' shoes for an extra bowl of soup.'[17] For all the horrors she experienced there, she never regretted the work she had done for the evaders in Belgium. 'I was fighting against the Germans and I accepted the consequences.' The two Elsie Maréchals, mother and daughter, carried on that undercover work as best they could, now trying to hide the inmates known as *les lapins*, the rabbits or guinea pigs. These were Polish women used by the camp doctors for hideous medical experiments. Young Elsie befriended one whose crippled leg dangled behind her because her sciatic nerve had been deliberately removed, With the Russians getting nearer to the camp in northern Germany, these living testimonies to atrocity were marked out for immediate liquidation. Most were caught and dispatched with a bullet in the back of the neck but, with help, some concealed themselves in the roof spaces. Then the killing widened out. Women were seized from their barracks indiscriminately by baton-wielding female guards and told they were being taken to Berlin, fifty miles to the south, to help dig defence trenches and build barricades. This was a lie, like so many before. The trucks they were crammed into were one-way 'black transports' to the crematorium. American-born Virginia d'Albert-Lake, caught by the Germans while guiding evaders to the Fréteval forest hideout in France, kept her shaven head down when the SS came hunting for victims. Personal survival was her only concern, now that Janette, her closest companion, a mutual mainstay through their haunted half-life in the camp, was dead.

I knew she was dying. Her eyes were expressionless and her skin yellow but as I laid her down she looked at me and her face began to glow with recognition. I realized she was not suffering any more. She was no longer cold, nor did she feel her hunger. 'Good night,' I said gently. 'Soon it will be time to go home to France. We will be there in time for the cherries. Good night now. Sleep well.' A slow smile crept over her face. I bent and kissed her and then stumbled out into the night.[18]

Lake's loss was profound. Just days before her friend's death they had come so close to being rescued at a satellite camp near the Baltic coast, where they had been part of a labour detachment carving out roads through dense forest. The work was crippling, the cold unbearable, the guards vicious. The women were barely holding on to their sanity. And then panic had swept through the German ranks. Russian planes were shooting up the airfield. The Red Army was closer than anyone had expected. The female SS officer in charge took off in a car at top speed, with her lover, an airman, at her side; the gates of the camp were open; there was not a guard to be seen. While the Polish and Russian prisoners went wild, ransacking the now-empty SS quarters, Lake walked through the gate and savoured freedom. Then she too went on the prowl and in a cellar found rooms crammed to the ceiling with crates, cans and boxes. Food. Tons of it. She froze in awe at the sight of this 'hoard of plenty', stored yards from where the prisoners had been forced to scrounge rotten cabbage leaves and raw beet.

What should I take from it? My eyes lighted on gallon tins of jam. We all craved sweet things. I grabbed as many as I could and hurried back to my hut. That night we had a wonderful supper. Lovely slices of bread spread with margarine and jam, and delicious creamy milk.

The post-prandial *digestif* was sickening. The door of the hut burst open and a girl staggered in, bleeding from a gunshot wound in the shoulder. Germans! An army patrol was in the camp. The inmates rushed to hide their plunder as the stamp of heavy boots resounded outside. 'We all tried to adopt an air of innocence, but we were quaking with fear inside.' An officer strode in and told them they were still prisoners and he still had the power of life and death over them. 'Anyone caught pillaging will be shot,' he declared. He left, with a warning that he and his men would be back. But the soldiers failed to return, and the girls ate more jam and relaxed. In an attic room in the SS quarters Lake stumbled on a store of uniforms for the women guards and snatched up a light blue blouse, a skirt and a smart grey gaberdine overcoat to replace the lice-infested rags she had been wearing for so long. Word spread that the Russians were ten miles away. 'If only they would *hurry*!' Lake said to herself anxiously as she changed into her new clothes. More news – the Russians were now within *three* miles . . .

Suddenly there was a great clamour in the courtyard. Men were shouting and women were screaming. Shots were being fired. Was it the Russians? My hopes soared. Then one of our girls ran in, looking as if she had seen ghosts.

'It's the Germans,' she cried. 'The SS from Ravensbruck. They've come to get us! They've ordered us to line up outside.' The joy that had welled up in my throat now choked me. It had been too good to last. There was more misery to bear.

The women stared at each other in disbelief. It had never crossed their minds that this could happen. The main camp was hundreds of miles away. It was inconceivable and irrational to drag them back there through a country on the verge of collapse. But in its bureaucratic madness as well as its brutality, the SS state-within-a-state would not let them go. A guard came through the door. 'All those not outside in five minutes will be shot,' he bawled. They hurried to obey. As she left the hut, Lake quietly discarded the gaberdine. This was no time to be caught wearing a looted German uniform. In the yard the women were hustled into a ragged column and then out through the gates with shoves and snarls. One who ran back to her hut for something she had forgotten – her name was Monique; everyone knew her – was shot dead. The SS were in a desperate hurry. They didn't want to be caught by the Russians. The stories from the eastern front of what Stalin's soldiers did to any German they captured, especially those in the elite Nazi force, spurred them on.

They acted like brutes. They knew they were finished but they still had us on whom to mete out their vengeance and despair. We knew that with men such as these our lives were not secure.

Gunfire came from the rear as stragglers were shot. Friends gripped faltering friends, held them up, carried them if necessary, to save them from the same fate. Janette, already weakened by illness, clung on to Lake as they tramped painfully south through wind and snow. 'I can't go any farther, Virginia,' she sobbed. 'I just want to die. Here in the road.' She was saved by the column's arrival at a railway siding, and then they were in cattle trucks and the next day back in Ravensbruck. There, an inmate who witnessed their return was appalled by their condition as they were hurled to the ground from the trucks. She thought they were corpses until the guards moved in with whips to force them to their feet. Janette was among the worst. 'She was but half alive,' Lake recalled. 'It was horrible to see her in such a state, a shapeless heap lying in her filth, unable to talk. There were others like her, but this was my friend.'

And now that special friend was dead, and Lake herself was consigned to an ever deeper hell in the overcrowded, dysentery- and typhus-ridden camp where all sense of order had gone in the fight to stay alive. Bodies lay uncollected. It was a horrific price to pay for daring to help the evaders – would any of them be spared? 'I saw all my friends about me growing weaker and weaker, drugged by the horrors that surrounded us – and I knew that I was just like them. We were on the border of life and death.' A guard picked on her. She demanded the wedding ring from her finger, though Lake's knuckles were so swollen it would not come off.

I showed her the condition of my hands, but that made no difference. She kept goading me. She was cruel and I hated her. Tears started running down my cheeks. I felt as if I could bear no more. My wedding ring was all I had left, all I had of Philippe [her husband], of love, of life.

I turned to another woman and blurted out, 'I'm an American. Does she steal from Americans too?' The woman spoke to the SS guard, who now looked at me as though she was seeing me for the first time. I was no longer just a stinking skeleton good only for the gas chamber. She looked startled, even concerned. I was told I could keep my ring.

This encounter was her salvation. A few days later, as her spirits dipped still further and yet more of her will to live leaked away, a shout summoned her from her dormitory. The SS had something for 'the American'. Without any explanation, she was issued with clean clothes. Three days later came another summons, this time to the camp office, where a secretary smiled and offered her a chair, 'an unbelievable consideration!' A guard smiled too. She was then led out through the main gate and into a building where an SS officer sat. 'You are an American?' she asked in perfect English. 'Then tonight you will be happy. You are going away.'

A great surge of hope and excitement rose in me. But could it be true? Were they playing with me? Were these more Nazi lies? I felt frightened and apprehensive. I muttered to myself: 'Is it true? Oh, God, is it true?'

It was. With an SS escort, she left Ravensbruck by train, a proper one, not a cattle truck, her destination an internment camp for civilians near the Swiss border. With her went one of the camp's VIP prisoners, Geneviève de Gaulle, niece of the head of the Free French forces who was now installed in Paris as the leader of a liberated France.[19] They travelled through a panic-stricken, bombed-out Berlin, a Munich reduced to rubble, an almost deserted Stuttgart. Air-raid sirens wailed and, though Lake was very weak, they walked miles when the tracks ended in craters. Tens of thousands of refugees flooded the stations and the roads, fleeing the Russians, the bombing, the war. Relentlessly, all three kept coming after them. As she trekked through this landscape of the damned, Lake saw for the first time the torment she herself had endured. During one overnight stop she caught her reflection in a mirror, a sight she had not seen since her deportation from Paris nearly a year ago. She reeled back in horror.

What ugly creature was this? A woman, yes, but with neither hips nor breasts, great lustreless eyes staring out of a grey countenance, the skin stretched like parchment over the skull and high cheek bones, beneath which were empty holes.

She was thirty-five and looked seventy. 'I turned away. Never in my life have I received such a shock. I shall never forget it.' But she was alive, and close to freedom – of a sort. She arrived at a relatively safe halfway-house, still inside the Reich and still behind locked gates, but 'paradise', as she called it, after where she had been. Her 500 fellow inmates were British and American women caught in the wrong country when the world went to war. She was an internee, not a detainee, a person again, not an animal. The regime here was relaxed. Lying peacefully on a comfortable bed, eating from Red Cross parcels, 'I could hardly bear the joy. It nearly suffocated me.'

★

For those helpers left behind in Ravensbruck, the killing and the battle to survive went on. Then, in the first week of March, the Maréchals and Nadine were among 10,000 inmates who were given minutes to collect their few possessions and then marched out, five abreast, through the gates and packed into cattle trucks. Ahead was a gruelling, freezing 400-mile journey south from one end of Germany to the other, to the Mauthausen concentration camp near Linz in Austria. It was a notorious place, high even in the ranks of Nazi infamy for its harshness, worse than Dachau and Buchenwald, some said. It was up in the mountains, among beautiful forests; the Danube glistened nearby. But its granite walls were studded with iron rings, to which men were chained, beaten and left to die. Here male prisoners laboured in the quarry until they dropped dead and unfed Russians were slowly starved to death. The brutality was not tempered by the arrival of women. On the five-mile uphill march from the railhead to the camp, Elsie saw exhausted women fall. 'A rifle shot told us that their sufferings were ended for ever.' One who almost died this way was Nadine. It was on this slog that her body buckled and she was tempted to lie down in the snow and let an SS bullet end her misery. The thought of the mother she still hoped to see one day kept her legs going, as it did when over the next months she laboured in the quarry in 'very, very bad conditions'.

Other women were spared this, assigned instead to the laundry or the sewing room – or to death. The camp commandant person-ally made the selections, picking out the young ones to work and sending the old, the emaciated and the weak to be slaughtered. But youth was no guarantee of survival. Young Elsie was sent on a *Kommando* to clear up a site wrecked by American bombers. She picked up a piece of material to wipe her nose and stuffed it in her pocket, where it bulged its presence when she was searched on her way back to camp. She knew her life was forfeit. She had seen a woman similarly caught with something 'stolen' kicked to death by the guards, while the other prisoners were ordered to walk round her, singing.

The guards ordered me to go to the top of a pile of wreckage and undress. I stood there in the freezing cold, naked. But then one of the other girls began screaming hysterically, and the guards pounced on her. They weren't looking at me so I put on my clothes and slowly got down, pulled my scarf over my head and made myself very, very small.[20]

The misery of Mauthausen worsened as thousands more prisoners arrived from other camps. The food ration was down to one mouldy slice of bread a day. They ate dandelions and drank from a stream polluted by their own excreta from the latrines. Hundreds died each day. 'The crematorium was continually in use,' Elsie recalled.

We heard the Russians were only sixty kilometres away, but days and weeks passed again. We became so weak and weary and apathetic that the guards had to beat us to make us move.

Liberation came – just. The French and Belgian political prisoners were isolated, amid rumours that the Red Cross were outside the camp. Was this too much to hope for? Young Elsie thought so. 'We were shut in the showers, and that night the commandant hesitated whether to gas us or not.' The next morning they were let out through the camp gates to sit and wait on a flat stretch of ground. Next to them was a massive hole. The crematorium could not cope any more and bodies were being thrown into this pit and covered with quicklime.

But, for all their fears that at this late stage they were to be cheated of life, this was not to be their fate. A deal had been done between the SS and the Red Cross. Elsie recalled:

We saw a white lorry with a huge red cross on it, then others. A long column of them was coming in our direction. We could hardly believe our eyes. The story of the Red Cross was true. They were taking us over. Tears came to our eyes, and we could not speak for the emotion.

They were little more than skeletons as they climbed aboard the lorries and for three days drove northwards past columns of retreating soldiers. There was a moment of drama on the German side of the Swiss border when the guards stopped the convoy and forced everyone out at gunpoint. 'There were orders to shoot us,' young Elsie recalled later. Negotiations began, phone calls were made, time stood still on that mountain road.

Then the Red Cross told the women to get back into the lorries, slowly, very slowly. When one lorry was full, the driver let off the brake and it free-wheeled silently downhill across no-man's-land to the border. The others followed before the Germans noticed and then shots were fired, killing some prisoners.

Suddenly we were in Switzerland, and the sun was shining. There was liberty, civility, peace. At a hospital, nurses washed us, brushed our hair, disinfected us, took off the lice. No more screaming, no more knocks. Then we sent a telegram to the family to tell them we were coming home.

# 13. We'll Meet Again . . .

Vera Lynn's was the emotional voice of Britain at war, accurately echoing the mood of the time with its throat-catching blend of sorrow and strength. In the rousing and confident opening bars of 'We'll Meet Again' was all the optimism that servicemen and civilians desperately needed. The second line – 'Don't know where, don't know when' – embodied the underlying uncertainty that gripped them too. When a man went missing in action, the strain on his family was immense. The dreaded 'Regret to inform you' telegram delivered to the door put wives and parents into shock, and then limbo. The postman brought a commanding officer's 'sincerest sympathy in these anxious days of waiting', words of comfort from the padre and then an Air Ministry missive with details of where the missing man's possessions were being stored. And after that, a sad and anxious silence, broken with good tidings or bad – a confirmation of death for some, an affirmation of life for others in a scribbled postcard from a POW camp. For the families of evaders, however, there was, perhaps, the worst fate of all – no news. Inevitably there were no communications, no sightings, no relief from the misery of not knowing. Were the men they loved alive or dead, wounded, prisoners? That they might be on the run and hiding was barely considered. The official letter from the Casualty Branch of the Air Ministry in London did not even list it as a possibility, so few put their faith in this outcome.[1]

They coped with the sudden vacuum in their lives as best they could. Some went into denial. Pilot Cliff Hallett's mother simply refused to accept that anything had happened to her son. To anyone who offered sympathy because he was missing, she said that he was perfectly safe – which he was, hiding in France. 'I'd know if he wasn't,' she told them.[2] But other families turned to each other in their distress. While RAF bomb aimer Tom

Wingham was living under cover for months on end in a Belgian mining village, at home in Herefordshire his mother sought some comfort in correspondence with the parents of the other members of his seven-man crew. Had they heard anything? Please get in touch if they did. They responded in letters of shared sympathy, scored with a remarkable politeness and dignity that belied the fears in their hearts. 'It is the greatest grief to have this silence and not know what has happened,' one mother wrote. 'Our home, like yours, seems to have lost all the sunshine out of it,' a father confided.[3] They wished each other well. They sent their prayers. They *knew* their boys were strong and good and would stick together and survive. Except they didn't know any such thing.

Weeks passed, then months, and at last some information drifted in. The rear gunner was in hospital in Holland with a broken leg, the flight engineer was a prisoner too. Their mothers passed on the good news, and those still waiting bit back their own disappointment and offered generous congratulations. Then they sent condolences when the pilot and the mid-upper gunner were confirmed dead[4] and sympathies when the wireless operator was reported alive in a POW camp but with his right leg amputated. For Mrs Wingham, the agony went on. She asked, but the Red Cross had no information on '156389 Flying Officer Sydney Thomas Wingham, although full enquiries are being made and every effort to clarify this distressing situation. Please accept our sympathy in your suspense.' There was an added twist. Of the two crew still unaccounted for, one was believed to be dead. Was it Tom? She hoped not – though she was painfully aware that the other missing man, Jim Lewis, the navigator, had a young wife and a newly born baby and that Nel Lewis was praying just as desperately as she was that her husband would be the one left alive.

And then, as if in a child's story book, they came marching home from war, Tom and Jim together, side by side. Wingham had been liberated by an advance column of American troops in September 1944 and was now in the King George V hotel in Paris, which MI9 had taken over as a debriefing centre for evaders. He was indulging in a forgotten French pleasure – white bread, his first for five months. 'It was surprising how much joy one could get from merely gazing on and then sinking one's teeth into a piece of crusty white loaf,' he recalled. Collecting his room key in the foyer, he was thumped in the back.

'Well, if it isn't Tom Wingham,' said a voice, and I turned round and saw the face of Jim Lewis looming over me. I had last seen him in the nose of our burning Halifax bomber as we wished each other luck before jumping.

They had been mates back on the squadron, regular drinking partners at the bar of the Half Moon in York. The reunion was as if they had been together there only last night, affable but restrained, a very English occasion.

There was no high emotion, not really. We weren't the sort for crying and slapping each other. We just went out for a beer with the escape money I still had left and laughed and joked like we had always done. Those months on the run – the scares and the fun – hadn't really affected us that much.

A sanguine Wingham assumed his family would have been told he was safe. They had not. Back in London, after unhurried days of interviews and medicals, he telephoned an aunt in Croydon to say he and Jim were coming to stay. He had to identify himself twice before an amazed voice cried out: 'Good God, you're back from the dead!' And then it was home on the train to Herefordshire. 'My family were mildly pleased,' he recalled diffidently, 'well, delighted really, I think.' Only later, as he read through his mother's correspondence file, did he realize what she had been through while he was missing, how she had 'clutched at straws' in the absence of information about her lost son, how she had suffered too, her agony prolonged because she was not notified he was safe.

'Ginger' Brown's parents were so unprepared for his return that he came back to an empty house. It was a Saturday afternoon and they were out. Excitedly he rang the bell but nobody came and he had to climb in through a window. They thought he was a ghost when they put the key in the lock and heard him call out: 'Hello, Mum, hello, Dad. It's only me.'

They just stopped in their tracks, and it took some time before I convinced them that it really was me, and even longer for the colour to come back into their faces. They were pretty emotional when they grasped that their son was alive. I tried to act the big boy, trying not to show my feelings but they were there, just below the surface. I was embarrassed because of all the heartbreak I must have caused them. I felt bad too that the first they knew I was alive was when they saw me. The shock could have killed them.[5]

Ray Worrall's parents had similarly been kept in the dark.

My parents had the telegram to say I was missing and that was it. When I got back, I rang up from King's Cross station. I put my tuppence in the box and called home. They had been out of their minds with worry. They just didn't know whether I was alive or dead.

I got a train to Leeds and my father collected me from the station. When we got home, my mother was waiting at the door, just standing there, the sign that my war was over and I was safe. It was really wonderful to walk into the house. There had been times when I didn't think I'd ever see it again.

The next day we went into town and it was lovely to look round the shops and not have to feel that any moment I was going to be picked up. Nobody was looking at me. I didn't have to remember I was an evader. I could chew gum if I wanted.[6]

But he was cross that his parents had been put through unnecessary suspense. For a week after he was liberated, no one had bothered to tell them he was alive, not the Air Ministry nor the intelligence officer who had debriefed him and promised to make the call.

On the other hand, Pilot Officer George Fernyhough was in trouble because the MI9 officer who interviewed him *did* pass on the news. After five months of anxiety, his wife Jessie had an official telegram saying her husband was in London. But it was another forty-eight hours before he walked through the door of their home in Coventry in the middle of the night and woke her up. 'Where have you been?' she demanded to know, angry and relieved at the same time. It was not the welcome he had expected. Thoughts of home and being reunited with his loved ones had kept him going during the boredom of being in hiding and those times when, head down, he had shared a train carriage with inquisitive German soldiers and felt his heart pounding with fear when an SS officer scrutinized his false papers. And, having survived all that, he was being interrogated by his wife!

I couldn't believe it. I had been thinking about her all that time and those were the first words. There were a few tears then – and it was fantastic to be safe back in my own home. Just where I wanted to be. It had all been worth it.[7]

There was disappointment, too, when he tucked into the gargantuan meal that, as he had eked out beans and black bread in Holland and drunk tea made from crocus bulbs, he had promised himself as soon as he got home. His stomach had shrunk, and he left the plate of food unfinished. He had a different joy to savour – cuddling his new daughter, born while he was in hiding. And a great sadness to bear – his father had died. And a relief – the entire crew of his crashed Halifax had survived (though some were POWs and injured).

Fernyhough was spared the awful duty that fell to Bill Knaggs when he returned – of visiting the families of crewmen still missing and trying to give them some hope and comfort. When he called on the mother of his navigator in Glasgow, she gently hushed him even before he had finished explaining why he had come. She knew her son was dead, she told him. On the night their plane had been shot down, she had been woken by a cow lowing. It was a sign of death. She had not needed official telegrams or visits from his friends. 'It was uncanny,' Knaggs recalled, 'and she was right.

Her son had gone just as she said, one of five from that flight who never came back.'[8] Only Knaggs and one other survived.

A visit to the RAF depository where the belongings of missing airmen were stored was a sharp reminder to another returning evader, George Pyle, of how lucky he was to be home.

I saw the huts with their rows and rows of shelves stacked with kit bags, boxes and cases, each the property of someone who had not returned, fate unknown. It was sobering and depressing. I wondered how many of their owners were still alive and how many, if any, managed to evade.[9]

He pulled out his uniform and put it back on, glad to be wearing it again despite the whiff of petrol that now attached to it. It had been packed in a cardboard carton that had originally contained two petrol cans. The off-putting smell was a small inconvenience compared with the pleasure of being alive and home.

For Terry Bolter – with whom this book began and to whose adventures on the run we have often returned – that feeling of elation at having evaded and survived was unsurpassable. His mother and brother danced round the kitchen table when the telegram arrived saying he was safe. Then Bolter phoned from the MI9 hotel in London with a cheery 'Hello, Dad. See you soon' and hopped on a number 2 bus from Baker Street to Finchley Central.

My father and brother came to meet me at the station. Pop saw me and was running towards me. It was a wonderful moment. As we walked down our avenue, all the neighbours came out from their houses, clapping and waving. A moment later and my mother and I held each other close, with my mother saying, 'Terry, is it really you?' and pinching me to make sure. It was exciting, a great feeling just to be back home. That's what the last six months had been about – that moment of being with my family again.[10]

For the Bolter family, the strain and uncertainty were over. Terry wrote later: 'They were able to look on the previous months as a nightmare and start to put it behind them.' There was, though, his other 'family' to tell of his safe return, the helpers he had left behind. The war was still on and France and Belgium occupied when Bolter crossed the Pyrenees and then returned to London. As promised, he sent a coded message via the BBC to the Resistance in Belgium: '*La cravate rouge et bleue est bien arrivée.*' ('The red and blue tie has arrived safely.') When the war ended in the early summer of 1945, it was time to see how many of his helpers, and those of the thousands of other evaders like him, had made it too. In Paris and Brussels, there would be reunions – but not for everyone.

★

Elsie Maréchal and her daughter came home to Brussels shortly after being released in Switzerland. As they stepped down from the train at the Gare du Midi they were still wearing their jackets from the concentration camp at Ravensbruck. The distinctive smell that clung to them was that of charred human remains. The smoke of the crematorium that had hung like a pall over the camp in Germany was not so easily left behind, any more than the memories of all they had endured. Starved, emaciated, her lungs riddled with TB and her skin covered in scabies, Elsie was a sick woman but she had refused to stay for medical treatment in Switzerland. She rested for three days and then was desperate to be home. She knew her husband Georges was dead, executed by the Germans, but there was still her teenage son Robert. Friends told her he had also been arrested by the Gestapo but had escaped the same fate by the skin of his teeth. She wanted to see him, to connect again, to know that, for all her sorrow, she was truly alive. The train journey across France with other French and Belgian survivors was tantalizingly slow. The younger Elsie recalled:

We were the first from the camps to get into the country and at each little station the train stopped, the local band played the 'Marseillaise' and the people gave us soup, wine, bread, cakes. We had too much! I was as sick as anything through overeating! To me, those long French baguettes were like priceless treasure.[11]

And then they were on the platform in Brussels, with Robert leading the family charge to run and embrace them. They needed to be gentle. The women were stick thin, their upper arms, he noted with alarm, wasted more than their lower arms, the bones clearly visible. As relatives crowded round, young Elsie kept a tight hold on her bread and was furious when her grandmother urged her to just throw it away. She could not do so. Food was precious in her eyes. But what distressed her as much was her grandmother's obvious failure to understand, a foretaste of how strangely and distantly many people would react to those returning from the camps. 'We were to speak very little of our adventures,' she said, 'because we encountered only incomprehension and it disturbed some people.' But she would never forgive or forget what had been done to her and to millions of others in those terrible places. 'To do so would be making cheap the life of every victim.'

At least they still had theirs, though they had a battle on their hands to get fit and well again. Both women were skeletons weighing not much more than five stones. They were also penniless and homeless. The problem of money was solved by a British government official, acknowledging the Allies' debt for what the women had done to provide shelter for evaders with an immediate and substantial grant. Rich friends put a luxury flat at their disposal and they took long, pampered baths in perfumed water and slept in soft beds like babies. Except that camp habits were not so easily washed and soothed away. 'I found I couldn't sleep,' Elsie recalled. 'I was too warm and comfortable, so I got out of bed and slept on the floor.'

Elsewhere in Brussels, a very sick Dédée de Jongh was also home from Ravensbruck, having arrived in the dirty striped dress she had worn in the camp. There the SS had come specifically for her at the end, singling her out for elimination. She hid and held on to her life. She was pitifully thin with the lined face of an old woman, according to an Allied official who encountered her soon after her release.[12] As they talked, she unconsciously took two pencils, a rubber and some paper clips from his desk and hid them, then realized what she had done and owned up. 'In camp we all stole,' she explained. 'Even the smallest things had barter value.' Now she had a father to mourn – shot, she learned, by a German firing squad a year earlier. So too did her friend and collaborator in the escape line, Nadine Dumon, feeling the empty space in her life that her father, who had not survived the concentration camp as she had done, had once filled. He died just three months before the war ended, after enduring so much pain and torture. That he almost made it but could not hold on still troubles her. 'To suffer for so long and finally not to come back,' she sighed. 'I ask myself if it would have been better for him to be shot straight away rather than die after such long months in the camp, but I don't know the answer.'[13] His death was a permanent sadness in her life. 'For years after, whenever I felt the slightest bit gay, suddenly I would think of those who didn't come back and particularly of my papa. He thought that after the war he would do this or that, and he never did, that he would go to this or that place that he never got to.' She too kept silent about what she had endured. 'For years I could not talk about the war and especially about the camps.'

There was sadness too for Virginia d'Albert-Lake. She had seen out the last months of the war in a civilian internment camp in Germany close to the Swiss border after being released quite unexpectedly from Ravensbruck.[14] There she was liberated by Allied troops on the last leg of their advance through Germany and a few weeks later was in a car being driven back to Paris. She sat silently, her head shaved, her body like that of a tiny bird. She was still physically weak but also emotionally confused.

I had never experienced such joyful anticipation, but the joy was mingled with fear, fear of the unknown awaiting me. What was I to find on reaching home? What had become of those I loved – my husband, my family – during this long year of unbroken silence? Did our little cottage in the country, our flat, and all the belongings to which one gets so attached, still exist after the storm?[15]

The sun was setting as the Citroën cruised into the streets of the French capital – 'the city I love' – and she looked around in wonder. She had last seen it through the bars of a German prison van. Now the grey and green uniforms of the conquerors had gone. 'Freedom had returned.'

Outside her flat she waited for a moment and reflected.

Soon I would know whether it had been worthwhile clinging on to life, or whether it might have been preferable to let myself sink quietly into the unknown which was constantly inviting us at Ravensbruck.

She was met at the door by her mother-in-law, who straight away confirmed that her husband Philippe was alive and well. After Virginia had been arrested escorting evaders, he had been spirited away to London to join the forces of the Free French. She would see him soon. The terrible news was that her American mother had died a month ago. She, it transpired, had worked ceaselessly behind the scenes to get her daughter released from Ravensbruck. 'She died without knowing that I was alive and safe. Poor Mother, who experienced only pain and anguish during those last days, and never knew that her efforts had not been in vain.' Virginia also learned that her own undercover work had not been wasted either. The evaders' camp in the Fréteval forest had cost her her freedom and very nearly her life but it had been a great success. Close to 200 Allied airmen had been liberated from it. She could take pride in that. In the end, she had won.

★

In his Church of Scotland manse in rue Piccini in Paris, the Revd Donald Caskie was on his knees in prayer. He commended the souls of the dead from the escape line he had been so instrumental in setting up in Marseilles back in 1940, 'the bright lights extinguished', as he called them. 'I thanked God for those who died that we might live.'[16] His obsequies were interrupted by news of a resurrection – Pat O'Leary was alive. The tough action man who had taken over his work, sent hundreds of Allied evaders home and then been betrayed to the Germans had against all odds survived three years in Dachau concentration camp. 'It was the first I had heard of him since he was taken by the Gestapo,' Caskie recalled. 'I thought he was dead.' Scores of those swept up with him in the arrests that broke the Pat Line were less fortunate. Dr Rodocanachi, whose flat above his surgery in Marseilles had been O'Leary's headquarters and home, would not be coming back from Buchenwald. Another stalwart, a man named Charles Morelle, had survived Dachau, lived past the end of the war, but never emerged from the camp hospital. General Jacques Leclerc, the Free French soldier who had accepted the Germans' surrender of Paris, came to his bedside, saluted and shook the dying man's hand. The gesture was greeted with a smile of pride, a sense of mission accomplished. Then Morelle fell back asleep and died a few hours later.[17] But O'Leary had made it through, and Caskie could have rung all the bells of Paris to celebrate. 'Your friend is alive,' he was told. 'He's not the kind that dies easily. But he is in pretty bad shape. At present he is in hospital in Bavaria, where the doctors are trying to put flesh back on his bones.' A reunion was promised when he was fit. It would be more agreeable than the one Caskie had just had with another person from that same distant past.

The minister, a survivor himself of inhuman treatment and torture in prison and still not fully recovered from the experience, had only the day before been summoned to a British army detention camp just outside Paris, where he was the visiting chaplain. He was asked to see what he could get out of a mysterious British soldier being held in custody. 'He's one of ours all right,' the camp commander said, 'and we can tell he's a crook. But he's a tough case and refuses to talk. We don't know who he is. I'd like you to have a chat with him.' Caskie walked into the cell and a face looked up. It was one he could never forget. Staring back at him was Harold Cole, the British sergeant who had infiltrated the Pat Line and then betrayed dozens of its workers. Men had died on the guillotine, in front of firing squads and in concentration camps because of him.

I saw that he recognized me too. 'Hello,' I said. 'We meet again in interesting circumstances. So many of our friends have been in jail – rather worse ones than this, I fear.' But he quickly pulled himself together. 'Name of Smith, padre,' he countered. 'You've made a mistake. What's more, preaching is not wanted here. Get out.'

His brazen falsehood enraged me. I shouted: 'You lie, you disgusting traitor. Are you quite without shame? You deserted your country. You sold your friends to the Nazis for money, God help you.'

Though the prisoner protested he was not Cole, Caskie reported what he knew to the camp commander, who whistled in amazement as he took in the information and promised to check it out. 'But watch him,' the minister warned. 'He's one of the trickiest scoundrels that have exploited this war. The devil is in the fellow. Keep an eye on him day and night.'

Cole was as difficult to hold down as the minister predicted. He escaped from custody after stealing a guard's uniform and went on the run. But this was one evader Caskie was not about to help. On the contrary, he felt hunted himself. Cole well knew the minister's evidence could send him to the gallows. He had sworn to kill him. The authorities told Caskie to be on his guard and not venture out alone at night. Nervously he shut himself up at home and waited.

One evening the telephone rang. Cole had been located in a flat on rue de Grenelle. The building was surrounded. Would I stand by to identify him when he was arrested? I agreed.

Later the phone rang again. 'He's dead, padre,' I was told. 'We expected him to put up a desperate fight. We sent half a dozen men in after him and he got two of them before the others filled him with bullets. Our two chaps are wounded but they'll be all right. He's as dead as he'll ever be.'[18]

It was fitting that O'Leary was back in Paris in time to confirm the dead body was that of Cole.

Thus ended a career of quite remarkable treachery and double-dealing. This time there was no escape for the man who switched sides in the twinkling it took to change his coat or his uniform. He had wriggled out of a string of tight spots. The leaders of the Pat Line had finally rumbled him and were about to shoot him when he made a daring leap from one house to another to escape. He got away too from the police in unoccupied France, who found him so obnoxious they put him on trial on the extraordinary charge (for Vichy, that is) of 'delivering French citizens into the hands of the Germans'. He was sentenced to death but saved his own life by denouncing his wife as a Resistance activist.[19] He was then seen in Paris, working with the SS at their headquarters in avenue Foch, where his activities were such that MI9's Airey Neave described him as 'the most dangerous of our opponents and the most callous of German agents, actually helping the Gestapo to torture those he had given away'.[20] And he was last glimpsed leaving the French capital in a hurry just before it was liberated by the Allies in the summer of 1944. He was in full German uniform. He had been helping catch evaders and their helpers right to the end.

The following year he was back in Paris, in an American uniform, posing as a US colonel and attaching himself to a special army unit recovering art treasures stolen by the Germans. He was caught doing a bit of stealing for himself, arrested and handed over to the British. Or so Caskie was told when he went to see him in his cell. But Neave had a different story. He reported that Cole had presented himself to an American regiment as a Captain Mason of British Intelligence and been put to work interrogating suspected Nazis. It was a chance for the habitual traitor to double-cross his old German friends by identifying to the Allies the SS and Gestapo officers he had once worked with. When he was killed there were few tears, except from some of the many girlfriends he had charmed into his bed. One of them, a Swiss woman, called him her 'Sonny Boy' and thought him kind and loving. 'I know you all think he is a swine,' she told the British authorities, 'but you are wrong.'[21] But to Neave, the Lothario was loathsome, a con man and a criminal, selfish, callous and devoid of any moral or patriotic feelings. He deserved his reputation as the worst Allied traitor of the entire war. Caskie the clergyman tried to be more charitable in his final earthly verdict.

Cole was now in the hands of God the omniscient and merciful judge and his life was over. I felt pity for him that he had wasted it and besmirched his soul so wantonly. He might have served as valiantly as Pat O'Leary, the generous leader he betrayed, but instead chose Judas. Justice had been done.

That same justice was handed out to others who had betrayed the evaders and their workers. The French Resistance disposed of the Pat Line's betrayer, Roger le Neveu, nastily and without bothering the due processes of the law. Prosper de Zitter, the Belgian collaborator with the missing finger, was properly tried and sentenced to death. He howled with terror in his cell before he was taken out to be shot, his behaviour a sharp contrast to the way many of those he denounced had met their end. Jacques Desoubrie, among whose hundreds of victims was Frédéric de Jongh, Dédée's father, and virtually the whole of the Comet organization in Paris, was also executed. These men were all out-and-out traitors who, whether for money or out of sympathy with the Germans, willingly and wilfully betrayed their own countrymen. They were dealt blood for blood, and rightly so. But in the frenzy of retribution and scapegoating that followed liberation there were excesses, mistakes, misunderstandings and the settling of private scores, and those who had helped evaders could be highly vulnerable. Sheltering men on the run had necessarily been a secret business, carried on behind closed doors, and there were those who had given the impression of cooperating with the Germans as a guise for such activities. Now they were suspected collaborators. There was an old farmer in Normandy in whose cottage an Australian airman he knew only as 'Danny' had hidden for months. The old man was a loner, a curmudgeon and unpopular in his village, and after the war his neighbours charged him with harbouring a German deserter. They wanted him tried and hanged. Fortunately 'Danny' was tracked down, brought half-way round the world from Sydney and rushed into a crowded courtroom just in time to exonerate his host. Terry Bolter did the same for one of his helpers, the manager of a casino in the Belgian city of Namur where the punters included German officers. He too was accused of collaborating with the enemy. Bolter's testimony to his patriotism cleared him. But in this atmosphere of suspicion, even fearless, patriotic Mary Lindell, escape-line organizer and Ravensbruck survivor, came under a cloud. Incredibly and irrationally after all she had been through, she was branded as a German sympathizer. In what had been occupied Europe, these were unforgiving times.

There were other figures in the story of the evaders who, under torture or out of fear, gave the names of those who had helped and sheltered them. Lives were lost as a result. After the war, nobody pursued them with recriminations. They had their own consciences to face instead of tribunals and courts. There was the soldier we have called Wicks,[22] whom Sergeant Harry Levy had encountered in St Gilles prison in Brussels and who identified a chain of local helpers to the Germans. He was said to have caused the arrest of more than forty Belgians. 'What the 'ell was I supposed to do?' he had pleaded in defence of his actions when Levy challenged him. 'Let those Gestapo bastards shoot me?'[23] But it was a different story he told when he came back from a POW camp at the end of the war. He had been on the run for two years after Dunkirk and then was caught, he told his MI9 debriefer. One of his helpers was arrested – not his fault – and the Germans told him she had given them a list of names and addresses where he had hidden. At St Gilles, 'people were brought in front of me and those who denied knowledge of me I pretended not to recognize'. Even if this was strictly true, it was a tacit admission of complicity – and more than most evaders ever did. It was a golden rule never to show any recognition of anyone, whatever lies the interrogators told you. But MI9 either did not pick up on what he had done or, in the absence of any direct accusation against him, chose to do nothing. And, anyway, his subsequent experience as a prisoner of war had been of the very toughest. He had escaped three times from work camps in Poland – or so he said – and each time been recaptured. He had got out again, squeezing under the main gate during an electrical failure, and joined a group of Polish partisans. The Russians 'liberated' him, but in reality kept him a prisoner for two months before sending him home via the Black Sea port of Odessa. It was May 1945 before he got back to Britain. He had been absent for nearly five years.

Whatever really happened in that Brussels jail he kept to himself to his dying day. He didn't tell his wife or his children. Was he ashamed? Had he washed his sins away with his years of terrible grind in far-flung POW camps? Were his escapes an attempt to wipe the slate clean? We will never know. He was an uneducated man, unable to read or write, and was out of his depth as an evader in a foreign country. Those who know his story are inclined to be generous. One wrote:

In mitigation, I would say that he was possibly abandoned at Dunkirk and made the best of the situation. In some ways we must admire his resourcefulness. We must also remember how he would have been treated after his arrest, almost certainly tortured or threatened with torture.[24]

Wicks is dead and we should now let him rest in peace. But for other evaders who spoke when they should not have done so, the agony goes on. RAF navigator Stan Hope, captured with Dédée de Jongh when trying to cross the Pyrenees, beaten and threatened with torture, blurted out details of his evasion. 'I hoped that I was just giving the Gestapo snippets of information but a family that sheltered me were caught. It made me feel pretty low.'[25] It still does. His eyes filled with tears as, sixty years later, he recalled the incident.

When I look back on those times now and the people who helped me, I feel a great deal of guilt. I often think about it and it's very disturbing. That through you, inadvertently or in any way at all, they have suffered. It's very upsetting.

I know they were fighting a war the same as we were fighting a war.

But that's not really a help to me. They tried to help me and they suffered for it. I felt as though I'd let them down. But there was nothing you could do, nothing . . .

His voice tailed off into a despairing silence. All he had left of those days was a photograph of the grave in Brussels of Maurice, his special friend seized by the Germans and never seen alive again – along with his guilt and his gratitude.

I'm immensely grateful to those who were willing to risk their lives for me. I do not know what motivated them because the risks were terrible, terrible. I'm still alive today because of them. You never forget it.

For him the incident will never be closed – but it was for Dédée. She knew one of her 'packages' had talked but after the war she refused to allow an investigation into which one it was or to press the matter. 'All is forgiven,' she said.[26]

*

In Brittany, Resistance fighter and Pat Line prodigy Geo Jouanjean, the man who had helped Gordon Carter escape across the sea to England back in 1943, was home, to the enthusiastic reception of his sister Janine and the rest of the family. He had been through hell since his arrest by the Germans. His prison camp number 185795 was embedded on his arm, a relic of Birkenau, Buchenwald and finally Flossenburg. He was, in his own words, 'derided, wounded, bruised, tattooed',[27] but free at last. American troops saved him when SS guards were herding the last of the inmates along forest roads in southern Germany. He had marched 400 miles – in bare feet, he thought, though he may have been wearing clogs. He could never remember for sure. Thousands from Flossenburg died on that notorious march, most dispatched without mercy as they fell behind, some killing themselves by dropping to their knees, stuffing dirt from the ground into their throats and ending their agony by choking to death. The deafening roar of tanks brought salvation. 'God bless you, soldiers of America,' he cried.

A train brought him home to France, and when he reached Rennes, railwaymen there telephoned the family home to say he was alive. And then they stopped a goods train going in that direction and attached a passenger carriage just for him. He arrived in style at midnight, to be greeted on the platform by his father. His mother and grandmother were at home to welcome him too, a relief for him since, as so often happened to the relations of Resistance workers, they had been seized by the Germans and imprisoned as hostages for him before his capture. They were safe and so was he. But, though home was a haven, it did not bring him peace. He found post-war France a disappointment. He resented the legions of fake resisters, the Jean-come-latelys who had appeared only when the outcome of the war was certain, claiming the glory of defiance when they had done nothing to earn it. Like so many of those who survived German hands, he was haunted. 'The shadows left by my dead friends follow my steps,' he wrote in his memoirs. 'I see their agony. My own began the day I saw men killed for no reason.' But there was happiness too. Another much wished-for reunion had already happened.

Squadron Leader Carter had been marching through the remnants of Hitler's Reich too, though he was at the other end of Germany – near the Baltic Sea and struggling along eastward towards the River Elbe in a column of British POWs held captive by their guards until the very last moments of the war. Hitler was dead in his bunker and Berlin had fallen to the Russians before a half-track from the Cheshire Regiment came to free them. It was another week before he was flown back to Britain and could cable his parents in Canada with important news: 'In England doing fine. *Checking on Janine.*' The sweet French girl he had met so briefly two years ago and fallen in love with was still at the front of his mind. But had she waited for him? Would she even remember him? He couldn't be sure. Was she even alive?

I hadn't had any contact with her since I escaped from France and had no idea what may or may not have happened to her. She may have been killed during the war. She could have been captured. She could have even, God forbid, met an American and gone off with him. That was the biggest risk of all.

I did know from my Aunt Dot that Janine had received the letters I wrote to her [and which his aunt had kept until after the liberation of France, when they could be delivered], but that was nine months ago. My overriding concern was to get back to her and pick up where I had left off. I had to go and find out if she still wanted me.[28]

He applied for permission to cross over to France and, after he explained why, wangled compassionate leave. 'My pals immediately abridged this to *passionate* leave.' He set off with a fourteen-day pass, took the ferry from Newhaven over the Channel – not so easy at a time when travel was largely restricted to urgent military needs – and arrived in Paris. He searched for her at a pastry shop in rue Blanche, where he had been told she once worked behind the counter, to learn that she had long since gone back to Brittany. He took the next train the 300 miles to Morlaix on the north Brittany coast in a first-class carriage reserved for Allied officers, a nervous overnight journey for him, unsure of what awaited him at the other end. He got there to be told there was no connecting service to Carhaix, twenty-five miles away, where Janine was living, until tomorrow. Disappointment. Another day and night of suitor's nerves stretched ahead. Then delight. He was offered a lift in a car instead and an hour later was on the main street of Carhaix, standing hesitantly outside the tailor's shop owned by Janine's grandfather, unannounced and unexpected. The door opened. An aunt stood there. She looked at him and turned her head back inside. '*Janine*,' she called out, '*c'est Gordon!*'

A bemused Janine appeared for what, given the circumstances and all the hope he had invested in it, was a 'subdued' reunion – his word. The details escaped him sixty years later.

I can't even remember what we said to each other. I expect there was a hug and a kiss but I don't think there was any great outpouring of emotions. Janine said that it was quite extraordinary that neither of us seemed surprised to see each other again.

Janine was not as calm as he thought. Nor was their meeting 'subdued'. Not for her, anyway. She had spotted him before her aunt went to the door and her heart had leapt.

I was looking out of the window of my grandparents' house and a car was stopping outside in the street. I saw him getting out, with his RAF uniform on! It was the first time I'd seen him in about two and a half years. Oh!

It was so amazing, I was overwhelmed by it. I couldn't really believe my eyes. I couldn't take it in. Last time he had been in this shabby French suit and here he was in full uniform, medals and all. It was such a change. My heart jumped when I saw him.

I started crying as I ran out towards him. I ran straight into his arms. I was crying but I don't think he was. He had a stiff upper lip! Typical Englishman. He'd come half-way across Europe to find me, straight from getting back from the POW camp. All my family were watching and they were so happy for us.[29]

Now was a chance to get to know one another properly. Over the next days, they went for walks, took moonlight strolls, dined with family and friends and gorged themselves on coffee-cream cake and a golden liqueur by the name of Vieille Cure. It was during this period – 'halcyon days', according to Carter – that Janine's brother Geo came home. Everyone was worried by his condition, and even more so by a brother-in-law who also returned from Germany, still in his striped uniform and so thin he was almost unrecognizable. The full horror of the concentration camps was evident and a shock for everyone. But there was joy in all being together again. Miraculously, the whole family had come through the war. And now it was to expand by suddenly taking in an extra, impetuous but determined member.

Carter's fortnight's leave was fast running out. He would have to be back with his squadron soon. He had waited years for the girl he loved. He saw no reason for further delay. And nor did Janine. She accepted his proposal of marriage. 'I didn't even think about it,' she recalled. 'I said yes straight away.' Her mother was not so sure. It all seemed so rushed. The couple barely knew each other. This man was a virtual stranger. There was much soul-searching before she and her husband gave their blessing. But it was to be a proper wedding, not a hole-in-the-corner occasion, the banns read out for ten days beforehand, the works, full and formal. The bridegroom-to-be showed his mettle. He and Janine raced to Paris, where he persuaded an RAF air marshal (one with a little romance in his soul, presumably) to extend his leave by another fourteen days. By chance they then ran into one of Carter's old RAF chums, a Norwegian pilot now working at his country's embassy in the French capital. He instantly fixed them up with the official 'certificate of celibacy' demanded by the law before a couple could marry, bypassing the usual slow-moving French bureaucracy. Then it was back to Brittany – and another piece of good fortune. They needed a waiver on that ten-day public notice of their wedding, and an official in the *mairie* obliged. 'He had just arrived back from a concentration camp and was in a mood to grant us anything we wanted.'

On the morning of 11 June 1945 – just twenty-three days after he stood outside her door wondering what her reaction would be at the sight of him, his past and his future all coming together in that one crucial moment – Gordon Carter married the woman of so many of his dreams, he in his uniform, she in a pretty blue frock. They celebrated with her family in a country restaurant, and then, his leave just days away from expiring, they took the train to Paris, on to Calais, and sailed for England and a new life. After so long apart, the Allied evader and the faithful French girl who had helped hide him were together at last. It had been love on the run when they met. Now they had all the time in the world.

\*

It was rare for the relationship between evader and helper to end up in romance, as it did for Gordon Carter and Janine, but the speed with which he renewed contact with those who had risked their lives to protect him was far from unusual. Back home, many evaders reflected on what had happened to them and were overwhelmed with gratitude – and the need to express it to those people who had befriended them in their days, weeks and months of great need. As soon as he heard that the Dutch town of Ede had been liberated, Arnhem veteran and evader Brigadier John Hackett made arrangements to fly to Holland. He loaded his bags with real tea, coffee, sugar and tinned food. Before they retreated, the Germans had cruelly starved the local population, reducing some, in their desperation, to forage in the fields for tulip bulbs to eat. As his plane landed, the rearguard of the Wehrmacht was still putting up resistance a little way in the distance, pounded by Allied guns. But Ede itself was free and *en fête*.

The houses were open, and there were orange flags and hand-painted union jacks everywhere. The streets, so long nearly deserted, were now thronged. Where only a few sad elderly people could be seen before, moving with slow steps and downcast eye, there were now people of all ages, smiling, laughing, shouting to each other. A pall of mourning had lain over this town when last I saw it. Now everything was as gay as a village wedding.[30]

It felt strange to be there.

Was I really driving along, dressed as a British officer, and unafraid, looking about me as curiously and freely as I pleased? Where were the uniforms of sombre grey? There were none. Instead there were khaki-clad soldiers. Little Dutch boys and girls would come up to them with smiling faces and say 'Hello, Tommy!' as if they were greeting a close relative they had heard about all their lives and were now seeing for the first time.

He came to the house of the de Nooij family, his home and his refuge for all those months. One of the aunts stood in the doorway.

There was no surprise upon her serene face, only shining happiness. She was in tears and laughter at the same time as I embraced her. Then the others joined us, everybody laughing and crying and talking at once.

Last of all came John [the son, who had led Hackett on his escape], grinning with delight and looking a proud and happy man as he grasped my hand. 'Mr Hackett,' he said, 'we are very pleased to see you again!'

He handed over his gifts, and soon a pot of coffee was steaming, and everyone crowded round the kitchen table to drink and talk. It was, he recalled, 'the gossip of a family in a troubled time when one of their number has been away and come back again'. Excitedly they told him how they had heard the coded message over the radio that he had made it safely home to England and they had danced a jig in delight; how John had been caught and put into forced labour on the Rhine defences but had got away; how an uncle whose head had been humiliatingly shaved by the Germans had at last managed to grow back his hair. Then Hackett went off to wander nostalgically around what had once been his domain.

Everything in the house was the same. The upstairs landing was festooned with washing above the trapdoor to the hiding place. I lifted the carpet and the boards and got in again. My own room was unchanged too and as I stood there by the bed, there came back to me the cold bite of dark winter mornings when I was dressing for a walk in the snow. In the barn outside, I thought I could almost see through the little window to the back of the house where the German Feldgendarmerie had been, and from which they had moved only the other day.

That evening he sat with the family again as they read the Bible together. His own copy, an English Authorized Version, was brought out from the cupboard, as it had been every night during his stay there, and placed in front of him. Afterwards he went to bed in his old room and slept once more beneath the embroidery sampler of the Sleeping Beauty. He felt at peace after so much war. 'Everything was just as it had been before but somehow a hundred times better.' He had to leave the next day, back to his regiment, but as he said his farewells at the white-painted garden gate, he knew he would return. This was the first of many reunions – with the de Nooijs and others who had been his protectors. He would meet again Dick Kragt, the secret agent he knew as 'Van Dyck', and the mysterious Dutch boatman who took him down the river, silently past the German sentry posts, on his final escape. He visited at least once a year, renewing friendships and expressing his heartfelt thanks for all 'the acts of faith, simple, unobtrusive and imperishable' that had been bestowed on him as an evader, until his death in 1997.

The ever-grateful Terry Bolter kept in touch too with the army of helpers who had got him home.

I've stayed very close to them ever since. They were very brave people, who had taken the deliberate and personal decision to risk their lives. To me and my wife, it's like having an extra Belgian family, French family and so on.

His dedication was echoed by George Fernyhough.

Those people risked their lives so I could get back to my home and family, and I'm incredibly grateful to them. There is an everlasting bond between the evaders and the helpers. I'm still in communication with them and their families, even the grandchildren of the people I stayed with. There's nothing I can do that will ever adequately repay them. But, oh yes, my gratitude to them is there for ever.

Ray Worrall thought their courage much greater than his own.

As an airman, you went out on a raid and, if you made it back, you could go down to the pub with your pals. OK, the next night you'd be out on ops again. But when it was over you were back in your Nissen hut and safe. But they were living with danger twenty-four hours a day. Even while they were sleeping, they feared the knock on the door in the middle of the night.

When I was on the run in France, I was pretty scared, but I knew my only real risk was that I would be captured and sent to a POW camp. But they would be tortured and shot, which was an immense thing to face. How they coped with that unrelenting pressure I'll never know.

Would I have done it for them if the situation had been reversed? Would I have shown the strength and fortitude they did? I hope so, but I sometimes wonder if I would have had the courage. Why did they do it? That's a big question. You'd have to ask people like Nadine about that.

But Nadine Dumon, a frequent face at reunions and deserved recipient of all the praise and thanks showered on her, was self-effacing when the question was put to her.

When I see these men now, I am very happy, but I wonder why people find what I did so special. I think of what *they* did during the war for me and my country. They were such young men and they baled out in the night in a foreign country without knowing the language. It was very difficult for them, and I just wanted to help. It's always the same when we meet each other again – they thank us and we thank them, because without the British we wouldn't be free.

Gratitude came in more tangible form too. On their return home, MI9 had asked successful evaders to list the details of anyone who had helped them, and Neave's final job for the organization (before he went off to be a prosecutor at the Nuremberg trials of the surviving Nazi leadership for war crimes) was to set up an awards bureau to recommend honours for those who had helped the cause. He passed the bulk of the work to Donald Darling, the British diplomat-cum-spy in Lisbon and Gibraltar, who had been a contact from the start for the Comet and Pat escape lines. Setting up his headquarters at the Grand Hôtel Palais Royal in Paris, he wisely did not advertise his presence or the job he was doing.[31] But word of mouth spread, and there were soon queues of people at his door with stories of their bravery and enterprise. Some were obviously genuine candidates and easy to cross-check with the reports given by evaders to MI9. The problem was that many evaders had never known the names of people who helped them – and rightly so if security was as tight as it should have been. The lists from London contained thousands of 'unknowns' or vague and unverifiable descriptions. 'A man who spoke good English came and gave me new identity papers' was a not untypical entry. Darling's job of giving credit where credit was due was not going to be easy. It was made harder too by the reticence of some helpers, used to years of silence about their activities. He went to visit a woman who reports said had hidden a total of twenty-three pilots in her attic flat. The location checked out. It was close to a baker's shop, which the evaders had remembered staring at longingly through the window. The front door matched their descriptions perfectly. He knocked.

A small, tired-looking woman half-opened it and in a frightened voice asked me my business. I said I wanted to talk to her about airmen she had sheltered, 'twenty-three of them, I believe, Madame'. She replied, 'I don't know what you are talking about,' and slammed the door shut.[32]

Old, furtive habits died hard, and, confused and scared, she had mistaken him for the Gestapo, though the Germans had long since left. Darling called out to her: 'But I have come from England to tell you how grateful we are to you.' His reassurance calmed her and she opened up. 'Did you say twenty-three men, Monsieur?' she asked. 'Well, there were actually twenty-four and here is a list of their names.'

I stared in astonishment at the tiny flat and wondered how she had found room for them. 'I looked after the boys as well as I could,' she said, almost in self-defence, as if I were inspecting the premises and might in retrospect find them unsuitable!

Darling asked if there was any help she needed, food, say, or clothes (copious supplies of which MI9 had amassed for just such contingencies). But she proudly said no, though it was obvious to him that she and her family were short of everything. 'We can manage,' she told him. As he left the building, he realized too that she was also short of recognition for what she had done. The concierge stopped him. Was there anything wrong upstairs? 'No,' he said. 'You have a heroine up there. Be proud of her.'

She gaped at me. She had not known about the evaders! I thought now was the time for the neighbours to hear about it and to regard the shelterer with the awe she deserved.

Others, of course, deserved nothing, and it was the bureau's job to weed out those looking for handouts or, more often, for official recognition from the Allies as a means of disguising what they had really been up to during the war. Some French people were shameless in promoting themselves. A retired general living in Bayonne, the collecting area for Comet Line evaders before their trip over the mountains to Spain, wrote to Winston Churchill saying he had helped and deserved 'a suitable decoration'. The order came from Downing Street to give him one. But Darling did some detective work and discovered the man had done nothing more than offer a few English paperback books to a woman who was actually sheltering airmen in her home – and he had done that rather late in the day when it was clear which way the war was going.

I wrote to MI9 protesting that the general deserved nothing. My letter was received with considerable annoyance and I was reminded that Churchill himself had asked for this award. Then my French colleagues told me that throughout the war the general had kept hidden in his garage a large car in excellent condition that could have been invaluable to the Resistance. This evidence turned the tables, and Churchill pressed the matter no further.

Darling sensed that, nonetheless, MI9 continued to distrust him and thought he was purposely doing down the toffs and upgrading the humble. But he was determined not to be swayed by snobbery of any sort. He would justly reward anyone who had rendered signal service, 'be he a baron or fireman, or she a countess or an abortionist'.

But then there were tricky (and very British) issues over what sort of awards foreigners were entitled to. Whitehall stuck rigidly to bureaucratic tradition. Servicemen – the commanders of the

Fréteval forest camp, for example – could have military decorations,[33] but the likes of Dédée were eligible only for civilian awards, as if they had not been real fighters at all. And what about those helpers whose roles had been minor? There were thousands of these, such as the tram driver who said he made an emergency stop to let off three men he guessed to be evaders and their female escort when he spotted Gestapo agents coming towards them checking papers. A 'certificate of gratitude' was drawn up on parchment for them. A special King's Medal for Courage was also struck. But all these fine distinctions produced yet more problems, and there were furious internal rows about whether a helper had done enough to earn a high-level or low-level award. In one drawn-out wrangle, the issue was whether the daughter of a family had contributed more than her brother. An exasperated official in Paris suggested honouring the family's pet parrot. 'Well, *it* didn't talk, did it?' The wording of citations could throw up difficulties too, since some were destined to be read out at Buckingham Palace. How, Darling pondered, was he to describe the occupation of Dédée's brilliant Pyrenean guide, the fearless Florentino, marked out for a George Medal? The man was a smuggler. 'In the end I described him as an "Import and Export merchant", and hoped the establishment in London would not notice.' And then there was a tawdry brouhaha over whose signature should appear at the bottom of the letters of thanks. Churchill offered his, promising, as a sign of respect, not to use a rubber stamp but to sign each one individually. But the Air Ministry wanted a piece of the glory, arguing that most of the evaders helped had been RAF boys, and an air marshal's squiggle was the one that eventually appeared – though it was a facsimile and not the real thing.[34]

Amid all the paper chasing and the wrangling, Darling had uplifting moments. Among the visitors who now came to the Palais Royal was Pat O'Leary, emaciated and exhausted still but excited and eager to race off to Marseilles to pick up with old friends. But first he had to go to his home in Brussels to see his parents. They had had no word from him since, as Captain Albert-Marie Guérisse, a doctor in the Belgian army, he fled in

1940 for Britain. They had no idea what he had been up to – that he had assumed a new name, been a Royal Navy commander, a secret agent, organizer of an escape line in France and, finally, an inmate in the Mauthausen, Natzweiler and Dachau death camps. Darling drove him to the Belgian capital and witnessed a tearful reunion. 'They all wept for joy and embraced. He had returned to them after five years, with a false name and a remarkable record.' Darling also introduced Pat to Dédée de Jongh. They had run escape lines on opposite French coasts but never met until now.

They had heard rumours of each other through the Resistance grapevine. They gazed hard at each other and then, laughing, they embraced. These two remarkable people, both back from the dead, had between them organized the evacuation of some 1,500 evaders to safety.

Dédée received a George Medal, presented in person by King George VI (though Sergeant Jack Newton, the first airman she spirited over the mountains to Spain, was convinced that, if anyone deserved its military cousin, the Victoria Cross, for valour, she did), and O'Leary the George Cross. Geo Jouanjean was awarded a British Empire Medal – the citation described him as 'a most devoted and courageous helper, whose excellent services contributed to the efficient working of a most important escape line'.[35] For others there were OBEs and MBEs, and 8,000 parchment letters of thanks were handed out.

And now life had to go on. The whole of Europe was recovering from its wounds, putting the war behind it, looking to the future not the past. Those coming back from concentration camps were no exceptions. Dédée became a nurse in a leper colony in Africa. O'Leary reverted to being a Belgian and an army medical officer. Virginia d'Albert-Lake became pregnant and had a son. 'That was my gift to myself for surviving the camps,' she said.[36] But the new world was not always easy. The two Elsie Maréchals, mother and daughter, were homeless and had to live with Georges's mother, sharing rooms in her tiny apartment. Some financial help continued to come from the Allies but the older Elsie, though disabled, had to find work too – as a humble accounts clerk, hardly the reward of heroines.

Official acknowledgement for their war work and their suffering was slow in coming and unworthy when it came. For all Donald Darling's efforts to be fair, there were glaring gaps in the awards system. From Britain, the Maréchals received letters of commendation for brave conduct, in effect, little more than a 'mention in dispatches', delivered by the ambassador in Brussels in 1948! This joined the medals and stars they had received just as belatedly from the Belgian government. They didn't mind. 'For us, the medals were superficial. We did what we did, and that was that.' For the redoubtable Mary Lindell, a senior figure in the escape lines, there was just a letter too, hopelessly inadequate for what she had done. But, as her biographer pointed out, she did have the personal affection of all those she helped, 'which in the long run has far greater meaning'.[37]

Financial compensation – or, rather, the lack of it – became an issue too. Madeleine Lamy, a French woman who had hidden, fed and clothed two American evaders in Le Havre for three months, angrily returned the cheque for 15,000 francs sent to her by the US authorities after the war. It was the equivalent of $125 – $1.50 a day, as she pointed out. 'I wouldn't insult my char woman by estimating her life at your miserable rate!' She listed all she had done. There was not only the price of food, 'most of it obtained through the black market and more valuable than gold', but also 'my sweat to get it (which meant miles to walk and over 100 steps to run down and climb every day), my sweat to get their clothes, my sweat to gather pieces of wood for their cooking, washing and bathing. And all this extra done on top of a hard day's work.'[38] The cost had come out of her own savings, as did the price of photographs for their false identity papers. She also had to pay out a fortune for two hard-to-come-by toothbrushes for them. She was in debt as a result.

And what about the lives of my father, my four brothers, their wives and children? My own too? We were in danger. The least we could expect was the torture chamber and the concentration camp at the end. My boss at work died in Buchenwald for sheltering sixteen airmen. We never thought of the risks, because we believed that the life of those aviators was of more value to the Allies' cause than ours.

Her motive was not mercenary, she insisted.

Be sure that if I were out for money, I would have worked for the Boches, who were more generous. Their price was 25,000 francs. Per head. In my case, that meant 50,000 francs – with no more danger, no toil, no sweat!!! Cash on the spot!!! That price was official. Huge posters were all over the city for anyone to be tempted.

How funny to see how little you Americans think of a decent girl who didn't bargain for the safety of your fellow men, compared to the way you treat some street girls who slept with any Boche (and with any Yankee afterwards). I fought in the Underground because I believed in democracy, in right, in justice, in the value of the human soul. I didn't lick the Boches' boots. I didn't hang my head under their law. So I am sending you back that cheque. It is burning my fingers. I need no charity.

Mme Lamy got a bigger cheque (which she used to pay for her passage to the United States, where she lived for the rest of her life) and an American Medal of Freedom. But the real issue she raised was not so much a monetary as a moral one. Allied officers clearly had no concept of what life was really like in occupied Europe. 'You have a very poor idea of the conditions of our lives under the Nazi heels,' she wrote. This was a far too common misunderstanding in the cosy reaches of Whitehall, as Donald Darling had discovered in his dealings with the pen-pushers in London.

They simply did not appreciate what the French equivalent of John Smith and his wife had done to assist evaders. They thought in terms of soldiers' wars, in which civilians took little part. But this had been a dirty war, and every civilian man, woman and child who took a part risked an equally dirty death.

Those disappointments for helpers over recognition for the work they had done and the risks they had taken were mirrored by rows in Britain over whether evaders deserved medals for getting home. Jack Newton, one of the first RAF crew to get back, was the subject of a letter from a senior officer to the Air Ministry recommending an award. He did not hear another word and was greatly disappointed.

The Air Ministry didn't think I had done anything particularly worthy. Did I think I deserved a medal, or a written commendation? Well, I was the only one of the six crew who bluffed his way through Belgium and France, across the Pyrenees, and into Spain. But in the eyes of my superiors, that was just a part of wartime's grief.[39]

Here again was that dismissive tone towards men on the run that characterized official attitudes to evasion. It was seen as unimportant, a side issue, not 'real' fighting and therefore not worthy of 'real' appreciation. Evaders who returned home often found medals and citations waiting for them, but usually for what they had done in the air rather than on the ground. The ever-belligerent Air Marshal Sir Arthur Harris, head of Bomber Command, took up cudgel and pen on behalf of his men. As early as 1942 he was complaining to the Air Ministry that bomber crew who successfully evaded were being fobbed off with a 'mention in dispatches' instead of a medal. 'This is a totally inadequate and inappropriate reward,' he wrote. 'It is my opinion that every escaper should receive an award.' Denying them showed 'a lack of appreciation of the resolution and skill required to escape from the enemy'.[40] The Royal Navy – whose total of evaders by the end of the war was fourteen against the RAF's 1,966[41] – stirred the pot unhelpfully by suggesting that evaders should most certainly be rewarded, but with civilian medals not military ones. The War Office thought evasions should be graded, and only for those where the man on the run had had to perform 'some action of a military nature' would he get a military medal. The silly dispute went on in memoranda and minutes and was never resolved. Sometimes both forms of award were handed out. If several evaders got home in a group, the senior man might get a Military Cross but the others an MBE. Equal services were unequally recognized. It was another example of what the MI9 historians M. R. D. Foot and J. M. Langley called 'the intricacies of the British system, which not even the British altogether understand'.[42]

Such rows ceased to matter much as evaders and their helpers came to the realization that their respect and admiration for each other were unshakeable and unbreakable. The RAF chipped in here – urged on by one of its very first evaders, Basil Embry (by then an air vice-marshal) – and gave its backing to an organization to help keep alive the flame. The RAF Escaping Society was born and with it regular reunions and visits that continued for the next fifty years. Those friendships have proved more enduring than metal and parchment. 'We were a band of brothers and sisters,' as a frail 'Ginger' Brown told us shortly before his death. 'When I look back on it now – those times when I was looking at the Germans, waiting for the knock at the door or a car to pull up, were incredible. Sometimes I can't believe it was me that did it. But it wasn't really down to me. My destiny was in the hands of the people who helped me. I am eternally grateful to them.'

★

There remains one awkward question that needs to be addressed. Was any of it worth it? There had been so much suffering, so many lives sacrificed, and for what, on the surface, appeared to be so little gain. Figures compiled by MI9's historians put the number who successfully evaded at 2,373 British and Commonwealth men and 2,700 Americans, a total of just over 5,000.[43] Crockatt, the MI9 founder and head, made claims that their return to active service was of great importance to the war effort. This is hard to sustain. In truth, their absence would hardly have made a large dent in the Allied military machine, and their return made a negligible difference to the outcome of the fighting. The majority of the airmen among them never flew in combat again – the RAF crew were assigned to other duties and the Americans were sent back home to the US straight away. The actual gain in 'pilot yield', as a Dutch historian of the underground war put it, was 'very disappointing'.[44] At one stage, the hard-pressed Resistance in Holland even tried to stop its members helping evaders because it thought too many of its fighters were being caught and executed for what it calculated was too little benefit.[45] Perhaps, it might therefore be argued, the grudging and unhelpful attitude of MI6 and the War Office was the right response after all. Airey Neave – not surprisingly – disagreed fundamentally. At Nuremberg after the war he interviewed many high-ranking Nazis. 'I was able to confirm that Hitler and Goering realized the impact on the Allied war effort of hundreds of trained airmen slipping through their hands. They attached importance to smashing the escape lines.' They also had to detach much-needed troops from other duties to hunt them down. At the very least, the evaders were a useful diversion. In the end, what destroyed Hitler's fantasy of European hegemony was that he chose to fight on too many fronts at once. An army of evaders and resisters, however small, had its part to play in his downfall.

And then there was the impact on the morale of the RAF. This should never be underestimated. When a long-lost man completed his home run and returned to his squadron or regiment, he was not just a hero with adventures to relate over free-flowing beer in the mess. He was also a marker to every one of his comrades due to set out on the next dangerous operation that this war was survivable. For Bomber Command, where the casualty rate was the highest of all, this was a vital message that helped Harris keep his strike force in the air over Germany to batter a resolute enemy until it finally crumbled.

Mary Lindell recalled a pilot she met in England just before she was sent to France to run an escape line. 'I wanted to say thank you for going over there,' the shy young man stammered. 'The boys have tremendous admiration for what you are doing.' She protested that it was nothing and that the airmen were the real heroes. He replied. 'Yes, but tonight I shall be back and sleeping in a warm bed without any fear. But where will you be? And you're

going out there for *us*, to help us back if we're shot down . . .' Here
was proof of the comfort men took from knowing there was help
out there. But wouldn't it have been better, it could be argued, if
the evaders had simply surrendered and gone to the POW camps
that many of them ended up in anyway? They would have been
safer, and fewer lives would have been at risk. And indeed there
were times when men on the run felt precisely that. To those
hiding in crannies under floorboards or buried in 'tombs' beneath
fields, the relative space and the comradeship of a prison compound
seemed attractive. Many of those actually behind the barbed wire
would have disagreed. Captivity, the loss of his freedom, his subju-
gation to another's will, ate into a man's soul and many came back
from the camps not only physically wrecked (particularly after the
ordeal of the marches at the end of the war) but psychologically
damaged. Nothing could compare with being free. Nothing could
better the idea of making it home.

Even more important, however, was the boost the evasions gave
to the morale of the conquered people of France, Belgium and
Holland. Helping Allied soldiers and airmen to escape was their
only chance to fight back in a way they had not found possible
when the German war machine rolled over them in 1940. The
cost-effectiveness of what they were doing, the actual gain to the
war effort, was irrelevant. They needed to defy the dictator. Denys
Teare recognized this in the people who hid him.

Why did they risk their lives and those of their families just so I could
get home? Because it was the only contact they had with the opposition
to the Germans. Our bombers passing overhead on their way to Germany
were a sign of hope for the future, of freedom, and that's what we
represented.[46]

It was a joint effort in a common cause. 'They were patriots
fighting for their own freedom alongside me,' said RAF pilot Cliff
Hallett. 'I saw the heights to which the human spirit is capable of
rising when there is a belief,' wrote US airman Jetty Cook.[47] Deep
human emotions – unquantifiable by the military theorists – run

through the story of the Second World War evaders, and their helpers are its essence. That most pragmatic of soldiers, the tough paratroop commander John Hackett, found the experience inspirational. He quoted scripture: 'I was hungry and ye gave me meat. I was thirsty and ye gave me drink. I was a stranger and ye took me in.' In his helpers he discovered 'a rare and beautiful thing, a structure of kindness and courage, of steadfast devotion and quiet selflessness. I had often seen bravery in battle. I now also knew the unconquerable strength of the gentle.'

It was indefatigable. On a dark street corner in Brussels, as we saw at the beginning of this book, a young man and a girl stood laughing in the rain, an English airman on the run and a Belgian art student who had adopted him and become his guide and protector. They didn't mind the downpour. They had just escaped the clutches of the Germans. They were free. Moments like this may not have won the war, but they were what it was all about. On that wet, windswept night, the evader and his helper together put a small scuff on the polished boots of tyranny – with the promise that eventually their shine would disappear completely.

# Epilogue

'What has become of those places where we spent so intensely so many months of our lives?'

*Gordon Carter, 2006*

Sixty years on, it takes just minutes for us to fly over the Channel, once an almost impenetrable barrier. We land on the flak-free north-eastern coast of Brittany at what is now a tourist airport and are soon bowling in a car along open roads and through towns and villages that were a battleground in the 1940s. There are no checkpoints thrown up to bar our way, no demands for papers from sullen, grey-uniformed soldiers, no guns levelled at us, no bullet-ridden bodies left lying on the ground or swinging from makeshift gibbets to intimidate us. Years ago, Allied evaders came this way, fearing for their lives and their freedom, hiding in the fields and woods, travelling secretly at night, heading for houses they hoped were safe before slipping aboard ghostly fishing boats that would, if their luck held, ferry them across the sea to home. We have come to explore the now-tranquil terrain that was the scene of so much toil and agony for them and their helpers. In a couple of hours we complete a journey that would have taken them days, weeks even, and are on the Atlantic coast in the pretty town of Quimper. Squadron Leader Gordon Carter (RCAF, retired), stooped now, slowed by illness and age, is at the door of his home to greet us. This unassuming gentleman in his eighties is the hero we have come to meet, his exploits in the mid-twentieth century a lesson for us all in the twenty-first.

We enter a smart but small flat in a sheltered home for the elderly, the irony of finding him in this last safe house not lost on us. On the back of a chair he has laid out his ancient blue RAF tunic. It is faded from long years hanging in the cupboard but, with its Distinguished Flying Cross ribbon (and bar), it is a thing of huge pride. Across it lies a piece of off-white fabric, silk, still soft to the touch despite its obvious age. It is the remnant of the parachute that lowered him, the navigator in a crippled Halifax bomber, reluctantly onto the soil of occupied Europe in 1943, a scrap he carried with him in his pocket on his evasion, through hard times in a POW camp, on the long march of hunger and fatigue that finally brought him to the end of his war. It travelled with him and his French-born wife Janine around the world in his post-war work for the United Nations agency UNICEF. It came home with them to France when he retired.

The room is packed with mementoes of a full life, both professional and private. Children and grandchildren smile out from framed photographs. Shared memories, he believes, that is what we all consist of, that is what our lives are constructed around. But it is Janine who still holds the centre of his life. There is a black-and-white snap of her from years ago, her long hair pushed to one side of an elegant face that could well have graced Hollywood. 'She looks like Veronica Lake,' he muses, referring to the 1940s American film beauty renowned for her peek-a-boo tresses. And she does. It is clear what drew him to her when he first laid eyes on her, a helper for her Resistance-fighter brother. This is the image that sustained him in their years apart and brought him back to her the moment he was a free man again. No wonder he could not wait to marry her. No wonder that she was all he ever expected and wanted.

Janine enters, small, neat, exquisite, as beautiful and gracious in old age as she must have been as a young girl. Her skin is perfect, as are her manners and her style. She apologizes for the inadequacies of her English. It is perfect too. They talk, we listen, and we are now back in a different time, the old days still fresh and vivid in their minds. How handsome Gordon was, she tells us, with his matinee-idol good looks, and how different from the other men she met. 'He was so polite. When he kissed me, he asked permission first. I found that so amazing.' No wonder she waited for him.

And then there were the love letters he wrote, posted for safe keeping to his aunt, who sent them to Janine when France was liberated and Gordon was a prisoner in Stalag Luft III. He grunts at the mention of them. He doesn't want to appear over-sentimental. (This from a man who still has the original pass for compassionate leave that allowed him to rush to France to find Janine in May 1945!) He can't remember what he wrote, he blusters, and tries to change the subject. They must have been thrown away, he suggests. 'Oh no,' she chips in brightly. 'I've still got them, all of them.' He looks at her quizzically, crossly even. 'I didn't know that,' he declares. '*Mais oui, chéri,*' she says. 'They are *dans le sac marron.*' She leaves the room, knowing precisely where to look, and is back in seconds with a muslin shoe-bag. The letters, scores of them, are tucked neatly inside a brown envelope. We ask if we can see them, and the request flusters Gordon. He looks embarrassed, like a schoolboy whose note passed across a classroom has been intercepted by a teacher. 'I've never read them,' he tells us unconvincingly. He doesn't want us to look at them. His French was no good then. They were just matter-of-fact accounts of what he had been up to, not interesting at all.

Finally, he grudgingly admits that, 'OK, they were love letters,' and we are allowed to see a handful. The years roll back. He is young again and full of fire and romance, all of which he poured out to her in letters that he never even knew she would see. But she did, and his words won her heart. He wrote of her eyes, her smile and that morning when he woke her from sleep and she was '*si chaude, si amoureuse*' ('so warm, so loving'). How could she resist when he pleaded for her to wait for him? When he came to find her, she knew they were meant to be together. Years after their whirlwind of a wedding, Janine's mother told her she thought she must have been mad to let her daughter marry someone she barely knew.

But it worked beautifully! If someone told you the story, you wouldn't believe it. You would think it was a film or a novel, that it couldn't happen in real life! But it did, and to me, and I was so very, very happy.[1]

But their love was only part of the story. There was, of course, danger and fear too. We drive to the sea at Tréboul, its harbour full of yachts and pleasure craft now. In 1943 it was a fishing port ringed by big guns and patrolled by German gunboats, and Gordon had come here by rail with sixteen other evaders and followed the leader from the station down dark streets to the quayside. Today the sun is shining in a blue sky and waves are lapping against the wall. Back then there was a fierce wind blowing across a rough sea. But the biggest difference was the German sentries – 'Over there,' Gordon tells us, pointing excitedly across the quay,

where that man is standing. They were armed and would not hesitate to shoot if they saw us trying to board a boat. We counted their steps as they marched up and down and then dodged past them when the timing seemed right. But we got safely on board and lay quietly in the hold. Then the boat had to get past the sentry point over *there* . . .

He is not just recollecting the moment, he is reliving it, as, he says, he does so often these days.

The past is not something locked away. As I get older, it becomes more and more prominent in my mind.

And then he sighs and quotes the novelist L. P. Hartley at us:

'The past is another country. They do things differently there.'

He is right. Men like Gordon Carter and all the other 'home run' heroes and their helpers whose stories we have told did indeed do things differently. They were put to the test in a way that later generations were not. They proved steadfast, brave, loyal. To this day, they are an inspiration to us all.

# Appendix

# TIPS FOR EVADERS AND ESCAPERS
## MEDICAL AND FIELDCRAFT HINTS
**(Issued by MI9 to escape and evasion lecturers, July 1944)**

## 1. MEDICAL

(i) The good escaper is the man who keeps himself fit, cheerful and comfortable. He is not a 'he-man' who boasts about his capacity to endure discomfort. He should be a man with sound common sense and above all a man of great determination. The following hints may be useful in helping to keep this determination.

(ii) CONSERVATION OF ENERGY
Know how to use your Aids Box. Ration out your Horlicks tablets and regard them as a meal; do the same with any other food stuffs you may be carrying. Be careful of water; use your sterilising outfit. Remember that thirst is worse than hunger. If you need to use your Benzedrine, follow carefully the instructions printed on the packet.

(iii) CARE OF THE FEET
You must pay special attention to your feet. They must be kept dry and clean. When you rest keep your feet elevated if possible. When you halt, and are in a safe place, wash and dry your socks and change them over from one foot to another. Leave your shoes off as long as practicable. When faced with the possibility of frost bite, wrap your feet in straw or brown paper or newspaper, and keep them as dry as possible. A change of socks is invaluable.

## (iv) SLEEP
Whilst it is possible to go for long periods without sleep, it is advisable
to get regular sleep. During the summer months this is no great difficulty.
A wind-break can be made by piling branches and grass against tree
trunks. A haystack is very warm and comfortable. If you cannot sleep
because of extreme cold, try to snatch odd half hours during the marching
at night whilst the blood is circulating well. When the cold wakes you
up, continue the march to get warm again.

## (v) BOWELS
It is possible that your bowels will not move regularly if you are living
on strict Escape Box rations. Do not let this alarm you.


# 2. FIELDCRAFT

(i) Keep close to hedges etc. wherever possible. Never walk in the centre
of fields. It is harder to notice a moving object if it is against a dark
background.

(ii) Keep to edges of woods rather than walk through the middle; this
improves your field of vision, and decreases the noise you will make.

(iii) Keep eyes and ears wide open, watch the behaviour of birds and
cattle well ahead. They are easily disturbed and will give your enemy's
position away as well as your own. (Especially jays, magpies, plovers and
blackbirds.) Your main dangers are ahead, but remember someone may
be following you.

(iv) Be wary of crossing the skyline.

(v) Whenever at a vantage point, survey the territory you intend to cross
and plan your route across the lower lying land. This saves time and
helps you to avoid danger spots.

(vi) Farm dogs bark easily at night but people rarely leave warm beds to investigate. Dogs barking in the distance may denote a guard or policeman.

(vii) Never take chances. If two are travelling together, always discuss your plans and take the more cautious advice.

(viii) Many rivers are fordable. Sluggish waters are deep. A ford is often indicated by a line of rippling foam over the shallow rocks below. This is rarely in a straight line and mostly is in a V formation pointing down stream.

(ix) Water is sometimes hard to find. Very green lush grass and plants often cover a natural spring. If you dig a hole there, clean water will soon seep through.

(x) A line of thicker herbage, bushes and trees following a valley often denotes a stream.

(xi) A moving object is more easily noticed than a still one. A person will often evade observation from a distance just by standing still.

(xii) If you hear a noise, crouch down and listen. Don't rush blindly away, for you may give yourself away by doing so.

(xiii) Try to keep a reserve of strength in case you are chased.

(xiv) Don't rush up steep hills, take them very slowly.

(xv) A cigarette is often as good as a meal, but do not smoke in the daytime, because the smoke may give your position away, or when on the march. Save your butt ends; you may be thankful for them later on.

(xvi) Generally speaking, a man can keep going as long as his will power lasts out. Many evaders and escapers from Germany have travelled the last kilometres to safety in a state of collapse.

## 3. WATCHES AND COMPASSES

Be careful that watches, compasses etc. are in a safe place. When travelling these things are easily lost or damaged.

## 4. DIRECTION FINDING

(i) Remember the dawn is in the East and sunset in the West.

(ii) Moss does not grow only on the Northern side of tree trunks, as is commonly supposed.

(iii) The Northern or Pole Star is a very accurate guide on cloudless nights.

(iv) In the Northern hemisphere, by pointing the hour hand of a watch at the sun, the point half way between 12 o'clock and the hour hand will point approximately South. Sun time must be used in these calculations.

(v) Churches on the Continent are not necessarily aligned East and West.

## 5. ANIMAL FOODS

All animals of the European continent are edible. Men should be impressed with the importance of forgetting old prejudices when they are faced with the necessity of eating anything they can get hold of. Moreover, they may discover that many animals so far neglected or despised as food are, in fact, good, tasty food when prejudice is forgotten. For example, people who like raw oysters are horrified at the idea of eating raw snails, although these are just as good food, just as tasty and much cleaner feeders than oysters because they live on wholesome foliage.

All animals may be eaten raw or cooked. Animal food is rather more wholesome and digestible when eaten raw than when cooked.

The above should be driven home before reading the following details because it is so important to sink all prejudice and every consideration excepting the bed-rock necessity of getting food somehow in order to keep going. All objections to wholesome food are hysteria.

Owing to their high food value when compared with most vegetable foods, small animals, even two or three snails or some frogs' legs, are worth collecting for adding to a meal of boiled leaves or roots. But the finding of animal food in quantity is uncertain, whereas vegetable food, especially wild plants, is virtually certain.

(i) RATS AND MICE are both palatable meat. Rats cooked in a stew might be mistaken for chicken. Skin them, gut them and boil them in a mess tin: rats about 10 minutes, mice 5 minutes. Either can be cooked with dandelion leaves for a stew. Be sure to include the livers.

(ii) BIRDS are all edible. Moorhens or coots may be found in ponds. The former are palatable, the latter tough and unpalatable but nevertheless good food.

(iii) FROGS. The flesh of all frogs is delicate and wholesome, but most of the meat is on the hind legs.

(iv) SNAILS. All of these are a real delicacy; can be eaten in two ways: (a) raw by cracking the shell and withdrawing the snail, (b) dropping them into boiling water for 5 minutes and pulling out the cooked snail with a pin.

(v) DOGS AND CATS. Providing so much food, they are worth some trouble in capture by friendly advances. The liver is the most valuable part. Either animal stewed with edible leaves will provide an excellent meal.

(vi) GRASS SNAKES AND LIZARDS. To eat the snakes, cut off the heads, skin them (easily done) and boil for ten minutes.

(vii) HEDGEHOGS would be a lucky find (in dry ditches). Turn them on their backs, tickle the body lightly with a stick or the fingers. It will then poke out its head and neck which can be severed by a stroke of a knife. Skin and cook as subpara (v).

(viii) EELS might be found in ponds or deep sluggish streams.

(ix) COARSE FISH – ditto.

(x) HORSE meat closely resembles beef.

# 6. VEGETABLE FOODS

Men who have to subsist on vegetable foods such as cabbages and other green stuff and especially wild vegetables must realise that owing to their comparatively poor food value, large quantities must be eaten to obtain sufficient calories. On the other hand, owing to their high vitamin and mineral value, edible leaves are very wholesome food and provide much bulk so that they satisfy the appetite. 'Short commons' on this form of diet may result in better health and strength than an equal shortage of the richer foods.

A considerable part of each day must be devoted to gathering and eating the foliage if it has to be eaten raw. Animals who subsist on it spend the greater part of their waking hours in eating and the welfare of men living on the wild vegetation of a country will largely depend on the time they are able to set aside for this purpose, including the preparation as well as the consumption of the food. Men in hiding should therefore take every opportunity for collecting food and take it to their hide-outs for preparation and eating. An average cabbage, weighing two lbs, if eaten raw cannot be chewed and swallowed in under half an hour, and at least nine cabbages would be needed.

## (a) CULTIVATED VEGETABLES
It makes no difference to health whether these are eaten raw or lightly cooked, but the advantage of cooking is that they can be eaten quickly. A cooked cabbage can be eaten in five minutes. Cabbages, cauliflowers,

broccoli etc. are tender after five minutes boiling (carrots and potatoes a few minutes longer).

There is a valuable hint regarding these vegetables. The stalks are usually left in the ground after the heads have been cut off. The stalks of last winter's vegetables are valuable. If the outer rind is stripped off with a knife, the centre will be found to be fleshy and excellent food, raw or cooked. Many of these stalks may be found in cottage gardens. All the cultivated roots may be eaten raw. The leaves of all the root vegetables, excepting potatoes, are first class food, especially turnips. Peas and beans are the most valuable of all the vegetables.

## (b) WILD VEGETABLES

This is a more serious subject than (a). It is most important for the men to recognise the chief edible plants and have some idea as to which provide the best food. Many, such as grasses, have only a minute quantity of food available through human digestion because their food material is enclosed in cellulose which our digestion cannot dissolve. But by searching in grass fields, ditches etc., several nutritious vegetables are commonly found.

(i) STINGING NETTLES when young and light green in colour, after six minutes boiling, are a tasty and wholesome vegetable, rather like spinach. One minute boiling entirely removes the sting. Older nettles would require longer boiling. The food value of nettles is very high.

(ii) CLOVER, which is not a grass, has a soft and rather fleshy leaf which can be chewed and swallowed rapidly. Most ordinary pastures contain clumps of it. The food value is probably about the same as an equal weight of dandelion. It has not the effect of stimulating the kidneys which is found in the dandelion.

(iii) BRACKEN FERN. The young, curly shoots, before they become upright, may be eaten lightly boiled, like asparagus. The roots of bracken are rich food but they must be dug down deep to get the whole root out. Should be boiled till tender.

(iv) SOW THISTLE – *Sonchus oleraceus*. Of all the edible wild plants, the sow thistle takes first place as a sustaining food. In many countries of Europe it is boiled for the table and its disuse in this country can only be due to ignorance of its qualities. Both the leaves and its thick succulent roots are delicacies. The fleshy part at the junction of leaves and root resembles the core of the Jerusalem artichoke. For the purpose of these directions its greatest recommendation is its plentiful occurrence throughout the fields, gardens and ditches of Europe. Eaten raw it is rather like lettuce, and the root is palatable.

Men could live well for a considerable period on this vegetable alone. The weed flowers with a yellow blossom. Five to 8 minutes boiling is ample.

(v) DANDELION. This is a well-known vegetable. The leaves are used for salads. The roots may also be eaten. The French name *Piss-en-lit* indicates the effect of this plant upon the kidneys. It is due to an alkaloid called taraxacin. If the leaves and roots are boiled for ten minutes and the water poured away, some of the taraxacin will have gone and the bitter taste of the plant much reduced. Owing to the certainty of finding this plant in large quantities and to its good food value, it must be regarded as one of the most important of the wild vegetable foods. The roots are at times very thick and fleshy. When many of the leaves are eaten raw the palate becomes accustomed to the bitter taste which is then less noticeable. The stimulating effect upon the kidneys need cause no anxiety.

(vi) ARROWHEADS. This plant, which forms large leaves, is found in marshy country. It has a tuberous root like a potato and a white flower. Follow the root down. The tuber is at its end. Called in China 'Anti-famine herb'.

(vii) MUSHROOM. Well known by its pink or brown under gills. A description of other edible fungi is omitted owing to the danger of mistakes in identification.

(viii) CORN. The ripe 'ears' should be broken off and rubbed between the hands. The husks can then be removed by blowing on them in the cupped hands; the grain will remain in the hands.

(ix) FRUITS. Apples, pears, plums etc. can be eaten – in moderation if unripe. They are valuable for the starch they contain. If over-ripe they are still wholesome and need not be feared. A slight mould on the over-ripe fruit need not cause anxiety. It is a penicillin and quite harmless.

(x) HIPS AND HAWS are valuable food and may be found in the hedges in and after August.

(xi) YEWS. Although the foliage is poisonous, the berries are wholesome food.

# 7. CATCHING ANIMALS

(i) SMALL BIRDS AND MICE. By far the best implement is the little 'break-back' mouse trap obtainable at any ironmongers. The structure can be concealed by sprinkling short pieces of dry grass (taking care to leave the spring free) and it should be baited with biscuit crumbs for sparrows and other finches, but for blackbirds and thrushes a large live worm impaled on the trigger is much the best bait. Being very light, the trap should be anchored to a peg in the ground with a piece of string.

(ii) EELS AND COARSE FISH. The former are the more valuable and easily caught in sluggish streams. Requirements are a roach hook mounted on gut and a short length of fine fishing line. A stick can be cut for a rod. The hook should be baited with a worm and allowed to sink to the bottom. The line can be hitched round a small piece of stick to act as a float, and attached so as to allow the required depth.

For fish, the float should be so adjusted that the bait is just off the bottom. Great care should be taken of the hook and gut – it may become precious.

(iii) RABBITS AND RATS. Snares set in the runs are best.

(iv) SNAILS may be found by 'combing' hay fields with the fingers. They will be on the stalks of the grass or on the ground. Standing hay is a rich finding ground for snails.

(v) CRAYFISH may be found by thrusting the hand into their holes at water level in streams with muddy banks.

(vi) SHELLFISH OF THE SEA SHORES. Mussels, cockles, winkles and razorfish can all be eaten raw. The commonest shellfish of the rocks are limpets. These are very tough when raw, but when chopped up and boiled with just enough water to cover them they are quite edible and are good food. Sea urchins are very palatable.

## 8. SEA WEEDS

In case of necessity these should not be neglected. The commonest is the 'bladder weed'. This is tough and unattractive but when boiled in two waters becomes edible.

Ulvas (long ribbon-weeds) are quite edible. They may be eaten raw, but are better boiled like other green vegetables, the water being strained off with much of the salt.

## 9. GENERAL DIRECTIONS

To skin rats, mice and birds, cut off the heads, make a skin-deep incision down the centre of the breast and abdomen. Peel off the skin from centre to sides, then pull the skin off the back from above downwards. Afterwards cut open the belly and draw out the guts, leaving the liver behind.

## 10. PRECAUTIONS

(i) WATER should be boiled for two minutes always if taken from ponds or ditches.

(ii) POISONOUS PLANTS
    (a) Unless a man has special knowledge of fungi, it is advisable to stick to mushrooms (which are easy to identify by their brown or pink under gills).
    (b) Some weeds with tempting leaves are poisonous because they contain oxalic acid. These include all the docks, sorrel (too commonly eaten in salads) and the leaves of rhubarb.
    (c) Buttercups are poisonous.
    (d) Cow parsley is an edible plant but several others of the same order which closely resemble it are very poisonous, e.g. hemlock.

(iii) ANIMAL FOOD
Great care should be taken to see that the meat has not putrefied, and it is advisable to eat any animals that have been killed fairly soon to make sure of this. Dead animals such as dogs found run over or horses killed in action should only be eaten if they are still warm when found.

*This document is available at the National Archives, ref. WO208/3268*

# Notes

Where a reference is given for an interview, book or document, that reference applies for the remainder of the chapter. For instance all quotes from Terry Bolter in the Preface (note 3) are from his private memoir and his interview with the authors in May 2005. Similarly, in Chapter 1, all quotes from Gordon Instone are from his book, *Freedom the Spur* (note 1). All other references are attributed as stated.

## Preface

1. General Sir John Hackett, *I Was a Stranger* (Chatto & Windus, 1977).
2. Anthony Deane-Drummond, *Return Ticket* (Collins, 1953).
3. Terry Bolter, private account and interview with JN and TR, May 2005.
4. The 'Royal Air Forces Escaping Society' [sic] officially disbanded in 1995 but surviving members still meet every year.
5. Official figures regarding the total numbers of evaders vary. The RAF Escaping Society estimated that 2,803 British and Commonwealth airmen alone (i.e. not including soldiers or sailors) made it home. M. R. D. Foot and J. M. Langley, the authors of the official history of MI9, give total figures of 2,373 for all British and Commonwealth servicemen and 2,700 Americans.
6. Again, official numbers are impossible to come by – many 'helpers' were killed by the German forces, many were never located or came forward. The RAF Escaping Society estimated that there were 14,000 helpers officially recognized in 1945.
7. MI9 briefing document, National Archives, WO208/3242/227857.
8. It has crossed the Atlantic too. When France refused to join the US and Britain in a coalition to invade Saddam Hussein's Iraq in 2003,

many jokes relating to 1940 were made at its expense. Some American commentators had great, if unedifying, sport in denouncing the French as 'cheese-eating surrender-monkeys'.

9. See John Nichol and Tony Rennell, *Tail-End Charlies: The Last Battles of the Bomber War, 1944–45* (Viking, 2004).

10. MI9 briefing document, National Archives, WO208/3242/227857.

11. James Davies, *A Leap in the Dark* (Leo Cooper, 1994).

12. Gordon Carter, private account and interview with JN and TR, September 2005.

13. MI9 briefing document, National Archives, WO208/3242/227857.

## Chapter 1: Left Behind

1. Gordon Instone, *Freedom the Spur* (Pan, 1956).

2. Debriefing by MI9, August 1940, National Archives, WO208/3298.

3. Wing Commander Basil Embry in Anthony Richardson, *Wingless Victory* (Odhams Press, 1950). Related by Richardson, this invaluable source was written in the third person from a verbal account given to him by Embry. Embry scrupulously checked the final manuscript and endorsed it. 'Richardson has related everything that happened to me and brought it to life exactly as I told it to him,' Embry wrote in the preface. 'The story is true and correct in every detail.'

4. J. M. Langley, *Fight Another Day* (Collins, 1974).

5. Quoted in Jonathan Fenby, *The Sinking of the Lancastria* (Simon & Schuster, 2005).

6. National Archives, WO208/3298.

7. Peter Scott Janes, *Conscript Heroes* (Paul Mould, 2004).

8. The Earl of Cardigan, *I Walked Alone* (Routledge & Kegan Paul, 1950).

9. This and what follows is taken from Captain R. L. Hulls, MI9 debriefing, 27 June 1940, National Archives, WO208/3298.

10. M. R. D. Foot and J. M. Langley, *MI9: Escape and Evasion, 1939–1945* (The Bodley Head, 1979).

11. Ibid.

12. 'Notes on the experiences of British personnel captured by the

enemy during recent operations and lessons learnt from their escapes', MI9 file, National Archives, WO208/3298.

13. Richardson, *Wingless Victory*, for this and the edited account that follows.

14. John Christie, private memoir, Imperial War Museum, 88/47/1.

15. The exchange at the time was 180 francs to the pound, but £3-odd was a goodly amount, given that 1lb of butter was the equivalent of six old pence (2.5p) and good champagne was three shillings (15p) a bottle (Christie's figures).

## Chapter 2: The Back Door

1. The Earl of Cardigan, *I Walked Alone* (Routledge & Kegan Paul, 1950).

2. Gordon Instone, *Freedom the Spur* (Pan, 1956).

3. Derrick Peterson, private account, Imperial War Museum, 98/4/1.

4. J. M Langley, *Fight Another Day* (Collins, 1974). The only consolation was that the Frenchman said he hated the Germans more!

5. John Christie, private memoir, Imperial War Museum, 88/47/1.

6. Captain D. B. Laing of the Cameron Highlanders, National Archives, WO208/330.

7. Instone, *Freedom the Spur*.

8. Colonel Sir Roderick Brinckman of the 3rd Battalion, Grenadier Guards, Imperial War Museum, 86/61/1.

9. Lisa Fittko, *Escape through the Pyrenees* (Northwestern University Press, 1991).

10. 'It was astounding that even the venerable old English travel agency Cook sold false transatlantic tickets. Soon every émigré in Marseille knew about it, and we also went to the big, elegant agency in the city center. We paid two hundred francs, and the genteel, rather supercilious official with the British accent sold us the fake tickets without turning a hair,' ibid.

11. M. R. D. Foot and J. M. Langley, *MI9: Escape and Evasion, 1939–1945* (The Bodley Head, 1979).

12. Langley, *Fight Another Day*.

13. Donald Caskie, *The Tartan Pimpernel* (Oldbourne, 1957).

14. According to Jimmy Langley, 'the French police must have been fully aware of most of the plots hatched within its precincts. In fact it was only allowed to stay open because it was such an excellent source of information about clandestine British activities.'

15. Apparently Caskie would at times complain that his intelligence contacts dragged him into activities he did not approve of and which put him in an embarrassing position with the French authorities. However, he made no such protestations in his autobiography, writing about how pleased he was by the approach from 'Major X'. 'I was heartened, feeling myself part of the large force which was fighting for freedom.' If he voiced embarrassment to the US consul about the money and that he felt compromised by it – as US sources say, according to author Derek Richardson in *Detachment W* (Paul Mould, 2004) – then he was probably just being diplomatic.

16. Donald Darling, *Secret Sunday* (William Kimber, 1975).

17. To be fair to Hoare, he had been told by Winston Churchill that his only priority was to keep Franco from joining the war on the German/Italian side. He was right to be paranoid.

18. Another Briton detained by the Spanish, Gordon Instone, listed the following nationalities as his companions: Poles, Belgians, French, Yugoslavs, Germans, Dutch, Armenians, Algerians, Hungarians, Romanians, Czechs and Greeks. Plus Spaniards.

19. Gordon Instone's description.

20. The record is unclear. In *I Walked Alone* Cardigan first describes the man as 'the British Military Attaché from Madrid' and later amends this to the 'Assistant Military Attaché'.

21. She was married to a local businessman named Fiocca. Under her maiden name of Nancy Wake, she would become better known for her activities later in the war as a star agent of SOE.

22. Helen Long, reporting on the recollections of the Rodocanachi family, in *Safe Houses Are Dangerous* (Abson Books, 1989).

23. Ibid.

24. Yvonne Daley-Brusselmans, *Belgium Rendezvous 127 Revisited* (Sunflower University Press, 2001).

25. The lady's name was Elsie Maréchal. William Etherington, *A Quiet Woman's War* (Mousehold Press, 2002).

26. Dumon's given name was Andrée, but she adopted 'Nadine' to distinguish her from Andrée de Jongh, who was to be the leader of this group of helpers.
27. Andrée (Nadine) Dumon, interview with JN and TR, June 2005.
28. Nadine stuck to her policy of non-violence. 'I know it sounds hypocritical because when I helped evaders to go back to England they would fight again and kill Germans but I could not kill,' she explained. 'Even after the war was over I could not kill a guard from the concentration camps I was in, even after everything that they did to me, everything I had seen . . .'
29. The evader's name is given as Colin Culpar in the official *MI9* history by Foot and Langley. Darling, *Secret Sunday*, however, gives the soldier's name as James Cromer, while Airey Neave, in *Little Cyclone* (Hodder & Stoughton, 1954), his biography of Andrée de Jongh, has him as Colin Cromar.
30. In *Fight Another Day* Jimmy Langley describes how he witnessed Dansey bawling out an officer for recruiting a woman agent in France: ' "They simply are not trustworthy. Do you understand?" he bellowed.'
31. Foot and Langley, *MI9*.
32. Airey Neave, *Saturday at MI9* (Leo Cooper, 2004).
33. Neave, *Little Cyclone*.
34. Etherington, *A Quiet Woman's War*.

## Chapter 3: Feet First

1. H. J. Spiller, *Ticket to Freedom* (William Kimber, 1988), and interview with JN, June 2005.
2. Harry Levy, *The Dark Side of the Sky* (Leo Cooper, 1996), and interview with JN, June 2005.
3. Ed Burley, private account.
4. George Duffee, private account.
5. Fred Gardiner, private account and interview with JN, July 2005.
6. Terry Bolter, private account and interview with JN and TR, May 2005.

7. Wayne Eveland, 'Memoirs and Reflections', unpublished private account.

8. Maurice 'Collie' Collins, private account and interview with JN and TR, May 2005. Sadly, Maurice Collins died before this book was completed.

9. MI9's Airey Neave was amazed by the way in which MI9 'failed to gain the cooperation of senior officers. This has always been something of a mystery ... but even in 1944 there were many whose background made them reluctant to accept the need for escape and evasion training. This was all the more surprising in the case of the Air Ministry.' Airey Neave, *Saturday at MI9* (Leo Cooper, 2004).

10. George Fernyhough, 'A Time to Remember', unpublished private memoir written with Tony Eaton (1998), and interview with JN, June 2005. The authors are grateful to Mr Eaton for providing copies of his work.

11. Some may think this a jaundiced view but even MI9's Airey Neave, its greatest advocate, admitted: 'The reaction of men to these lectures was unpredictable. Most followed their instructions and some took them sufficiently seriously to learn languages and study the countries where they were due to go on operations. Others assumed that nothing would happen to them' (*Saturday at MI9*). Donald Darling, who interviewed every airman who made it home via Gibraltar, backed up this conclusion. He wrote: 'Quite often men paid little attention to [parachute] training matters until they heard their captain's order to bale out and then there was no time to recall instructions they had hoped never to require. Similarly, men were unaccountably careless about their escape kits (were they considered sissy?), which they were instructed always to carry with them but too often neglected to do so.' Donald Darling, *Secret Sunday* (William Kimber, 1975).

12. For example Gordon Carter, private account and interview with JN, August 2005.

13. Frank Haslam, private account.

14. John 'Ginger' Brown, private account and interview with JN, May 2005. Sadly, John Brown died shortly after this interview.

15. Internal 4 Group memo, National Archives, AIR 14/1864.

16. MI9 briefing document, National Archives, WO208/3268.

17. Ibid.

18. MI9 debriefing of Major John Mackintosh-Walker (Seaforth Highlanders) and Major Thomas Rennie (Black Watch), National Archives, WO208/3298.

19. 'A Warning from the Past', National Archives, WO208/3412.

20. Not certifiably mad, of course, but certainly eccentric and with a fine sense of humour. When a mysterious caller once asked to meet him secretly, Hutton suggested the *top* of Nelson's Column. See Clayton Hutton, *Official Secret* (Max Parrish, 1960).

21. The answer was bribery. Houdini paid the appointed carpenter to build the box in such a way that he could pivot the planks and slip out. Ibid.

22. Ibid.

23. Paper had proved useless for the maps – it rustled and creased into illegibility. The only paper that worked was a specialist product from Japan made from mulberry leaves. The experiment with silk almost failed, too, when the ink ran. Mixing in pectin, a substance used to set jam, solved the problem.

24. Anthony Richardson, *Wingless Victory* (Odhams Press, 1950).

25. The description is that of the 'senior man' concerned, Robley Winfrey. Lloyd R. Shoemaker, *The Escape Factory* (St Martin's Press, 1990).

26. George Buckner, 'Down and Out in 1944', unpublished private account.

27. Ed Burley, private account.

28. Eveland, 'Memoirs and Reflections'.

29. M. R. D. Foot, *Resistance* (Granada Publishing, 1978).

30. This and all quotations below from MI9 documents in National Archives, WO208/3268.

31. Authors' italics. The advice seems to be that 'disposing' of the enemy was all right as long as you weren't seen doing it!

32. Hugh Dormer, *Diaries* (Jonathan Cape, 1956).

33. Ralph McKee, private account and interview with JN, July 2005.

34. Spiller, interview.

35. John Christie, private memoir, Imperial War Museum, 88/47/1.

36. Many RAF pilots did their initial flying training abroad, most in Australia, South Africa and Canada, some, like Duffee, in the USA.
37. Howard Harris, 'Vive la France and French-fried Potatoes', unpublished private account.
38. Squadron Leader Wally Lashbrook, 'Some Anxious Moments in World War II', unpublished private memoir.
39. Story told by Fred Gardiner, who was the other airman.
40. Quoted by Bob de Graaff in *Stepping Stones to Freedom* (privately published, 2003).
41. LMF stood for 'Low Moral Fibre' and was the designation given to airmen who refused to fly. In the RAF it was seen as tantamount to cowardice, and those accused of LMF were severely disciplined, some publicly cashiered in front of their squadrons and assigned to the most menial and humiliating duties. For more on this, see Chapter 6 of the authors' *Tail-End Charlies* (Viking, 2004).
42. De Graaff, *Stepping Stones to Freedom*.
43. Marguerite Brouard-Fraser, private account and interview with JN, August 2005.

## Chapter 4: Over the Top

1. Another ploy was to be seen flicking through an obviously pro-German magazine. George Duffee did this on trains in Holland, occasionally allowing himself a little smile as if he was enjoying every word. 'One sight of that and no one wished to speak to me,' he recalled; private account.
2. But they did. American airman Ralph McKee couldn't believe the Gestapo officers checking his train wouldn't think *four* deaf-mutes in the same carriage odd. 'My heart beat faster and there were butterflies in my stomach.' But the Germans worked down the coach and moved on; private account.
3. Jack Newton's story is told in full by Derek Shuff in *Evader* (Spellmount, 2003). The authors are grateful to Mr Shuff and to Spellmount for allowing us to use material from this excellent book.
4. The detail of such questioning was amazing. Lancastrian Kenneth

Skidmore was asked the colour of bus tickets in his home town of St Helens and the cost of the train fare to Liverpool. In Namur in Belgium, Terry Bolter was interrogated by a man who identified himself as a British agent and quizzed him on the price of whisky (3*s*. 4*d*.), the route of the Northern Line underground from West Finchley and the number of mounted sentries outside Horse Guards in Whitehall.

5. 'It was like a comic book adventure,' Levy recalled, 'almost unreal. It seemed as if all those I met were playing some kind of game . . . culled from a boy's book of adventures.' Harry Levy, *The Dark Side of the Sky* (Leo Cooper, 1996).

6. Ibid.

7. Helen Long, *Safe Houses Are Dangerous* (Abson Books, 1989).

8. Wayne Eveland, 'Memoirs and Reflections', unpublished private account.

9. Anthony Read and David Fisher, *Colonel Z: The Life and Times of a Master of Spies* (Hodder & Stoughton, 1984).

10. Terry Bolter, private account and interview with JN and TR, May 2005.

11. The dangers of the Bidassoa were not to be underestimated. In the winter of 1943, Count Antoine d'Ursel, a member of the Comet Line, was swept away and drowned while trying to cross.

12. The same crossing point was used at other times when the river was too deep and fast to ford. George Duffee came over the Pyrenees this way in the late autumn of 1943, nearly two years after Newton. He too was guided by Florentino. Dédée had long been under arrest by then and it was her successor, François Northomb, who had taken her place. See Chapter 5.

13. In all, eleven British and Empire servicemen made home runs from Colditz.

14. Airey Neave, *They Have Their Exits* (Leo Cooper, 2002).

15. MI9 debriefing report, National Archives, WO208/3298.

16. Jim Murray, private account and interview with JN, July 2005.

17. National Archives, WO208/3242.

18. Airey Neave, *Saturday at MI9* (Leo Cooper, 2004).

19. H. J. Spiller, *Ticket to Freedom* (William Kimber, 1988), and interview with JN, June 2005.

20. Kenneth Skidmore, *Follow the Man with the Pitcher* (Countyvise, 1996).

21. Maurice 'Collie' Collins, private account.

22. This was unusual. For security reasons the usual drill was that Bomber Command and Fighter Command men on the run who got home were not allowed on operational flying again. They were deemed to have too much top-secret information to risk being shot down and captured again, and became instructors or were sent on non-front-line duties. But, as Collins explained, 'that was only if you had got out on an escape line. It was different for me because I made my own way out.' There were other examples of evaders being sent back on flying duties – Gordon Carter, for example (private account).

23. Wayne Eveland, 'Memoirs and Reflections', unpublished private account.

24. Howard Harris, 'Vive la France and French-fried Potatoes', unpublished private account.

25. Ed Burley, private account. For the record, Burley made contact with another guide and crossed the Pyrenees in horrendous conditions. Twelve days of non-stop snow delayed the start and when the party finally set out it was through deep drifts. Burley saw a frozen arm sticking out of the snow at one point. A fellow crewman lost a shoe without knowing it and walked on a bare foot for hours before he realized. By then he was irreparably frostbitten. The same man went into convulsions after eating snow and then fell into a coma. An exhausted Burley left him for dead. A Basque guide went back to rescue him.

26. Everett Childs, private account and interview with JN, August 2005.

## Chapter 5: Betrayed

1. Andrée (Nadine) Dumon, interview with JN and TR, June 2005.

2. Hélène de Champlain, *The Secret War of Hélène de Champlain* (W. H. Allen, 1980).

3. Terry Bolter, private account and interview with JN and TR, May 2005.

4. George Buckner, 'Down and Out in 1944', unpublished private account.

5. Harry Levy, *The Dark Side of the Sky* (Leo Cooper, 1996), and interview with JN, June 2005.

6. Ibid.

7. M. Kauffmann was eventually sent to Dachau concentration camp, which he miraculously survived.

8. Not his real name. The man in question died only within the past ten years, and the authors understand the wife and family he acquired after the war never knew about his activities. To avoid causing them distress, we have changed his name.

9. Fortunately, Levy never had to find out. The Luftwaffe eventually came for him and took him to a proper POW camp. By then he had been in prison for ten long weeks, lonely and depressed. He had been beaten up a couple of times by guards who discovered he was Jewish, but otherwise his race and religion seem not to have made his treatment worse. It might not have been the same in SS or Gestapo custody, as he well knew. But the mental torture had been tough, and he had survived only by entering into an 'inner world' in which he 'struggled to push away the thick strands of my fears closing my mind to futile conjecture.'

10. National Archives, KV2/415.

11. *The Blue Noon* (Review, 2003), Robert Ryan's novel about Cole, is a terrific read and much to be recommended. But, though based on actual events, it is fiction. The author is the first to acknowledge that it was his decision to make Cole a sympathetic character rather than a total villain, and that this was for dramatic reasons rather than based on documentary evidence or historical accuracy. But we suggest that you read it anyway and make up your own mind.

12. Sir Denis Crowley-Milling, cited in Helen Long, *Safe Houses Are Dangerous* (Abson Books, 1989).

13. Twenty years after the war, Garrow revealed that he had not been totally fooled by Cole and, after at first defending him to Caskie and O'Leary, had changed his mind. He didn't think Cole had

betrayed anyone at that point, but 'was convinced of his potential danger and decided after much thought to kill him'. In order to avoid a police investigation that might expose the escape line, he sought the advice of Dr Rodocanachi, a fellow helper, on how to make Cole's death appear to be from natural causes and was told a massive injection of insulin would put him in a coma and then he could be dropped in the sea to drown. A hypodermic was prepared, a place in the port chosen where he could be dumped and all was ready to go when Garrow was arrested. Letter from Garrow to Donald Darling, May 1965, quoted in Long, *Safe Houses Are Dangerous*.

14. Donald Caskie, *The Tartan Pimpernel* (Oldbourne, 1957).

15. Long, *Safe Houses Are Dangerous*.

16. It is even questionable whether Cole had ever actually enlisted in the army. In his book, *Fight Another Day* (Collins, 1974), Jimmy Langley suggested – without proof – that, to escape the police in England, Cole had fled to France in 1940 in a stolen sergeant's uniform, after which he made off with the mess fund.

17. Ibid., quoting *The Way Back*, by Vincent Brome (Cassell, 1957).

18. Long, *Safe Houses Are Dangerous*.

19. Ibid.

20. This work was vital for security too as the Gestapo tried to insert spies disguised as evaders. Darling personally detected two, posing as volunteers for the Free Belgian and Free French forces.

21. Donald Darling, *Secret Sunday* (William Kimber, 1975).

22. Had Cole always been a traitor? O'Leary believed so, as did Jimmy Langley, and there is some indirect evidence to support this. When she was temporarily held in prison, Elizabeth Haden-Guest heard rumours that the group's 'man in the north' was not to be trusted. Perhaps he had been a double agent, working for both sides (but chiefly for himself) right from the beginning, though those airmen he brought south and who credit him with saving their lives think not. Nor is there any proof that he betrayed Garrow. Cole may not have actually betrayed anyone until this point when, willingly or unwillingly, he fell into German hands.

23. Ian Dear, *Escape and Evasion* (Cassell, 2000).

24. Ibid. The interrogator was a Dutchman named Cornelius Verloop.
25. The third was a genuine British evader, a pilot, who had nothing to do with Cole's plot.
26. According to Donald Caskie, though it is unclear how he knew this.
27. Derek Richardson, *Detachment W* (Paul Mould, 2004).
28. This happened more often than is generally believed. Bob de Graaff, in *Stepping Stones to Freedom* (privately published, 2003), cites examples in Holland. On 9 July 1944 three airmen caught in the home of a family in Tilburg were taken onto the terrace and shot. On 2 October of the same year an American, Robert Zurcher, and a British airman, Kenneth Ingram, were found with a local Resistance group in Apeldoorn and executed, their bodies hung up for public display for three days with the word 'Terrorist' on labels round their necks.
29. See Chapter 7.
30. Or was it in the evening? Some accounts say Garrow left with the night shift of guards in the morning, others that he came out with the day shift in the evening. Since Helen Long's account in *Safe Houses Are Dangerous* was based on conversations with O'Leary – and he was there – we have followed her version of events.
31. Langley, *Fight Another Day*.
32. Long, *Safe Houses Are Dangerous*.
33. He was placed in the care of the Red Cross and returned to his mother when she came back, a concentration camp survivor, after the war.
34. 'I had to confess our serious sin of omission in failing to check Cole's bona fides,' Langley wrote in his memoirs. He was amazed that O'Leary did not complain about this or offer any words of recrimination. Donald Darling also confessed to British Intelligence's lamentable failure to stop Cole. In *Secret Sunday*, published in 1975, he revealed that Cole had been wanted for con-artistry in France before the war, when he had posed as an RAF officer on a secret mission. 'His photograph had even figured in the rogues' gallery at French Security police offices at their Channel ports. Had MI5's London office known of this in 1940–41 and through me passed a warning

to Garrow and O'Leary, Harold Cole could have been disposed of before he had time to betray so many French patriots. Somebody had been more than negligent.' Darling had only just discovered this himself in 1975. 'That this information should take 30 years to surface, as it did, is more than shocking,' he added.

35. Count Greindl – see below. Quoted in Dear, *Escape and Evasion*.

36. De Graaff, *Stepping Stones to Freedom*.

37. Sherri Greene Ottis, *Silent Heroes* (University Press of Kentucky, 2001).

38. Airey Neave, *Saturday at MI9* (Leo Cooper, 2004).

39. Ibid.

40. Stan Hope, interview from the Second World War Experience Centre, Leeds, and with JN, June 2005.

41. Or were they German field police in grey uniforms? That's how Airey Neave recorded them in *Saturday at MI9*. However, in *Little Cyclone* (Hodder & Stoughton, 1954), the same author called them 'gendarmes', which seems more likely. It is possible that both French and German forces took part in the raid, though, given the nature of the tip-off on which it was based, and that this was seen at the time as a routine arrest of evaders rather than the smashing of an entire line and the capture of its leader, there is no reason why it should have involved anyone other than the local police.

42. Neave, *Little Cyclone*.

43. See Chapter 2.

44. Marguerite Brouard-Fraser, private account and interview with JN, August 2005. After the war there arose some doubt about whether the two were spies – see Chapter 13.

45. *Saturday at MI9*.

46. De Graaff, *Stepping Stones to Freedom*.

47. William Etherington, *A Quiet Woman's War* (Mousehold Press, 2002).

48. Dear, *Escape and Evasion*.

49. The sentence was never carried out. He died when Allied bombers hit the Brussels army barracks he was imprisoned in – an ironic end for a man who had helped to rescue so many airmen and send them

home to continue the war. On the other hand, as Donald Darling wrote in *Secret Sunday*, 'perhaps it was a merciful release from the torture of the Gestapo'.

50. M. R. D. Foot and J. M. Langley, *MI9: Escape and Evasion, 1939–1945* (The Bodley Head, 1979).
51. Neave, *Saturday at MI9*.


## Chapter 6: Love on the Run

1. Joe Sankey's private account (recorded with 'Peter Waters of Lancaster' in 1991 – no other details) was provided by his daughter Joanna.
2. Joanna Jones, interview with JN, June 2005. The authors are grateful to Mrs Jones for so freely discussing in such detail what must have been a highly emotional aspect of her life.
3. Gordon Carter, private account and interview with JN and TR, September 2005.
4. Gordon Instone, *Freedom the Spur* (Pan, 1956).
5. Harry Levy, *The Dark Side of the Sky* (Leo Cooper, 1996), and interview with JN, June 2005.
6. Peter Scott Janes, *Conscript Heroes* (Paul Mould, 2004).
7. See Chapter 1, p. 16.
8. Literally, 'a little bit of meat, sold without coupon', meaning 'a bit on the side'.
9. This was before Cole's split with Pat O'Leary. Janes thought Cole did a good job escorting the party to Marseilles, though it must have looked odd at the station nearest to the demarcation line 'when nine fellows, all between 20 and 30 and all carrying suitcases, dived off the train and, studiously avoiding each other, made straight for the same little pathway. On the road we were all strung out but plainly visible to each other.' Janes made it home eventually – via the Pyrenees and a spell in Spanish custody and at Miranda del Ebro concentration camp before being released to the British embassy. A liner converted to a troopship ferried him to the Clyde in Scotland and he arrived by train in London along with others of his

vintage chanting, 'We are the last of the BEF [British Expeditionary Force].' It was the middle of January 1942, seventeen months after Dunkirk!

10. H. J. Spiller, *Ticket to Freedom* (William Kimber, 1988), and interview with JN, June 2005.

11. Group Captain Frank Griffiths, quoted in Helen Long, *Safe Houses Are Dangerous* (Abson Books, 1989).

12. Richard M. Smith, 'Hide and Seek with the German Army', unpublished private memoir.

13. Hélène de Champlain, *The Secret War of Hélène de Champlain* (W. H. Allen, 1980).

14. See Chapter 2.

15. Derek Shuff, *Evader* (Spellmount, 2003).

16. Ibid.

17. Janine Carter, interview with JN and TR, September 2005.

18. The decree came into force on 16 February 1943. Before then the Germans had simply picked men off the streets; now they were required by law to 'volunteer' themselves.

19. Gordon Carter, private account and interview with JN, August 2005.

20. He discovered their thoughts when he went back to the house fifty-two years later and in an old teapot found a yellowing piece of paper on which the girls had recorded their impressions of his stay in 1943. 'We were the only airmen they came across during the war, despite many aircraft crashing in the vicinity in the following months.'

## Chapter 7: Rule Britannia

1. Ron Scales, 'One Man's War', unpublished private memoir.

2. Airey Neave, *Saturday at MI9* (Leo Cooper, 2004).

3. J. M. Langley, *Fight Another Day* (Collins, 1974).

4. He had come to Europe from the US originally as a member of the American Red Cross.

5. Langley, *Fight Another Day*.

6. The doctor stuffed Straight's ears beforehand with a mixture of brick-dust and soap, which looked like a discharge of pus when he was examined. Rodocanachi was well schooled in deceptions like this and was able to get seven other airmen repatriated in the same way – Helen Long, *Safe Houses Are Dangerous* (Abson Books, 1989).

7. Lucien Dumais, *The Man Who Went Back* (Leo Cooper, 1975).

8. George Buckner, 'Down and Out in 1944', unpublished private account.

9. Dick Smith, private account.

10. André Hue and Ewen Southby-Tailyour, *The Next Moon* (Viking, 2004).

11. It is unclear whether this was Alphonse's house, as in the previous operations. The description does not seem right. It may be that the assembly place had been changed for security reasons.

12. Buckner did not know the man's name, but the authors' assumption is that it was Dumais.

13. See Chapter 3. In effect, a division of labour was agreed. MIS-X would concentrate its efforts on the war in the Pacific, leaving the European theatre to MI9.

14. Kenneth Skidmore, *Follow the Man with the Pitcher* (Countyvise, 1996).

15. James Armstrong, *Escape!* (Honoribus Press, 2000).

16. Yvonne Daley-Brusselsmans, *Belgium Rendezvous 127 Revisited* (Sunflower University Press, 2001).

17. Andrée (Nadine) Dumon, interview with JN and TR, June 2005.

18. Bob de Graaff, *Stepping Stones to Freedom* (privately published, 2003).

19. Roy Davidson, private account and interview with JN, July 2005.

## Chapter 8: Digging In

1. The aircraft was a Lysander of No. 161 SOE (Special Operations Executive) Squadron, and the pilot was Squadron Leader Hugh Verity. His book, *We Landed by Moonlight* (Crecy, 1998), records this and many other similar operations.

2. Fred Gardiner, private account and interview with JN, July 2005.

3. MI9 debriefing report, National Archives, WO208/3242/227857.

4. Denys Teare, *Evader* (Air Data Publications, 1996), and interview with JN, May 2005.

5. Tom Wingham, private account and interview with JN, May 2005.

6. A. B. Smith, 'A Place Remembered', unpublished private memoir.

7. Terry Bolter, private account and interview with JN and TR, May 2005.

8. Airey Neave, *They Have Their Exits* (Leo Cooper, 2002).

9. Airey Neave, *Saturday at MI9* (Leo Cooper, 2004).

10. Ray Worrall, *Escape from France* (Silver Quill, 2004), and interview with JN, April 2005.

11. Cliff Hallett, interview at www.rafinfo.org.uk and with JN, August 2005.

12. Other witnesses dispute Hallett's version of events, but they arrived at the camp later on in its existence, and possibly after the split had been made, whereas Hallett was there almost from the start and saw more than most. Such animosity between Allied servicemen was not unusual – their commanders were often bickering, so why shouldn't the men? In the close confines of the forest camp, differences could easily become exaggerated. If Boussa had to split the camp anyway, a division along these lines would have made some sense.

13. Website: www.hilaroad.com/RCAF/freteval/freteval.html. June 2005.

14. Hallett had been injured in the bale-out and his injury caused him various problems throughout his time as an evader.

15. Virginia d'Albert-Lake, 'Autobiography of an American Woman in France', unpublished private memoir.

16. See Chapter 10.

17. James Davies, *A Leap in the Dark* (Leo Cooper, 1994).

18. John Vallely, Imperial War Museum, 85/38/1.

19. Walter Farmer, 'World War II Experiences', unpublished private memoir.

20. Dubious because this applied to most evaders. And he had, after all, been officially logged as missing. Frankly, the explanation he was given doesn't wash and his return to front-line duties remains something of a mystery. Perhaps it was just another wartime snafu.

21. Gordon Carter, private account and interview with JN and TR, September 2005.
22. Gordon and Janine Carter's private letters; the authors are grateful to Mr and Mrs Carter for allowing them to read such personal correspondence.
23. Graham Pitchfork, *Shot Down and on the Run* (National Archives, 2003).

## Chapter 9: Libération!

1. Specimen lecture for Army units on conduct if cut off from unit or captured. MI9, April 1944. National Archives, WO208/3242/227857.
2. The tips make fascinating reading in full. See Appendix. p. 459.
3. Interview recorded at the US National Museum of the Pacific War, Admiral Nimitz Historic Site, Fredericksburg, Texas, October 2002.
4. Frank Haslam, private account.
5. Denys Teare, *Evader* (Air Data Publications, 1996), and interview with JN, April 2005.
6. John 'Ginger' Brown, private account and interview with JN, April 2005.
7. Airey Neave, *Saturday at MI9* (Leo Cooper, 2004).
8. Ray Worrall, *Escape from France* (Silver Quill, 2004), and interview with JN, April 2005.
9. Website: www.hilaroad.com/RCAF/freteval/freteval.html.
10. Cliff Hallett, interviews at www.rafinfo.org.uk and with JN, August 2005.
11. There is a conflict of evidence here. Ray Worrall's version was of a large force of American trucks, armed jeeps and armoured cars arriving in the forest, having been summoned by the crews of the two US tanks who had first made contact and already taken some men away. He said the majority were now taken away in this convoy. 'There was the sound of gunfire all around us and the American drivers and their mates grabbed their rifles and started

firing back. I thought we were all going to be caught up in the fighting and be killed, just as safety was looming up. However, after a little while the firing died down and we moved off. As we did so, we passed a convoy of buses all decked out with the Free French insignia and French flags. It was Airey Neave, head of MI9, who had come to rescue us, only to arrive after most of us had left on the American transport. He was able to collect the remaining few who had not got aboard the American vehicles.'

Did Neave exaggerate his rescue mission? Possibly. He was not a politician for nothing in the years after the war. And there are some inconsistencies in his several accounts. In his book *They Have Their Exits* (Leo Cooper, 2002), first published in 1953, he acknowledged with irritation that the two US tanks had got to the forest first and stated that they had radioed for trucks. By the time he came to write *Saturday at MI9* in 1969, the tanks were still in the story, but all mention of trucks had disappeared. At the same time, the camp itself and the plan to liberate it were his babies, and he had been snubbed by the Americans in Le Mans when he asked for help. If they had indeed got there first with their convoy, as Worrall describes, one might well sympathize with Neave if he subsequently decided to spin the story in his favour. MI9's official history by M. R. D. Foot and Jimmy Langley squares the circle by diplomatically stating that the men in Fréteval 'were rescued by Neave himself and the American Captain Coletta, under guard of a big SAS patrol, by a bus convoy from Le Mans'. It is an explanation that covers all the bases but has the ring of a fudge about it (*MI9: Escape and Evasion, 1939–1945*). (The Bodley Head, 1979)).

12. George Pyle, *Broken Mustang* (Blaisdon Publishing, 2001).
13. Bill Knaggs, *The Easy Trip* (Perth & Kinross Libraries, 2001).
14. William L. Cupp, *A Wartime Journey* (Sunflower University Press, 2002).
15. Quoted in Worrall, *Escape from France*.
16. The ambush that had led to the reprisal was apparently carried out not by 'partisans' but by the SAS detachment that had parachuted into the area.

17. George Fernyhough, 'A Time to Remember,' unpublished private memoir written with Tony Eaton (1998), and interview with JN, June 2005.
18. Tom Wingham, private account and interview with JN, April 2005.
19. Janine Carter, interview with JN, September 2005.

## Chapter 10: Paying the Price

1. Len Bareham, private account, Imperial War Museum, 97/23/1.
2. Marshal and head of the Luftwaffe.
3. Harry Levy, *The Dark Side of the Sky* (Leo Cooper, 1996), and interview with JN, June 2005.
4. Donald Darling, *Secret Sunday* (William Kimber, 1975).
5. William Etherington, *A Quiet Woman's War* (Mousehold Press, 2002).
6. Eric de Menten de Horne, quoted in Airey Neave, *Little Cyclone* (Hodder & Stoughton, 1954).
7. Andrée (Nadine) Dumon, interview with JN and TR, June 2005.
8. Neave, *Little Cyclone*. This book, Neave's biography of Dédée de Jongh, is a very good read and generally accurate, if rather fanciful in its reproduction of dialogue he can never have witnessed or had reported to him.
9. Ibid.
10. Recounted in a private memoir supplied by Gordon Carter.
11. Pierre d'Harcourt, *The Real Enemy* (Sphere, 1970).
12. Barry Wynne, *No Drums . . . No Trumpets: The Story of Mary Lindell* (Arthur Barker, 1961).
13. Virginia d'Albert-Lake, 'Autobiography of an American Woman in France', unpublished private memoir.
14. Donald Caskie, *The Tartan Pimpernel* (Oldbourne, 1957).

## Chapter 11: Lost in the Garden

1. Anthony Deane-Drummond, *Return Ticket* (Collins, 1953).
2. Deane-Drummond added: 'My system started to function again quite normally as soon as I started to eat when I got out. My only legacy was a series of bad boils, followed by styes, which persisted for about a year afterwards.'
3. Leo Heaps, *The Evaders* (Bluejacket Books, 1976).
4. Ibid. The group was led by Sergeant-Major Robert Grainger.
5. Quoted in Deane-Drummond, *Return Ticket*.
6. MI9 debriefing notes, Imperial War Museum, Department of Documents IS9/WEA/1/274/2366; General Sir John Hackett, *I Was a Stranger* (Chatto & Windus, 1977).
7. Squadron Leader Y. R. W. Lovegrove, private account, Archive of the RAF Museum, Hendon, X001–2324/003.
8. Article in *The Royal Army Ordnance Corps Gazette*, January 1945, from the archive of the Second World War Experience Centre, Leeds.
9. His real name was Dick Kragt, a Briton with a Dutch father and an English mother. Frans Hals was a seventeenth-century Dutch portrait painter, most renowned for *The Laughing Cavalier*.
10. Airey Neave, *Saturday at MI9* (Leo Cooper, 2004).
11. Heaps, *The Evaders*.
12. By now MI9 was working alongside IS9 (WEA) – which stood for Intelligence School 9 (Western European Area) – whose job was to liaise with Allied Supreme Headquarters over the welfare of escapers, evaders and POWs. The two organizations, while officially separate, became virtually indistinguishable.
13. Heaps, *The Evaders*.
14. One group of a dozen paratroopers had amassed five anti-tank mines, a Bren gun, three Stens, three rifles and twelve hand grenades; ibid.
15. Heaps had jumped from a train of cattle trucks taking POWs to Germany, hidden with the Resistance and then made a daring solo escape over the River Waal in a small boat while German machine-

gunners blazed away at him from the north bank. He pulled himself out of the water, gripped by 'a deep sense of rapture, mystical and mysterious' at being free; ibid.

16. Heaps, *The Evaders*.
17. Neave claims he was put under pressure 'on all sides' to mount this second operation. Others, however, especially Leo Heaps, say the primary impetus came from Neave himself.
18. David Ward, interview with JN, June 2005, and Mel Rolfe, *Bomber Boys* (Grub Street, 2004).
19. Ray Kubly, 'One More River to Cross', unpublished private memoir, and interview with JN, July 2005.

## Chapter 12: Fleeing the Ruins of the Reich

1. MI9 briefing paper, National Archives, WO208/3268.
2. Tony Johnson, *Escape to Freedom* (Leo Cooper, 2002), and interview with JN, June 2005.
3. Ron Carabine, private diary, courtesy of his son Bob.
4. Carabine was in a POW camp near Munich, liberated by the Americans at the end of April 1945.
5. Hal Naylor, private account and interview with JN, July 2005.
6. General Sir John Hackett, *I Was a Stranger* (Chatto & Windus, 1977).
7. Dick Kragt, alias Frans Hals, but known to Hackett as 'Van Dyck'.
8. Lipmann-Kessel made it through the lines.
9. Ray Kubly, 'One More River to Cross', unpublished private memoir, and interview with JN, July 2005.
10. David Ward, interview with JN, June 2005, and Mel Rolfe, *Bomber Boys* (Grub Street, 2004).
11. For the full story of this exodus, see John Nichol and Tony Rennell, *The Last Escape* (Viking, 2002).
12. Gordon Carter, private account and interview with JN and TR, September 2005.
13. The prisoner was Welsh airman Jim Davies, who had been an evader in Holland for four months before he was betrayed to the Gestapo. See Chapter 8.

14. When he finally did take off his boots, he discovered to his horror that he had lost all his toenails.
15. Army doctors examined Scales when he finally got back to England. He weighed 74 pounds, just over 5 stones.
16. Ron Scales, 'One Man's War', unpublished private memoir.
17. Andrée (Nadine) Dumon, interview with JN and TR, May 2005.
18. Virginia d'Albert-Lake, 'Autobiography of an American Woman in France', unpublished private memoir.
19. Geneviève de Gaulle had been an active Resistance fighter for three years in France before being betrayed to the Germans and sent to Ravensbruck.
20. William Etherington, *A Quiet Woman's War* (Mousehold Press, 2002).

## Chapter 13: We'll Meet Again . . .

1. The letter received by Tom Wingham's mother told her that her son was missing after his plane set off to bomb Düsseldorf 'and was not heard from again. This does not necessarily mean that he is killed or wounded, and if he is a prisoner of war he should be able to communicate with you in due course . . .'
2. Cliff Hallett, interview at www.rafinfo.org.uk and with JN, August 2005.
3. Tom Wingham, private account and interview with JN, April 2005.
4. By the International Red Cross, after notification by the German authorities that the bodies had been retrieved and buried.
5. John 'Ginger' Brown, private account and interview with JN, April 2005.
6. Ray Worrall, *Escape from France* (Silver Quill, 2004), and interview with JN, April 2005.
7. George Fernyhough, 'A Time to Remember', unpublished private memoir written with Tony Eaton, and interview with JN, June 2005.
8. Bill Knaggs, *The Easy Trip* (Perth & Kinross Libraries, 2001).
9. George Pyle, *Broken Mustang* (Blaisdon Publishing, 2001).
10. Terry Bolter, private account.

11. William Etherington, *A Quiet Woman's War* (Mousehold Press, 2002).
12. Donald Darling, *Secret Sunday* (William Kimber, 1975).
13. Andrée (Nadine) Dumon, interview with JN and TR, June 2005.
14. According to Terry Bolter, the Americans paid a ransom for her release from Ravensbruck. He was in a position to know. He was helped by d'Albert-Lake while evading and became a family friend and frequent visitor, 'with much mutual affection', after the war.
15. Virginia d'Albert-Lake, 'Autobiography of an American Woman in France', unpublished private memoir.
16. Donald Caskie, *The Tartan Pimpernel* (Oldbourne, 1957).
17. Story told by Airey Neave in *Little Cyclone* (Hodder & Stoughton, 1954).
18. True to the mystery that still surrounds Cole, there were various accounts of his death and numerous unresolved inconsistencies. According to Neave, Cole was found by two French gendarmes who knocked on the door of the flat he was living in above a bar looking for deserters. They were not specifically looking for him. He came out brandishing a pistol, fired three times, wounding one of them, before they shot back and killed him. Even the year of his death is unclear. Documents in the National Archives put it in 1946, but Caskie and Donald Darling of MI6 (who helped locate Cole) say it was in 1945.
19. He was set free on the promise that he would track her down and kill her but he failed. She was helped to escape to England, where she joined SOE.
20. Airey Neave, *Saturday at MI9* (Leo Cooper, 2004).
21. Quoted in Darling, *Secret Sunday*.
22. Not his real name; see Chapter 5.
23. Harry Levy, *The Dark Side of the Sky* (Leo Cooper, 1996), and interview with JN, June 2005.
24. Private correspondence with authors.
25. Stan Hope, interviews at the Second World War Experience Centre, Leeds, and with JN, June 2005.
26. Quoted in Sherri Greene Ottis, *Silent Heroes* (University Press of Kentucky, 2001).

27. Geo Jouanjean, private account.

28. Gordon Carter, private account and interview with JN and TR, September 2005.

29. Janine Carter, interview with JN, September 2005.

30. General Sir John Hackett, *I Was a Stranger* (Chatto & Windus, 1977).

31. To have done so, he was warned, would have attracted collaborators trying to disguise their treachery. He and his staff would have wasted much time proving their claims invalid.

32. Darling, *Secret Sunday*.

33. There was a DSO for Jean de Blommaert and an MC for Lucien Boussa.

34. The signature was that of Lord Tedder, deputy commander of the Supreme Allied forces. His boss, General Eisenhower, signed the American letters of thanks – using a rubber stamp.

35. Official citation in the possession of the Carter family.

36. Virginia d'Albert-Lake, interview in *Philip Morris Magazine*, November 1989.

37. Barry Wynne, *No Drums . . . No Trumpets: The Story of Mary Lindell* (Arthur Barker, 1961).

38. From Lieutenant Joseph Murphy and Lieutenant James McCurley, 'Our Wartime Adventures in France', unpublished private memoir.

39. Derek Shuff, *Evader* (Spellmount, 2003).

40. Letter to Under-Secretary of State, Air Ministry, April 1942, National Archives, AIR 2/5684.

41. Figures from M. R. D. Foot and J. M. Langley, *MI9: Escape and Evasion, 1939–1945* (The Bodley Head, 1979).

42. Ibid.

43. Official figures regarding the total numbers of evaders vary. The RAF Escaping Society estimated that 2,803 British and Commonwealth airmen alone (i.e. not including soldiers or sailors) made it home. Such discrepancies in the figures surprise many people but were inevitable in wartime conditions, particularly in the post-D-Day period when some evaders may well have slipped back over the lines and returned to their regiments and squadrons without units such as MI9 and IS9(d) logging them. Also, MI9 tried to distinguish between 'evaders' and 'escapers', and therein lay inevitable

inaccuracies. The end of the war brought even more administrative chaos, as prisoners of war made their way home; many, in their exuberance at being free, did their best to bypass the bureaucracy waiting to debrief them. And after the war? Well, no one wanted the trouble of cross-checking the statistics held in all the various departments and trying to reconcile them. And who can blame them? For a further discussion of this, particularly in relation to returning POWs, see 'Appendix 4 – The Numbers Game' in John Nichol and Tony Rennell, *The Last Escape* (Viking, 2002).

44. Bob de Graaff, *Stepping Stones to Freedom* (privately published, 2003).

45. 'Helping Dutch civilians, even Jews, hide was not punished as harshly by the Germans. When hiding Jews one was at least saving them from certain death, whilst airmen, should they fall into German hands, would only be made prisoners of war'; Ibid.

46. Denys Teare, interview with JN, April 2005.

47. Jetty Cook, private account.

## Epilogue

1. Janine and Gordon Carter, interview with JN and TR, September 2005.

# References

## Published sources

Armstrong, James, *Escape!* (Honoribus Press, 2000)

Bott, Lloyd, *The Secret War from the River Dart* (Dartmouth History Research Group, 1997)

Burgess, Alan, *The Longest Tunnel* (Bloomsbury, 1989)

Cardigan, Earl of, *I Walked Alone* (Routledge & Kegan Paul, 1950)

Caskie, Donald, *The Tartan Pimpernel* (Oldbourne, 1957)

Cooper, Alan, *Free to Fight Again* (William Kimber, 1988)

Cupp, William L., *A Wartime Journey* (Sunflower University Press, 2002)

d'Harcourt, Pierre, *The Real Enemy* (Sphere, 1970)

Daley-Brusselmans, Yvonne, *Belgium Rendezvous 127 Revisited* (Sunflower University Press, 2001)

Darling, Donald, *Secret Sunday* (William Kimber, 1975)

Davies, James Arthur, *A Leap in the Dark* (Leo Cooper, 1994)

de Champlain, Hélène, *The Secret War of Hélène de Champlain* (W. H. Allen, 1980)

de Graaff, Bob, *Stepping Stones to Freedom* (privately published, 2003)

Deane-Drummond, Anthony, *Return Ticket* (Collins, 1953)

Dear, Ian, *Escape and Evasion* (Cassell, 2000)

Dormer, Hugh, *Diaries* (Jonathan Cape, 1956)

Dumais, Lucien, *The Man Who Went Back* (Leo Cooper, 1975)

Etherington, William, *A Quiet Woman's War* (Mousehold Press, 2002)

Fenby, Jonathan, *The Sinking of the Lancastria* (Simon & Schuster, 2005)

Fittko, Lisa, *Escape through the Pyrenees* (Northwestern University Press, 1991)

Foot, M. R. D., *Resistance* (Granada Publishing, 1978)

Foot, M. R. D. and Langley, J. M., *MI9: Escape and Evasion, 1939–1945* (The Bodley Head, 1979)

Gill, Anton, *An Honourable Defeat* (Heinemann, 1994)

Goodall, Scott, *The Freedom Trail* (Inchmere Design, 2005)

Gulbenkian, Nubar, *Pantaraxia* (Hutchinson, 1965)

Hackett, General Sir John Winthrop, *I Was a Stranger* (Chatto & Windus, 1977)

Hawes, Stephen and Ralph White, *Resistance in Europe* (Penguin, 1976)

Head, Louis, *Dancing in the Dark* (Writers Club Press, 2002)

Heaps, Leo, *The Evaders* (Bluejacket Books, 1976)

Hearn, Edward, *The Chronicle of a Passer-by* (privately published, n.d.)

Hue, André and Ewen Southby-Tailyour, *The Next Moon* (Viking, 2004)

Hutton, Clayton, *Official Secret* (Max Parrish, 1960)

Instone, Gordon, *Freedom the Spur* (Pan, 1956)

Johnson, Tony, *Escape to Freedom* (Leo Cooper, 2002)

Jones, Francis, *The Double Dutchman* (Corgi, 1977)

Knaggs, Bill, *The Easy Trip* (Perth & Kinross Libraries, 2001)

Langley, J. M., *Fight Another Day* (Collins, 1974)

Lasseter, Don, *Their Deeds of Valour* (Xlibris, 2002)

Leslie, Peter, *The Liberation of the Riviera* (J. M. Dent, 1981)

Levy, Harry, *The Dark Side of the Sky* (Leo Cooper, 1996)

Long, Helen, *Safe Houses Are Dangerous* (Abson Books, 1989)

McCaig, Dennis, *From Fiji to Balkan Skies* (Woodfield, 1999)

Meynell, Laurence, *Airmen on the Run* (Odhams Press, 1963)

Millar, George, *Horned Pigeon* (Cassell, 2003)

——, *Maquis* (William Heinemann, 1945)

——, *Road to Resistance* (The Bodley Head, 1979)

Moore, William, *The Long Way Round* (Leo Cooper, 1986)

Neame, Sir Philip, *Playing with Strife* (George Harrap, 1947)

Neave, Airey, *Little Cyclone* (Hodder & Stoughton, 1954)

——, *Saturday at MI9* (Leo Cooper, 2004)

——, *They Have Their Exits* (Leo Cooper, 2002)

Nichol, John and Tony Rennell, *The Last Escape* (Viking, 2002)

——, *Tail-End Charlies: The Last Battles of the Bomber War, 1944–45* (Viking, 2004)

Oliphant, John, *Mad Rebel* (privately published, 1998)

Ottis, Sherri Greene, *Silent Heroes* (University Press of Kentucky, 2001)

Pitchfork, Graham, *Shot Down and on the Run* (National Archives, 2003)

Pyle, George, *Broken Mustang* (Blaisdon Publishing, 2001)

Read, Anthony and David Fisher, *Colonel Z: The Life and Times of a Master of Spies* (Hodder & Stoughton, 1984)

Richardson, Anthony, *Wingless Victory* (Odhams Press, 1950)

Richardson, Derek, *Detachment W* (Paul Mould, 2004)

Rolfe, Mel, *Bomber Boys* (Grub Street, 2004)

Routledge, Paul, *Public Servant, Secret Agent* (Fourth Estate, 2003)

Ryan, Robert, *The Blue Noon* (Review, 2003)

Scott Janes, Peter, *Conscript Heroes* (Paul Mould, 2004)

Shoemaker, Lloyd R., *The Escape Factory* (St Martin's Press, 1990)

Shuff, Derek, *Evader* (Spellmount, 2003)

Skidmore, Kenneth, *Follow the Man with the Pitcher* (Countyvise, 1996)

Smith, Sydney, *Wings Day* (Pan, 1970)

Sniders, Edward, *Flying in, Walking out* (Leo Cooper, 1999)

Spiller, H. J., *Ticket to Freedom* (William Kimber, 1988)

Taylor, Geoff, *Piece of Cake* (Peter Davies, 1956)

Teare, Denys, *Evader* (Air Data Publications, 1996)

Verity, Hugh, *We Landed by Moonlight* (Crecy, 1998)

Worrall, Ray, *Escape from France* (Silver Quill, 2004)

Wynne, Barry, *No Drums . . . No Trumpets: The Story of Mary Lindell* (Arthur Barker, 1961)

## Letters, diaries and accounts

Ablett, Patricia
Anthoine, Roger
Armstrong, Jim
Arthur, Douglas
Barckley, Bob
Barclay, Phil
Bareham, Len
Barlow, Patrick
Baum, Irv
Benoit, Virgil
Berthelsen, John
Bevan, Pauline

Bolter, Terry
Brigden, Jim
Brinckman, Sir Roderick
Brouard-Fraser, Marguerite
Brown, Bertie
Brown, Fred
Brown, John 'Ginger'
Brydon, Geoff
Bubenzer, Gus
Buckner, George
Burley, Ed
Burley, Miriam

Butler, Joan

Canning, Bob

Carabine, Bob

Carabine, Ron

Carter, Gordon

Carter, Janine

Chaster, Barry

Childs, Everett

Christie, John

Churches, Ralph

Clark, Nobby

Clinch, John

Coles, Bob

Collins, Maurice

Comley, J.

Constable, Peter

Cook, Jetty

Coverley, Roger

Croxson, Hal

Cullen, Thomas

Cupp, William L.

d'Albert-Lake, Patrick

d'Albert-Lake, Virginia

Daley-Brusselmans, Yvonne

Davidson, Betty

Davidson, Roy G.

Davies, Jim

Davies, Tony

Dawson, Rowland

Deane-Drummond, Anthony

Dell, Frank

Dench, R.

Donaldson, Peter

Donnelly, Peter

Dothie, William

Duffee, George

Dumon, Andrée (Nadine)

English, Ian

Enver, Harry

Etherington, Bill

Eveland, Louis

Eveland, Wayne

Farmer, Walter

Fernyhough, George

Fisher, Harry

Foster, Jack

Franklin, John

French, Fred

Fryer, Stanley

Gardiner, Fred

Graham, Dominick

Hallett, Cliff

Harding, William

Harpin, Lorraine

Harrington, Ralph

Harris, Howard

Harris, Jeanette R.

Harvell, Tom

Haslam, Frank

Hayes, Bill

Heaps, Adrian

Hearn, Edward

Heathfield, Fred

Hetherington, Brid

Hewitt, Ian

Hirst, Glenn

Honor, Dudley

Hope, Stan

Hurrell, Stan

Johnson, Ian

Johnson, Tony

Jones, Bertram

Jones, Joanna

Jones, John

Kirk, George

Knaggs, Bill

Kubly, Ray

Laing, D. B.

Lambert, Deryck

Lashbrook, Wally

Lawrence, Jack

Leonard, Norman

Levy, Harry

Lovegrove, Y. R. W.

MacDougall, John

MacKenzie, Mac

Maloney, Joe

Marco, Virgil

Martin, Sidney

Maxwell, Thomas

McCaig, Mac

McCurley, James

McKee, Ralph

Metcalf, Derek

Mills, Milton

Milner, Eric

Munns, Stanley

Murphy, Dot

Murphy, Joe

Murray, Jim

Naylor, Hal

Neff, Kenneth

Neff, Midge

O'Donnell, Joe

Palmer, Bill

Parkinson, Bob

Parton, Thomas

Percival, Sue

Peterson, Derrick

Potten, Josie

Potts, Phil

Pritchard, Arthur

Purvis, Joe

Pyle, George

Racy, Ray

Rafferty, Jean

Rainsford, Jim

Randall, Wally

Reynolds, Vic

Rose, Sylvia

Rosser, Jim

Rowe, Sandy

Sankey, Joanna

Scales, Ron

Schwartz, Jennifer

Scotchmer, Grace

Sheffield, Oscar

Sims, Brian

Smith, A. B.

Smith, Dick

Smith, Martin

Smith, Nigel

Spiller, Bert

Squire, Kathryn

Starks, George

Tanner, Bob

Taplin, John

Teare, Denys

Thompson, Harold

Titus, Bob

Torrans, J.

Tunstall, Pete

Vallely, John

Vandegriff, Robert

| | |
|---|---|
| Ward, David | Wood, George |
| Weir, Charles | Woolcock, Steve |
| West, Granville | Worrall, Ray |
| Weston, John | Wright, Ken |
| William, Rowland | Wynes, Christopher |
| Wingham, Tom | Zinck, Ray |

## Permissions

The authors and publishers are grateful to David & Charles for permission to reproduce text from The Earl of Cardigan, *I Walk Alone*; Pen & Sword Books Limited for Airey Neave, *Saturday at MI9*; Birlinn Ltd and The Church of Scotland for Donald Caskie, *The Tartan Pimpernel*; the author and Spellmount (Ltd) Publishers for Derek Shuff, *Evader*; The Random House Group Ltd for General Sir John Hackett, *I Was a Stranger*, published by Hogarth Press.

We would also like to acknowledge the following sources which have made an invaluable contribution to this book; Hélène de Champlain, *The Secret War of Hélène de Champlain*; Donald Darling, *Secret Sunday*; Lucien Dumais, *The Man Who Went Back*; M. R. D. Foot and J. M. Langley, *MI9: Escape and Evasion, 1939–1945*; Gordon Instone, *Freedom the Spur*; Jimmy Langley, *Fight Another Day*; Helen Long, *Safe House Are Dangerous*; Airey Neave, *Little Cyclone* and *They Have Their Exits*; Anthony Richardson, *Wingless Victory*.

Every effort has been made to trace or contact copyright holders. The publishers will be pleased to make good any omissions or rectify any mistakes brought to their attention at the earliest opportunity.

# Index